# Understanding Object-Oriented Software Engineering

**IEEE PRESS Understanding Science & Technology Series**

The IEEE PRESS Understanding Series treats important topics in science and technology in a simple and easy-to-understand manner. Designed expressly for the nonspecialist engineer, scientist, or technician as well as the technologically curious—each volume stresses practical information over mathematical theorems and complicated derivations.

**Books in the Series**

**Understanding the Nervous System**
***An Engineering Perspective***
Sid Deutsch and Alice Deutsch

1993 Softcover 408 pp IEEE Order No. PP2915
ISBN 0-87942-296-3

**Understanding Digital TV**
***The Route to HDTV***
Brian Evans

1995 Softcover 256 pp IEEE Order No. PP4366
ISBN 0-7803-1082-9

**Understanding Lasers**
***An Entry-Level Guide***
Jeff Hecht, Sr.

1994 Softcover 448 pp IEEE Order No. PP3541
ISBN 0-7803-1005-5

**Understanding Telecommunications and Lightwave Systems**
***An Entry-Level Guide, Second Edition***
John G. Nellist

1996 Softcover 272 pp IEEE Order No. PP4665
ISBN 0-7803-1113-2

**Understanding Electro-Mechanical Devices**
***An Introduction to Mechatronics***
Lawrence J. Kamm

1996 Softcover 416 pp IEEE Order No. PP3806
ISBN 0-7803-1031-4

Ideas for future topics and authorship inquiries are welcome.
Please write to IEEE PRESS: The Understanding Series.

# Understanding Object-Oriented Software Engineering

Stefan Sigfried

*Objective Ideas AB*
Senior member IEEE

IEEE PRESS



IEEE
COMPUTER
SOCIETY
PRESS

IEEE
Understanding Science & Technology Series
PRESS

The Institute of Electrical and Electronics Engineers, Inc., New York

**IEEE Press**
**445 Hoes Lane, PO Box 1331**
**Piscataway, NJ 08855-1331**



**IEEE Press Technical Reviewers**

Phil Laplante
*Burlington County College/New Jersey Institute of Technology*

Gene F. Hoffnagle
*IBM*

**IEEE Computer Society Press**
**10662 Los Vaqueros Circle, PO Box 3014**
**Los Alamitos, CA 90720-1264**

Dr. Barry W. Johnson, *Technical Editor*

This book may be purchased at a discount from the publisher when ordered in bulk quantities.
For more information contact:

IEEE PRESS Marketing
Attn: Special Sales
PO Box 1331
445 Hoes Lane
Piscataway, NJ 08855-1331
Fax: (908) 981

**ISBN 0-7803-1095-0**
**IEEE Press Order Number: PP4507**

Information on special prices and services for IEEE Computer Society members may be obtained by contacting:

IEEE Computer Society Marketing
Attn: Special Sales
PO Box 3014
Los Alamitos, CA 90720-1264
Fax: (714) 821-4010
Phone: 1-800-CS-BOOKS

**Computer Society Press Order Number: RS 00015**



Printed in the United States of America
10 9 8 7 6 5 4 3 2 1

**Library of Congress Cataloging-in-Publication Data**

Sigfried, Stefan (date)
Understanding object-oriented software engineering/Stefan Sigfried.
p. cm.—(IEEE Press understanding science & technology series)
Includes bibliographical references and index.
ISBN 0-7803-1095-0
1. Object-oriented programming (Computer science) 2. Software engineering. I. Title. II. Series.
QA76.64.S54 1995
005.1′2—dc20 95-1226
CIP

*Revolutions are not made; they come. A revolution is as natural a growth as an oak. It comes out of the past. Its foundations are laid far back.*

Wendell Phillips

*To him who looks upon the world rationally, the world in its turn presents a rational aspect. The relation is mutual.*

Georg Wilhelm Friedrich Hegel

*A book that furnishes no quotations is,* me judice, *no book—it is a plaything.*

Thomas Love Peacock

# Contents

## Part II
## *Building Large Systems*

### Chapter 4 Building Large Systems
#### *Software Engineering*

# Acknowledgments

A lot of people have helped me make this book a reality. A great THANK YOU is extended to you. I especially thank Göran Östlund at Sveriges Verkstadsindustrier, a major trade association in Sweden, who made the book possible by giving me the opportunity to conduct three studies. The studies were initiated by Sveriges Verkstadsindustrier, and they collected experiences from Swedish industry regarding the use of object-oriented technology. The studies involved more than 100 persons. The sharing of ideas and experiences with them has greatly contributed to make the book what it is today.

I also acknowledge the help I had from ideas and knowledge in books by other authors.

A special *thank you* must also be given to Kerstin Sundquist who gave me numerous suggestions on how to improve the English in my book. Any remaining faults are of course the sole responsibility of the author. Eliza Sigfried has drawn many of the figures and helped prepare the index and other items to finish this book—a big *thank you* to you, my dear.

Fourteen people read earlier versions of the book and gave suggestions. A warm *thank you* to all of you! I would like to give a special thanks to

Stefan Frennemo, ABB Automation
Göte Liljegren, FMV ADB
Mats Medin, ABB Automation
Arne Morell, Ellemtel
Rei Stråhle, Nobeltech systems AB
Kjell Svensson, ABB Automation

Lastly, but not least, I thank the persons I have met when consulting, writing articles and at my seminars. Your feedback when discussing the possibilities of object-oriented technology has been invaluable.

# Acknowledgments—IEEE Press Version

This book is an updated and augmented version of a book published by Industrilitteratur in Sweden.

Again I must extend a great *thank you* to my wife, Eliza, who has not only shown me great patience when the book has taken all my spare time but also helped me with the book by drawing all the new illustrations and also helped me in numerous other ways. A *thank you* is also extended to Lars Nordgren who has been instrumental in making the new example chapter, Chapter 7, what it is today. Of those who read the earlier Industrilitteratur version and made significant contributions to this new version, I would like to give a special *thank you* to the following:

Lars Wiktorin, IT Plan AB
Stig Berild, Swedish Attaché for Science and Technology
Per Grape, Enea Data AB

I would also like to extend a special THANK YOU to all at IEEE Press for the help, encouragement, and patience they have shown me during the process of preparing this book.

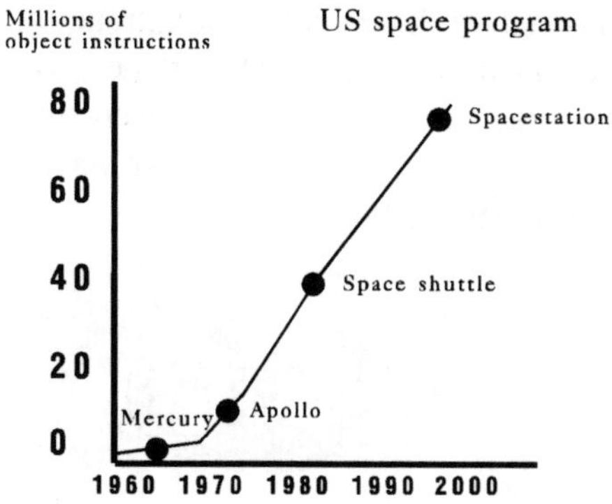


**Figure 1.2** (*Source: IEEE Computer,* Sept. 1987)

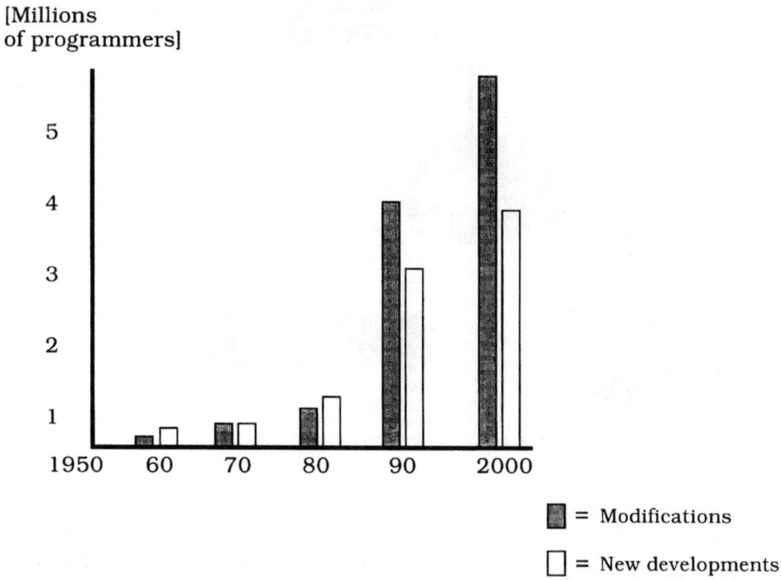


**Figure 1.3** (*Source:* Utlandsrapport Sveriges tekniska attacher. U.S.A. U3-8803)

There are even a few pessimists who think that before long all programmers will be modifying old software. We can conclude that it is beyond all reasonable doubt that the present state of the software industry does not meet our needs and expectations. Software has also become a critical technology for most enterprises and we thus conclude that we have a software crisis.

It is not the first time in history that we have had such a situation. When the present state of scientific knowledge is unable to meet our expectations, we encounter a crisis. This crisis is always followed by a revolution greatly changing the scientific knowledge, that is, our way of doing/modeling something. Figure 1.4 illustrates this idea.

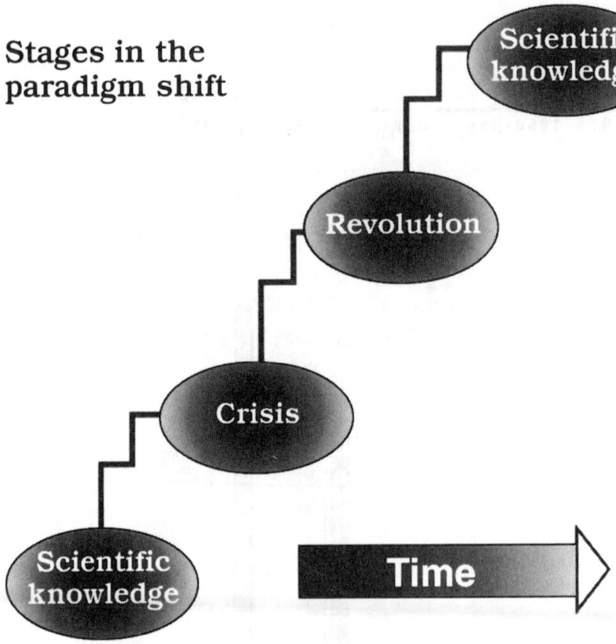


**Figure 1.4** Kuhn's paradigm shift.

Our changing perception of our universe is a good example of this principle. When the idea of having the earth as the center resulted in too complex models, the model was eventually replaced by one where the sun was at the center instead. When not even this was enough to explain astronomical observations, the sun lost its role as center and we had a model much closer to the one we use today. Thus, the situation we have today in the software industry is not unique at all.

There are other aspects of these changes too. For example, they are seldom painless or without losers. Those who have a stake in an existing technology seldom give it up but try to enhance it. New ways of doing things are slowly accepted whether they are models of the sun or the way we build systems.

## MODELING REALITY

*Good order is the foundation of all good things.*

— Edmund Burke

### Method and Methodology

We always use a "method" when we work. In its simplest form a "method" can be something we are not even fully aware of, a set of vague undocumented ideas or rules of thumb in the heads of some people. However, preferably, a method is something we can describe and communicate to our co-workers in a precise way, a documented system of principles and procedures that help us work in an orderly, systematic, and logical way. This is often called a methodology. By *methodology* we mean the system of rules, practices, and procedures we apply to a specific branch of knowledge.

In practice it is common to use the word *method* to denote the same thing. If we want to separate the concepts we can say that a methodology is the theoretical foundations for a method, whereas the method represents the systematic manner in which we work. However, there is no well-established practice for the use of these two concepts. We will thus use the words as synonyms but prefer the word method and we will adopt the following definition:

**Definition.** A *method* is a well-organized way of working in which we apply a defined set of rules, practices, and procedures.

A method should build on experiences gathered in earlier projects. It should help us both to find the information we need and to structure it. The method should also give us a work plan to ensure that all necessary activities are performed and performed in a correct sequence. However, a method should not be rigid, but should be like rules of thumb that help us to achieve our goals.

Note that in object-oriented terminology the word method is also used to denote a service that an object can deliver. In practice there is no problem with this double meaning, because the context makes it clear what we are referring to.

### Complexity

A serious problem we encounter when we start building a model of something is the multitude of things that exist for us to model. Being more formal, we can say that our *Universe of Discourse* encompasses many details (see Figure 1.5).

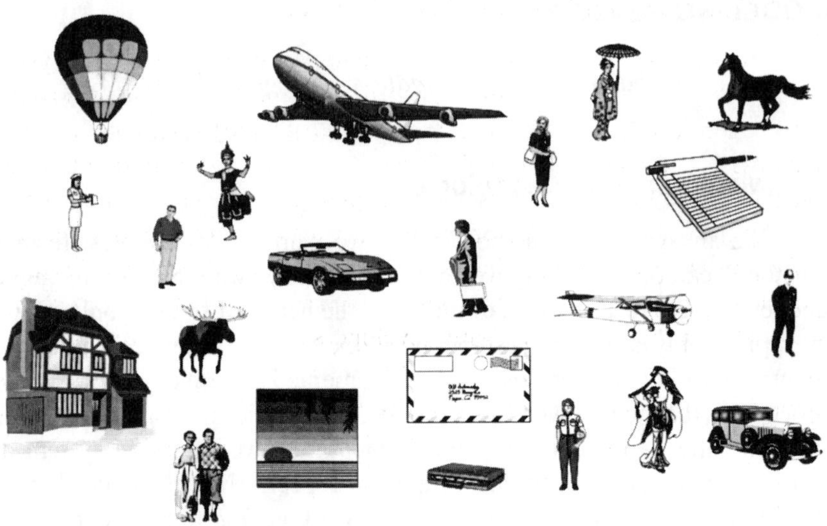

**Figure 1.5** The world is full of things.

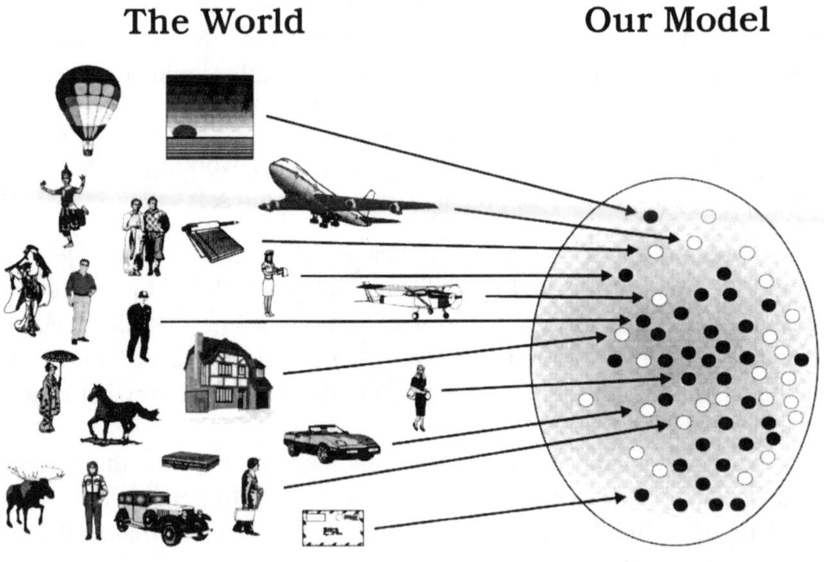


**Figure 1.6** Thus, a model of reality must also contain a lot of things.

The second thing we have to take into account, if we want to make a model of reality that includes many details, is that this will result in a model that is also full of details, which is illustrated in Figure 1.6.

The word we choose for this situation is *complex*. Note that it is not the number of details, as such, that contributes to complexity, but the number of details of which we have to be aware at the same time.

## Modeling Implies Handling Complexity

A small system is often easy to understand. However, as a system grows it soon becomes extremely difficult, if not impossible, to understand. The mental process of storing knowledge about the system and comprehending it becomes too difficult. We say that the *cognitive load* imposed on the system analyst becomes unacceptable. We need a better way of storing information. If we store some information with the least possible effort, we say that we have achieved *cognitive economy.* The way to bring this about is by imposing structure on the information we put into a model.

Most experienced software developers have encountered situations in which the model we make soon becomes so complex that we cannot handle it properly. It cannot be overstressed that this is the major problem in all medium- or large-scale software development projects, which is the reason why we are going to deal with the concept of complexity in some detail here.

What exactly do we mean when we say that a situation is complex? A typical entry in a dictionary could be as follows:

**Complex:** Something that is composed of several parts; complicated.

Why is complexity so difficult to handle? Let us consider a few facts. The first fact is the 7±2 rule. This rule states that a human being cannot properly handle more than seven plus or minus two things simultaneously, where things might be numbers, ideas, etc.

Please note the word *simultaneously.* The inability to handle many things simultaneously is a limitation of the human brain involving our short-term memory. Thus, it is a limitation that we cannot get away from by training. We can only learn how to handle it. For example, if we can form a new idea around some of the concepts we are trying to handle, the number of concepts will be reduced.

---

**Example**

We try to remember the digits 8, 1, 9, 5, 5, 7, and 3. If we have a friend Alex born in 1955, we can form a new set of concepts: 8, year of Alex's birth, 7, 3, giving us only four concepts to handle.

---

The situation is, however, very difficult for us, because we insist on developing large systems that contain many more than seven items.

The difficulty in handling large sets of facts is increased if they interact with each other—that is, if we have to deal not only with isolated facts, but also with interactions between these facts. This is a real "complexity bomb," as illustrated in Figure 1.7. In the figure we have considered a simple example where we presume that different things always interact in (only) one way. If we have two things, we have one way of interacting. If we have three things, we have three ways. Four things can interact in six ways, and so on. The number of combinations increases as *n* squared, significantly contributing to the complexity.

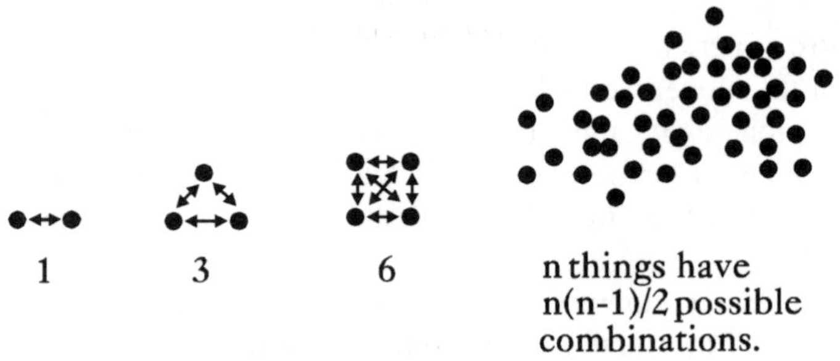


**Figure 1.7** Complexity is proportional to the number of items and how they interact with each other.

A simple measurement of complexity could thus be as follows:

*Complexity is proportional to the sum of the things we need to consider plus their interactions.*

We adopt this simple measurement of complexity because it is true, and because we have found it to be a workable model when explaining problems related to software development. If we presume that things interact in only one way and if we use the sign ~ for "is proportional to," we get

$$Complexity \sim n + n(n-1)/2 = n + (n^2)/2 - n/2 = (n + n^2)/2$$

If we skip the factor 1/2, we have

$$Complexity \sim n + n^2 \quad (1.1)$$

where *n* is the number of the items that need our attention.

If *n* is very large, we get

$$Complexity \sim n^2 \quad (1.2)$$

If we apply this discussion to a typical model, as discussed in books today, the items are the lines, the circles, the squares, etc., used in the model.

Note that in a graphical model, all items—such as lines, squares, or circles—would often have to be included in $n$. Using (1.2), we understand why it is important to divide a system into smaller *independent* parts. Dividing a system into smaller parts helps to conquer its inherent complexity. For example, dividing a system containing $n$ items into two independent parts with $s_1$ and $s_2$ items, respectively, would give us the following measurement of complexity:

$$Complexity \sim s_1^2 + s_2^2 + 3 \tag{1.3}$$

The 3 in the equation is added because dividing the system into two parts introduces two new concepts (the two parts) and one new way of interaction (if we follow our simplification that parts should only interact in one way). However, this number is small compared to the rest of the equation and we can ignore it. If we divide the items we had into two equally large parts we get

$$s_1 = \frac{n}{2} \tag{1.4}$$

$$s_2 = \frac{n}{2} \tag{1.5}$$

Combining (1.3), (1.4), and (1.5), we arrive at

$$Complexity \sim \frac{n^2}{4} + \frac{n^2}{4} \tag{1.6}$$

or

$$Complexity \sim \frac{n^2}{2} \tag{1.7}$$

(assuming $n$ is large).

Thus, simply dividing a system into two independent parts reduces the complexity by approximately 50%. Dividing the system into more parts will reduce the complexity even more. Note that having two independent parts means that there are no dependencies between parts (except our simple interaction).

It could be argued that the greater the number of lines, circles, etc., the better, as they are put there to give us important information. It is true that they give us information, but we cannot handle the information they give us if we have to view them all at the same time.

It could also be argued that having many different types of lines, boxes, and so on, will give us many modeling possibilities, which is good. The argument could thus be made that having many notational possibilities gives us modeling strength. However, there is no contradiction between the need for having great modeling strength and having low notational complexity. The solution is to find a notation that is simple but that gives us the modeling possibilities we need, thus also giving us great modeling strength.

We conclude that it is the inherent complexity of our systems that is our key problem. We summarize the problem of complexity as our first problem:

> **Problem 1.** A model usually presents us with too many things *simultaneously.*

### Change Is Killing Us

The systems we build are seldom finished. Demands for new abilities keep coming.

To change a system to make it include new abilities we must first understand the system. If someone beside the original designers will implement the changes, the need for an easily understood system increases even more. The problem with change can be expressed as a maintenance problem:

**Definition.** *Software maintenance* is the process of modifying a software system or component after delivery to correct faults, improve performance or other attributes, or adapt to a changed environment [IEEE].

A good requirements specification can protect us from many changes, but not even a perfect requirements specification can protect us from all changes, because the world itself changes with time:

- The real world changes something that requires our system (and model) to change with it.
- The perception of what the system should do changes. This occurs especially when a customer gets a chance to use a system when it is only partly developed. He or she then soon learns more about the capabilities and possibilities of the system, getting many new ideas during the learning process.

Unfortunately, the systems that we have built until the present do not gracefully respond to a "simple" change in customer requirements (our reality). The customer wants a small and simple change, but the simple change is often transformed into several changes of the software system, as illustrated in Figure 1.8, which is always expensive.

Hence, we can define our second problem:

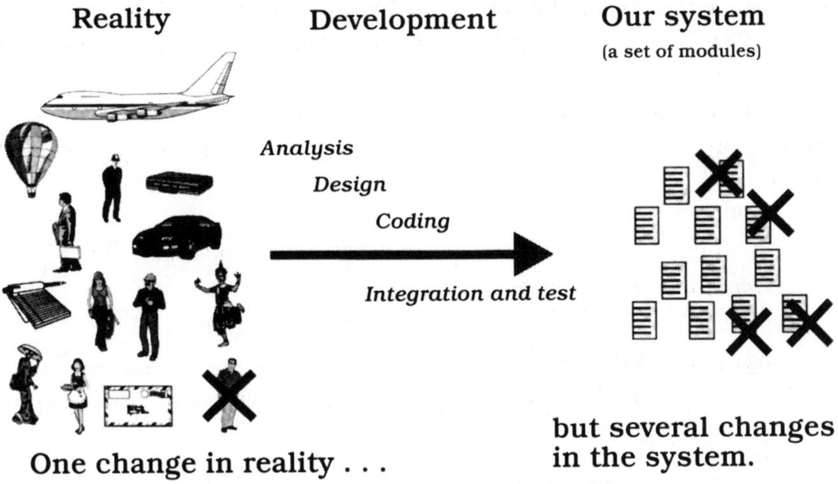


**Figure 1.8** Changes are often difficult to handle.

**Problem 2.** A simple change in reality often results in the need for *several changes* in the software system.

## The Tower of Babel

*The Lord said: "If as one people speaking the same language they have begun to do this, then nothing they plan to do will be impossible for them. Come, let us go down and confuse their language so they will not understand each other." So the Lord scattered them from there over all the earth, and they stopped building the city. That is why it was called Babel—because there the Lord confused the language of the whole world.*

—Genesis 11:6–9

Yes, as if the problems already mentioned were not enough, we have the problem of not understanding each other. The great difficulty we have in describing what a system should do is illustrated by the facts found in Figure 1.9. The figure shows, for example, that more than half the errors we have in a system are introduced during requirements analysis. On the other hand, we discover only a minority (5%) of the errors we have in a system during requirements analysis. Ramamoorthy mentions in *IEEE Computer* 10/84 that 55% of the faults are introduced in the first phase of the software development project. In his book *A Professional's Guide to System Analysis* [28], Martin E. Modell mentions that perhaps 80% to

| Software development phases | Errors introduced | Errors observed |
|---|---|---|
| Requirements Analysis | 55% | 5% |
| Design | 30% | 10% |
| Construction and system test | 15% | 40% |
| Acceptance test and operations/maintenance | ca 0% | 45% |

**Figure 1.9** (*Sources:* Boehm, Barry W. *Software Engineering Economics.* Englewood Cliffs, N.J.: Prentice Hall; Hughes DOD composite Software Error History.)

90% of the changes after implementation are due to incomplete or inaccurate front-end analysis in the original project. Many other sources say the same thing: Most of a system's faults are due to faults in the requirements specification.

The effect of this is expensive, because we do not detect the errors at the beginning but later, when it is much more expensive to fix them. These errors are largely caused by a communication gap between the customer and the developers. This communication gap occurs because customers and software developers do not talk about the same things. While the customer thinks about his or her world, perhaps a world of invoices, records, and the like, the software developers too often try to map what they hear directly into detailed code designs. We illustrate this problem in Figure 1.10.

A third problem is found:

**Problem 3.** We have a communication gap between customers and software developers.

## SOLUTIONS

### Abstraction

*The art of being wise is the art of knowing what to overlook.*

—William James

Let us take a closer look at the first problem. We said that reality could be described as something that consists of a large set of things and that the

**Figure 1.10** Communication between user and developer is often a problem.

human being is unable to take in such a large number of details. If we are to conquer complexity, we must thus find some way of organizing the complexity in a way that the human brain can handle it. Is there such a way? A simple answer is the answer we introduced earlier: Reduce the number of items we have to deal with simultaneously. We have found a first solution:

> **A Tentative Solution.** Use a technique that reduces the number of facts with which we have to deal simultaneously.

Comprehension is not automatic. The time we need to comprehend something is inversely proportional to the number of things with which we are presented and to the relevance of those items. The process is analogous to when a physician meets a patient the first time. If he or she is first given a summary written by another physician, the new physician will understand the situation much faster than if he or she has to make a full investigation of the patient. This situation is true because irrelevant items have been abstracted away, and only the relevant items remain in a summary. A high-quality model fills the same function as a summary, whereas a model that confuses us is like a report stating every conceivable fact. This does not mean that we have to take away details from our model, only that we must use a technique that somehow hides *irrelevant* details.

Figure 1.11 illustrates how we can get a simpler model by ignoring details. That is, if we can hide most of the details that we have to consider

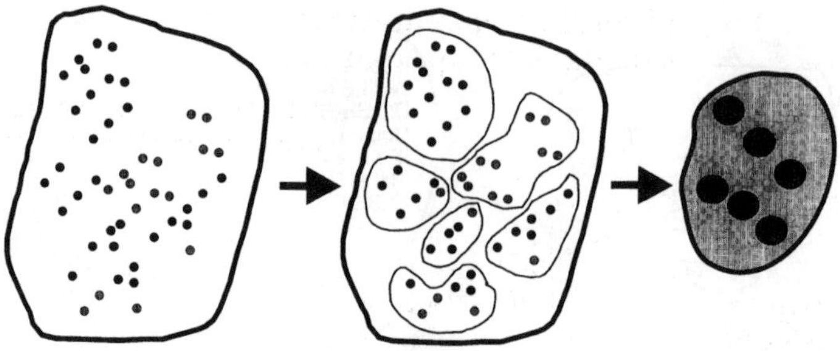

**Figure 1.11** Hiding details improves comprehension.

at a given moment, we can successfully deal with what remains. This is called abstraction.

**Definition.** To *abstract* is to separate mentally, to consider apart from other things, to summarize, to extract the essentials of several things.

Using this knowledge we restate our first tentative solution:

**Solution A.** Use abstraction to hide *irrelevant* details, thereby reducing the number of things with which we have to deal *simultaneously.*

This solution is extremely important. However, for some obscure reason, abstraction is not used much in many popular object-oriented modeling techniques. We will see in this book, however, that (good) object-oriented techniques rely heavily on this solution and that different ways of doing abstractions tend to appear in many different forms.

## Having a Close Mapping

*What is reasonable is real; that which is real is reasonable.*

—Georg Wilhelm Friedrich Hegel

As mentioned earlier, the experience of maintenance is that one change in the requirements often leads to many changes in the software system. If we could have a simpler mapping between reality, model, and software system, the maintenance would be easier. Figure 1.12 illustrates the idea of having a simple connection between reality, model, and implementation.

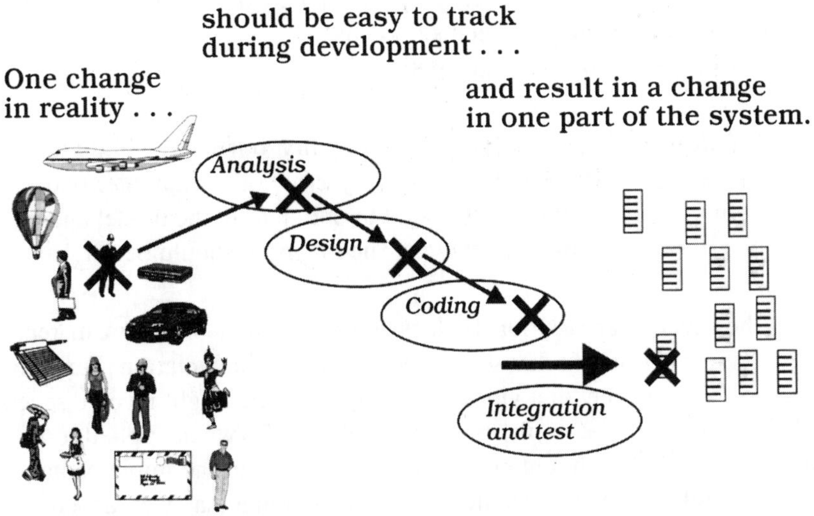


**Figure 1.12** A simple connection between reality and model minimizes work due to changes.

That is, *if* our way of modeling makes it easier to relate between reality and our system, we have found a second solution:

> **A Tentative Solution.** The mapping between reality, our model, and the implemented system should be simple and straightforward.

Why is this mapping so important? To answer that question, let us recall the paradox about the barber who shaved everyone in his little village who did not shave himself and only those people. With this sentence we have built a little model of reality, but we have a problem: Who shaves the barber?

- If he shaves himself, he is not allowed to shave himself, because he did not shave those who shaved themselves.
- On the other hand, if he does not shave himself, he should shave himself, because he is supposed to shave everyone who does not shave himself.

Is this a problem? In reality, there is not a problem, because the beard on the barber will grow longer and longer unless someone cuts it! That is, the real world *does not tolerate paradoxes*. The world is inerrant—infallible—and the problem is to be found in our model, because it does not describe the situation properly. When the model is not close enough to reality, we get problems like this.

So let us state our second solution:

> **Solution B**. The mapping between reality, our model, and the implemented system should be very *close*. For example, one item in reality should correspond to one item in the model and one item in the implementation. The mapping should be 1:1:1.

Note, however, that solution B does *not* imply that one item in reality must correspond to one low-level item in the implementation. For example, the behavior Play of a video recording machine might involve several low-level items in the implementation. Solution B (when applied to Play) says only that there should be one high-level item in the implementation, grouping relevant low-level items into something that we can connect with Play.

### *Close Mapping and Traceability*

Close mapping covers *all aspects* when we transform reality to a model and then to implementation. Traceability, on the other hand, normally applies only to the ability of tracing from one item in an early phase of system development to an item in a later phase, and vice versa. Thus, traceability between a functional requirement in an early phase and how it is realized in later phases is not enough to say that we have close mapping. Close mapping also means, in addition, that a functional requirement should be connected to a particular user or group of users. This is so because in reality it is a particular user that needs this functional requirement and we should not lose this information when we build our model.

Having close mapping also means that as we develop an item, from phase to phase, it should continue to exist as a single idea. Traceability, on the other hand, does not have this restriction, and the implementation of a functional requirement could be found in several unconnected parts of a system. Traceability is thus a more limited idea than when we say that we shall have close mapping.

## Structures

A third solution is found if we consider that the human brain, while not very good at remembering a lot of facts, nevertheless is very good at navigating in structures. A technique called *mind mapping* uses this fact.

If we look at Figure 1.13, we see that what makes it easier for a human being to handle this set of facts is that the parts are related in a mindmap. That is, starting with a certain fact it is possible to get to another fact using associations between the facts.

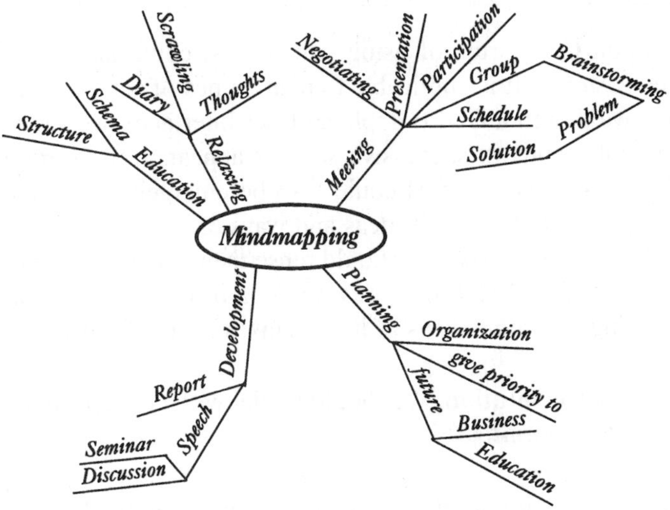


**Figure 1.13** Structures improve comprehension.

This means that *if* we can use knowledge of how facts are similar or how they relate in some way, it is easier to navigate between them. The human brain is very adept at using these different kinds of associations for handling large sets of facts. Summarizing, we state our third solution to the software crisis:

> **Solution C.** Structure the parts (things) in the (software) model using *similarities* and using *structures*—that is, by using the fact that parts often relate in structures that are natural to us.

Actually we have two solutions: We can apply the idea of similarity both to the contents of a model and to the form of modeling, that is, the convention we apply to our modeling.

---

**Example**

*Contents*: If we find many similar things, we can group them and refer to the group rather than to all the members of the group.

*Form:* We might decide that certain names should always start with an uppercase letter and that words in a name should always be separated with a blank underline (_). We could also define a documentation standard. Such a standard is an excellent help when we try to grasp the information in a document. With such a standard we know—even before we start reading a document—roughly where we can find information considering different aspects.

---

Solution C, the rule of using similarities, could also be called the *rule of consistency.* It is applicable to many types of activities. For example, when we design a GUI (Graphical User Interface), we should design in a way that menus in successive screens appear in the same position. The rule of using similarities could also be enlarged to include a more general experience. That is, if ideas and ways of arranging things used in everyday life already exist, we should reuse them when we model. Generally speaking: If we want to express an idea or concept, then we should use something that reminds us of it. This takes us to a fourth solution.

> **A Tentative Solution.** We should model with concepts that are *natural* and *intuitive.*

This idea is sometimes referred to as having a minimal *semantic gap* between what we model and the model.

**Definition.** *Semantics* involve the relationships of symbols or groups of symbols to their meanings in a given language [IEEE].

**Definition.** *Syntax* involves the structural or grammatical rules that define how the symbols in a language are to be combined to form words, phrases, expressions, and other allowable constructs [IEEE].

Thus semantics relate to the meaning of something, whereas syntax deals with the rules of using symbols for denoting that meaning. The closer our model and implementation are to how something is normally described, the smaller our semantic gaps are for model and implementation, respectively. A small semantic gap is, of course, advantageous.

---

**Examples**

(a) If a system handles invoices and we need to indicate them on a monitor, we should model them with something that reminds us of invoices, such as icons that resemble typical invoices.

(b) If we need to express an equation, using approved standard mathematics notation yields better results.

(c) If something is best represented with a figure, use a figure. If something is best represented with text, use text.

(d) If a customer uses a particular word for a concept, use that word in the model rather than some other invented word.

---

Because we want our customer and developer to speak the same language, we restate this fourth solution as follows:

> **Solution D.** We should model with concepts that are *natural, intuitive,* and *close* to the customer.

Note that this rule deals with the concepts we use, whereas solution B is a more general solution mapping items in reality, model and implementation. As illustrated in Figure 1.14, the object acts as an interpreter between customer and developers, helping them to achieve solution D.

All solutions introduced in this chapter could be regarded as specializations of a more general solution.

> **Solution E.** KISS (Keep It Simple, Simon!)*

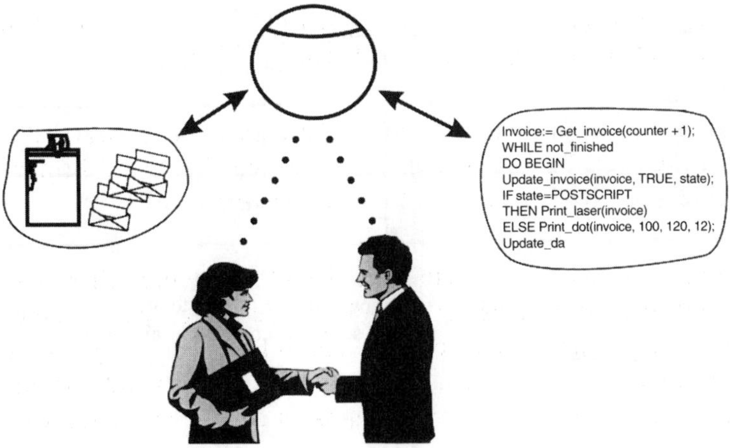


**Figure 1.14** An object, represented with a circle in the figure, acts as an interpreter, helping the user and the developers to focus on the same thing.

---

*Sometimes also translated as Keep It Simple, Someone or Keep It Simple, Stupid.

In the rest of the book we will use these solutions when we try to judge whether a certain modeling technique is good or bad. Object-oriented modeling should always be performed in such a way that we apply the solutions we have introduced in this chapter. These solutions will thus be important tools for us when we select and discuss object-oriented modeling techniques in the rest of the book.

Figure 1.15 shows roughly how the problems and solutions mentioned in this chapter are related. *Reuse,* listed in this figure as a problem, has not yet been discussed. Reuse is a multifaceted problem, and we will discuss it at various points in the rest of the book. Let us here just say that reuse will be facilitated by the solutions we have mentioned. For example, abstraction will help us create parts that are not very dependent on other parts in an application, which helps us when we want to reuse an object in a new application. The use of natural concepts will help us find reusable parts that can be applied in more than one situation. Using structures—for example the class structure introduced in Chapter 3—helps us create new components reusing designs found in old components. Close mapping helps us trace a part in analysis to the actual code representing it, and so on.

| Problems | Solutions |
|---|---|
| 1 Too many things | A Use abstraction<br>C Use structures |
| 2 Too many changes | B Have a close mapping |
| 3 Communication gap | D Use natural concepts |
| 4 Reuse | A, B, C and D |

**Figure 1.15** General solutions and how they are related to problems connected with the software crisis. These solutions are the axis around which discussions in this book will revolve.

## SUMMARY

In this chapter we have seen that the software industry is in the midst of a crisis. Three important problems related to this crisis were discussed in detail:

- The systems developed today involve an enormous number of details, which create a complex situation that the human brain cannot easily handle.
- We cannot properly handle changes in systems that have already been developed.
- As software developers, we are often unable to speak the same language as the customer.

Four important solutions to the software crisis were also discussed:

- By using abstraction to hide details, we can simplify our task of handling the complexity.
- Our model and implementation should be closely related to reality. The maintenance will then be easier, because one change in reality will lead to only one or a few changes in the corresponding part of the system and not too many changes in the system.
- We should build the system with structures that are natural to our way of thinking.
- The customers and the software developers should use the same terms.

These solutions will be the basis for judging object-oriented modeling techniques presented in this book.

# 2

# Basic Concepts

## *Modeling Reality*

> *Human subtlety . . . will never devise an invention more beautiful, more simple or more direct than does nature, because in her inventions nothing is lacking, and nothing is superfluous.*
>
> —Leonardo da Vinci

### INTRODUCTION

In this chapter we introduce basic modeling concepts used in object-oriented modeling: objects, classes, attributes, methods, and messages. We also discuss related ideas, such as information hiding; modularity; what a model is; how to draw objects and classes; how to use nouns, verbs, adjectives, and adverbs to find objects, methods, and attributes.

Both data-intensive and function-intensive software development are adopting object-oriented ideas, but they differ in their approach. Both areas make interesting contributions, however. We start by taking the perspective of the DP (Data Processing) world. This is followed by a more technical approach to object-oriented modeling.

### THE MODEL

In the previous chapter we introduced the idea that modeling reality implies handling complexity. But what do we mean by reality and what is a model?

**Definition.** A *model* is a representation of a real-world process, device, or concept. [IEEE-729]

When we start building a system, we might find items such as invoices, bank accounts, monitors, and input/output devices, but we also find items that are not very tangible, such as the ideas the user employs in his or her business. All these must be put in our model. Thus we are interested in anything perceptible to the senses—something tangible, but also in those things that are perceptible only to the mind—abstract notions.

We also have to invent new ideas to make the system do what we want it to do. We illustrate this in Figure 2.1. We put objects in our model because they exist as tangible things or as abstract notions but also because they result from the creative thinking done by the developers. If from this you infer that the clear line between analysis and design disappears, you are correct. The line between analysis and design is much less well defined when using object-oriented techniques.

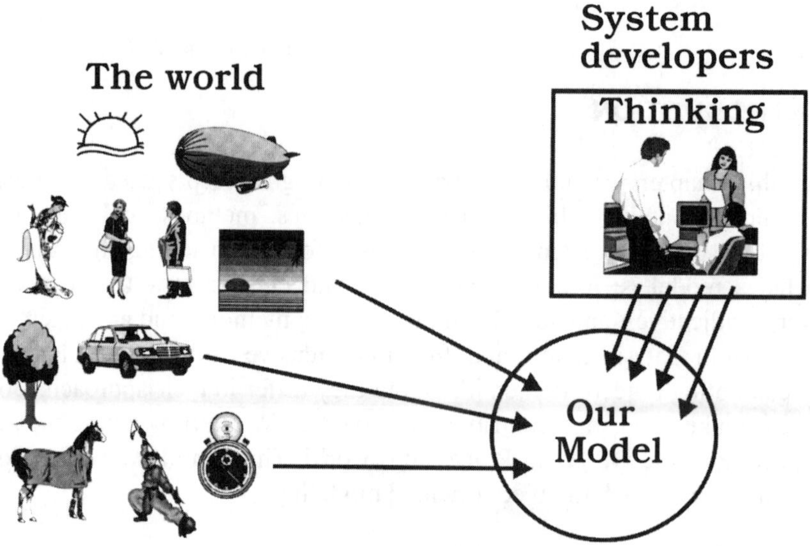


**Figure 2.1** Both existing ideas and new idea objects are put in the model.

Often the difference between tangible and abstract objects is vague. For example, an invoice is the result of earlier human creativity although it now exists. The important point here, however, is that our drawing will contain objects from several areas when we try to put the model on paper: tangible objects, abstract notions and new idea objects, which are objects created by system developers.

Before we continue, let us define a few important concepts:

- The drawing that we make of the system to be constructed is called a *model*. A model represents a system in graphic and narrative form. A first high-level model will show the major parts of a system, how they interact, and how they relate to the environment where the system is to be used. We refer to a drawing of this first-high level model as a *context drawing*. An expanded part of this drawing will show subparts of the model and how they interact.

- *Modeling* is the act of creating a model.
- The *world* is everything in our universe.
- The part of the world in which we take an interest is our *reality*. A word sometimes used for this is UoD (Universe of Discourse).

When we investigate reality, we frequently expose technical aspects of the system. Often there is a heated debate whether we should allow this type of information in our model or not. We should strive to avoid having objects dependent on some particular technical solution. However, we are not living in a perfect world, and if we have an important technical limitation we can represent this fact in our model—even at a high level of modeling. If we ignore an important technical implementation detail, we could end up with a nice model, but a model that we cannot implement. After all, we are trying to model reality; if technical limitations or hardware parts are part of that reality, why not put them in our model? We should try to avoid being fanatical about issues like this. Instead, we should try to exercise good judgment based on our experience.

We can make models of both application software and system software.

**Definition.** *Application software* is software designed to fulfill specific needs of a user; for example—software for navigation, payroll, or process control [IEEE].

**Definition.** *System software* is software designed to facilitate the operation and maintenance of a computer system and its associated programs—for example, operating systems, assemblers, and utilities [IEEE].

The techniques outlined in this book apply to both these types of software. (The principles and ideas outlined in this book can, in fact, be applied to handle any complex system whether it concerns software or not.) Our general definition of software is

**Definition.** *Software* covers all instructions and data that are input to a computer to cause it to function in any mode. This includes operating systems, compilers, test routines, application programs, etc. The documents used to define and to describe the programs are also included. For example, program listings, specifications, test plans, test data, test results, user instructions, etc.

## INFORMATION MODELING

In the data processing world, different data models are very important. So, let us see what an earlier technique called information modeling* has to offer. This technique starts by stating that our reality is full of things. In the next step information modeling recognizes the following:

1. There are many things out there, but many of them are similar, as illustrated in Figure 2.2.
2. The things in our model should have a direct one-to-one mapping to things in reality (see Figure 2.3).

**Figure 2.2** Similar things can be grouped.

The idea that things are alike (item 1) is an idea meeting solution C introduced in Chapter 1. The idea that things in reality and the model should have a simple and direct relation (item 2) is a restatement of solution B found in the same chapter.

---

* A more thorough comparison of object-oriented modeling and information modeling is found in Appendix 1.

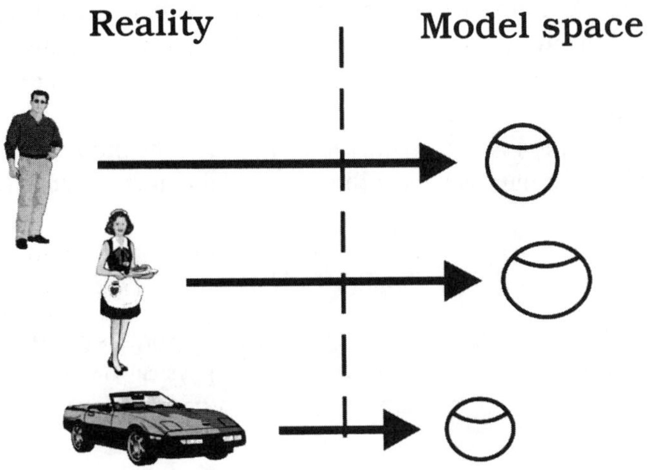


**Figure 2.3** Reality and model should be closely related.

Even if these ideas are simple, they are seldom completely followed in system development. Why? The ideas are simple, but they are often difficult to apply. This situation is especially true for technical systems. For example, the idea that all elements in the model should be directly and easily related to things in reality might sound reasonable. Achieving this goal might be another thing altogether. With the object-oriented modeling techniques described in this book, it is easier to accomplish this goal, however.

When modeling we are sometimes using views. A *view* is a particular way of regarding something. We might view a system in different ways, and each view will yield a presentation suitable for a particular purpose.

---

**Example**

Let us describe a book. A possible approach would be to describe the book as consisting of covers with several pages between them. Each page is then described as made up of several lines, sometimes including pictures. Each line can be described as a series of characters. Another view could be more logical. A rough sketch of this view is as follows: The book contains several chapters. Each chapter has one or several subchapters. A subchapter might contain smaller subchapters (and headers), until we find paragraphs. A paragraph is made up by grouping one or several sentences. Sentences and headers are made up by grouping words and a word is made up by one or more characters.

---

The problem we are considering here is the problem of achieving a close mapping between reality and our model. If we can get different models starting from the same reality, how can we preserve a close mapping? We find part of the solution to this problem when we consider that we can always connect each view with a certain purpose. Thus, behind each view is a unique purpose. We discuss the importance of the purpose more in Chapter 3.

The solution is thus mainly to be aware of the problem: If we model with an unclear purpose, we will get a model that is a mix of several distinct views.

---

**Example**

A model of a book with parts like pages, lines, and words is probably not a good model. (It mixes two views: a logical view and a physical view).

---

## ATTRIBUTES

What do we mean when we say that things are similar? We simply mean that they should have the same characteristics.* For example, when we are dealing with people, we might concern ourselves with a specific group. In that group we might be interested only in the name, age, and occupation of the members in the group. We could make a *table* for these attributes as in Figure 2.4. The table can be used to list similarities between several things. This table actually becomes our definition of what attributes (characteristics) someone should have *if* he or she belongs to the group we call Person.

Person

| Name | Age | Occupation |
|---|---|---|
| | | |

**Figure 2.4** A table summarizes facts concerning a group of things.

It is important to distinguish between the table as such and data we put into the table. The table does *not* represent any thing(s) from reality until we have filled it with values as shown in Figure 2.5. Thus the table is

*Because we have not yet introduced methods for describing the behavior, we concern ourselves only with attributes. Introducing behavior would not alter the discussion.

**Person**

| Name | Age | Occupation |
|---|---|---|
| Elisa | 22 | student |
| Stefan | 37 | consultant |
| John | 36 | programmer |

**Figure 2.5** Specific instances are described by stating their values.

only a description or illustration of what attributes a thing should have to be placed in this particular table.

Each row of values represents one "thing" in reality—in our example, a person. The values define characteristics about this specific thing. We call this thing an *instance* and the different characteristics *attributes*.

**Definition.** An *instance* is an occurrence of *one* individual person, act or thing (abstract or concrete). It has certain characteristics, that may be unique or the same as other instances, but it can always be referred to in a nonchanging and unique way.

**Definition.** An *attribute* is a descriptor of an instance. It tells us something important and significant about the nature of an instance.

Examples of attributes include length, weight, color, date of birth, price, place of work, name, sex, and age. So, when we say that things are alike, we mean that the attributes we have picked are the same, not that the *values* of those attributes are the same. (The values might be the same, but only by coincidence).

We can say that if we know that an instance belongs to a certain table, we know what attributes the instance must have, but we do not know their values. Only when we put values into the row have we described the instance completely.

---

**Example**

An *instance* weighs 27.13 kg. The attribute *weight* is a consequence of the *table* defining the instance, but the value 27.13 is (probably) unique for this instance.

---

Because this book deals with object-oriented modeling, we rephrase the previous example using the definition of *class*.

**Definition.** A *class* describes what attributes and (as we shall soon see) methods an object shall have.

---

**Example**

An *object* weighs 27.13 kg. The attribute *weight* is a consequence of the *class* defining the object, but the value 27.13 is (probably) unique for this object.

---

In our studies [2] we found that we lost nothing by making the words instance and object synonyms. That is, an object is an instance and not a class. The word entity is also often used for the word thing. In this book we use the words entity, thing, instance, and object interchangeably.

### Domain

The possible values of an attribute are often restricted in some way. In this case an attribute is allowed to accept only a specific set of values or a certain range of values. We call the values we allow the attribute its *domain*. In Figure 2.6 the domain is 1 to 65 years for Age, $0 to $100,000 for Salary, and so on. Note that a domain is equivalent to a *data type* as this term is usually used in modern programming languages.

| | | |
|---|---|---|
| Age | : | Integer [1 .. 65] (Year) |
| Salary | : | Integer [0 .. 100,000] (US$) |
| Name | : | String [1 .. 100] (Char) |
| State | : | [Ok, Idle, Error, Warning] |

**Figure 2.6** Examples of domains for the attributes Age, Salary, Name, and State.

It is common to define a set of values to be included in a domain as in the preceding examples. However, the domain can also be defined in other ways, such as by giving a rule or rules or by referring to something. In initial stages (analysis, top-level design), it is a good idea not to be too explicit about the domain. For example, "Name of dog" gives more freedom in later stages (low-level design, coding) than a "String 1 to 60 characters."

Often several of the attributes we use are related in some sense. We could, for example, have a group of attributes that describe an address.

This implies that we need the ability to group attributes into subgroups. We call such attributes *complex attributes* or *composite attributes*.

Domains of scalar values are thus more accurately referred to as *simple domains* in order to distinguish them from *composite domains,* used in connection with complex attributes. A composite domain is basically just a combination of simple domains. No such distinction is adhered to in this book, and when we refer to a domain (or a type) it could be a simple domain or a composite domain. Synonyms for simple domains and composite domains are atomic type and composite type, respectively:

**Definition.** *Atomic type* is a data type, each of whose members consists of a single, nondecomposable data item [IEEE].

**Definition.** *Composite type* is a data type, each of whose members is composed of multiple data items. For example, a data type called PAIRS whose members are ordered pairs (x,y) [IEEE].

The normal case is that an attribute has an associated domain. A (simple) attribute thus normally has three parts:

1. Its name
2. Its domain (or data type)
3. Its value

The name describes the attribute, the domain restricts the values the attribute can take, and the value describes what the attribute is at the moment.

A complex attribute can be described by grouping several simple attributes inside brackets []. For example:

```
[YearofBirth, Name, Age, {Comment}]
```

where italic implies values that can be *derived* (*Age* = current year - YearOfBirth) and curly brackets {} implies one or several attributes of the same type.

### Other Attributes

Besides distinguishing between simple and complex attributes, it is often of help to think about attributes as having three different roles in a model. We use *descriptive attributes, state attributes,* and *referential attributes* to describe these roles. A descriptive attribute describes an important and relevant characteristic or property of an instance. A state attribute describes some important state information connected with the instance, and referential attributes are used to implement relationships. A referential attribute has a type that makes it possible for the attribute to reference other objects. These two latter types of attributes are discussed in more detail in connection with state transition diagrams and relationships, respectively. It is also common to refer to attributes as *instance attributes* or *class attributes*. An instance attribute describes an instance, whereas a class attribute is connected with the class as such. A class attribute is typically used to share data between objects of the same class. It is like a global variable, except that it cannot be accessed by objects created from other classes.

---

**Example**

We have a class describing cars. A typical instance attribute is the registration number. A typical class attribute for the class is the number of car objects created using the class.

---

When we reach implementation, we might encounter variations of this. For example, in Smalltalk we have instance variables, class instance variables, and class variables. *Instance variables* and *class instance variables* correspond to instance attributes and class attributes, respectively. (A *class variable* has a scope that includes the defining class, subclasses of that class, and all instances of these classes).

## METHODS—AN INTRODUCTION

Methods make it possible to connect algorithms (behavior) with an object. Using object-oriented terminology, we say that an object has both attributes and methods. In the same way that we use attributes to describe static characteristics of an object, we use methods to describe behavior of an object—that is, the services or actions that an object can supply. Each method has a *name* and a *body*. The body carries out the action (or behavior) associated with the method name.

A method is very similar to a *procedure* or a *function*—that is, some named code that is executed when called. This code can then check or change the attribute values of the object and/or call other object(s). A key question when deciding about what methods objects should have is, "What is a proper distribution of responsibilities among the objects?"

## THE CLASS AND THE OBJECT

We can consider the class to be a development of the table mentioned earlier. The objects correspond to the "entities" used in information modeling. Entities are things in reality (our instance, a row in the table).*

---

*Also, see Appendix 1.

The class is our description—or definition—of the attributes and methods an object will have. The name of a class should be a singular noun. Note that it can be a good idea to state *inclusion criteria* and *exclusion criteria* to describe a class. This is especially true when we are in the early stages of describing a class and we have not decided what attributes and methods the class should have. Inclusion criteria tell us how objects belonging to the class are alike and exclusion criteria tell us when an object should not belong to a class. Such criteria help us to select the right mix of attributes and methods for a class.

We say that we create or *instantiate* object(s) using a class. The class states what attributes *and* methods an object *should have* (if it is to belong to the class in question). Figure 2.7 illustrates the idea: Using a class, we know what methods and attributes an object should have (but not what values these attributes will get).

```
IF "an object  is created using this class"
THEN BEGIN
          Give it attribute A
          Give it attribute B
                 :

          Give it method no. 1
          Give it method no. 2
                 :

          Give it a unique identity

          END
```

**Figure 2.7** A class is a description defining objects.

In some books the concepts type and class are used interchangeably. We do not follow this practice; instead we regard the class as an augmented form of the type concept. We use the type to describe—or rather to restrict—the values that an attribute can take, whereas we use the class to define the objects we create. Why we connect the type concept with attributes and the class concept with objects is explained in more detail in the section, *The Class and the Type Concept,* later in this chapter.

An object can be viewed as an encapsulated program operating on its own local data (attributes), a little self-contained computer or software machine able to remember its state. However, an object in a model represents an occurrence of something. This implies that we can regard an object as a model of its own as it models something. A better metaphor is, therefore, to view an object as an independent microworld able to remember things—a microworld with well-defined responsibilities, created to model something specific, and collaborating with other objects to achieve its goals.

The object has a unique *identity.* The identity of an object is independent of its state or its behavior. Thus, as long as the object exists, there is a way of handling it via its identity. The object is given this identity by the system when it is created, and the identity will not be reused for any other object. The identity cannot be changed during the time of execution and it distinguishes the object from every other object in the system. This is different from how an identity is constructed from attributes in traditional database systems. (A comparison between the identifiers used in information modeling and the identity of an object is found in Appendix 1).

Note that an object can model tangible things, abstract notions, or new ideas.

---

**Example**

We can model both people and invoices with objects in a system. If, when designing a system, we find that we need to manage collections of invoices, we can also model this new idea with an object. (As a rule, it is good design to avoid creating too many new objects that are not easily related to reality.)

---

Two key questions we should ask ourselves when we introduce an object are, "Why should the object exist?" and "What obligations should the object have?"

When an object is created, memory is allocated for it. If memory is not managed automatically, often called *garbage collection,* special constructions for destroying objects must exist so that allocated memory can be released. In some object-oriented languages—such as C++, which is without garbage collection—this allocating and deallocating of memory is a major source of errors.

## DRAWING THE OBJECT

Figures 2.8 and 2.9 show varied ways of drawing an object.

The area above the line contains the *interface* of the object. Other objects can use what we put here. For example, other objects can call

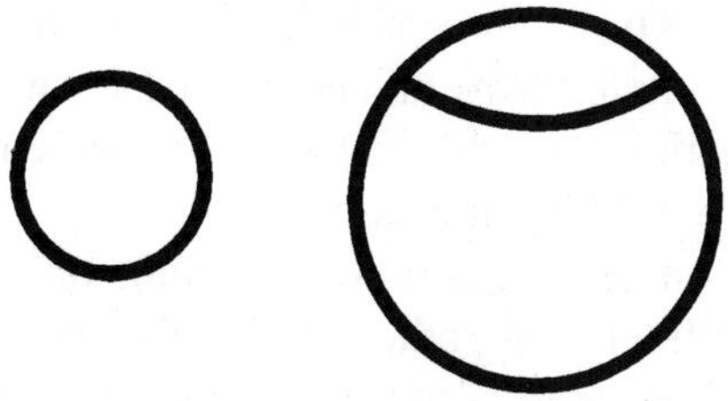

**Figure 2.8** Two simple ways of drawing an object.

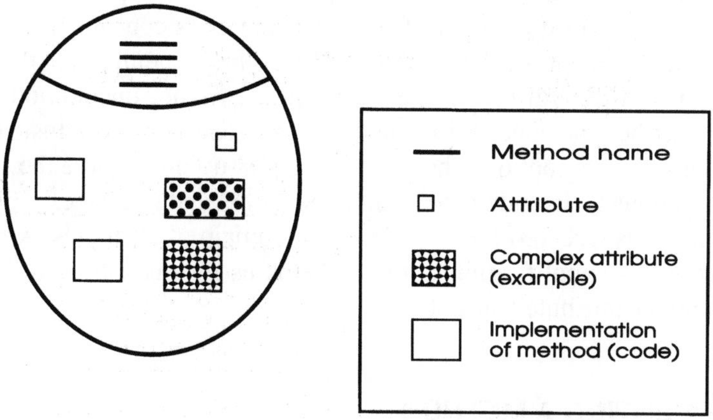


**Figure 2.9** A more elaborate way of drawing an object.

those methods whose names are placed here. We say that such externally visible or available methods (or attributes) have been *exported*. Note that if we have a method in an object but its name is not placed above the line, then this method can still be used by the object itself. Below the line, we place details (attributes, subobjects, etc.) that enhance the understanding of the object. As always, we should put a *relevance test* to this and not display things unless they really aid in our comprehension of what the object is all about. Also see the section "Selecting Good Interfaces" in Chapter 4.

## THE CLASS AND THE TYPE CONCEPT

When we refer to a class we mean both the interface and the implementation of the class. This is true because as a class defines the methods of an object, the class also defines the object's interface. However, different classes may have the same interface even if their implementations are different. Sometimes the type concept is introduced to denote the interface of a class. For example, "two objects have the same type (because their interfaces are identical) but have different implementations (because they are instantiated from different classes)."

When we build an application by grouping objects together the focus is always on the interfaces rather than the implementations. Thus, we seldom need to differentiate between the interface of a class and the class as such. Also many languages do not make this distinction explicit.

Thus, if we need to refer to only the interface of a class we will simply refer to the "interface of the class" rather than the "type of the class." This leaves us with the option of reserving the class concept for objects and the type concept for the attributes. We will thus neither use the type concept as a synonym to the class concept—as is not uncommon—nor will we use the type concept to denote the interface of a class. Instead we select the following option: The class concept is used to denote the specification of objects, including both implementation and interface, while the type concept is reserved for describing the domain of attributes. A major reason for this simplification is that it helps us distinguish between the object and the attribute concept.

## IMPLEMENTING A METHOD

A method has a name and a corresponding *implementation*, earlier referred to as the body. When we draw this, we indicate the method name with a line and the implementation with a square or rectangle. We may also write the method name instead of using a line (see Figure 2.10). The implementation of a method is typically small, 10 to 25 lines. However, method implementations may be much larger than that.

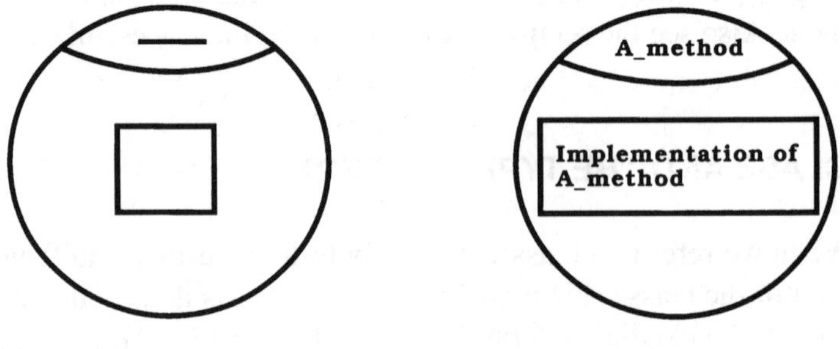


**Figure 2.10** Detailing an object drawing can be done in different ways.

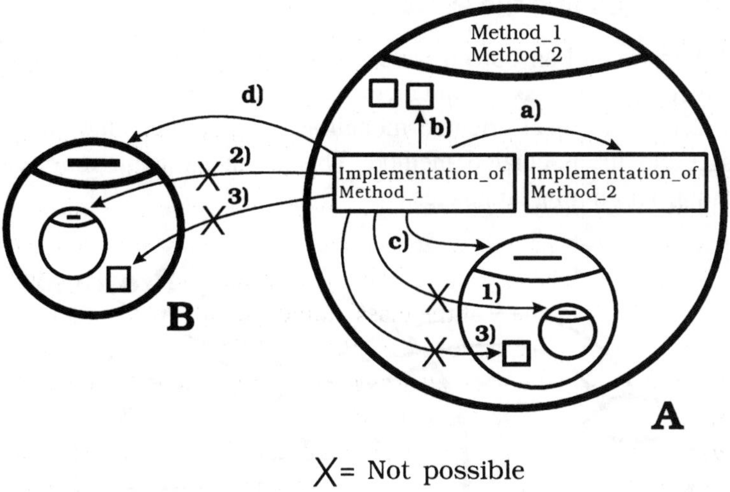


**Figure 2.11** Implementing a method using attributes and other methods.

Figure 2.11 illustrates how we may implement a method belonging to an object A. We may use

a. Methods belonging to A
b. Attributes available in A
c. Methods belonging to subobjects of A
d. Methods belonging to objects outside A

Option d should be used with caution because it has a tendency to give us unstructured code.

It is *not* possible (directly) to use

1. Methods to subobjects inside subobjects
2. Methods to subobjects belonging to objects outside A
3. Attributes other than those belonging to A

For further discussion, see the section "Information Hiding" later in this chapter. This way of structuring objects is very similar to how other technical fields have structured their components. For example, if we think of A and B as circuit boards and their subobjects as the integrated circuits mounted on these boards, we immediately see similarities. It is, for example, normally not possible for an integrated circuit on A to use something inside another integrated circuit (option 1) or directly use integrated circuits mounted on B (options 2 and 3). On the other hand, it is normally perfectly all right to use what is available on A (options a, b, and c above) and often to use another circuit board (option d).

## Messages and the Protocol

When we call an object, we say that we send a *message* to it. The object receives the message and a corresponding method is executed (see Figure 2.12). In object-oriented modeling we give the same name to a message and its associated method. This is also true in most object-oriented programming languages.

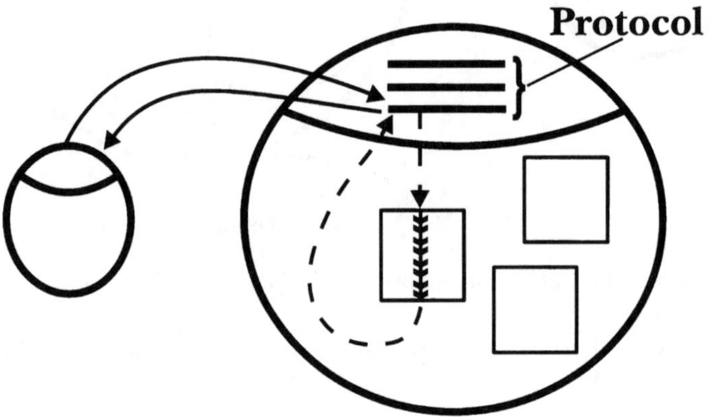


**Figure 2.12** Illustration of a message call.

The set of available messages that an object can receive is called its *protocol*. Note that in other technical fields the protocol is often understood to include more than this. For example, the rules about the format for calling are often included in the protocol.

It is common that a call to a method returns a result. However, it is not a requirement that a method should return a result. We adopt the calling possibilities outlined in [IEEE]:

**Definition.** *Call:* (1) A transfer of control from one software module to another, usually with the implication that control will be returned to the calling module. (2) A computer instruction that transfers control from one software module to another as in def. 1 and, often, specifies the parameters to be passed to and from the module. (3) To transfer control from one software module to another as in def. 1 and, often, to pass parameters to the other module [IEEE].

Note that defs. 2 and 3 are only variations of def. 1.

When we send a message to an object, a method with the same name will start to execute. Figure 2.13 shows two different ways for an object, B, to handle the return of a method call. In alternative 1, B immediately

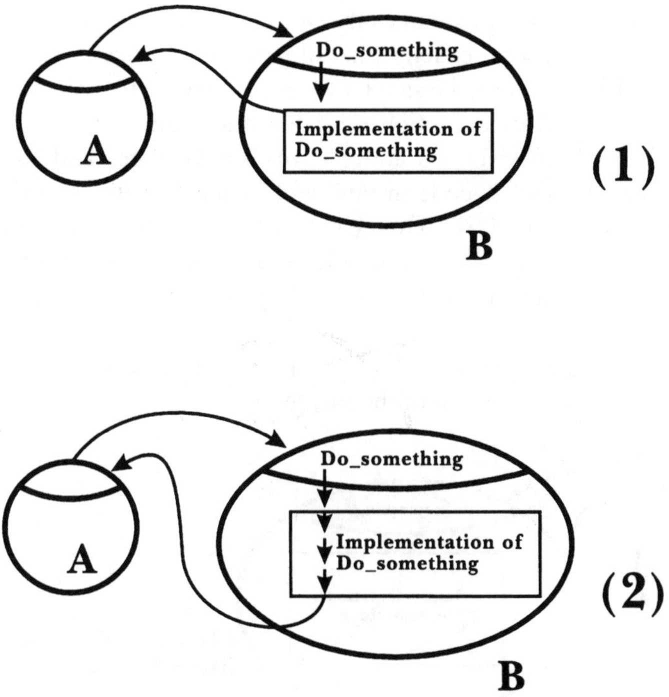


**Figure 2.13** Returning a method call.

returns control to A. In alternative 2, B returns control when the method has been completely executed. Alternative 1 is a good solution in some situations—for example, when we want to print something on a print queue. If B is a print queue, a call to it could look something like this:

```
B.Print_file(a_file);
```

In this case it is very natural for B to take care of the printing, allowing A to continue with its execution. (Note that we are assuming that it is possible for B and A to execute in parallel.) Alternative 1, however, is not always safe. Let us assume a call is made in a system managing a hoisting mechanism for an elevator. We also assume that B is in charge of handling the doors of the elevator rather than handling a print queue. What will then happen when the following call occurs?

```
B.Close_doors;
```

If B immediately returns control to A, before it has successfully closed the doors, it could have serious consequences. For example, suppose a person is in the doors, stopping the doors from being closed. It is not safe to move the elevator before the doors have been successfully closed, but if the system assumes that the call `B.Close_doors;` successfully closed the doors, exactly that situation could occur. On the other hand, alternative 2 would be safe (if we could assume that the method will not reach the end of execution until the doors have been successfully closed). Thus both solutions above have disadvantages and advantages. The strategy for pseudocode in this book is that we are returned from a call when this is safe. It is up to the called object to decide when it is safe. Thus, in the example with a print queue, solution 1 would probably have been chosen. In the case with the hoisting mechanism, solution 2 would have been chosen.

A third case is shown in Figure 2.14. In this case the return of a call occurs during the execution of the method.

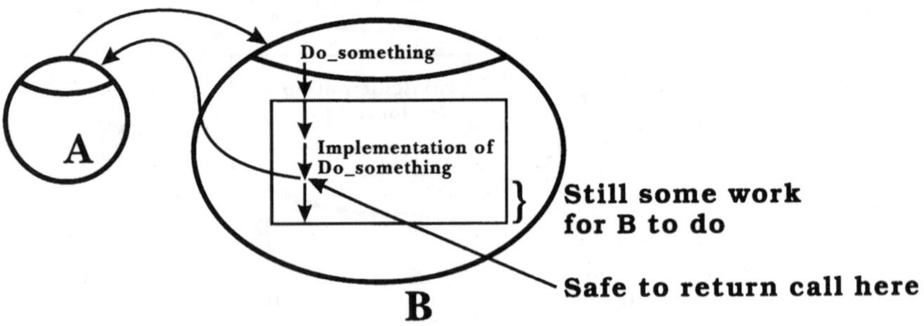


**Figure 2.14** Returning a method call during the execution of a method.

Note that this discussion pertains to possible ways of modeling in analysis and design. It may be a good idea to look at the selected implementation language before choosing between the possibilities just outlined, because the difficulty in transforming from design model to implementation depends on how easily the constructs available in the selected language can be used to implement the design.

When we need to call one of the object's own methods we do not prefix the method name with the name of the object we call.

---

**Example**

We have two objects, A and B, with the methods a1, a2 and b1, b2, respectively. When we write the implementation of a1, we need to call a2 and b2. The call to A.a2 could then be written as "a2," whereas the call to B.b2 would have to be coded as "B.b2." . There are also other ways of expressing these constructs. For example, in Smalltalk we find the reserved word self. Making the calls in Smalltalk would look like this:

```
self a2.
```

and

```
B b2.
```

respectively. (The dot . is in Smalltalk used to end a statement.) Thus when an object needs to send a message to itself, it sends it to self.

---

## DRAWING THE CLASS

Figure 2.15 shows a typical way of drawing a class. At the top we find the name of the class. Below we find boxes where we can write the names of the methods, attributes, and other important things for the class. The idea of having a special section at the bottom for business and control rules is taken from Ian Graham [7]. In this box we can put information about constraints on objects created by the class, if the objects will be persistent or not, and so on. *Persistence* tells us whether an object will exist for the duration of a single given execution of a system or if it will continue to exist between particular executions of a system. The idea of persistency can also be applied to things other than objects, such as attributes. (Persistence is discussed in more detail in Appendix 1, in the section on databases.)

We have put the methods above the attributes to have them in the same place as the method names of an object. This differs from the notation used by Coad and Yourdon [4], for example, but is similar to the notation used in *Design Patterns* [35]. Note that methods are exported by default but not the attributes. If a method is not exported, we can indicate this by putting its name in parentheses. If an attribute is exported, we have to indicate this explicitly. (Note, attributes are not exported in this book.)

There are several other possible ways of representing a class. A simple way is to put the class name inside a square or rectangle, as shown in Figure 2.16. In the lower part of the figure, we see how we can add attributes and methods to this square or rectangle. This representation is particularly easy to use when we make a hand drawing of a class. During analysis or design, we often need to change our model. Maybe we need to add a new attribute or a method. If we confine the attributes and methods to boxes, we will soon run out of space when we hand draw a class. This does not happen if we use the representation found in this figure. To add a method, just make the vertical line longer and add the method to the right. Attribute B in the figure illustrates how we can show subgroups of attributes (complex attributes).

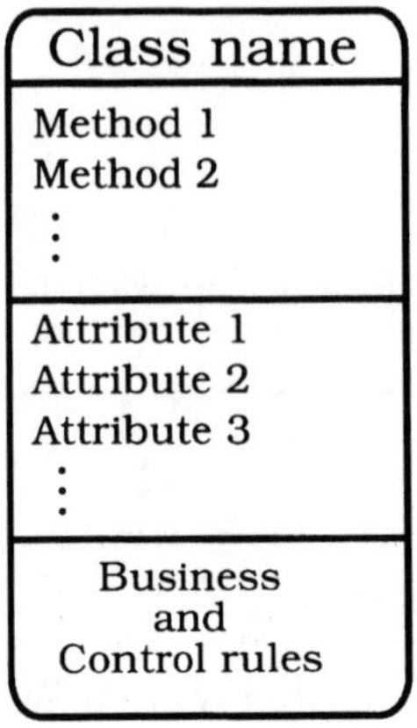


**Figure 2.15** A common way of drawing a class.

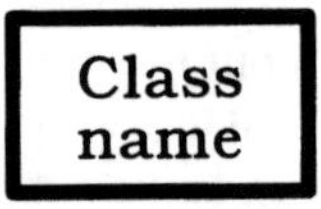


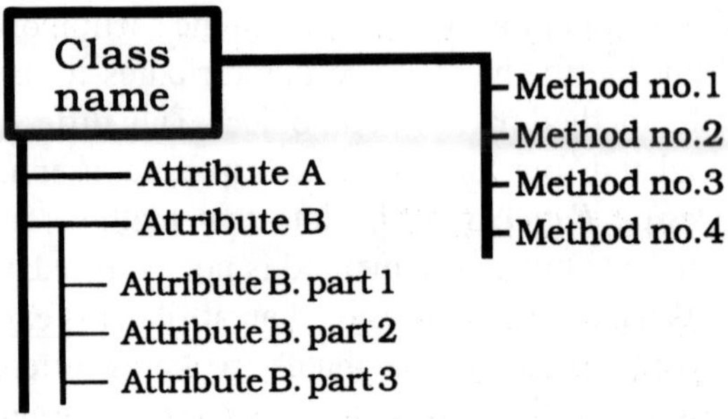


**Figure 2.16** Drawing a class.

Figure 2.17 shows how a class can be described on a computer system. By clicking on various items, we get more information. For example, by clicking on "Description," we get a friendly description of the class and the information we earlier called business and control rules. The same is true of the list of the method names; by clicking on the name of a method, we can get more information about this method, such as how it is implemented and an example of how it is called. By clicking on an

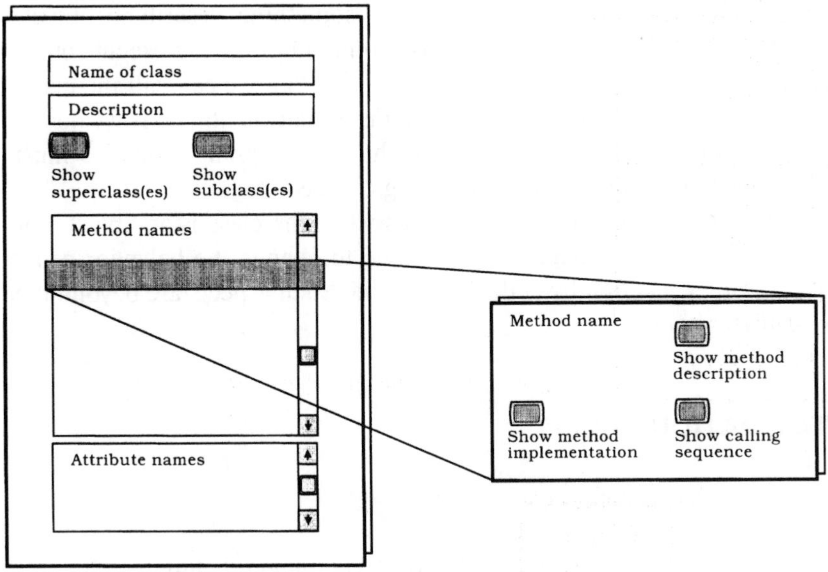


**Figure 2.17** A typical computer-based description of a class.

attribute name, we get a description of the attribute and information about whether it is a simple attribute or a complex attribute having its own structure, etc.

## THE CLASS AS AN OBJECT?

We can select a group of classes with some common characteristics and make a description of these characteristics. We have then made a class description that describes other classes. Classes describing objects that are classes are called *metaclasses*. From an object-oriented modeling perspective, we do not gain much by introducing metaclasses. It is the experience of this author that the use of metaclasses makes it difficult to distinguish between the ideas class and object. We will thus not use metaclasses in this book. The main reason, however, for clearly separating object and class structures is the experiences gained in the studies referred to earlier [1,2].

If we take the perspective of object-oriented programming instead of object-oriented modeling, the situation is a bit different. A few object-oriented programming languages such as Smalltalk allow the class to be an object. This means the class is not only something describing objects needed to build our application, but also something that can execute on its own in the computer. One advantage of this is that we can call the class, because it is an object, when we want to instantiate an object. If we do not permit the class to be an object, then the programming language must include special constructions for creating objects.

There can also be other differences when the class is an object. For example, in some languages it is possible to change the behavior of an object during execution by adding a method. Such aspects are beyond the scope of this book.

## INFORMATION HIDING

We begin with two definitions.

**Definition.** *Encapsulation* is a software-development technique that consists of isolating a system function or a set of data and operations on those data within a module and providing precise specifications for the module [IEEE].

**Definition.** *Information hiding* is a software-development technique in which each module's interfaces reveal as little as possible about the module's inner workings and other modules are prevented from using information about the module that is not in the module's interface specification [IEEE].

Note that the concepts encapsulation and information hiding are often used as synonyms, which is a simplification we adopt in this book. What does encapsulation signify when transferred to object-oriented modeling? One important advantage of information hiding is that something inside the object being changed does not necessarily need to be reflected in the interface.

When attributes and method implementations are encapsulated, other objects cannot directly see or use them. For example, Figure 2.18 shows that attribute values can be changed only by the object itself. This means that if we want to know (or change) the value of a certain attribute, there must be a method available that can read (or change) this value.

The actual sequence of actions that must occur when we want to know the value of an attribute, illustrated in Figure 2.19, is roughly the following: We send a message (1) to the object, that starts the correspond-

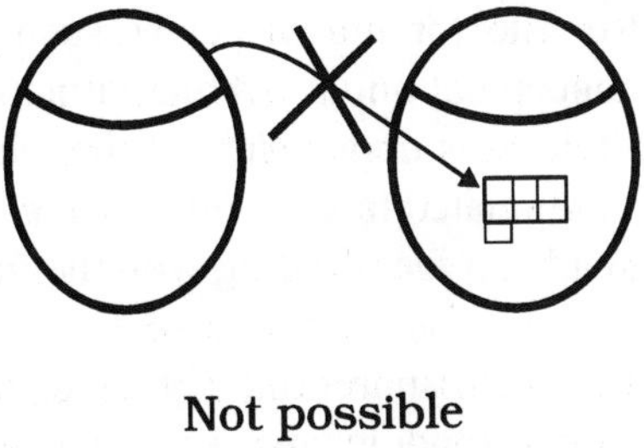


**Figure 2.18** Information hiding stops access of attributes inside other objects.

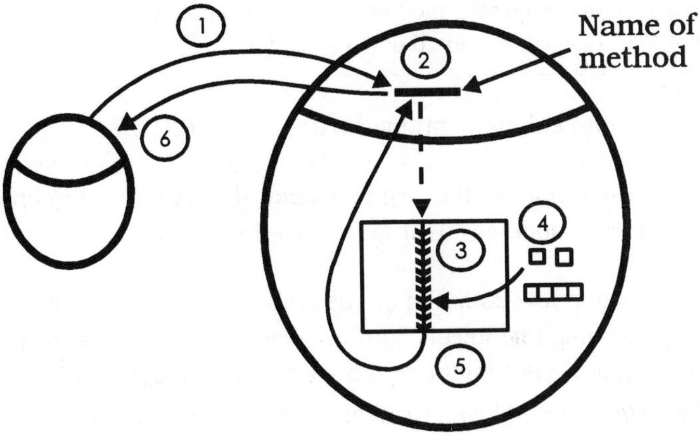


**Figure 2.19** We can access attributes only through method calls.

ing method (2). The code for that method begins to execute (3), and the value of the attribute is read (4). The execution ends (5), and the read value is returned (6). The actual sequence of actions is hidden from the user. The user cannot see whether the returned value is the result of some computation or the result of just reading the value of an attribute. This is good because it means that when modeling, the method is our conceptual unit—rather than a lot of details

a. A set of attributes plus
b. Their values plus
c. The implementation details of the method

That is, we have a good abstraction technique because we can think of the whole (the method) instead of all its details.

The same is also true for the object as such. The object can be regarded as a single conceptual unit, a whole, rather than a set of details. When creating this whole, it is important that the methods and attributes included in the object are related to each other, which is a *cohesion* property. Cohesion is originally an idea dealing with the functions of modules.

**Definition.** *Cohesion* is the manner and degree to which the tasks performed by a single software module are related to one another [IEEE].

---

**Example**

A module that incorporates only functions that deal with file access has a good degree of cohesion. Should the module one day also be given a function for digital filtering, the cohesion would go down considerably.

---

Cohesion is seldom mentioned without also referring to coupling:

**Definition.** *Coupling* is the manner and degree of interdependence between software modules [IEEE].

High cohesion and low coupling are desirable properties for objects, too.

Low coupling for objects implies that they should be independent microworlds that do not interact with each other unless absolutely necessary. This can be restated as an important design rule:

- Try to separate things that change independently of each other.

For example, it is always a good idea to separate those parts that deal with the interface (for instance, a windowing system handling the dialog with a customer) and other parts of the system. Later in this book we will discuss how objects are often dominated by data or behavior aspects. We will call these two types of objects information objects and system objects, respectively. This is still another example of how we try to separate independent things, thus decreasing the coupling between parts in a system.

Transferring the idea of cohesion to our objects yields these rules:

- We should find only necessary attributes and methods in the object.
- They should be properly related.

Thus, the object must have a well-defined purpose and not deal with many disparate tasks. For example, if we have an invoice object, we should find attributes for expressing a typical invoice (customer name, ordered items, date, prices, etc.) and methods that use those attributes. We should not find attributes describing hobbies or other unrelated attributes.

Keeping data and functions together is a very important aspect of object-oriented modeling. Looking at earlier software-development methods, we find that data and functions that belonged together were not kept together. It was left to the designer or the programmer to keep track of the data (the certain characteristics) and what was done with it (the functions applied to the data). Figure 2.20 illustrates how we used to separate related data and functions. This separation is not a good idea, because we usually apply a function (operator) to some particular *group* of data (operands), and this coupling between function and data should be retained in the model. The old operand/operator approach did not explicitly record such dependencies between function and data. Because such dependencies are typically difficult to understand, conflicting assumptions concerning them were often made. Thus, a procedure could easily be made to operate on data having the wrong format or data not even intended for the procedure. During maintenance, these undocumented (implicit) assumptions made the maintenance harder. In an object, on the other hand, we should find groups of related attributes and methods that are encapsulated.

To show that we have grouped and encapsulated a set of objects, we enclose them with a circle or an ellipse. If the objects inside the circle (ellipse) can be called directly from objects outside the circle, the enclosing line is dotted. We call these two ways of grouping *strong* and *weak aggregation*, respectively, and they are illustrated in Figure 2.21. That is,

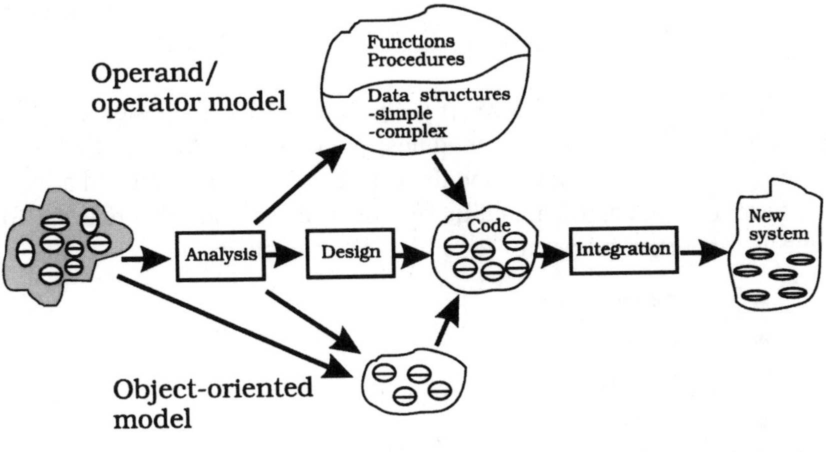


**Figure 2.20** Objects preserve connections that typically exist between data and functions.

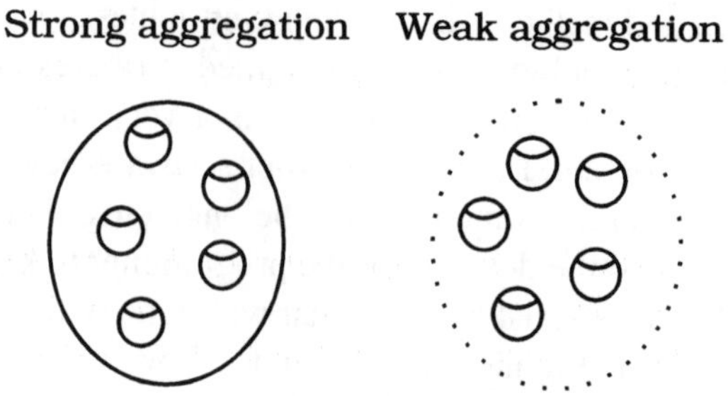


**Figure 2.21** Aggregation with information hiding (left) and without it.

if we use information hiding to hide the details of the objects we group together, we have a strong aggregation. On the other hand, if objects can be accessed directly from objects outside the aggregation, we call it weak aggregation. Aggregation is discussed in Chapter 3.

## MODULARITY

From IEEE we extract the following definitions:

**Definition.** A *Module* is (1) a program unit that is discrete and identifiable with respect to compiling, combining with other units, and loading. (2) A logically separable part of a program [IEEE].

**Definition.** *Modularity* is the degree to which a system or computer program is composed of discrete components such that a change to one component has a minimal impact on other components [IEEE].

Boehm et al. [34], Meyer [6], and others have suggested different properties that good software (modules) should satisfy. An object is sometimes referred to as a typed module. Consequently, an object and a module have a lot in common, and these properties are thus also relevant for objects. Important properties for a module or an object are

- Understandability
- Decomposability
- Composability
- Continuity
- Protection
- Linguistic modular units

*Understandability* basically implies that the objects, when used as modeling tools, are close to the way we are used to thinking.

---

**Example**

A mathematician is to implement an algorithm. The algorithm involves vectors of different dimensions. The element number $m$ in a one-dimensional vector is referred to by $a_m$. For example, the second element is referred to by writing $a_2$. An implementation of $a_2$ as A[2] is then more understandable than an implementation of $a_2$ as A[1]. This concept is simple; note, however, that in C++ vectors start at zero, so A[1] thus refers to the second element and not the first element.

---

If an object is *decomposable* it can be divided into new subobjects. This process must be repeatable and thus enable us to divide subobjects into secondary subobjects. *Composable* is the opposite of decomposable: the possibility of combining objects to form a larger object. Note that it should be possible to take objects developed for other applications and combine them with our newly developed objects into a larger object. Objects having this property are sometimes called *universal* objects.

*Continuity* is a vital property. It means that small changes in a specification should result in limited changes to a system. For example, a small change in our specification should affect only one or possibly a few objects in the implementation and definitely not the whole object structure. Continuity is closely related to solution B, having a close mapping, introduced in Chapter 1.

If objects have the *protection* property, then an abnormal condition occurring at run time in one object will affect few, if any, other objects.

Modules that correspond to syntactic units in the programming language, program design language, the specification language, etc. are called *linguistic modular units.*

Objects will not automatically satisfy the properties just introduced, but if we use the type of object-oriented modeling presented in this book, we will indeed get objects that have these properties. The objects will be understandable and satisfy the linguistic modular units property, because they are modeling concepts that are close to reality and because we select natural and intuitive concepts. They will satisfy the decomposability and composability properties, because we use the aggregation technique introduced in this chapter and elaborated on in the rest of the book. Our system will display continuity because we apply solution B, having a close mapping. We achieve the protection property by adhering to solution A, hiding details.

Another principle, introduced by Meyer [6], states that a module should be both unchangeable and open to changes. It should be closed to changes because persons using the module in a system do not want it to change suddenly, for obvious reasons. On the other hand, someone designing a new system might be interested in a slightly changed version of an existing module. This principle is called the *open/closed principle*. It is not possible to satisfy this principle using conventional means of designing a system. With object-oriented modeling, however, we have the class concept, which is ideal for resolving this problem. Completed systems will use existing classes for instantiating their object structures. If a new system needs a slightly changed object, a subclass to an already existing class can be developed. The new (changed) object is instantiated from this subclass, leaving the "old" class unchanged.

## NOUNS, VERBS, AND ADJECTIVES

> *Look to the essence of a thing, whether it be a point of doctrine, of practice, or of interpretation.*
>
> —Marcus Aurelius Antoninus

We have sometimes used the words *thing* and *object* as synonyms. Thinking about objects as things implies that they are closely related to nouns. However, the simple rule that a noun is automatically an object is too inexact. It is the experience of the author that there has been some confusion about this subject, so let us try to straighten things out. One source of difficulty is that it is possible and easy to turn a verb into a noun, and vice versa.

---

### Example

If we are going to measure something, we might say, "...and then the measurement is done."

---

The word measure is a verb, but the word measurement is a noun. To solve problems like this, we must try to look behind the scenery and ask ourselves if we have a description of an action or if we have a "thing." That is, if the text is about a measurement being done, then we should not consider measurement to be an object but find the object that is doing the measurement. When we have found the object that is responsible for the action, we can attach a method "measure" to that object.

On the other hand, if the text implies that we shall store the result of the measurement somewhere, we must ask ourselves another question: Is the measurement result important and/or complex enough to become an object of its own, or should the result instead belong to an object as an attribute? Remember that we have the option of using complex attributes in object-oriented modeling. That is, attaching the result to an object as an attribute is a possible solution not only for single values.

If we are thinking about attaching a complex attribute a1 to an object B we should consider whether it might not be a good idea to turn a1 into an object A1 instead. If we turn a1 into an object, we can then put this information object, A1, inside B, as illustrated in Figure 2.22. The information is then not directly accessible inside B, as in the case with having a complex attribute, but it is easier to manage and protect the information. (If we turn a1 into an object, A1, the information will be accessible only if A1 has methods for accessing a1.)

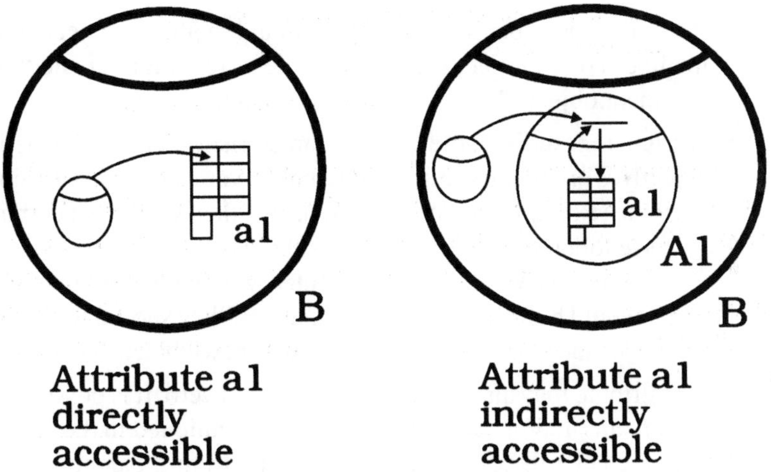


**Figure 2.22** Two different ways of modeling a complex attribute.

Common sense must, of course, always be applied. Look at the following extracts from sentences in a specification:

1. . . . the car *is* red . . .
2. Those who *work* at the Gold Oil Inc. office in Dubai . . .
3. The main parts of the system *weigh* about 10 pounds.
4. The sensor *connects* to the system via a long connecting cable.
5. The sensor *has* a reset mechanism activated . . .

The words *is, work, weigh, connects,* and *has* are all verbs, but only in the last example is it probable that we have found a method. In examples 1 and 3 it is quite likely that we have found the attributes *color* and *weight,* respectively. Example 2 might suggest a classification structure (employee is_a person) or an aggregation structure (employee is_part_of Dubai_group) and example 4 might be an indication of an aggregation structure (sensor–cable–system). A tip is that a rewrite can often make things clearer. Summarizing, we have the following guide:

- An object might appear as a noun (example: measurement) or disguised as a verb (example: measuring). We should then ask ourselves if we have a thing. If we really have a *thing*, then we have an object.
- A method might appear as a verb (example: investigate) or be disguised as a noun (example: investigation). The key question is whether something is being done or not. If the word implies some kind of action or work, then we have found a method.
- It is also possible that we have found both an object and a method. For example, the method "measure" might create "measurement objects."
- Attributes describe some kind of characteristic, and we find them as adjectives or other modifiers for nouns or verbs. If we have a single attribute (examples: color, weight, price), then with great certainty we have found an attribute that will belong to an object. If we have found a set of several *related* attributes, we should ask ourselves if these should build a complex attribute or if they should form a new idea. This idea is then the beginning of a new object.
- An attribute may also imply a noun and/or a verb. It is possible that such nouns and/or verbs are not directly mentioned in the text, but they are nevertheless understood to exist from the context of the text. These nouns and verbs should be listed and treated in the same way as nouns and verbs that are explicitly mentioned in the text.
- We can often derive adjectives from nouns and verbs respectively. For example, beautiful from beauty (noun), and qualified from qualify (verb). The reverse of this process is often also possible, turning a noun into an adjective. For example, "with responsibility (noun) to" can be changed to "responsible (adjective) for." An adjective turned into a noun is often better turned back into an adjective because it is more likely that it represents an attribute than a (new) object.

Thus the process of mapping nouns into objects, verbs into methods, and adjectives and adverbs into attributes is not a straightforward process. Common sense must always be applied.

## OVERLOADING AND POLYMORPHISM

The aim of this section is not only to explain overloading and polymorphism, but also to show that, even though it is a great advantage having a language that implements these ideas, there is really nothing new as such with the ideas. We apply these ideas every day during our normal lives. Thus, using the ideas during analysis and design is natural, but there is no need to explicitly refer to the terms overloading and polymorphism during these phases.

**Definition.** To *overload* is to assign an operator, identifier, or literal more than one meaning, depending upon the data types associated with it at any given time during program execution [IEEE].

In the following we discuss overloading and polymorphism using two examples.

---

### Example 1

We ask a person to write two integers, add them, and write their sum. A (part of a) simple model for this activity could be

```
write(518, 202)
write ("The sum of these numbers is:")
write(720)
```

---

We implement this model using a computer and a computer language. If the language lacks a write operation, we need to implement suitable write operations. Writing an integer is not the same thing as writing a string. We thus need different implementations for our write operations. A possible implementation for the part of the model shown is

```
write_two_integers(518, 202);
write_string("The sum of these numbers is:");
write_an_integer(720);
```

If the compiler is able to decide from the number and types of arguments which implementation of write to use, a possible implementation could be

```
write(518, 202);
write("The sum of these numbers is:");
write(720);
```

If this implementation can occur in the language we use, we say that it is possible to *overload* an operation. The operation "write" is thus now overloaded. In the example, the binding of name and implementation can be done before execution. We call this binding of name and implementation before execution (at compile time) *early binding,* or *static binding*. The advantage of overloading is that implementing a model is simpler as the semantic gap is smaller between model and implementation.

---

**Example 2**

We have a group of persons, some of whom are students. We instruct the students to give us their name and the school they attend when asked to present themselves. The rest of the group give us only their name when asked to present themselves. We make an object-oriented model of this group by introducing two classes Person and Student. Each class is given attributes and methods. For example, we give Person a method Present_yourself that prints name and Student a method Present_yourself that prints the name of the student and the school the student attends.

---

In reality *and* in our object-oriented model, it is understood (implicitly) that an object of the class Person, when asked to Present_yourself, will write name. It is also clear that when an object of the class Student is asked to Present_yourself, he or she will write name and school. However when we are to implement this model, we might run into problems because the computer is not good at using context to understand what to do. This can be illustrated by the following example: We want to construct a list of mixed Person and Student objects interactively and then let the objects write their information. The pseudocode for this could be as follows:

```
// Construct list interactively when running the
// application.
// Let the objects write their "information":
FOR an_object := first_object TO last_object
an_object.Present_yourself;
END_FOR;
```

The list of objects does not exist at the time we write the code, and thus we will not know at compile time what objects we will have in the list. If we do not know what objects we have, it is not clear *at compile time* which implementation of `Present_yourself` should be used when we call `Present_yourself`:

```
an_object.Present_yourself;
```

However, at the time of execution, the list will exist. If the system is able to choose the correct implementation (of `Present_yourself`) at the time we execute the program, the problem is solved. This possibility is available with object-oriented languages. We call this binding of method name and method implementation during execution of a program *dynamic binding,* or *late binding*.

Dynamic binding thus makes it possible for several different kinds of objects to respond to the same operation but with different implementations for the operation, which means that different objects will display different behavior when they receive the same message. This is possible because the receiving methods in the objects have the same name but different implementations. We call this ability *polymorphism* (rather than overloading) and it needs dynamic binding. (Polymorphism is related to the adjective polymorphous: having, assuming, or occurring in various forms, stages, or the like).

## SUMMARY

This chapter gives us the tools we need to model single things (objects) and groups of similar things (the class). Summing up, we learned in this chapter that

- A class is a description used when instantiating objects.
- An object shall have
  1. Name and an identity
  2. Attributes and *values for those attributes*
  3. Methods
- An object models an idea found in reality (tangible or abstract) or an idea created by people.
- The object hides (encapsulates) related attributes, their values, and the implementation details of the methods.

Figure 2.23 summarizes some of the things we have learned in this chapter. At the top of the figure we have two notations for a class. If we are interested only in indicating that we have a class, we draw it as a rectangle, possibly filled with the name of the class. If we want to show the class in a more detailed way, we write the name of the class at the top and

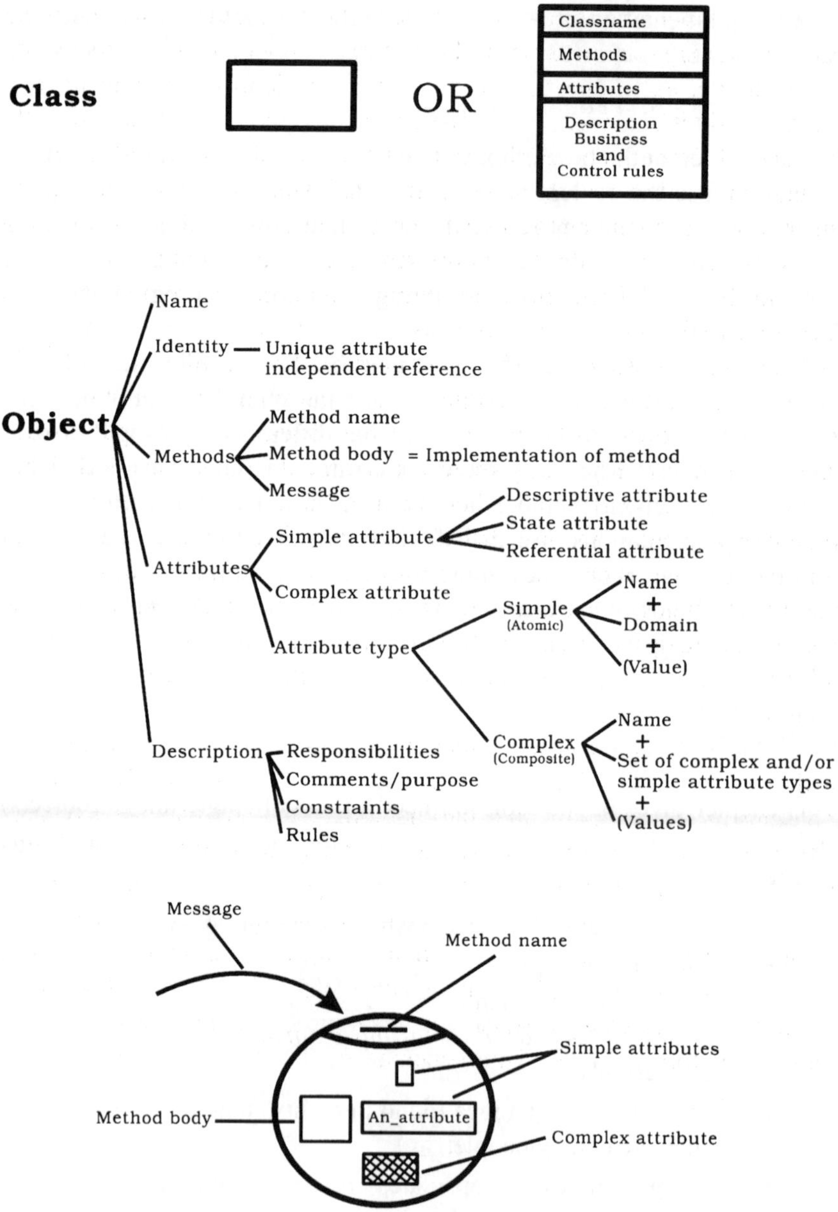


**Figure 2.23** Summary of the important concepts in Chapter 2.

below it write the names of the methods and the names of the attributes. At the bottom we put a description, business, and control rules for the class.

The class is used to create objects. In the middle part of the figure we see a mind map relating what we have learned about the object. As we see in the figure, each object has a name and an identity. The identity is a unique attribute-independent reference to the object. An object typically has several methods and attributes. Each method has a name and an implementation (method body), which is activated when we send a message to an object. We divide attributes into simple attributes and complex attributes. We further divide the simple attributes into descriptive attributes, state attributes, and referential attributes. A descriptive attribute describes a characteristic of the object, whereas a state attribute describes an important state that we want to model. Referential attributes will be described in detail in the next chapter. The figure also shows the corresponding types for simple attributes and complex attributes, respectively. We put "value" and "values" into parentheses because a type does not usually define a value. However, an attribute, when it exists, has a value or a set of values (complex attribute), and it is, therefore, appropriate to indicate this in our mind map. Synonyms for simple attributes and complex attributes are atomic attributes and composite attributes, respectively. Attributes can also be divided into instance attributes and class attributes (not shown.) We describe an object by stating its responsibilities and constraints, giving comments, etc.

Below the mind map we show the notation we use for an object. A call to a method, sending a message to an object, is indicated by an arrow pointing to the object owning the method. A method name is indicated either by a line—as seen in the figure—or by writing the name of the method in the upper part of the object. A simple attribute is indicated by a little square, a little rectangle, or a long rectangle with the name of the attribute inside it, as shown. A complex attribute is indicated with a square or a rectangle filled with some pattern. Finally, the body of a method is indicated by a square or rectangle, possibly with the method name at its top or the text "Implementation of," followed by the name of the method.

# 3

# Structures

## *Navigating Complexity*

> *The whole of science is nothing more than a refinement of everyday thinking.*
>
> —Albert Einstein

### INTRODUCTION

Chapter 2 introduced basic concepts used in object-oriented modeling—objects, classes, attributes, methods, and messages—and important concepts such as information hiding. We use these concepts to build our models.

The need to arrange a model in a way that we can grasp it, navigate in it and change it arises for all but the smallest system. We thus need techniques that we can use to arrange our model so we can look at it both in detail and, when needed, in larger chunks, hiding its internal details.

The mind-mapping technique is an excellent example of how good structures can increase our ability to manage a large number of details (see Figure 3.1). Object-oriented technology gives us several ways of handling complexity by introducing structures. Understanding how to use these structures is an important key to successful object-oriented modeling.

We make the following working definition of the concept *structure.*

**Definition.** A *structure* is a tool that helps us handle complexity by organizing and arranging items into patterns and larger wholes.

The first structuring paradigm discussed in this chapter was presented in Chapter 2: the *class*. The class is a way of grouping a set of methods and a connected set of attributes into a new idea forming a whole. If we have made a good abstraction, we can stop here and forget about its details. Instead we can think of the class as such, forgetting its

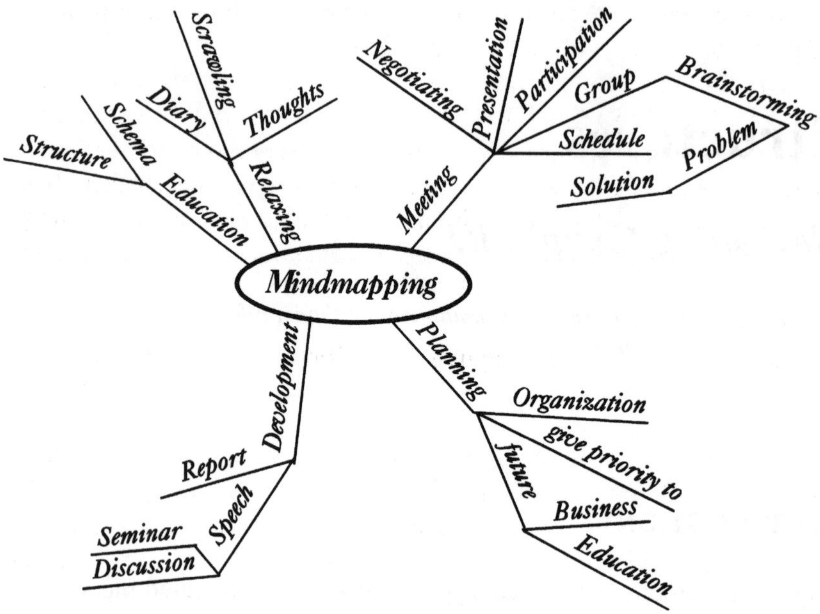


**Figure 3.1** We need structures to help us navigate in our complex models.

implementation details. The class is clearly one important structuring mechanism. In Figure 3.2 we see an example of another structuring mechanism discussed in this chapter, the *class structure*.

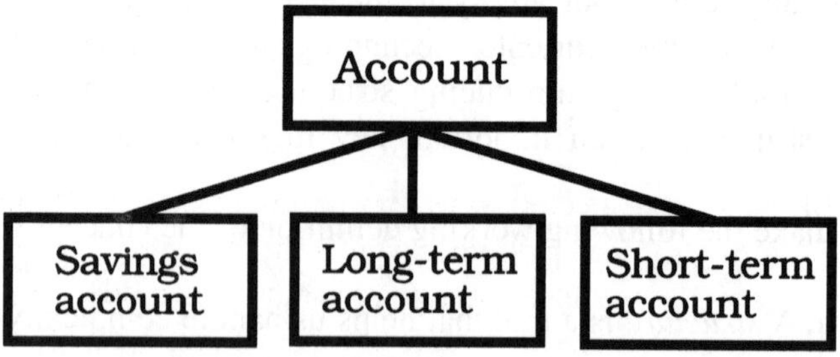


**Figure 3.2** A class structure.

A third important structuring mechanism is the grouping of several objects in levels using aggregation. This grouping is often referred to as *nested objects*. It is also possible to aggregate classes or both objects and classes. We will discuss aggregation of classes in Part II. We do not discuss aggregation of objects and classes because in our investigations [1,2] we found that we should separate them.

Our last structuring paradigm is *associations*. Hierarchical associations can be used to set up class structures and nested object structures. Nonhierarchical associations are widely used to set up other types of connections between classes and objects. As we will see in this chapter, these latter types of associations are of limited use in object-oriented modeling.

In this chapter we shall thus look in detail at the following structures:

- The class and the class structure
- The object structure (aggregation of objects, nested objects)
- Associations

However, we begin this chapter by discussing some questions concerning how we should go about forming an object-oriented model. For example, one important question we must ask ourselves before we start structuring our model is, What objects and classes shall we choose to put in our model in the first place? We will see that the purpose controls this choice to a high degree. Although this is often understood it is a point seldom applied.

## MODELING BASICS

### Naming

*The chief merit of language is clearness, and we know that nothing detracts so much from this as do unfamiliar terms.*

—Galen

One of the most neglected ways of bringing about a good model is to give good names to the things we put into the model. If we give good names to the classes, objects, attributes and so on, our model will be readable or almost readable without putting comments or any additional information into the model. The extra time spent on finding good names is well-spent effort. Few rules can be given concerning the selection of names, but here are some that might help:

- A name should feel right. Trust your instinct.
- Finding good names is an iterative process. If a first try does not produce satisfactory results, try again later.

- Avoid inventing a new name if the customer already has a name for a concept. In the same way, if you have invented a new name and discover that the customer has a well-established word for the concept, replace your invention with the word the customer is using.
- Avoid overused words, such as task, form, operation, and system.
- Finally, try to find words that are clear, defining the soul of what you are trying to describe.

## Subjects

Peter Coad has introduced an idea called subjects [4]. A *subject* is a grouping of various parts of a model in a way that helps a reader of the model understand it. The groupings (subjects) consist of classes and/or objects, and various groupings might contain the same part(s). Because of the experiences gained in the studies mentioned in the preface, this book takes a new approach. The differences will be evident as we continue our discussion, but let us mention two main points that form object-oriented modeling in this book:

- We separate object structures and class structures. The former represent the applications that we design, whereas the latter are best viewed as a library or a store of reusable components. It is our experience that these two functions should be carried out by two separate activities in a company.
- We stress the general solutions presented in Chapter 1. For example, when mapping, the relation between reality, our model, and the implemented system should be 1:1:1. This requirement makes it difficult to have the same part in several subjects.

## Thinking about Objects

When we try to understand a business, for example, we find things. Let us call these things our *potential objects*. The difficult question we must answer is: Which of these potential objects should become objects in our model?

The warning here is that we have to reeducate ourselves if we are going to be good at finding *reusable* and *usable* objects. We have been thinking about objects since childhood. The problem is that we, the system developers, have been taught to find data and functions and to separate them when we do our system development. This way of working is not easily changed. Some people—perhaps 10%—have great problems in switching to the object-oriented paradigm.

Returning to our potential objects, it is important to point out that the potential objects we have found might be something other than objects. For example, if we have found something simple, it is very possible that we have found an attribute instead of an object. In object-oriented analysis and design, attributes and objects are different modeling concepts. An object-oriented language might blur this clear distinction, however. For example, in C++ and Smalltalk, attributes are commonly used to implement subobjects. This mix of two different modeling aspects is not recommended. It simply illustrates the great influence of programming languages on our thinking.

Note that even if we have a collection of related attributes, we cannot be sure that we have found a new object. Maybe the attributes should just be added as a complex attribute to an existing class.

## The Importance of Purpose

*The secret of success is constancy to purpose.*

—Benjamin Disraeli, Earl of Beaconsfield

We find a lot of things when modeling—but what do we find? Remember the two different views of a book we presented in a previous chapter. The two views, one logical and one physical, gave two different models. Each view had a unique purpose. Consequently, purpose is a key. Thus, what we find when modeling depends on several things:

1. What is our *purpose*—our intention—when we describe something?
2. How much do we know about the area of interest?
3. What set of values do we hold? It is quite possible that people with different sets of values would choose entirely different purposes.

These ideas are not new, but we often forget them or take them for granted. A consequence of this is that we fail to define a clear purpose. If the purpose is not defined well enough by those who design the model, confusion or even project failure could result.

Thus, our purpose governs our selection when we look at reality and decide what we shall include in a model. This statement is also true for areas other than software development. A famous example of this fact is the discussion about the nature of fundamental particles (i.e., electrons, protons, neutrons, etc.) that took place early in the 20th century. It became evident that the particles did not always behave as something that had a well-defined shape and size—that is, as something we would call particles (see Figure 3.3).

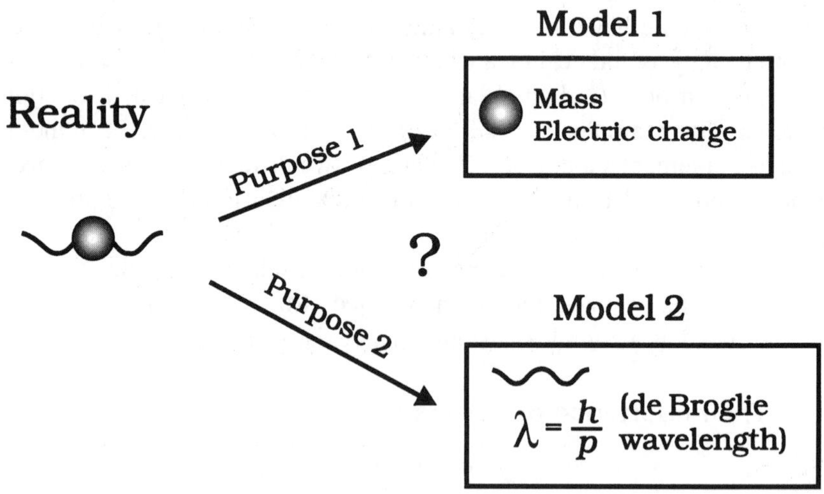


**Figure 3.3** Is an electron a wave or a particle? What about a proton?

Apparently, the fundamental particles in some experiments behaved as particles with characteristics like mass and electric charges, whereas in other experiments they behaved as waves producing diffraction patterns. The model needed to explain an experiment depended on the intent or purpose of the experiment.

A way for us to explain this problem is to say that reality is our only complete model. When we build a model to explain something, we get a fragmentary model. If we are lucky, this model will suit our purpose but probably not much more. We can state this explanation in another way:

- The model we make will be a true abstraction because it does not include every detail from reality.
- The main point is that the details we include depend on our purpose.

Figure 3.4 illustrates how the purpose governs the selection of details from the world. In all the cases in our example, reality is always the same, but our understanding or description of it changes according to our purpose, our knowledge of the situation, and other things such as the set of values we honor.

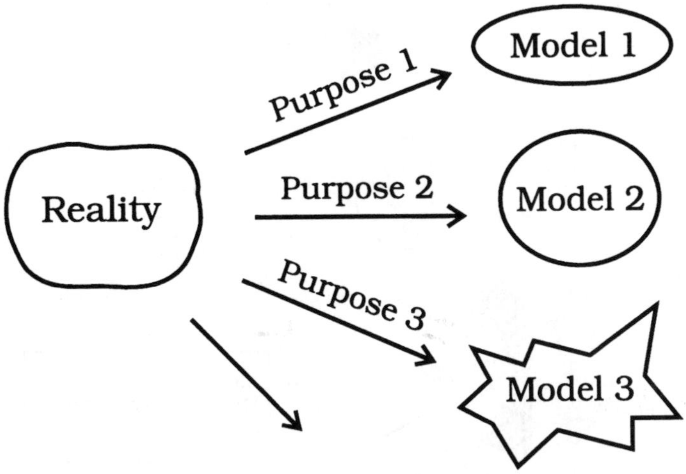


**Figure 3.4** How reality is modeled depends on the purpose.

---

**Example**

Classification of airplanes. The taxation authority will classify airplanes in one way, whereas the local village group will find another type of classification. This difference occurs because the village group has decided to write a complaint about the noise that the airplanes make, but the taxation authorities have another purpose in mind. We can be very sure that the airplane maintenance group would classify the airplanes in still another way.

---

Figure 3.5 illustrates yet another example. Describing the orbit of a satellite would yield one model, and describing the heat balance of a satellite would yield another model. A third and different model would have to be used if we wanted to describe the chances of a satellite being destroyed by another orbiting satellite.

Various purposes also yield various models when we try to describe computer systems. To a systems analyst, a system consist of jobs, programs, files, etc. A user would probably regard the system as something composed of reports, computer terminals, screens, etc. A good design rule is to take the user's perspective using the user's words and his or her definitions and understandings of the meaning of those words. However this only partly solves the problem; we always have to define a clear purpose, or the modeling situation will soon become very awkward indeed.

The solution is to stop looking for the one "true" description and to understand that we must start with a clear and exact definition of the

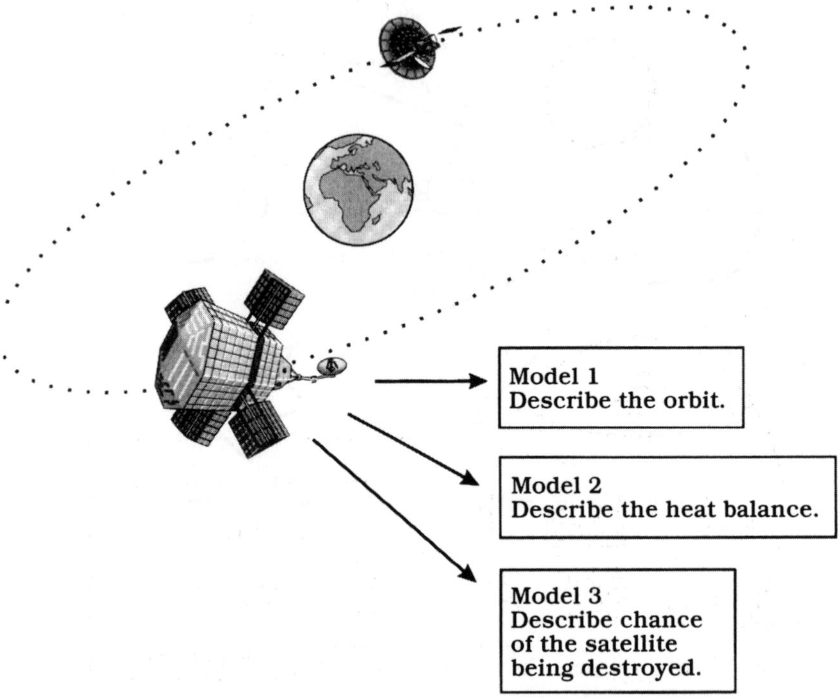


**Figure 3.5** To describe a satellite, we need several different models.

purpose of our modeling activity. The more exactly our purpose is defined and the more uniform our understanding of something is, the more alike our models will be. The purpose is often documented by writing a *problem statement,* that is a short text outlining the objectives with the system.

## Keep It Simple

*Our life is frittered away by detail . . . Simplify, simplify.*

—Henry David Thoreau

Let us look at a sensor to illustrate two basically different ways to model something. We imagine a system where we use a particular type of a sensor to take temperature readings but also store several sensors of this type in a store. To model this situation, we could make one big complex object of the sensor. This solution is shown at the top of Figure 3.6. Thus when we, in our model, need to use the sensor as something stored in a store, we select relevant parts for that. When we need the sensor as something that makes measurements, we select from the complex object those things that are relevant for this purpose. This approach is often referred to as having different *views,* or perspectives, of the same data. Another approach is to skip the large, complex object and instead directly make a separate object in our model for each use of the sensor, as in the lower part of Figure 3.6. The advantage with the first solution is most apparent

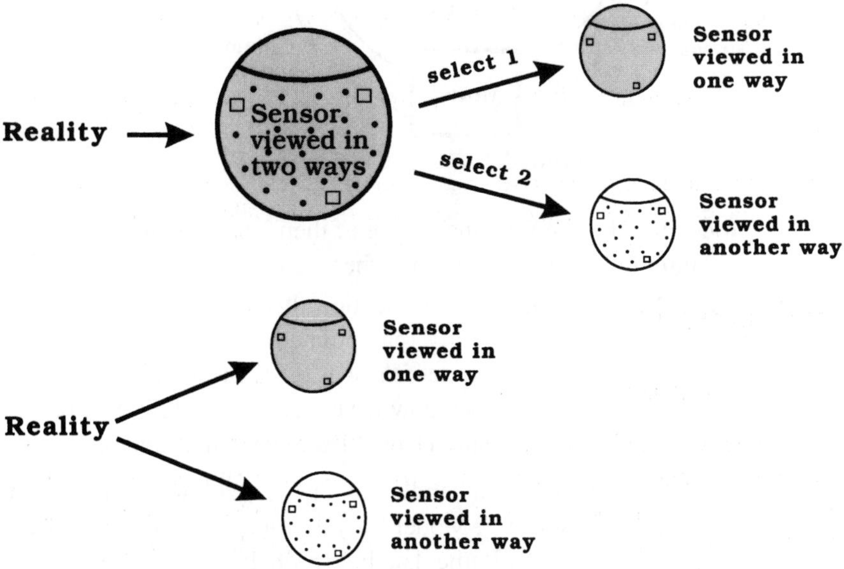


**Figure 3.6** Two different ways to model.

when we have information that is shared by both views. With the first solution this information is stored in one place, the large, complex object. With the latter solution, we have to store this information in two places. In our example of a sensor, this is probably not a big problem. However, we might end up with a lot of redundant information if we construct a separate object for each use of something. The second solution is simpler and, in this author's opinion, is often the best way to model. Note that the preceding discussion does not exclude a use of view modules such as in the Model/View/Controller (MVC) technology developed by XEROX PARC. This technology is used in Smalltalk, for example (see Figure 3.7).

The basic idea with this technology is to partition a program into three parts:

- *Controller.* The controller coordinates input from users with View and Model. It is thus responsible for coordinating between the

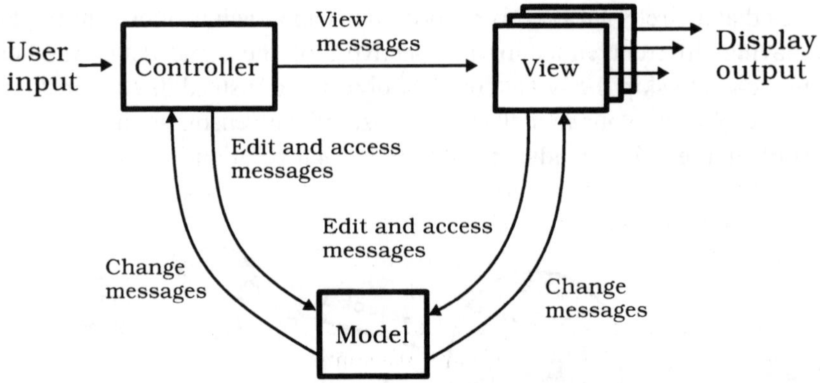


**Figure 3.7** The MVC technology.

Model and the View, so that if one of them changes, it knows how to communicate that fact to the other.

- *Model.* Model is the basic application. It is responsible for managing the information being manipulated. Model captures some relevant feature(s) of some real-world situation. For example, things to be shown in a window have a corresponding data representation. Model then handles this data representation.
- *View* transforms the data handled by the Model into an image that can be seen by user(s). A Model can be connected to several different views showing the same data but (probably) in different ways.

When this technology is used in systems other than Smalltalk, View and Controller are often combined into one unit often referred to simply as View. One advantage with the MVC technology is that a data structure and the values contained in it need be changed only if we have a real change. For example, rotating a drawing does not change the drawing's underlying data structure, and thus the Model need not be updated in this case. Another advantage is that the Model can easily be reused for different GUI's.

---

**Example**

In a CAD application, the data representing our drawing would be kept in the Model. If the user added a circle, the Controller would pass this information on to the Model, that would pass the information on to the used View(s). However, if the user wanted to, for example, rotate the drawing, this request need not be passed to Model because the data are unchanged. This request could thus be passed directly to View(s), that then would change the image appropriately.

---

Using the MVC technology is very much like the situation just described with a large complex object (Model) of which different Views are made. However there is no real contradiction between using the MVC technology and avoiding the use of the large, complex object when we model something, because the idea is to skip the large, complex object *when the purposes are fundamentally different*. The purpose of modeling a sensor because we shall store a sensor in a store is very different from the purpose of modeling a sensor because we need it in a measurement system. The purpose of modeling a sensor showing it full view in a CAD system and the purpose of modeling the same sensor showing it in part view is, on the other hand, not very different. We summarize the ideas in Figure 3.8.

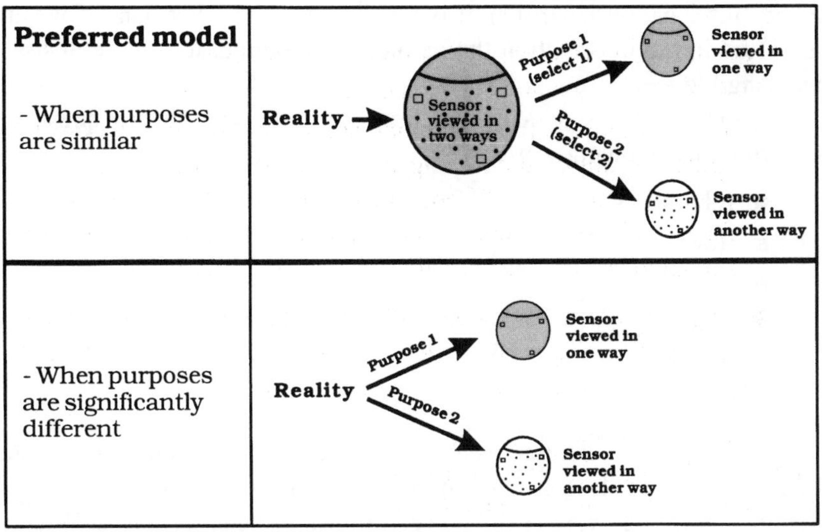


**Figure 3.8** A summary of two different ways of modeling.

## Brainstorming

*If a man will begin with certainties, he shall end in doubts; but if he will be content to begin with doubts he shall end in certainties.*

— Francis Bacon

Brainstorming is a technique used to increase creativity by having people blurt out whatever turns up in their minds. Everyone must be positive, and no suggestions should be stopped. At a later stage the suggestions are evaluated and discarded if they are not considered to be of interest. Brainstorming is described more in Appendix 3.

At first we can practice the idea of brainstorming and view anything that we find as a potential object. What we find might be tangible or more abstract, representing some information the model must remember. Examples of tangible objects are devices, systems, users, or other things with which the system must interact or at least keep track of. Examples of more abstract objects are invoices, registration cards, organizational units, physical locations, data about people, or things or events that the system must remember. The borderline between what is tangible or abstract is not always clear. For example, if we need to keep track of a paper where invoice information is written, it is tangible. On the other hand if we are interested in the information the invoice is modeling, it is more abstract than tangible.

Good questions to ask in a brainstorming session are questions involving the following words:

- What?
- How?
- Why?
- Who?
- When?
- Where?

These keywords can be used as tools to make a discussion take a new and different direction. It is always important to find fresh ways of viewing a system, and the keywords can be used to form sentences such as: What is going on? What do we have here? Why did this happen? Why did the user say what he or she just said? Who does what? When does he or she do what he or she does? How is something processed?

### Modeling Behavior

> *The truth is, the science of Nature has been already too long made only a work of the brain and the fancy: It is now high time that it should return to the plainness and soundness of observations on material and obvious things.*
>
> —Robert Hooke

Should a pen be able to draw symbols by itself? Should a stack of cards be able to shuffle and deal its own cards? Or, should a plant be able to water itself? The question we are addressing here is the behavior for which an object should be responsible. There is no simple yes or no answer to this question. However, if we decide to follow the solutions introduced in Chapter 1, having a close mapping to reality and using natural ideas, the answer is no. It is not natural and close to reality for a stack of cards to shuffle and deal cards by itself. On the other hand, it could be a smart design to let a stack of cards shuffle itself. We recommend minimizing such smartness. Always try to make a model as close to reality as possible. Someone else must water a plant or draw symbols with a pen. It may help to first find a manual solution, that is then mapped directly into a modeling solution. An example of this technique is found in the section, "State Transition Diagrams" in Chapter 4 where we introduce an elevator operator to mimic a manual solution.

If we insist on adding "unnatural" behavior, it should give us significant modeling advantages. Such behavior should also be independent of the user, because an object should always be completely responsible for the behavior it supplies. That is, if the behavior we add to an object has to adapt itself to the user, then this behavior should not be added to the object. An object should thus not have to know who is calling it—only how to perform the requested behavior. For example, does a stack of cards shuffle and deal its card independently of the game going on? Probably not. Thus, we should not put the behavior, "Shuffle cards and deal" in an object "Stack_of_cards." Note this reasoning is also applicable to attributes and objects in general. Thus, we get the general modeling rule that *if* we add unnatural methods, attributes, or objects it should give us significant modeling advantages. In practice it is very unusual to have to use a solution with unnatural methods, attributes, or objects.

Not all potential objects should be put in a model. Next we look at an example illustrating this selection process.

## A Simple Example

When we look at reality we might find people, cars, etc. All these things are our potential objects. Figure 3.9 illustrates the starting point for our example. (Note, we do not *explicitly* define a purpose in this simple example.)

The next step is to sort out things and details in reality that we can ignore. We must sort out the details that will not contribute to our purpose and keep those details that are within the scope of our purpose. For example, we might only be interested in certain people, so we decide to ignore everything but them. In Figure 3.10 we have selected the objects in which

**Figure 3.9** Starting point for our example.

**Figure 3.10** The purpose determines what objects to include in a model.

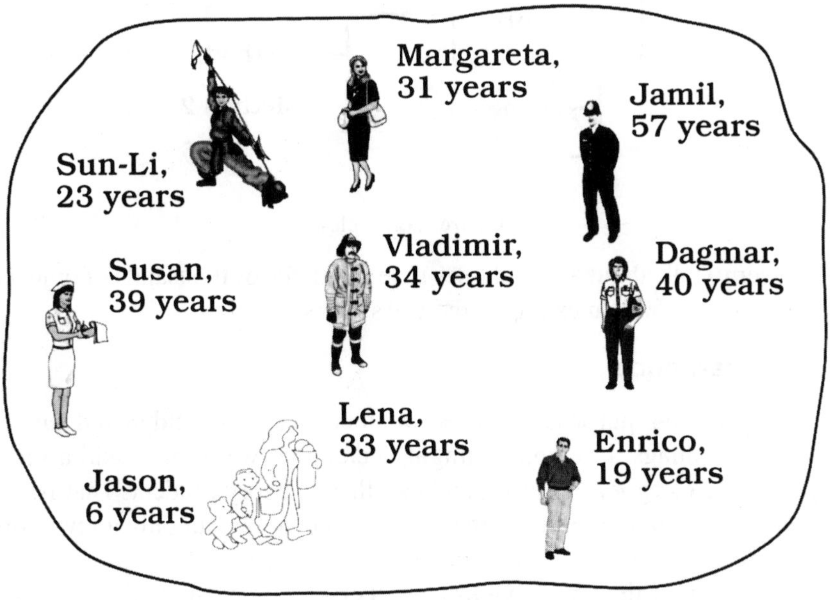


**Figure 3.11** The purpose also determines the selection of attributes.

we are interested.We have made an abstraction on the "object level" as we singled out the things (objects) in which we were interested.

It is also likely that we are not interested in all possible attributes of the selected objects. In our next figure we illustrate this selection. We single out certain attributes, always following our purpose (see Figure 3.11). We have made an abstraction on the "attribute level." (We should also have methods, but for the sake of simplicity we ignore them here). The difficulty in selecting objects, attributes, and methods varies between projects. No definite rule can be given, except that the selection process tends to be easier when modeling data-intensive systems than when modeling function intensive systems.

In the end we find that we have selected certain objects and that these objects have certain attributes and methods. This is the first step in deciding what class structures we need.

## THE CLASS STRUCTURE

We recapitulate the basics of a class. A class is a description of the attributes and methods an object shall have. Objects belonging to the same class must have the same attributes and methods. The class is here simply an abstraction principle: Instead of keeping all the objects in mind, we care only about what is common among a group of similar objects. It

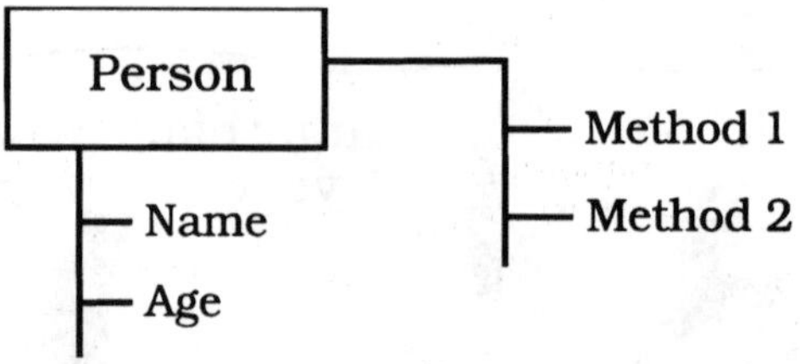


**Figure 3.12** A class.

is easier to talk about a few classes than hundreds or thousands of objects. Figure 3.12 shows an example, the class "Person."

## Inheritance

We use our purpose to sort out what classes we should include in our model. As things develop, we might decide that we want to add a more specialized category of Person and call that category Student. That is, we want to have another class called Student, probably with only a few more attributes.

We realize that the previous class, Person, has most of what we need. If we can start by giving the class Student all that is contained in the class Person, we would have an easy way of designing the new class, Student. This is exactly what we do in object-oriented modeling when we use inheritance to create a new class (see Figure 3.13).

Figure 3.14 shows a class structure. In this figure we have employed a simpler way of drawing classes, because we have left out the boxes and other details, keeping only the names of the classes. Leaving out the boxes is recommended unless we have few classes. However, if the class structure is very large, this style of drawing a class structure soon also gets cumbersome. An indented outline is then preferable. It takes much less space, is easier to handle, and is about as informative as a drawing.

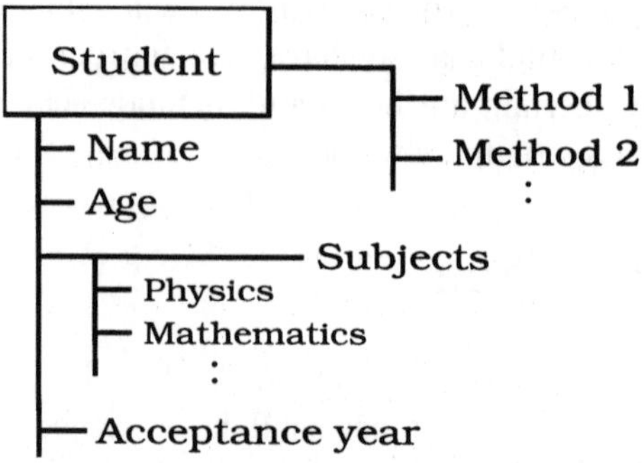


**Figure 3.13** Class Student reusing parts from the class Person.

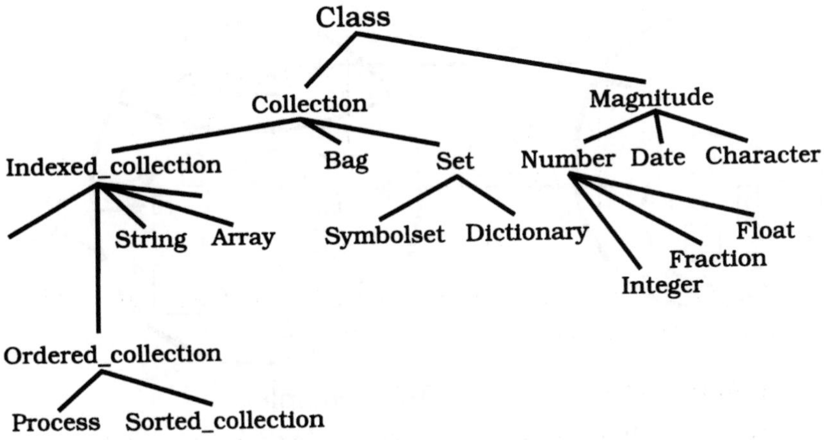


**Figure 3.14** A class structure showing how classes are related in Smalltalk. (Simplified and adapted).

The topmost classes are often referred to as *root classes*. Note that some object-oriented languages, such as Smalltalk, normally only have a single root class whereas other object-oriented languages, such as C++, allow several root classes.

The rules for designing a new class using an earlier class have traditionally been as follows:

1. The new class must have the same attributes as the old class. The attributes may not be changed, but new attributes may be added.
2. The new class must understand the same protocol (set of messages) as the old class.
3. The method implementations in the new class may be altered and new methods may be added. If new methods are added, messages for them are added to the protocol.

We use the word traditionally, because in some languages we may find other rules. For example, in the AI community it is common, when we create a new class, to inherit not only the attribute but a default value for it. In this book we ignore unusual rules like that. Note that experience indicates that we should not allow our class structures to become too deep. The design rules are illustrated in Figure 3.15.

In the following we discuss inheritance in more detail. Starting with class A we make two new subclasses B and C (see Figure 3.16). We call classes B and C *subclasses,* whereas class A is called a *superclass*. A superclass is sometimes called a *base class*, because it is the base from which a subclass is derived. In the same way, a subclass is sometimes

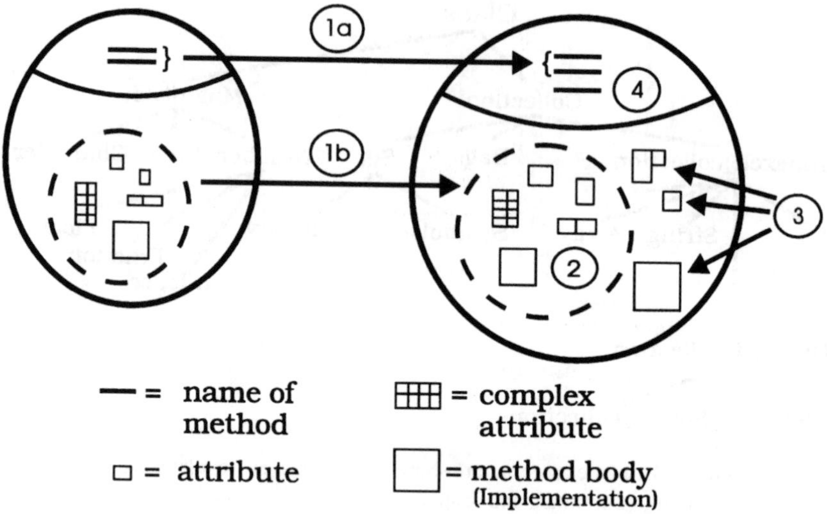


**Figure 3.15** We inherit attributes and methods(1). The methods can be changed(2) but not the attributes. Both attributes and methods might be added to the new class(3). Adding a method affects the protocol(4).

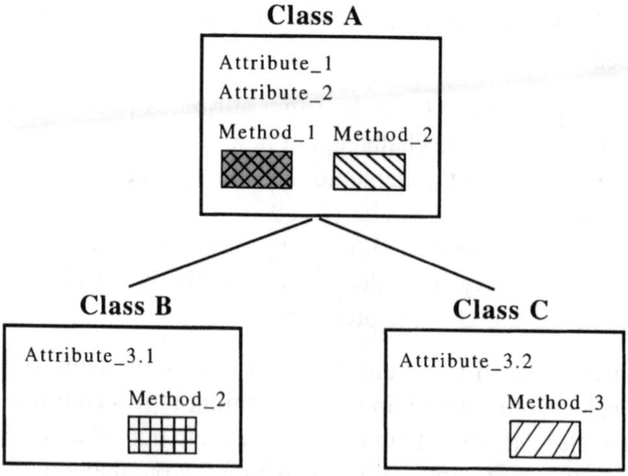


**Figure 3.16** Inheritance, implementors' view.

referred to as a *derived class*. We say that a subclass *inherits* (or reuses) all that has already been built when the superclass was built. Figure 3.16 illustrates what an implementor of an example class structure would see. However, a user will experience the situation in Figure 3.17, because all

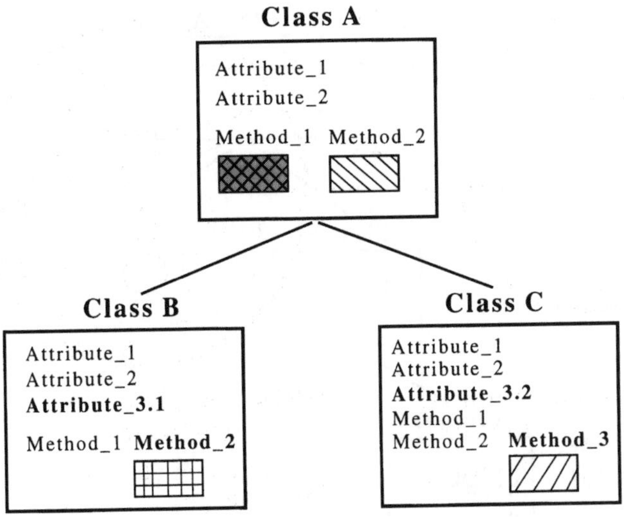


**Figure 3.17** Inheritance, users' view.

attributes and methods of class A are available in both class B and C. For example, even though only Attribute_3.1 is defined in class B, Attribute_1 and Attribute_2 are also available for use in class B.

Class B illustrates how we can add an attribute (Attribute_3.1) and that we may change the implementation of a method (Method_2). Class C shows the adding of an attribute (Attribute_3.2) and the adding of a method (Method_3). In class B the implementation of method_2 has thus been substituted by another implementation. This redefinition is generally referred to as *overriding*. Overriding of attributes is available in some object-oriented modeling techniques. However, in this book we allow overriding of methods only. In a class structure we build a hierarchy of classes, where the classes are related in child-parent relations. We say that subclass B is_a A and that C is_a A.

When a class D inherits from a class B, *all* attributes available in B are inherited by D. Thus, if class B originally inherited an attribute a1 from a class A, then attribute a1 is now also an attribute of D (see Figure 3.18). However, the rules for inheritance have not been standardized. For example, in some object-oriented modeling techniques, inheritance can be stopped along the hierarchy chain or a class can selectively inherit properties from a superclass. In this book we do not use *stopped inheritance* or *selective inheritance,* because they make it much more difficult to understand

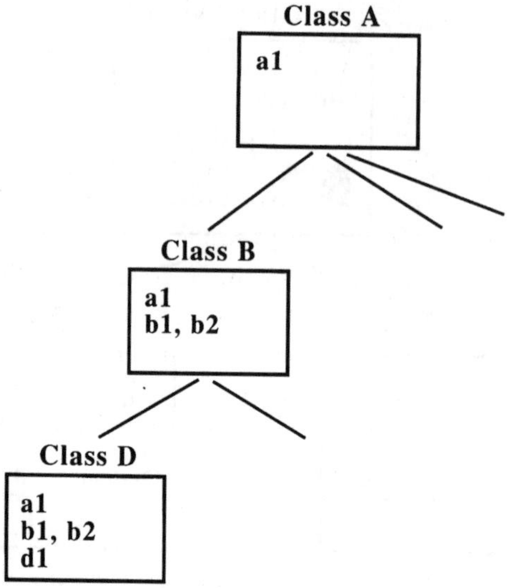


**Figure 3.18** All attributes are inherited, users' view.

inheritance. Whether we allow such options in a project or not is not as important as a clear definition of the rules we use. It is always a good idea to check if such options will make the implementation harder. For example, most object-oriented languages lack constructs for directly implementing stopped and selective inheritance.

## Abstract Class

An *abstract class* is a class that is used only as a base class for other classes or subclasses. Only these subclasses are then used to create objects.

An abstract class is often introduced to make it possible to store a set of attributes and methods common to several classes in one place, the abstract class.

---

**Example**

Instead of having copies of the same set of attributes and methods in several bank account classes, we can put them in a class of their own. If this abstract class is then used only as a superclass from which our subclasses inherit their common set of attributes and methods, we have an abstract class.

---

An abstract class should be introduced only if it increases the semantic contents of a model. Thus, introducing an abstract class is a good or a bad idea, depending on the classes involved. For example, the abstract class introduced in our bank account example is probably a good idea because bank accounts have a lot of modeling aspects in common. However, if we find the same set of attributes and methods in classes dealing with separate things—for example, a windows system and bank accounts—these classes should not be derived from the same abstract class. Thus, it is not enough that methods and attributes are similar; their corresponding classes must also be semantically related if they are to be derived from the same abstract class. The reason for this is that a clear is_a association should always exist between subclass and superclass. If two subclasses are semantically different, it is not likely that they can have true is_a associations to the same superclass.

A class that is not abstract is sometimes referred to as a *concrete class.* More common, though, is to refer to a concrete class just as a class.

Because an abstract class is incomplete—unable to instantiate usable objects—some complementary addition to it is needed if it is to be changed into a concrete class.

## Multiple Inheritance

With *single inheritance,* a class inherits from one superclass; with *multiple inheritance,* a class inherits from more than one superclass (see Figure 3.19).

A special case of multiple inheritance is *repeated inheritance,* where a class inherits from the same class twice. This is shown to the right in Figure 3.19, where class C inherits twice from class A. This type of inheritance can be tricky. For example, if a method defined in a class A has

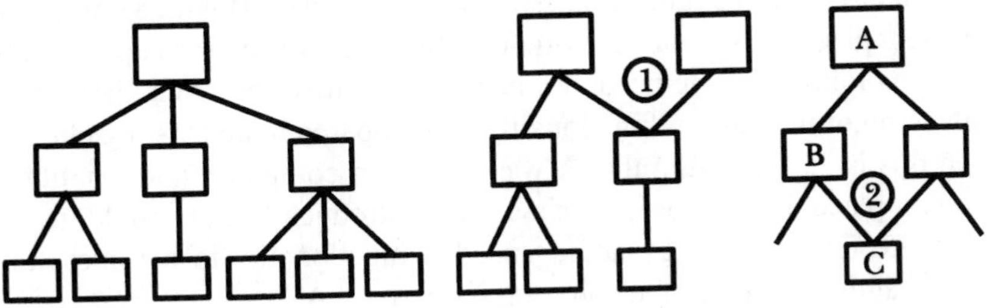


**Figure 3.19** Single, multiple inheritance (1) and repeated inheritance (2).

been changed in a subclass B, what method will be used in C? (See (2) in Figure 3.19). In object-oriented modeling, multiple inheritance should be used sparingly and repeated inheritance should be avoided. If these possibilities are available in the implementation language they should be used with caution. See also the section, "Problems with Inheritance."

## When Shall We Introduce a New Class?

It is not too uncommon that two projects can use the same class. However, it is much more common that a project needs a class *almost* identical to a class that was developed in an earlier project. Using the object-oriented technology of inheritance, we can take an already developed class and inherit everything from it into a new class, where we make the necessary changes. This solution is usually good. There are, however, several arguments against making new classes with just *small* variations as compared with existing classes:

- If every project is going to make small variations of the same base classes, we will get a lot of classes.
- If a class already exists with complete functionality, the chances are greater that it will be used than if we have to add some functionality to it before we can use it.

When should we introduce a new class? Look at the example illustrated in Figure 3.20. We presume that we have a base class, A, and two variations of it, A1 and A2, with the small additions a1 and a2, respectively. (Additions can be one or several attributes and/or methods.) We may then encounter a situation where we need another class B equal to A but having *both* the additions a1 and a2. Now, are we going to use A1 and add a2 or A2 and add a1? Would it not have been better if we had kept A and just added a1 and then a2 to it? (We are presuming that a1 and a2 will not make A1 and A2 fundamentally different. That is, B with a1 and a2 is able to replace A, A1, and A2 without difficulty.) We can sum up the arguments as follows: If the need of a new class B arises and that class needs only a minor increase in functionality, as compared to an existing class A, then this is an indication that A was not given complete functionality in the first place. In this case, we should not introduce B, but should give A complete functionality by adding needed functionality to it (unless this significantly de-creases the cohesion property of A).

Often the needed abilities of classes increase as a project develops. If a class is developed with a complete set of functions, it is probable that the functionality needed already exists in it. This is another reason why a

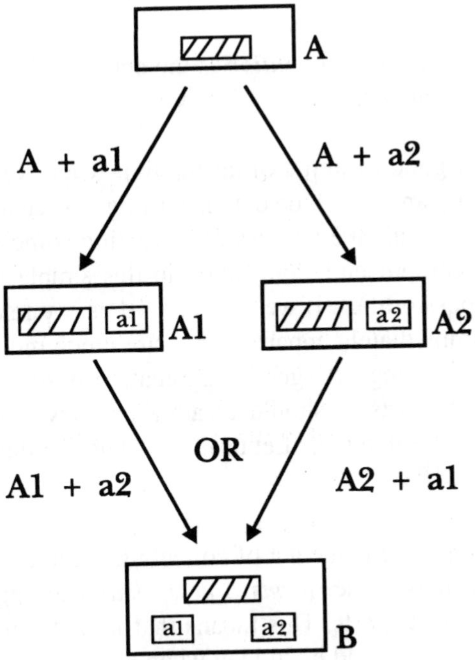


**Figure 3.20** Two alternative ways of creating the same class, B.

base class with complete functionality is preferable to a set of classes that are variations of the same base class.

## AGGREGATION

> *All intelligent thoughts have already been thought; what is necessary is only to try to think them again.*
>
> —Johann Wolfgang von Goethe

### Introduction

With the class mechanism we can group related attributes and methods, and with inheritance we have a way of organizing the classes into class structures. Such a class structure makes it easier for the human brain to comprehend and navigate among the classes.

Another structure we employ for beating complexity is called *aggregation,* and it deals mainly with objects. Sometimes we aggregate classes too, but we will deal with this in Part II. We have already briefly discussed aggregation, but let us now discuss it in detail.

**A Tentative Definition.** *Aggregation* is the act of collecting together; the state of being aggregated.

Aggregation is a good example of abstraction when we combine it with information hiding and thus hide details (strong aggregation).

Is aggregation just the process of collecting some things? Unfortunately we often comprehend aggregation in this simple way, but then we miss important possibilities. If we look around us, we find many aggregations, but as is immediately apparent, they are much more than mere random collections of things. A (good) aggregation is something more than just the sum of its parts. It should create a new level of understanding, forming a new and usable idea. Let us thus restate our definition of aggregation.

**Definition.** *Aggregation* is the act of collecting together in a way that the collection, when it is made, *forms a new idea*. The aggregation should also hide details of its parts. This means that new details should appear, whereas other details should be hidden when we form the aggregate.

Let us elaborate some on the important point, *forms a new idea*, by looking at existing aggregations.

### Real-World Examples

A trivial example of aggregation that illustrates the preceding point was given in Chapter 1. We discussed how we could increase our capacity to handle concepts if we could construct a new idea using concepts we already knew. We showed how seven things (8, 1, 9, 5, 5, 7, 3) could be handled as four things if we formed the idea "birthday of a friend to us" using the knowledge that we have a friend, Alex, who was born 1955. We then had the concepts: 8, year of Alex's birth, 7, 3. The idea, year of Alex's birth, is an aggregation of the digits 1, 9, 5, 5, and it forms a new idea—which was our definition of aggregation.

A simple example is how we can talk about our earth, a continent, a country, or parts of this country. The earth can be viewed as an aggregation made up of its continents, and so on. It is clear from this example that we can select a level of detail that suits our purpose. For example, when an astronomer talks about the earth he or she often ignores details such as

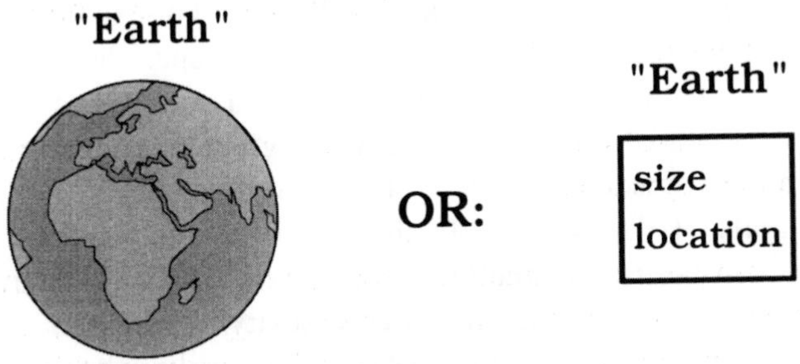


**Figure 3.21** The concept Earth is an abstraction.

what continents the planet has. Also, when the astronomer makes the "aggregate earth," new characteristics belonging to the aggregation as such appear. These new characteristics are quite meaningless if they are not connected with the aggregation. Examples of these characteristics are the shape of our planet, its size, and its location in our solar system (see Figure 3.21).

In the same way, mentioning a country does not mean that we have to think of all its details. For example, a European might ignore most of or all cities of the United States when referring to the United States. Thus we see that (good) aggregation is a form of abstraction in which we ignore some or many details. We also see that we get something new and very useful when we make this type of abstraction. The aggregation meets a need that none of its parts could fully meet on its own. That is, the key idea of an aggregate is that it helps us handle complexity in a way that none of its parts can.

---

**Example**

At the lowest logical level in a computer we find bits (zeros and ones). We group these into bytes. A byte is usually a group of eight bits. A collection of several bytes is called a file. We usually group these files into different directories. A set of directories with their files might be called a volume.

---

Each "higher" concept in the example is a grouping of smaller parts, but it also introduces something that is greater than the sum of the details it contains. A file is not just hundreds of bytes—it is something we can deal with in an easy way without thinking about bits or even bytes. It is a new "whole" that is different from the sum of its details. It is thus a new idea with its own, new characteristics, such as file name, file type, and file size.

The same is true for the idea we call Earth. For example, nowhere in its details do we find that Earth has a spherical shape. The aggregate Earth is a new idea that can be used and handled in a new and easy way. It also has new characteristics. For example, it is a globe rotating around its axis. Earth is an immensely complex system, still the concept, Earth, captures the essentials of this system. In this author's opinion, the aggregation technique can be used to reduce the complexity of any complex system regardless of the system's degree of complexity.

The aggregate has its own attributes that need *not* be directly derived from its parts. Good aggregations made during software development illustrate this idea. That is, if an aggregation does not give us a new and useful concept, then there is something wrong with the aggregation.

The association *is_part_of* is often used to describe explicitly, by drawing lines, the parts that belong to a specific aggregate. In this book we prefer to use circles or ellipses to express implicitly how we aggregate. The alternatives are illustrated in Figure 3.22.

If an aggregate can be given new attributes of its own then, it is undoubtedly a new object in itself. In Part II we will see that it is often very convenient to group a set of objects together into an aggregate, give the aggregate some new attributes and methods and regard it all as a new object. We sum up the discussion with a definition of an aggregate.

**Definition.** An *aggregate* is a collection of parts that together form something new that is more than just the sum of its parts. It introduces new

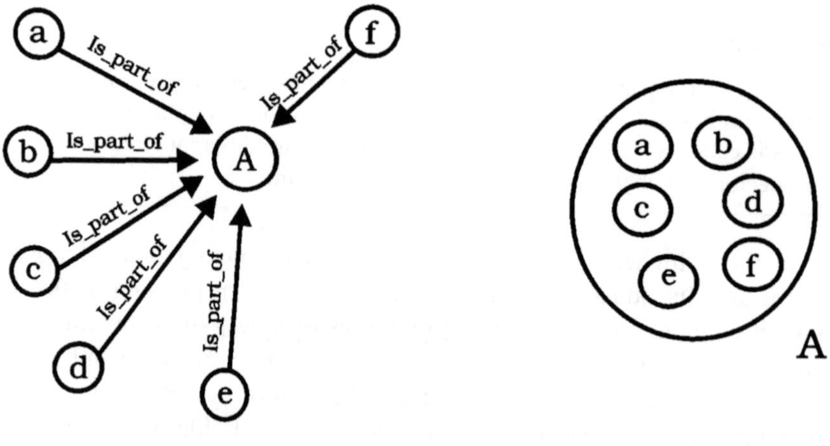


**Figure 3.22** Two ways of drawing aggregation.

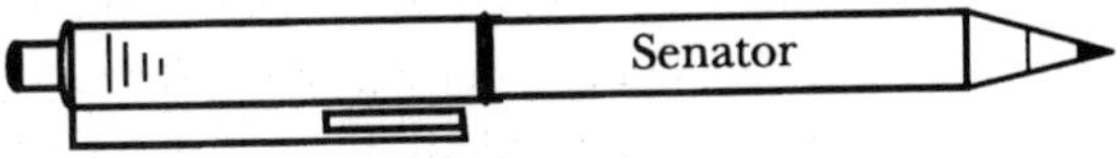


**Figure 3.23** A pen.

characteristics belonging to the whole rather than the parts. It is an abstraction that helps us ignore details and thus helps us conquer complexity.

Unfortunately aggregation is often misunderstood or not much used. Therefore, let us look at some more real-world examples. We do this to show how aggregation is a very natural abstraction technique used in our everyday life.

***A Pen***

Figure 3.23 shows a pen. We select some attributes for the pen: price, color, and brand.

This is, by definition, an abstraction, but we have actually already also employed aggregation as an abstraction technique. When we chose the attributes for the pen, we ignored the fact that the pen consists of many parts (see Figure 3.24). We ignored the parts and referred to "the whole"—the pen.

***An Invoice***

We can describe an invoice by mentioning only the invoice as such or by including details (see Figure 3.25). The description is meaningful even if we ignore most of the details. The invoice has its own attributes, which are not attributes of its parts but are attributes of the whole. Such an attribute is the invoice total. This attribute is a characteristic better described as belonging to the invoice than to any of its parts.

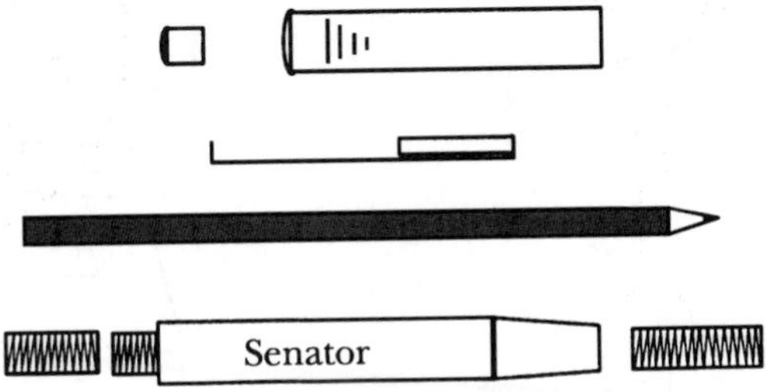


**Figure 3.24** The pen actually consists of many parts.

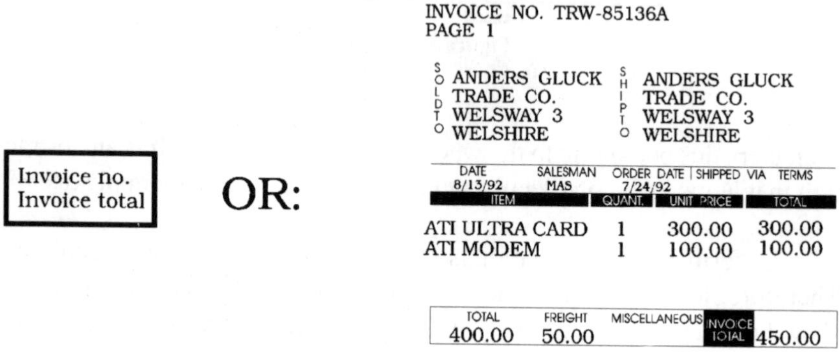


**Figure 3.25** An invoice.

***A Letter***

A letter can be thought of as one entity or as something consisting of many parts, as illustrated in Figure 3.26. This example is trivial, indeed, but it still illustrates the main point of an aggregation very clearly.

***A Computer***

A computer is more complex than a pen, an invoice, or a letter. How are we going to describe the computer? What if we are going to make an

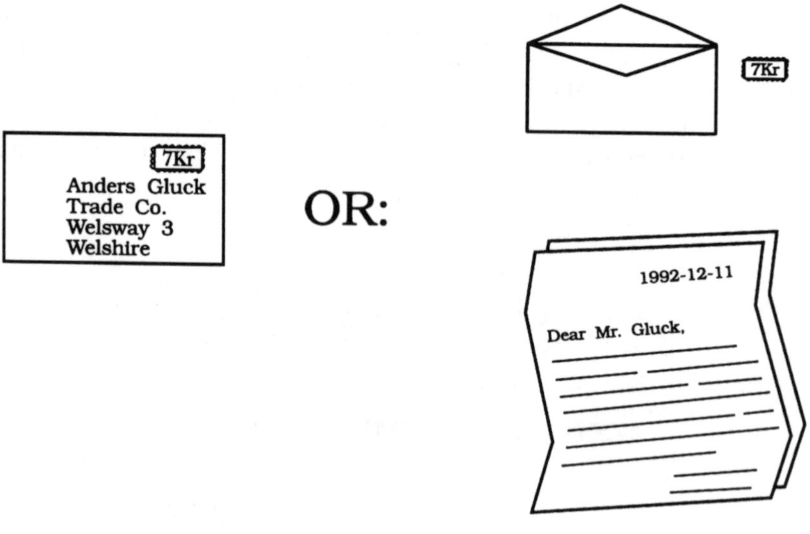


**Figure 3.26** A letter.

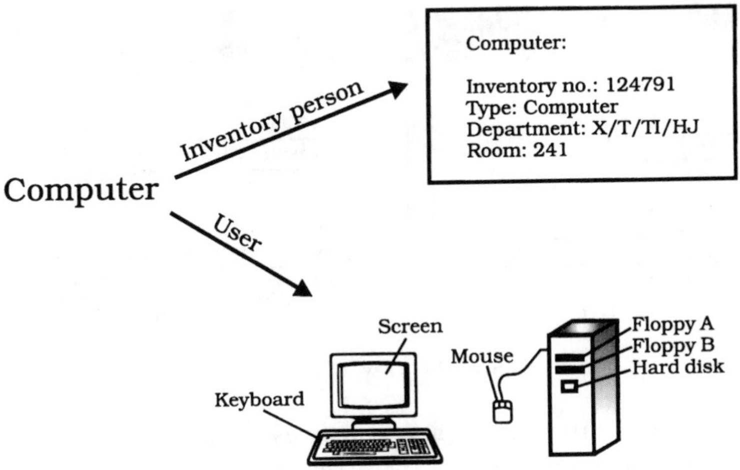


**Figure 3.27** A computer.

inventory,* service the computer, or simply use the computer? Again, we must consider our purpose. Figure 3.27 illustrates how we might see quite different things, depending on who we are. A computer user would not see the same computer as someone responsible for the inventory. A computer technician would see the computer in still another way. We can often build a hierarchy such as the one shown in Figure 3.28. This figure does *not*

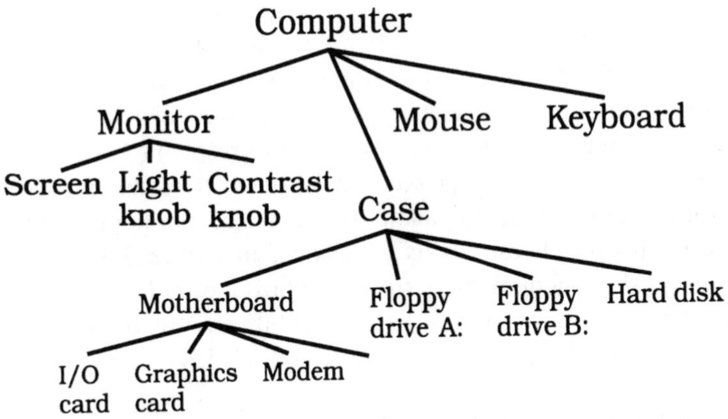


**Figure 3.28** A hierarchy of components. (Not complete.)

*An inventory is a detailed list or catalog of goods and movable properties.

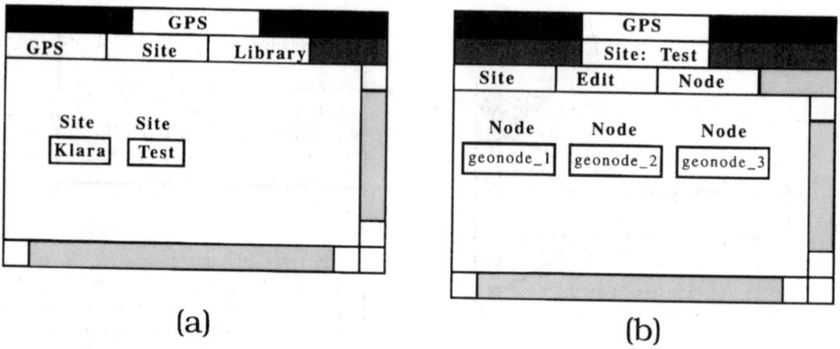


**Figure 3.29** Views of the railroad.

describe a class structure. We have simply used the same notation as for class structures to illustrate how reality can be mapped into hierarchies of aggregations. (This is actually a good illustration of how notation can deceive us when we are used to interpreting it in a certain way but use it for something else.)

***A Railroad***

As a final example, based on a system in use in Sweden, we will show how we can use aggregation techniques to keep track of details in a railroad. We can use the idea of a railroad without referring to all the details of a railroad. On the other hand, someone keeping track of the traffic on that railroad must deal with the details. There are many details in a railroad, so a natural way of partitioning it has appeared. To begin with, a railroad operator will say that a railroad consists of several sites. Figure 3.29(a) exemplifies this. Each site is composed of several nodes. If the operator is using a computer system he or she could probably access a site by double-clicking on a site-icon. We see the result in Figure 3.29(b). Double-clicking on a node-icon would take the operator to an even more detailed level. Double-clicking again would take him or her to the lowest, most detailed level. These levels are shown in Figure 3.30. The most detailed level shows a drawing of the actual layout of rails, signals, and so on. This last figure is, by the way, an excellent illustration of how the close mapping rule, introduced in Chapter 1, can be applied.

## Overlapping Aggregations

As we mentioned in connection with our discussion about purposes and views (in the section "Keep it Simple"), we often prefer to model each view of something with a separate object. This approach is in con-

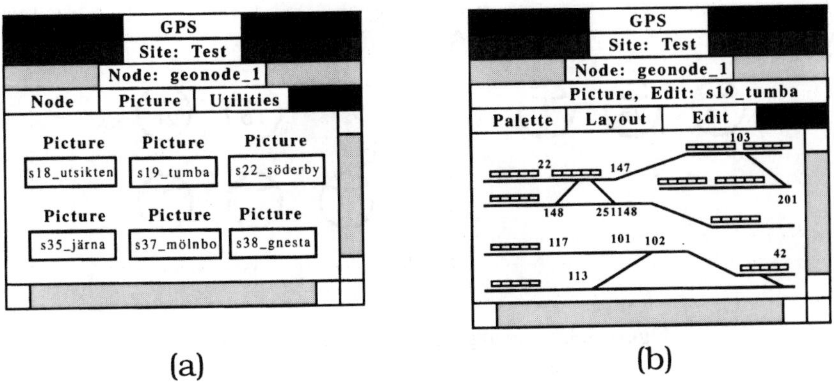


**Figure 3.30** Lower levels of detail.

trast to modeling something with a large, complex object, letting that object represent all aspects of this something. Using several objects results in a simpler model, even though we might end up with some redundancy in it. In a similar way, we try to avoid overlapping aggregations. The idea is illustrated in Figure 3.31, which shows two aggregations, A and B, where some of the objects take part in both aggregations. We avoid this type of overlapping aggregations to preserve a one-to-one mapping between reality and our model. The situation we try to imitate is that of using different drawings for different purposes. For example, if we are building a house, we could have a basic drawing showing rooms, doors, windows and so on and special drawings for the electrical installation and the sewage disposal system. A situation with objects being in two aggregations could occur if the objects were modeling more than one aspect. For example, if each object in Figure 3.31 models a room, aggregation A is our electrical installation drawing and B is our sewage disposal system, it must be that objects 1 and 2 model both the electrical

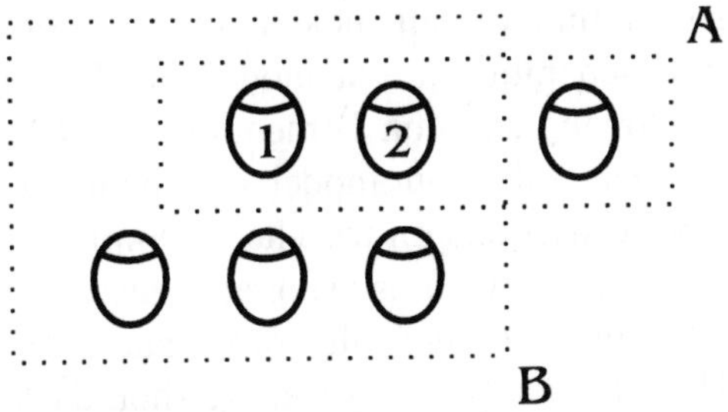


**Figure 3.31** Two aggregations sharing two objects

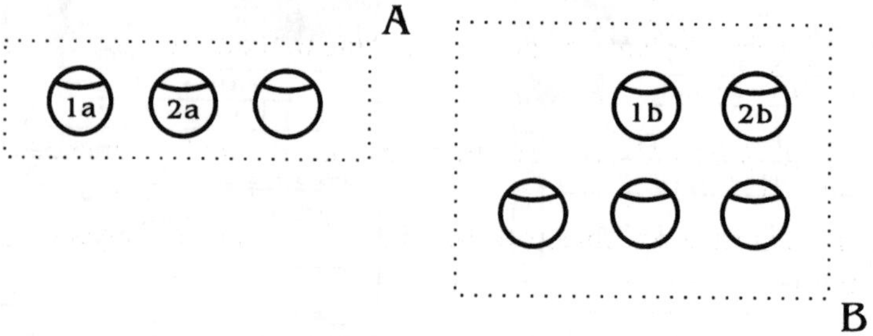


**Figure 3.32** Two aggregations with separate objects.

installation and the sewage disposal system. Figure 3.32 shows a changed model, where we model each view with a separate object. Thus, instead of letting objects represent two aspects, we now have objects 1a and 2a representing the aspect of electrical installation and objects 1b and 2b representing the aspect of sewage disposal system. This latter modeling approach is the preferred way to model in this book.

## Aggregation, Attributes, and Adjectives

It is possible to build an object structure implicitly by allowing the types of attributes to be equal to classes. It is then possible to use attributes to represent subobjects. (See also the section "Complex Class.") However, we do not use this approach in this book because we want to limit the use of an attribute to describing a characteristic of an object. The characteristic of something is described primarily with adjectives or other modifiers for nouns or verbs, and it is natural to reserve the use of attributes for this.

In spoken languages we repeatedly find adjectives, nouns, and verbs. If we allow attributes to describe object structures, we confuse the situation because objects are basically taken from nouns. Separating adjectives from nouns and verbs is common to all spoken languages of the world so it is natural to keep this separation in our model too. This choice is a direct consequence of following solution B mentioned in Chapter 1: having a close mapping between reality, our model, and the implemented system.

There may be restrictions on the chosen implementation language, forcing us to build object structures using attributes. However, we should not let such restrictions automatically propagate from implementation into design and then into analysis, instead, we should deal with them only when we have to and not before.

### Complex Class

Previously, we have made two statements that we now find are in some conflict:

1. The class describes what attributes and methods a created object shall get.
2. It is important for objects to be able to be grouped in layers—nested objects.

The problem is that if groups of objects are to be objects themselves—and we do want this to be possible—then the first description of the class is not sufficient. That is, the class as we have described it until now is not sufficient because it does not describe the (nested) object structure. In C++ and Smalltalk, this problem is typically resolved by having the attributes describe objects by allowing the type of an attribute to be a class. However, we need a more general solution because we do not want attributes to describe the object structure but do want to restrict attributes to describe characteristics of an object. Therefore we introduce the idea of a *complex class*. A complex class is a class that not only contains information about methods and attributes, but also contains information about an object structure. When a complex class is used to instantiate an object, this created object will also contain a specified object structure. The object structure is encapsulated by the object in the same way as attributes. The idea is illustrated in Figure 3.33, where we have an augmented class description to the left and an example of an instantiated

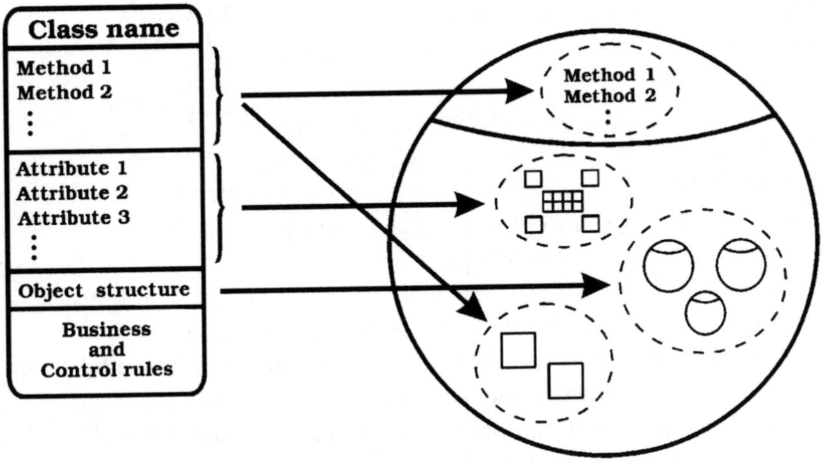


**Figure 3.33** A complex class defines an object structure.

object to the right. The objects in the object structure are themselves specified by other classes or complex classes. The object structure may thus be nested. It should be noted that when we use the word class in this book we put no restriction on it. Thus, the word class may refer to a *class* or a *complex class* as just described—whatever is appropriate.

## Delegation

We explain the idea of *delegation* with the following example. A class Linked_list has the methods First, Last, as well as other methods, making it possible for us to insert and take away elements in any place in a linked list. We need a new class Stack with the methods Push and Pop. We decide to inherit from the class Linked_list because it can supply us with much of the functionality we need (see Figure 3.34). However, inheritance gives our new class, Stack, all the methods of Linked_list, even though we want to have only the methods Push and Pop, because they define our Stack. The figure shows the situation. Someone might use these extra methods (First, Last, etc.) possibly making the whole system crash. A better solution is to use delegation. *Delegation* is a simple form of

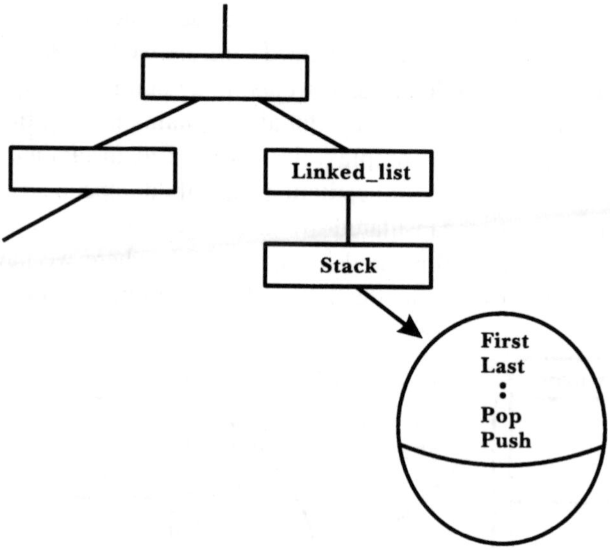


**Figure 3.34** Creating class Stack using inheritance.

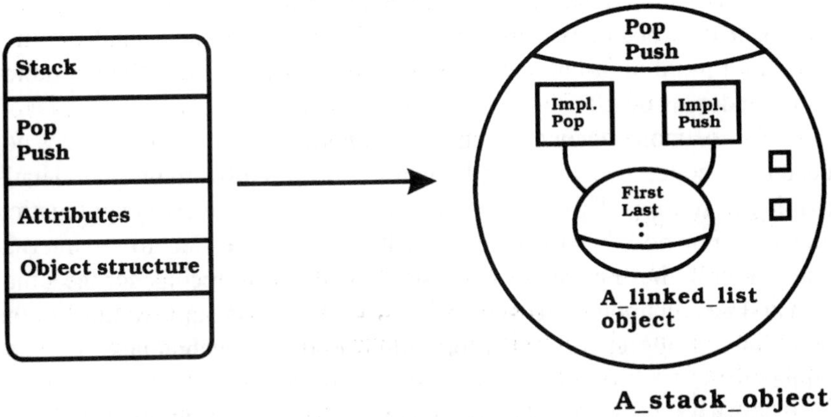


**Figure 3.35** Creating class Stack using delegation. (Only parts of implementation shown).

aggregation, where we put an object inside another object. In Figure 3.35 we show this solution. Note that Stack is now a complex class. With this solution, an object instantiated from the class Linked_list is available to Stack, and its methods can be used when we implement the Stack methods Pop and Push. At the same time, the Linked_list methods are hidden from someone using a Stack object. Figure 3.35 does not show where the class Stack should be put in a class structure because there are several possibilities. One possible location could be to give Stack the same superclass as Linked_list.

### Object Structures and Class Structures

The classes and the way they are related make up a class structure. Each class is the blueprint for one or several objects used to set up our application and *maybe several other applications*. Because we can normally connect the classes not only with our application but with a whole set of different applications, it is not practical to mix the class structure with the object structures that make up our application(s). That is, we should keep class structures separated from our application model(s). There are also other reasons for not mixing class structures and object structures too closely. (We deal with this topic at various points in this book.)

### Summary

In an aggregate we group objects that belong together and form a new idea, something whole to which we can easily refer. The "whole" is easier to understand than the set of its parts. When we make a good aggregation, it thus becomes possible for us to understand and handle something in a more high-level way, because we can refer to the whole rather than the details of it.

For example, when a user talks about a computer, he or she does not need to be concerned with details such as the motherboard or other details (irrelevant to him). This is a very important point. If we do an aggregation and it is not possible to understand it without referring to its internal parts, then we have gone awry. We should then try to reconsider the situation and design another aggregate. This situation is in stark contrast to the modeling of aggregation in information modeling techniques. Also see Appendix 1.

We have also seen, as in the examples with the computer and the railroad, that it is natural and necessary to have a nested structure of aggregations. We called these nested structures object structures.

## PROBLEMS WITH INHERITANCE

Now that we have introduced aggregation, it is time to look at inheritance again. Inheritance is a simple and powerful tool as we do object-oriented modeling and a simple way of reusing code when we do the actual implementation of a system. The former way of using inheritance is popular in Europe, whereas inheritance in the United States appears to be largely used to reuse code [2]. If we use inheritance as a modeling tool, we will, of course, reuse code, too. However, it is not the primary aim, just a nice secondary effect. Note that reuse of code through copy and paste is also a viable method when doing object-oriented development.

Unfortunately the simplicity of inheritance is mostly on the surface, which is shown by the misuse of inheritance. An example of misuse is when we miss the essential aspects of something. As a trivial example, consider the inheritance of "have legs" from a superclass to two classes, Cat and Table. Two classes should inherit from the same superclass only if they inherit the same property. Having legs is a property of both tables and cats, but this property stands for quite different characteristics in cats than in tables. This example is simple, but errors of this type do occur.

In most implementation languages, a subclass has full access to the contents of the superclass. This fact poses a basic problem with inheritance when we get to the implementation phase, as it tends to destroy information hiding. The problem is more related to available implementation languages* than to object-oriented modeling as such. However, the problem can also be viewed as a modeling problem, because changing a superclass can create problems. Suppose we have two subclasses X and Y with the same superclass S and that X and Y are used in separate projects. Changing a method in S affects both X and Y (unless the subclasses have overridden the method). Thus if a first project changes the superclass S, we might achieve a result with X that is wanted in this project. But what about the other project? Is the change all right for them too? The solution to this problem is to enforce a bureaucracy (configuration management) that prevents a project from making changes in a class used by other projects unless the changes have been approved by all concerned. If this problem applies to a class, the problem could also apply to subclasses of this class (because a derived class probably depends on its base class).

A common cause of problems when we are using inheritance is the use of the is_a association for something that is not a true is_a association. An example of this was discussed in the section "Abstract Class," where we noted that true is_a associations must exist between a superclass and all its subclasses. Let us look at another example.

---

**Example**

A car and its doors have some things in common—for example, their color and owner. If we let a class Door inherit from a class Car that has these attributes, we would give the Door the color and owner attributes, which is all right. The problem is that the Car class probably has many other attributes that we should not have in the Door class.

---

The is_a association implies exactly "is a." Because a canary *is a* bird, everything that is true for a bird must also be true for our canary. That is, it is correct to let a canary class inherit everything from a bird class. A door, on the other hand, is *not* a car. The examples are trivial, but the principles they illustrate are often violated in real-world situations. This misuse occurs particularly when a possible code reuse appears. When we inherit from classes because they contain things we need, we call it "inheritance by accident" if we do it in badly envisioned and badly structured ways.

*C++ is one of the few object-oriented languages that has some support for information hiding via the "private" construct.

Misuse of inheritance is also often connected with situations where we try to use multiple inheritance to design new classes but should have used aggregation instead.

---

**Example**

We are designing a Dialog_handler. Requirements are that it should be able to accept data, do local processing, output data to a remote computer, etc. A class, Input_handler, exists that has data input ability, and we decide to inherit from it. This will give our Dialog_handler data input ability. But what if we later need to add a second data input ability to our Dialog_handler? If Input_handler can only handle one set of inputs, what shall we do then? Do we inherit a second time?

---

If we think about this example we soon realize that our Dialog_handler is not really an Input_handler. That is, the is_a association is not appropriate here; the is_part_of association should be used instead. If we use the is_part_of association, we can take one instance of the Input_handler and let it be a part of the Dialog_handler. When we later decide to add a second input-handling capacity, we just create a second instance of the Input_handler and make that a part of our Dialog_handler too.

Multiple inheritance was a bad solution in the previous example. Referring to the preceding discussion, we conclude that as a first rule, we should not use multiple inheritance if we have is_part_of associations rather than is_a associations.

A second rule is that we should use multiple inheritance only from classes that have *different independent characteristics*. Borrowing a word from mathematics, we can say that we should inherit only from classes that are *orthogonal* regarding their characteristics.

## ORTHOGONALITY

In geometry, we have the vector as a concept. (A vector can be considered to be simply a directed quantity or an arrow.) If we have a set of different vectors $\{a_1, a_2, a_3, \ldots a_n\}$ we can construct new vectors by adding them in different ways. For example we could make a new vector b:

$$b = a_1 + 0.4*a_2 + 5*a_3$$

If it is possible to construct such a new vector, b, using vectors {a1, $a_2, a_3, \ldots a_n\}$ in only one way, we say that the set $\{a_1, a_2, a_3, \ldots a_n\}$ is linearly independent. A stricter definition is as follows: A set of vectors is said to be a linearly independent set if each vector in the set is linearly independent of the remainder of the set.

The idea of orthogonality can be applied to classes as well as methods and attributes. If an attribute can always be replaced (simulated) by other attributes, we say that it is dependent on those attributes. On the other hand, if an attribute cannot be replaced by other attributes, we say that the attribute is independent, and we call it a *primitive* attribute.

---

**Example**

If the value of the attribute age can be calculated using some other attributes in a class (such as the birth date) and/or available system value(s) (such as the date of the current day), it is not primitive. However, it can be made primitive by removing the attribute(s) it depends on.

---

In the same way, a method is primitive if there is no other method or set of methods that can perform the same function as the method in question.

A class is primitive if there are no other classes or sets of classes available that can be used to substitute for it. Orthogonality implies that classes should have different attributes and methods. However it does not only suggest that all attributes and all methods (in the same class) should have different names. It also means that names for attributes and methods, respectively, should not be synonyms.

---

**Example**

We have the attribute owner in one class and the attribute holder in another class. These attributes are probably not orthogonal, because they probably denote the same thing.

---

We make the following general definition:

**Definition.** We consider a class, an attribute, or a method *primitive* if it cannot be replaced by one or several other classes, attributes, or methods, respectively. We say that a set of primitive classes, attributes, or methods, respectively, is *orthogonal*.

It is a good idea to construct primitive attributes, methods, and classes. For example, if we are going to construct a new class C by multiple inheritance from the classes A and B, we will avoid a lot of problems if A and B are primitive in the sense described here, because we will avoid methods and attributes that conflict with each other.

In practice it is often not possible to only have primitive attributes, methods, and classes.

---

**Examples**

(a) We might have to introduce a new attribute such as total amount for efficiency reasons.

(b) The functionality of a set of primitive methods might be too low-level to be of practical use.

(c) The functionality of two classes might overlap because they were bought from different vendors or because they were developed in different projects.

---

## ASSOCIATIONS

### Introduction

Object-oriented modeling is full of different types of associations. Common associations are the is_a, consists_of, contains, is_part_of, use, and knows associations. A model using these associations is drawn much like the entity-relationship diagrams used in information modeling. We see an example of an object-oriented model using typical associations in Figure 3.36

The *is_a* association is a very important type of association. It is often simply called inheritance because we use it to show how one class inherits from another class. Sometimes a distinction is made between is_a and a_kind_of associations. Inheritance of features by class is then treated as an *a_kind_of* association and inheritance by objects as an is_a association. For example, the class Employee is a_kind_of Person, whereas the object Margareta is_a Employee. No such distinction is used in this book, however, and we use only one name for the association, is_a.

The *consists_of* association shows in what way things are put together.

---

**Example**

We can model the parts of an airplane with the consists_of association. That is, the airplane consists of a tail, two wings, a fuselage, and so on.

---

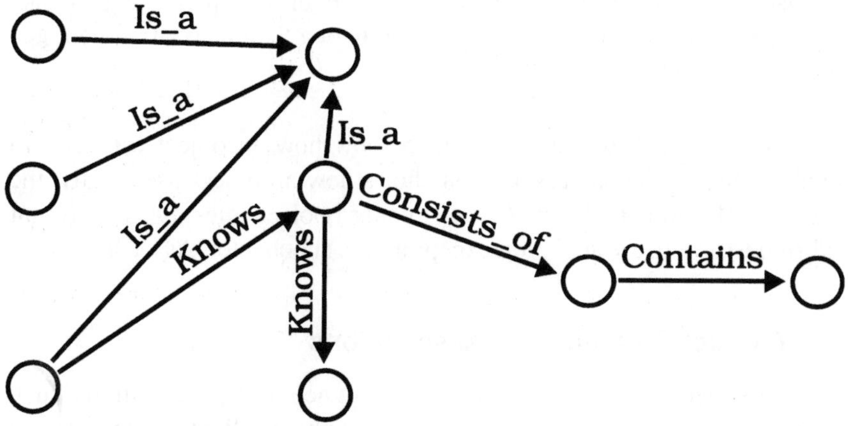


**Figure 3.36** Typical associations used in object-oriented methods.

Another name for the consists_of association is thus *aggregation*. Still another name is *composition*. (In this book we use the word aggregation).

The *is_part_of* association gives exactly the same information as the consists_of association but viewed from the other direction. For example, the tail is a part of the airplane.

The *contains* association is a looser type of aggregation, where the parts of the aggregation have been collected just because we want to keep them together.

---

**Examples**

Car contains Passengers; Database contains Records.

---

In most cases it is possible to replace the contains association with the is_part_of association without losing any information. We might, in fact, get more information by replacing the consists association with the is_part_of association, which we illustrate in our next example.

---

**Example**

We have the association Car contains Passengers. It does not make much sense to transform this into Car is_part_of Passenger (or Passenger is_part_of Car). Instead, if we transform Car contains Passenger into a model without the contains association, we could end up with Car is_part_of Transport and Passenger is_part_of Transport. That is, we become aware of a third object Transport, getting a more complete model in the process.

We use the *knows* association to show how an object can refer to another object. The *use* association shows how an object uses (calls) the methods of another object. (Note, in this book, a message call is not referred to as a use association except in this subchapter, Associations.)

### A Major Problem with Associations

An object-oriented model is often designed using associations, such as those just mentioned, to relate classes and objects. We then get a model with circles and lines much like the one shown in Figure 3.36, but much larger. (We can draw classes and objects in another way, but we would still be using the same principle.) To model a system in this way is to ignore some of the more powerful abstraction mechanisms available to us. Let us look at a simple example to illustrate this point.

In Figure 3.37(a) we see an example representing a typical model full of associations. The problem with this type of model is that when it

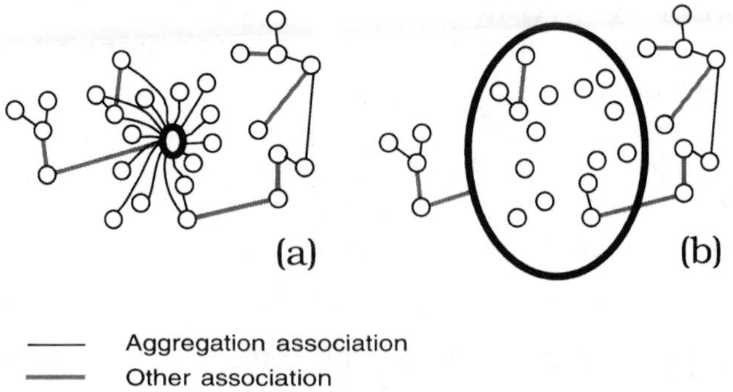


**Figure 3.37** The same aggregation drawn in two different ways.

grows, it soon becomes so full of details that we have trouble grasping the important overall structure. Removing most of the explicit associations gives us a much cleaner model, as shown in (b). Here we have a model that is easier to understand because we have hidden details and/or made them implicit. For example, we have made most of the aggregation (is_part_of) associations implicit. Thus, instead of showing every is_part_of association explicitly with a line, we understand how the corresponding aggregation is meant to be from the way we group the objects inside an ellipse. (If they are inside the ellipse, we understand that they belong together.)

If the grouping inside the ellipse forms an idea of its own, we can summarize the grouping using an empty ellipse. That is, we can make the model even better by hiding the details of the grouping. This model is easier to grasp, because we have fewer details to comprehend when we see it (see Figure 3.38).

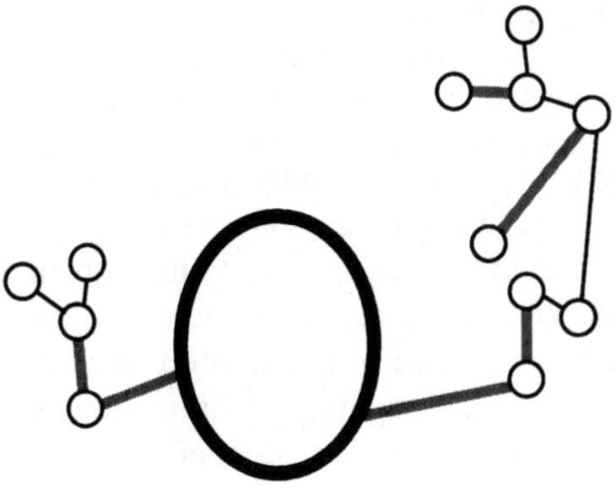

**Figure 3.38** The aggregation in Figure 3.37 simplified.

We can show how an object calls (uses) another object either explicitly, as in the previous model, or implicitly, by knowing that objects that are inside an ellipse can call and use each other. (When an object A calls another object B, then A is requesting B to perform some behavior associated with B.)

If we want to show explicitly that an object is calling another object, we can show this with an arrow or simply by drawing a line without arrowheads between them (see Figure 3.39). The simple line (without arrowheads) is a good way to start. The line then shows only that two objects call each other in some way.

To start with a less exact description (a simple line) instead of a more exact description (arrow/arrows) is a natural way of modeling. At first we might understand only that we should connect two objects. We might lack information whether object A should call B, object B should call A, or calls should be made in both directions. We then note our present understanding with a line, and if we see the need for further clarification, we add arrowheads when we have the knowledge to do so.

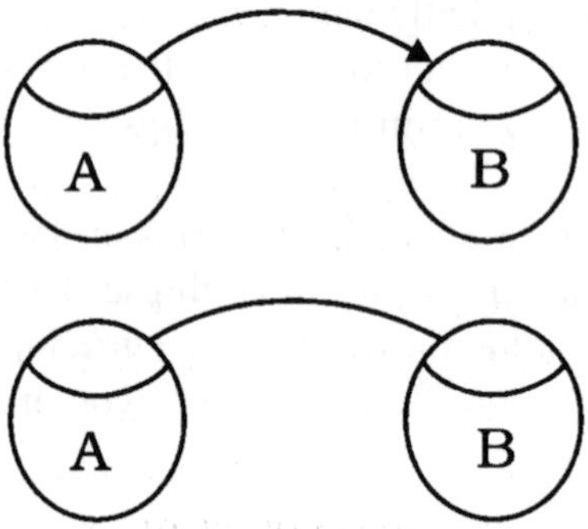


**Figure 3.39** Showing method calls in a drawing.

This discussion takes us to an important point: We draw a particular association because we want to add some information to the model. *But do we really need to add this information?* The problem with drawing too many associations is that we soon lose the general picture. *What is significant information* that we need to put into our model and what are just unimportant details? At the beginning of a modeling session, we often find many facts about the model but no good structure. It is then important to group the objects in ways that ease understanding, ignoring less important facts by doing abstractions. For example, if we feel the need to group a set of objects into an aggregate, it is probable that the objects inside this aggregation use each other in different ways. In particular, we will probably find that we have *knows* associations between some of them. But why should we explicitly show these associations in our model? If we do so, we gain in exactness, but we lose in understanding.

---

**Example**

In an industry we might have several employees. One employee probably knows other employees. Should we then indicate in a model exactly whom the employee knows, or is it enough to show that he or she belongs to a certain division and let this *imply* that the employee knows the other employees?

---

Too much or too little will spoil everything. *If* we are satisfied by recognizing that objects that we group together may refer to each other, we do not have to draw any *knows* associations at all. The need for showing associations explicitly then turns into a matter of modeling style, and we can skip the associations if we decide to. Our rule is as follows:

If an association adds needed information to the model, add it. Otherwise, leave it out.

We can treat the case of associations that show how objects call each other in the same way we treat *knows* associations. However, showing how objects call each other often significantly helps us to understand a model. It is not necessary, however, to show all these arrows and lines in the same picture. We can use several pictures with the same objects but with different sets of arrows and lines showing how the objects call each other. Such pictures showing how objects call each other in a given situation are often called *message traces* or *interaction diagrams*.

A go-to statement in code is viewed as a bad construct because it transfers the flow of execution in an unstructured way. This makes the code difficult to understand. However, an association often transfers the flow of attention in an unstructured way when we are trying to understand a model. Thus, associations could be called the go-to's of object-oriented modeling. This fact is one important reason why we should use associations sparingly.

## How Should We Use Associations?

*The more wise and powerful a master, the more directly is his work created and the simpler it is.*

—Meister Eckhart

We found in the previous subchapter that there are many different types of associations in use today and that models tend to be very complex and hard to comprehend because of the use of these associations. To rectify the situation, we will next give a definition of the concept of association and try to introduce some structure into the use of associations.

**Definition.** An *association* sets up a connection. The connection is some type of fact that we want to note in our model.

An association setting up a connection between classes also sets up corresponding connections in the object structures created from these classes. Thus, we can illustrate associations between classes using examples of object structures.

---

**Example**

A car has four wheels. If we use classes, we can illustrate this by saying that there is a 1:4 (one-to-four) association between the class Car and the class Wheel. If we

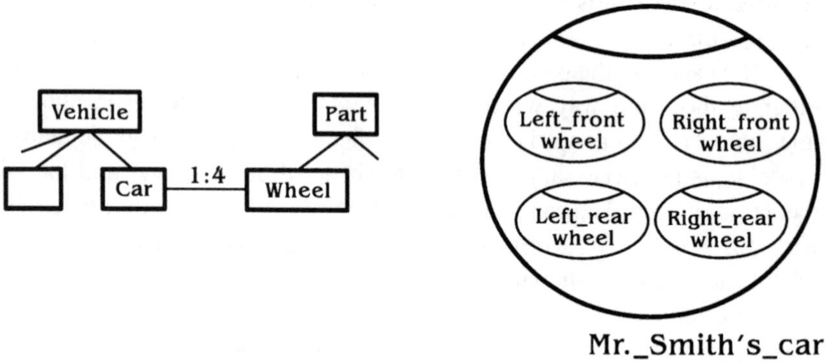


**Figure 3.40** Illustrating the same association using classes and objects, respectively.

use objects, we can illustrate this by saying that the object Mr._Smith's_car has the following four Wheel objects: Left_front_wheel, Right_front_wheel, Left_rear_wheel, and Right_rear_wheel. The examples are illustrated in Figure 3.40.

---

There is some tension between our class structure described with is_a associations and the corresponding object structure described with is_part_of associations. This tension can be understood by the following reasoning about Mr._Smith's_car. When we are about to construct the car —which corresponds to an application—we use parts such as wheels, which we get by instantiating them from classes. We keep on adding objects (doors, windows, steering-wheel, etc.) until we have built the car. At this moment—if not earlier—we realize that the car in itself is also an object and that it should have a corresponding class. (Note that in object-oriented languages, an object such as Mr._Smith's_car must typically be created from a class. However, in object-oriented modeling or if we use a programming language such as Ada, this is not necessary.) The example illustrates that there is an aspect of time involved in the construction of the car. First, lower-level classes such as the Wheel class must be available. We then shift our attention to the object structure where we build our application by instantiating objects from these available low-level classes. In the end we shift our attention back to the class structure and try to figure out if the newly created object structure (or parts of it) should constitute reusable parts to be described by new classes. If the answer to this question is *yes,* we update our class structures, adding new classes such as the class Car. Showing is_part_of information, such as the 1:4 association between Car and Wheel in the class structure, is thus wrong. This type of information is best acquired by working with the object structure—not the class structure—and should thus exist only in the object-structure.

The preceding example also explains to some extent why mixing is_a and is_part_of associations can be very confusing. An important conclusion is that the class structure should be kept as clean from associations other than the is_a association as possible. We now continue the discussion of associations, taking a more general viewpoint.

We divide associations into hierarchical associations and nonhierarchical associations.

**Definition.** *Hierarchy* is a structure in which components are ranked into levels of subordination; each component has zero, one, or more subordinates, and no component has more than one superordinate component. [IEEE]

A hierarchical association connects in a hierarchical fashion. A nonhierarchical association connects in an arbitrary manner. We use two hierarchical associations, is_part_of and is_a. Nonhierarchical associations are discussed in the section, "Relationships."

Other types of hierarchical associations can be constructed. For example, Dillon and Tan in their book *Object-Oriented Conceptual Modeling* [25] refer to an association called *instance_of*. This type of association connects an instance with the class that created it.

To decide if we need more hierarchical associations than the is_part_of and is_a associations, let us consult the Encyclopedia Britannica (as Coad and Yourdon did in their book, *Object-Oriented Analysis*. [4]):

In apprehending the world, men [people] constantly employ three methods of organization, that pervade all of their thinking:

(1) the differentiation of experience into particular objects and their attributes—e.g., when they distinguish between a tree and its size or its spatial relations to other objects;
(2) the distinction between whole objects and their component parts—e.g., when they contrast a tree with its component branches; and
(3) the formation of and the distinction between different classes of objects—e.g., when they form the class of all trees and the class of all stones and distinguish between them.*

The is_part_of and the is_a associations correspond to (2) and (3), respectively. We discussed constructs necessary for modeling (1) in the

*[From "Classification Theory" in *Encyclopedia Britannica,* 15th edition (1984), 4:691] (Reprinted with permission).

previous chapter when we discussed attributes. Thus, we can invent other types of hierarchical associations such as the instance_of association, but we do not really need them in our model, because we should use the same type of constructions when we model as when we think about a problem—nothing more and nothing less—if we are to follow the close mapping rule introduced in Chapter 1. An association such as an instance_of association can be understood to exist from the very fact that an instance is (normally) created from a class. When we need to know which class created which instance, this information can be available elsewhere—and not in the model of our application. (Preferably CASE tools keep track of such information for us.)

Of the many associations used in various object modeling techniques we thus need but a few. We need the is_part_of association. In this book we prefer to represent an aggregation with a circle or ellipse enclosing the objects that we aggregate rather than showing the aggregation explicitly with several is_part_of association lines. This solution reduces the amount of details and gives a more intuitive picture of what we are really trying to show.

We also need the is_a association, but it is not meant to be used much in the application model. It is, instead, the main association in the model of our storage of components that we build—the class structure(s).

When we need to show how different objects call each other, we draw an arrow or a line. Finally, we sometimes need to establish arbitrary connections between classes, which is the topic of our next section.

## Relationships

*Two things are identical if one can be substituted for the other without affecting the truth.*

—Gottfried Wilhelm Leibniz

In order to clearly distinguish between nonhierarchical associations and hierarchical associations, we will refer to nonhierarchical associations as *relationships.* This is *not* a well-established practice, and the words relationship and association are often used as synonyms. However, we reserve the word relationship for nonhierarchical associations, because it is convenient.

A relationship thus states some nonhierarchical fact that we want to include in our model. Relationships are used frequently in information modeling; we show some typical relationships in Figure 3.41. The capitalized words used in the examples are names of relationships. The set of

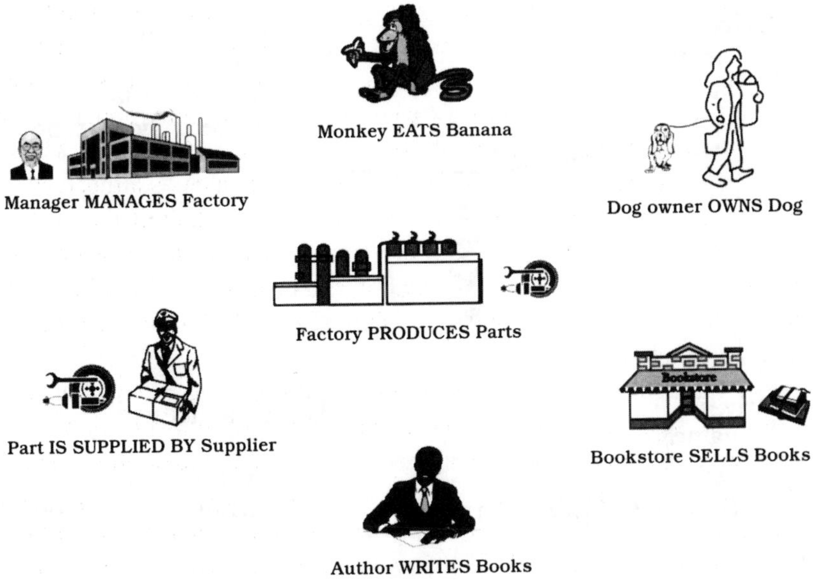


**Figure 3.41** Examples of relationships.

possible relationships is infinite and not restricted to the examples shown in the figure. Numbers can be used to show the *multiplicity* of the relationship. For example 1:1 implies that an object is always related to one object. 1:M implies that an object is related to one or several other objects. For example, if an object is always related to four other objects we write 1:4. The word *cardinality* is sometimes used instead of multiplicity, but this word is less standardized than multiplicity, and hence we prefer the word multiplicity.

We also sometimes use an *object connection* (often called *instance connection*). This is actually a misnomer. If we accept the idea that classes include all information necessary to create objects, then the information that an association exists must be included in corresponding classes. For example, if an object connection tells us *what* Monkey EATS *what* Banana, then there should be a corresponding relationship giving us the more general information that Monkey EATS Banana.

With object-oriented modeling we have special constructs available for our hierarchical associations: is_a and is_part_of. Note, however, that this does not imply that it is impossible to simulate aggregation or class structures using relationships. The point of not copying this way of modeling into object-oriented modeling is analogous to the point in favor of using high-level languages instead of assembler: Whatever you program

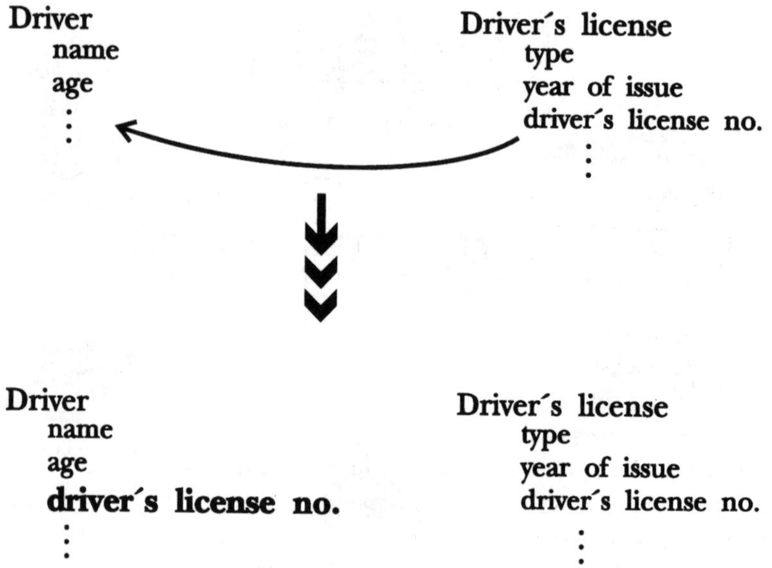


**Figure 3.42** Using attributes to implement a typical relationship, "Driver OWNS Driver's license".

using a high-level language you *can* program using assembler but why do it if you have high-level constructs readily available? The same type of reasoning can be applied to why we should not use relationships to simulate hierarchical associations when more direct constructions such as is_a and is_part_of are readily available.

Object-oriented models can have relationships, but they are much less in focus than with information modeling.

Figure 3.42 illustrates how we implement a typical relationship, Driver OWNS Driver's license. We take an identifier from one object and we make it into an attribute in the other object. Relationships are thus implemented by attributes. We sometimes refer to such attributes as *referential attributes*. Because relationships are implemented by attributes, we need not use them as they are used in information modeling (drawing connecting lines), but we can model them directly as attributes, which we put into relevant classes.

Unfortunately, the previous paragraph is not completely true, because the relationship concept is somewhat more complicated than we have assumed. That is, it is not always possible to model a relationship with an attribute. We discuss this in the following paragraphs.

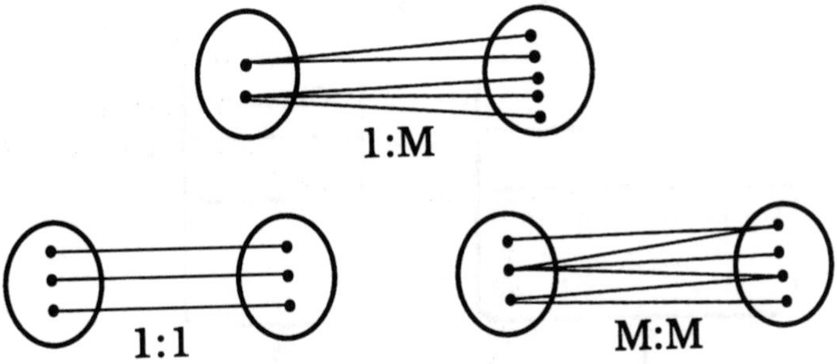


**Figure 3.43** Unconditional relationships. Dots represent objects, lines represent relationships.

Relationships are classified as binary relationships if they involve two objects or as higher-order relationships if they involve more than two objects. We also classify binary relationships as one-to-one, one-to-many or as many-to-many. This is illustrated in Figure 3.43. Furthermore we can classify our relationships as unconditional or conditional. Figure 3.43 shows unconditional forms. All objects participate in unconditional relationships. In a conditional relationship, there may be objects that do not participate, which is shown in Figure 3.44.

Note that we put the *c*, for conditional, where we have the uncertain connection. In some books the *c* is put on the opposite side (for example, 1:1c instead of 1c:1, and so on). Putting the *c* on the opposite side would violate our close mapping rule, so we put the *c* where it applies.

A *simple relationship* models a connection between two classes, whereas a *complex relationship* also models additional facts. Let us look at some examples that model relationships.

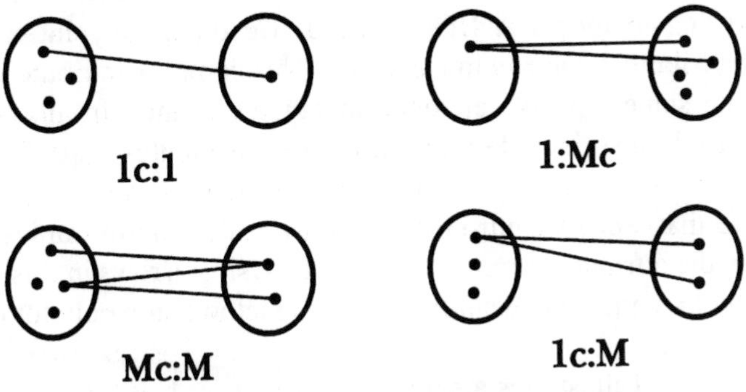


**Figure 3.44** Conditional relationships.

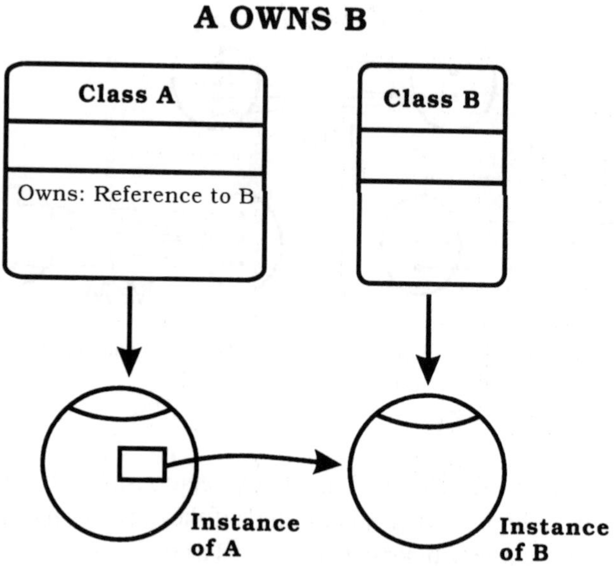


**Figure 3.45** Modeling a relationship.

If we have a simple relationship, as for example, A OWNS B, we can model it as illustrated in Figure 3.45. In the figure, we have introduced the attribute Owns. The name of the attribute describes our relationship and the type of the attribute is such that it can hold a reference to objects of class B. At the top of the figure we show class descriptions. When an instance of class A is created, the value of the attribute Owns will point to a particular object created from class B. This is illustrated in the lower part of the figure, with an example of an object structure.

In Figure 3.46, we have a more complex situation. We still have a one-to-one relationship, but we want to add some information to the relationship such as the date we created the relationship. We could, for example, be trying to model A BOUGHT B. We do this by introducing a complex attribute, as shown in the figure. This complex attribute will then contain the same type of reference to objects created from class B as before but will also include other descriptive attributes important to our model.

Note that we have introduced the arrows in the examples only to show how the attributes connect the objects. Using arrows in this way in a model is not recommended, and we use this method here only for explanatory purposes.

Figure 3.47 illustrates a solution in which we have chosen to represent the information we want to add to the relationship with a class of its

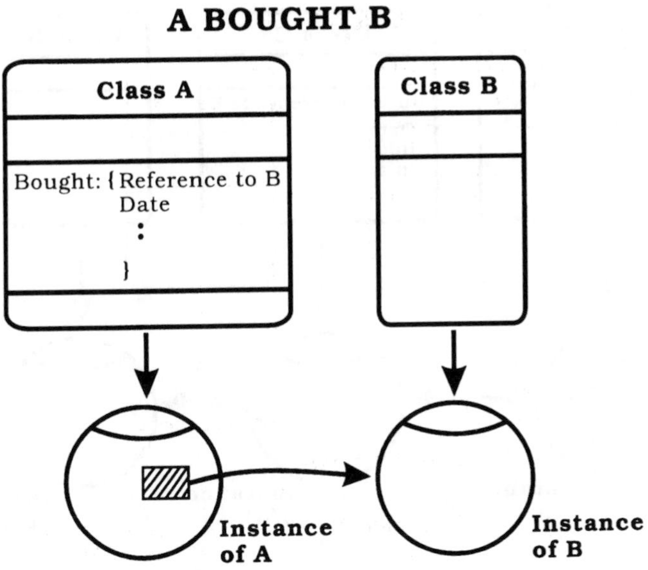


**Figure 3.46** Modeling a relationship with some information attached to it.

own. We thus have the possibility of modeling information connected with a relationship either by using a complex attribute, as shown in the previous example, or by introducing a new class, C, as shown here. Below the classes, we show an (example) object structure.

The preceding examples dealt with one-to-one relationships. We can implement one-to-many relationships in a similar way, except that the reference type must be able to accommodate several references. For example, if we have A OWNS (several) B's, we could implement this with an attribute called Owns of type References_to_B_objects:

```
References_to_B_objects is Array of References to B;
```

We illustrate this situation in Figure 3.48. Again, note that we use the arrows here only for explanatory purposes; we do not recommend that arrows be used like this when we make a model.

If we have a many-to-many relationship, a new class should be introduced. This class will then have to contain the information needed to model the relationship.

Summing up, we arrive at the recommendation that, when using object-oriented modeling, we should not implement associations using attributes if they correspond to hierarchical associations. Nonhierarchical associations, relationships, should be modeled using attributes, as shown

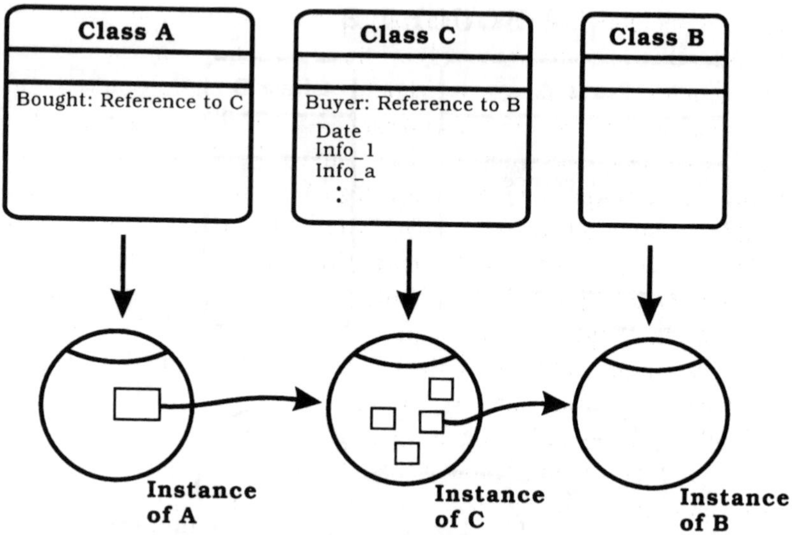


**Figure 3.47** Modeling a relationship using a new class, C.

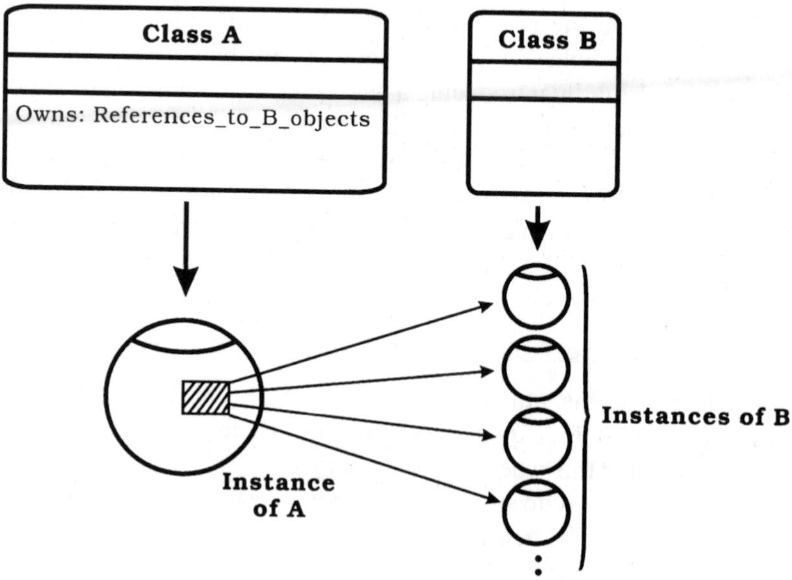


**Figure 3.48** A relationship referencing several class B objects.

above. This includes complex relationships but not the use association (which is modeled as a message call.) If this way of modeling is not possible for complex relationships, we should use a list to store information about how objects are connected with each other. This list can be modeled as a complex attribute or as a new object. A more detailed discussion about modeling relationships is beyond the scope of this book, and the reader is referred to a standard text such as *Object-Oriented Systems Analysis* [18] or *An Introduction to Database Systems* [10]. Also, see Appendix 1.

A final note: If possible, we should not talk about "relationships" at all, because thinking in relationships is not very natural. That is, if we own a dog we think that we have the ownership (attribute) of the dog, not that we have the relationship Dog owner OWNS Dog. Also, because we are to implement this ownership as an attribute anyway, it is better to do that directly without going through the relationship-modeling stage. This way we can preserve more easily a one-to-one mapping between reality (some characteristic) and model (an attribute).

## PURE OBJECT-ORIENTED MODELING?

In some languages, notably Smalltalk, a pure object-oriented approach is adopted and most things are viewed as objects. The reason for not adopting this simple paradigm in this book is *not* that it is an impossible one. For example, it is easy to implement an attribute as an object. An attribute has data, and we normally want to operate on it in some ways. For example, an attribute of type integer is connected with operations such as add, subtract, multiply, and so on, and a string is also typically connected with some specific operations, such as "size of string."

Thus, with a pure object-oriented approach, we could say that we send the message "+" to the object 2 when we want to add 3 to it, getting a new object, 5, as the result:

```
2 + 3 → 5
```

If we want to know the size of a string, we can say that we send it the message "size," getting an object, representing the size of the string, as the result:

```
"A string of 25 characters" size → 25
```

Letting attributes be objects also gives us a way of implementing subobjects because a subobject can then be added as easily as an attribute. This is, in fact, also the way we have to implement a subobject structure in Smalltalk and C++, for instance.

The major reason we do not adopt the paradigm that everything is an object, is that we as human beings do distinguish between attributes, values of attributes, classes, objects, and object structures. For example, we normally feel that there is a difference between the attribute age, the attribute value "25 years" for age, and the person (object) Sam having this age. We likewise treat the facts "Sam has two arms, a head, a body and two legs" (object structure) as different information from the fact that "Sam is 6 feet tall" (attribute) or that "Sam is a student" (class information), and so on. Hence, there are strong reasons to keep these distinctions when we do analysis, design, and (if possible) coding—it will help us because we are used to think in that way. Keeping these distinctions is also fully in accord with the close mapping rule introduced in Chapter 1. Using the "everything is an object" approach will give us problems partitioning the model into manageable parts, distinguishing between more important facts and less important facts, and so on, because we will lack the tools we are used to apply. The problem with a pure object-oriented approach during analysis and design is that we do not get a good model. However, as partly illustrated before, there is often no great problem implementing an object-oriented design model that distinguishes between attributes, objects, object structures, etc. in Smalltalk, for example.

Note that the parallel computing suggested by the way messages can be sent between objects in object-oriented analysis and design models cannot be directly implemented in Smalltalk. However, parallel processing can be simulated by making instances inherit from a class such as "Process."

## SUMMARY

We began this chapter with a discussion about some modeling basics. For example, we discussed the importance of having a well-defined purpose when we select objects and classes: The model we build is formed by our purpose and our knowledge of the problem area.

We then discussed the class from a modeling perspective and continued with a discussion about the class structure and inheritance, showing how it can help us navigate in a complex reality. We dealt in detail with the use of aggregation to build new concepts.

- We thus discussed the following structures:

  1. The *class* used as a way of keeping related attributes and methods together.

2. *Hierarchical associations,* where we in detail discussed the *class structure* used as a way of ordering and managing different classes and the *object structure*. The latter represents the *aggregation* technique.
3. *Nonhierarchical associations,* which we called relationships.

These structures take us closer to the goal of structuring the complexity we find in reality.

- We apply the following rules when we make a subclass:
  1. We inherit the names and the implementations of attributes and methods.
  2. The implementation of a method may be changed, but attributes may not be changed.
  3. We can add attributes and/or methods to the subclass.
- We also pointed out the importance of separating object structures and class structures when we build our model.
- We use the concepts primitive and orthogonal to represent a class, an attribute, or a method if it cannot easily be replaced by other classes, attributes, or methods, respectively.

Some of the things we have learned in this chapter are summarized in Figure 3.49. At the top we show notations for the class. The class idea was augmented in this chapter, and we now have both (simple) classes and complex classes. The difference is that a complex class also defines an object structure. This difference is illustrated in the figure with two examples: an object created from a simple class and an object created from a complex class. Note that the word class can indicate both a simple class and a complex class in this book—whatever is appropriate.

We can implement the structures we have discussed in this chapter with hierarchical associations and nonhierarchical associations. We use two hierarchical associations, the is_a and the is_part_of associations. The first one describes class structures, whereas the other one is typically used to describe object structures (also called aggregations) or nested objects. We illustrate these two structures in the figure with examples.

We called nonhierarchical associations for relationships. We illustrate the use of relationships in Figure 3.50 with examples of object structures. The first example is a simple one-to-one relationship, where we relate an object A to an object B by stating that A OWNS B. To implement this relationship, we use a referential attribute, OWNS, and we see two ways of illustrating this in the figure, (1) and (2).

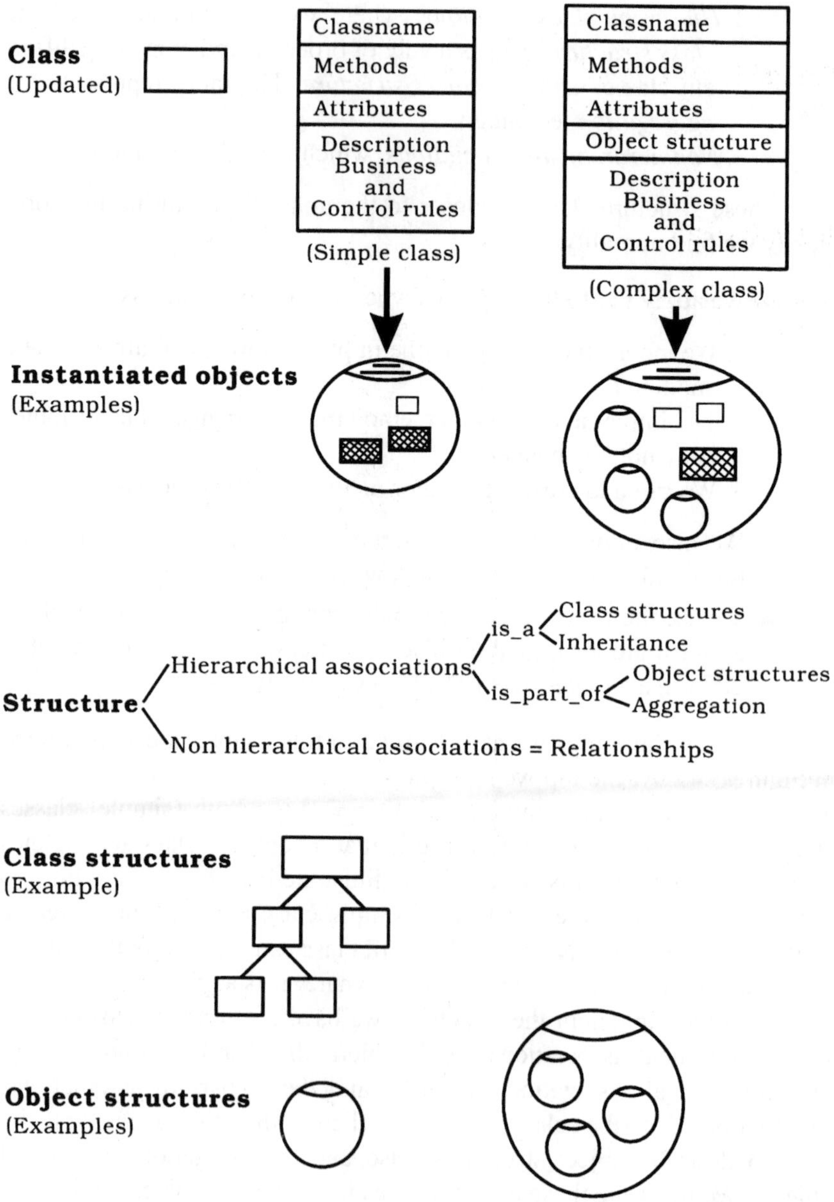


**Figure 3.49** Class and object structures, summary.

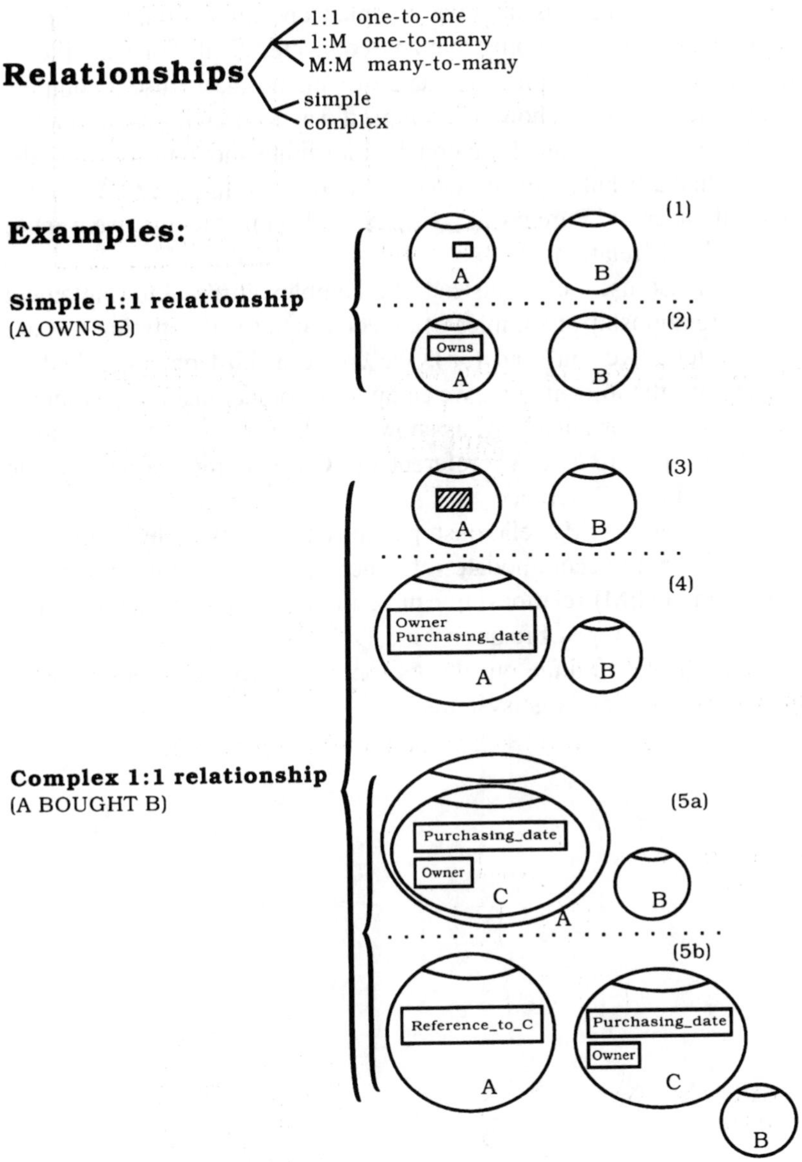


**Figure 3.50** Relationships: A summary.

The next example is about a complex one-to-one relationship. A complex relationship has some features connected to it. For example, if we also want to note the purchase date of something, we use a complex attribute. Alternative (3) shows the simplest way of drawing this. In alternative (4) we have expanded the complex attribute showing its internals: We see the first attribute, Owner, which is used as a reference to B, and we see an attribute called Purchasing_date, exemplifying a feature we want to connect with this relationship.

We can also use a class instead of a complex attribute to implement a complex relationship. Examples of object structures illustrating this are shown in alternative (5a) and (5b). We create a third object, called C, which contains the information. We can put this object inside A, as shown in alternative (5a), or outside A, as shown in alternative (5b). If we put it outside A, we have to give A a reference to C by giving A a new simple referential attribute: Reference_to_C.

One-to-many (1:M) relationships can be dealt with by letting the referential attribute accommodate references to several other objects. A many-to-many (M:M) relationship can be modeled by introducing a new class modeling this type of relationship.

In Part II we continue our discussion about structures but with the perspective of building large systems.

# Part II

# Introduction

## *Building Large Systems*

*When we build, let us think that we build forever.*

—John Ruskin

I was once given the task of testing several hundred pages of assembler code. The code contained algorithms for digital filters, and values for these had been changed. The company where I worked wanted me to test the updated code. I thought about it. What did my colleagues mainly working with electronics equipment do? Could I shake the listing of software as they shook the electronics equipment in their testing? What about putting the software listing in the weather chamber? My colleagues regularly put sophisticated electronics equipment into that testing chamber, running it at different temperatures and at different levels of humidity. Of course, none of those test methods seemed to offer any solution to my testing problems.

A solution to the problem was urgent. Thus, only a few days passed before the quality department called me. They asked me when I could have the verification and validation (their words for the testing) completed. Using my experience I said I thought I would probably be able to finish it in four or six months. It would be of help, however, if I could just get some documentation . . .

Their response was, "*Please have it tested in a few days will you? And you have the software listing, do you not?*" Well, I did have about ten pounds of code listings—but no comments.

A few days later they called me again and told me to verify that the code was validated and verified. Then they tried to push me, but my answer was the same, and I eventually turned to another employer. Could I have done what they wanted? Of course not.

This brings us to some interesting questions regarding software development, questions to which I have been collecting answers ever since that event occurred many years ago. In fact, there are many of us who have been collecting such answers for quite some time. We call these answers *software engineering*.

There are those who believe that object-oriented techniques can be used to replace the experience we have gained during the last decades. This is not the belief of the author.

Basically, Part II of the book shows how the chaos of software development and maintenance can be beaten with object-oriented techniques. This part of the book aims at three things:

- Building a bridge between the experience gained in software projects since the 1950s and the object-oriented techniques that we find at least partly in languages such as C++, Eiffel, and Smalltalk, but also in Ada.
- Clarifying and enlarging the ideas outlined in Part I.
- Adding ideas that can be used when doing object-oriented software development, such as mini-uses and use-cases.

# 4

# Building Large Systems

## *Software Engineering*

*Draw from others the lesson that may profit yourself.*

—Terence, *Publius Terentius Afer*

### INTRODUCTION

In Part I we introduced modeling concepts such as the object, the attribute, the method, and the class, and we discussed how we could arrange them in a model using different types of structures. We also discussed, for example, how a well-defined purpose helps us find relevant objects and classes.

In Part II we enlarge on this knowledge and relate it to the building of large or very large systems. This takes us to a discussion of object-oriented modeling from the viewpoint of software engineering.

**Definition.** *Software engineering:* (1) The application of a systematic, disciplined, quantifiable approach to the development, operation, and maintenance of software—that is, the application of engineering to software. (2) The study of approaches, as in (1). [IEEE]

In this chapter we discuss how object-oriented modeling improves the development process, how to define good interfaces, and how different types of objects tend to appear when we make an object-oriented model. In particular, we discuss how objects often are dominated by data (information objects) and by behavior (system objects) and how some objects handle different types of interfaces (interface objects).

The important topic of how to partition a system into subsystems is discussed in Chapter 5, Subsystems.

**Definition.** A *System* is a collection of components organized to accomplish a specific function or set of functions. [IEEE]

**Definition.** A *subsystem* is a secondary or subordinate system within a larger system. [IEEE]

However, note that when we refer to a system in this book, we are referring to an application that is to be developed in order to meet the requirements of a customer. The system includes everything that is necessary, such as hardware and software, but when we use the word *system* in this book we typically refer only to the software part of the system. Thus our working definition of a system is as follows:

**Definition.** A *system* is an application software developed in order to meet the requirements of a customer.

It is popular in some modeling techniques to view a system in three ways, information, processing, and time sequence behavior. The basic idea is illustrated in Figure 4.1. Three models of a system are then built,

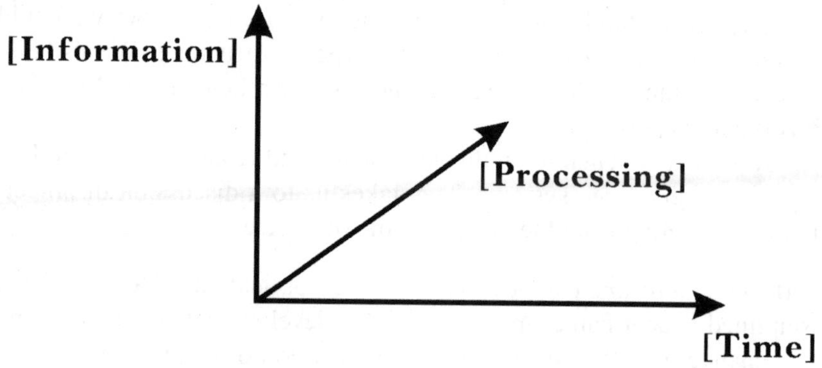


**Figure 4.1** Three different viewpoints on a system.

each representing one of the viewpoints. Entity-relationship diagrams can be used to describe the information in the system, data flow diagrams can be used to describe the processing or the work being done, and state transition diagrams can be used to describe the time sequence behavior. A problem with this approach is that the user has to integrate these three different models in his or her mind before gaining a complete picture about what is really going on.

This approach has been a common and popular one, so it is not very surprising to see traces of this thinking in many object-oriented modeling techniques today. A similar problem occurs if we start with the structured analysis and design method introduced by Yourdon and then try to find or derive the objects needed from the structured "stuff" resulting from using that method. For those who use the structured method, this is a very appealing approach. However there is not much practical evidence that this approach is a workable way into the object-oriented world. Working with objects is such a radical change in the way we work and think that we must regard object-oriented modeling as a paradigm shift, a basic change in the fundamentals. An object integrates behavior and information and is to a great extent responsible for the work it is doing. Object-oriented modeling thus integrates the three different viewpoints just mentioned, whereas the structured approach separates them from the beginning. Thus, we conclude that it is difficult to believe that structured analysis and design techniques—and similar techniques—can be used together with object-oriented techniques. The experience of this author, and others, points to this conclusion. See, for example, [2] and [26]. Thus, when we outline how to build systems in this book, we use an object-oriented approach, integrating information, processing, and time sequence behavior.

## THE PHASE MODEL

The phase model or some variant of it is one of the most commonly applied ideas in software development. In this chapter we discuss what it is, mention why it came to exist, discuss its advantages and disadvantages, and finally, show how it is changed by the object-oriented paradigm.

### Basics

Software development is traditionally done in a series of finished steps or, as they are commonly called, "phases."

**Definition.** A *phase*, in traditional software development, is a set of activities that uses one set of documents as input and produces a new and possibly changed set of documents as output.

Thus, software development is primarily a question of writing and refining documents. Large contracts for software development frequently call for a phase model. The phase idea is illustrated in Figure 4.2. The documents are reviewed when a phase is concluded; if the documents are approved, they are *frozen*. This means that we may not change the

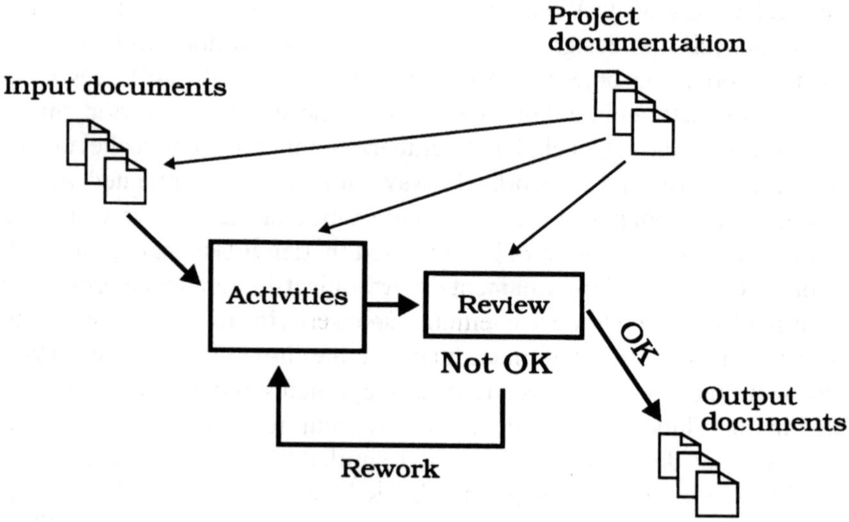


**Figure 4.2** A phase.

documents without first taking some formal steps. Having a configuration control board meeting is a typical way of regulating a change. A set of such frozen documents is often called a *baseline* because it is the base from which we start our next activities (the next phase). Using documents in this way is called baselining the documents. That is, we have established a bureaucracy that will keep track of software (and hardware items) and decide if suggested changes may or may not be done to these items. This activity is called *configuration management* (abbreviated CM) because the bureaucracy manages the (configuration) items (= mostly documents) that we have agreed to manage.

When the activities of one phase are completed to our satisfaction, we have another set of documents as the result. The phase model demands that these be verified before they may be frozen and used in the next phase.

**Definition.** *Verification* is the process of evaluating a system or component to determine whether the products of a given development phase satisfy the conditions imposed at the start of that phase. [IEEE]*

**Definition.** *Validation* is the process of evaluating a system or component during or at the end of the development process to determine whether it satisfies specified requirements. [IEEE]

*This is one of two possible definitions given in [IEEE].

We could thus say that validation is done to make certain that we have built the right system, whereas verification is a set of controls to ensure that the system is built right. Verification and validation are very time-consuming activities, and often they are not done or are done only in part because of tight schedules. Note that the difference between validation and verification is not too well understood in practice, and the words are often used as synonyms.

A common misconception is that it is possible to verify and/or validate a system by testing it. This is seldom possible; see, for example, *The Art of Software Testing* by Glenford G. Myers [11]. The solution to this dilemma is to build a system with techniques that ensure or at least make probable that the final system will be of high enough quality. This is called quality assurance.

**Definition.** *Quality assurance* (QA) is (1) a planned and systematic pattern of all actions necessary to provide adequate confidence that an item or product conforms to established technical requirements and (2) a set of activities designed to evaluate the process by which products are developed or manufactured. [IEEE]

Object-oriented modeling (that conforms to the solutions mentioned in Chapter 1) greatly facilitates quality assurance, but we still need to describe the software process. For example, we have to list the items (particularly documents) we produce in each phase and how to check them using checklists and other tools. (See Appendix 3).

## Phases

In the analysis phase we have to be a reporter, a detective, and an artist. We have to investigate and simplify, solve puzzles, and uncover facts that are not apparent. We must also have enough creativity to portray things in new and better ways. During object-oriented design we continue this work, but in this phase we have to give more concern to the software architecture, components, detailed interfaces, and so on. Coding takes place when we implement objects. Coding can take place during analysis and design, too, but then mainly in the form of sketching overall structures. We test interfaces and perform unit tests, testing the objects.

**Definition.** *Testing* is the process of analyzing a software item to detect the differences between existing and required conditions (that is, bugs) and to evaluate the features of the software items. [IEEE]*

---

*This is one of two possible definitions given in [IEEE].

It is the experience of this author and others [11] that the most productive approach to testing is to try to prove that what we are testing has bugs. In short, this approach is more productive, because we tend to get what we aim for. If we try to prove that a software item works, we will prove this—but the errors are still there. If we instead try to prove that something does not work properly, we will find more errors per working hour, which results in a more productive approach.

There are many similarities between a more traditional functional analysis approach and the approach suggested in this book. However, we do not separate functions and data but connect them together with objects. The focus is also on the needs of identified users rather than on functions listed in a requirements specification. With the object-oriented approach, we also work a lot with the structure of the system and we try hard to link it to reality. Our approach is basically top-down.

**Definition.** *Top-down* pertains to an activity that starts with the highest level component of a hierarchy and proceeds through progressively lower levels. [IEEE]

**Definition.** *Bottom-up* pertains to an activity that starts with the lowest level components of a hierarchy and proceeds through progressively higher levels. [IEEE]

One advantage of a top-down approach is that it gives us a better structure because it gives us a clearer perspective of the system and because it shows us early how parts of the system interact. It also helps us to avoid duplication of effort. A bottom-up approach is much more limited in these respects. For example, it is much easier to avoid building the same component twice if we start from a high level than if we start at a low and detailed level. With a bottom-up approach, we get some parts early, but integrating the parts will always be very difficult.

We can connect several phases to form a series, which yields a phase model (see Figure 4.3). It is typical for this model to have phases such as analysis, design, coding, and integration and test.)

### Why Use the Phase Model?

Let us take a short look at history. The first software model was the code and fix model (see Figure 4.4). The idea was to write some code and then fix the problems. Unfortunately, this simple model never works well when we develop large systems. It is still in use, and it still often produces chaos. The problems with this simple model are many:

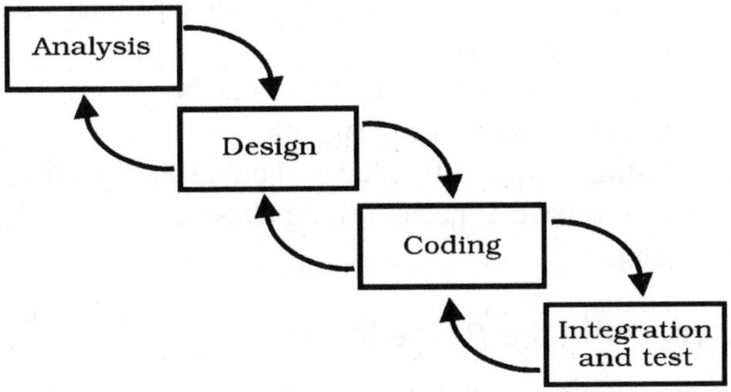


**Figure 4.3** A phase model.

1. After several fixes, the code is so poorly structured that subsequent maintenance, if possible, becomes very difficult to understand and/ or implement (that is, expensive).
2. This model does not start by asking the customer what he or she really needs. Thus, even when we get a "working" system, the customer might not want it.

The code and fix model is still very common, and the chances that we will meet it in one form or another are great. It will be disguised and probably have a fancier name than code and fix. On the other hand, the code and fix model is not always the wrong model to use. It can work out fairly well if we know what we want to build and the system is not too large. Spending two to three man-months implementing a system in Smalltalk in a strongly iterative way can, for example, turn out to be quite a productive experience if done by professionals.

As early as 1956 recognitions of problems like those just mentioned led to the development of a model called the *stagewise model.* This model took these problems into consideration by introducing some ideas:

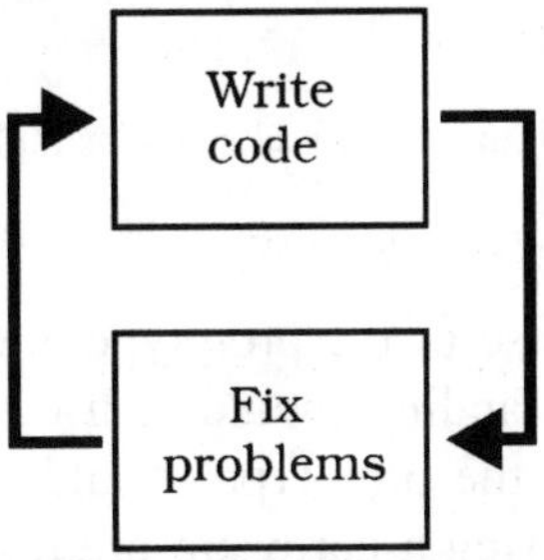


**Figure 4.4** The code and fix model.

1. Let us have a first stage in which we ask the customer what he or she wants (the analysis phase).
2. Let us think about the structure of the code before we start the actual coding (the first version of a design phase).
3. Because testing is very difficult, we should start planning for it from the start. Let us have a special testing phase at the end, planned from the beginning.

## Problems with the Phase Model

A refinement of the stagewise model was the *waterfall model,* popular during the 1970s and the 1980s. It had two primary improvements:

- An initial incorporation of prototyping via a step running in parallel with the analysis phase.
- A recognition of the feedback loops between the phases—that is, a recognition that it is hard to work the phases strictly in sequence. For example, when we code, we might find errors that were introduced in an earlier phase, leading to the need to make corrections in the analysis and prototyping phase and/or the design phase. This feedback is called *breakage,* and it is illustrated in Figure 4.5.

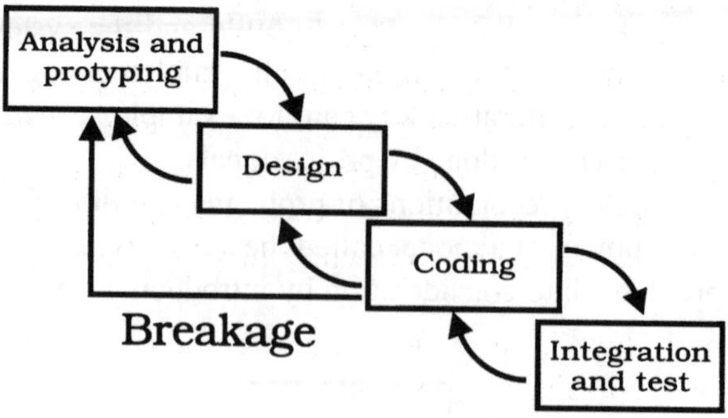


**Figure 4.5** Breakage. (Example.)

Note that the purpose of the prototype is to understand the system better. This better understanding should be used to write a better requirements specification, and the prototype should then be thrown away. No one would think about using a hardware prototype spread out on a floor with parts loosely connected. However, software prototypes are frequently used, even though their structure is often comparable to such a hardware prototype structure, because the bad structure is not evident. (A set of floppies with badly structured prototype code cannot easily be distinguished from a set of floppies containing a well-structured system.)

A basic reason for retaining ideas from the phase model is thus that the phase model represents a continuous development where we have collected experience and systematized it to get a practical way of working. And the work continues. For example, one attempt to improve the model is called the *spiral model* [19]. This model, developed by Boehm, tries to solve some problems with the waterfall model. For example, it tries to solve the problem with too much documentation, a problem often experienced during the development process.

## THE PHASE MODEL AND OBJECT-ORIENTED MODELING

> *What experience and history teach is this—that people and governments never have learned anything from history, or acted on principles deduced from it.*
>
> —Georg Wilhelm Friedrich Hegel

Today we see many code and fix models in use; the reason for using these models is, "We use object-oriented techniques; the phase model is dead." Those who give this reason forget that the phase model is a set of solutions based on experience gained in earlier projects. Ideas such as early prototyping, and using a user's manual to check requirements and specifications are old ideas. They are often presented as innovations, but they are not. These cases are too common to be ignored. They bear testimony to the fact that we have great difficulty in taking advantage of earlier experience.

We should thus keep earlier experience in mind when we discuss object-oriented modeling. For example:

- We still need an initial phase, probably with prototyping, where we try to understand what our customer needs (analysis phase).
- We still need to give our system a good architecture, before coding, to facilitate easy change (design phase).
- We still need to prepare for the difficult testing (test phase).

Having agreed on this, let us discuss how object-oriented modeling can contribute to good software development. We start this discussion by showing how object-oriented techniques help us to preserve a close mapping between reality, analysis model, and design model.

Today we have a better understanding of what a modeling technique must support and of the human mind and its limitations. As human beings we want to work in an iterative way with a fairly limited set of items.

We thus continue the discussion by showing how object-oriented techniques help us to work in an iterative way and how object-oriented ideas help us to partition a system.

Finally in this section, we take a look at how the phase and the phase model are changed by the object-oriented paradigm.

## Mapping

In the introduction we discussed the idea of having a close (1:1:1) mapping between reality, our model, and the implementation. Such mapping usually has not existed in the systems we have built. The main reason for this is that going from one set of representations used during one phase to another set of representations used in a following phase is often done through experience only. A typical example of this situation is when we go from structured analysis to structured design. This transition has a taste of magic. In fact, we sometimes hear statements such as "...and then the magic begins" in connection with work being done on these transitions.

There are also other reasons for not succeeding with a close mapping, but the main reason is this "magic" when we proceed from one phase to the next. Now, if we are going to call our work software engineering we cannot use magic. With the object-oriented technique, we can use the same concepts in analysis, design, and implementation (that is, objects, attributes, methods, etc.), which reduces the magic. We next discuss why object-oriented modeling gives us a much better chance to preserve a close mapping during analysis and design.

### *Object-Oriented Analysis*

The purpose of the analysis phase is to define the system we shall build. Analysis is sometimes presented as an activity where no consideration is taken of the implementation environment—for example, the selected programming language, database, or hardware. This first model, completely free from technological issues, is often called a *logical model,* or an *essential model,* because it is supposed to be a view of the system without technology clouding the issue. Later, a model often called a *physical model,* or an *implementational model,* is made. This latter model recognizes the tangible physical implementation units, whatever they may be. It is a good idea to try to build a model this way, starting with a model independent of the underlying technology. However, in practice it is seldom possible to fully realize an essential model. Inability to make an essential model should not be regarded as a failure, but rather as a fact of life. In our defense, we can also refer to solution B introduced in Chapter 1, the mapping between reality, our model, and the implemented system should be close. We can interpret this as follows: If reality comprises important technological conditions and/or limitations, it is only natural if this is reflected in an analysis model. This approach may not be very elegant viewed from a theoretical standpoint, but it is a very practical one. The final argument for allowing technological issues to influence our model of reality is thus that technological issues are also part of reality. The key to making this work is to use good judgment, leaving out most technological aspects but not the ones that are unavoidable.

With the object idea, we get a perfect vehicle for encapsulating hardware dependencies. Expressed in another way, the difference between an essential and an implementational model can be made small with an object-oriented approach if we put in some hard work. The reason that we try to minimize the difference between the essential and the implementational model is that it will minimize the transformation costs when we go from one model to another model (see Figure 4.6). By linking our analy-

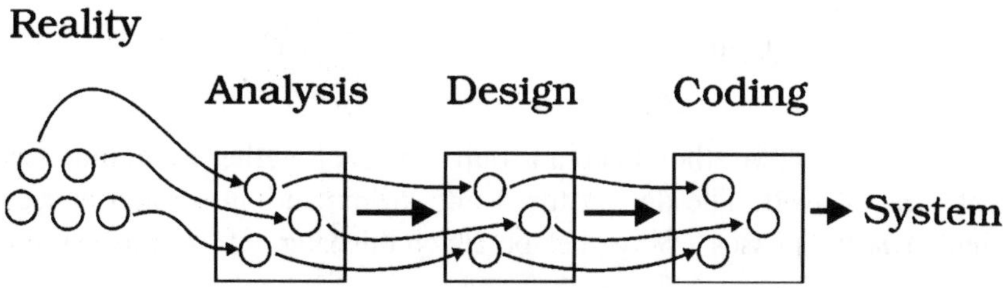


**Figure 4.6** Preserving the mapping between reality and system.

sis model closely to reality, we minimize the transformation costs between reality and analysis model. When we try to link the essential analysis model closely to our implementational analysis model, we minimize the transformation costs for going between them, and so on.

In object-oriented analysis we work with objects rather than more or less unconnected parts of data and parts of functions. We can keep related data and functions together nicely with the object idea. We can also (if we have done our work properly) relate them to ideas we use when talking, ideas we find in nouns, verbs, etc. As we explained earlier, objects in our model are related to real things (abstract or tangible) or to new ideas. Thus the step between objects in reality and objects in our analysis model is simple. A one-to-one mapping is often possible.

***Object-Oriented Design***

The design is often also straightforward. It might result in new objects and in a partitioning of objects into several layers, but the one-to-one or one-to-many mapping often remains (see Figure 4.7). Aggregation is used for

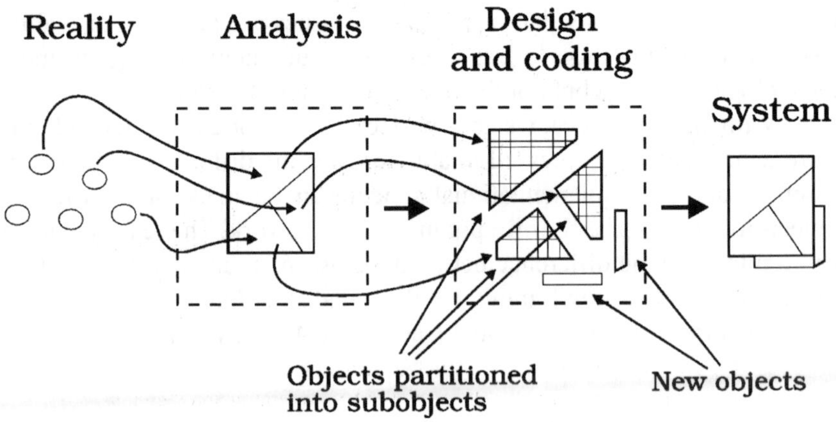


**Figure 4.7** Preserving the mapping, continued.

this partitioning. We then keep a group of parts together as an independent idea in itself. The design turns into an expanding of large objects found in earlier phases. (We will elaborate on this later in this chapter.)

## Finding Solutions by Iteration

*It is a bad plan that admits of no modification.*

— Publilius Syrus

If we know the end product, the production of it is often a straightforward process. For example, if we are to build a house, the process is mostly straightforward. However, the situation when we build computer systems is different because they are often very hard to understand and imagine.

Human beings do not want to or cannot work in a predetermined way if they do not clearly know the end product. For example, the human being is not well suited to follow a phase model that works best if each phase is completely finished without errors before the next phase is begun. Stated in a more concrete way, very few of us write a class correctly the first time.

The difference between building a known product and an unknown product is illustrated in Figure 4.8. When we start a problem-solving process, we seldom know the exact nature of our goal. We then prefer to start by trying something and then learn and make adjustments as the process proceeds. Thus, thinking leads to doing, which leads to a new understanding, which leads to more thinking, and so on. The object-oriented technique gives us some techniques for doing this. For example, we can start with an existing class and make a new subclass from it that better meets our needs. The first class can then be regarded as a first iteration, and the subclass becomes our next iteration, taking us closer to our goal.

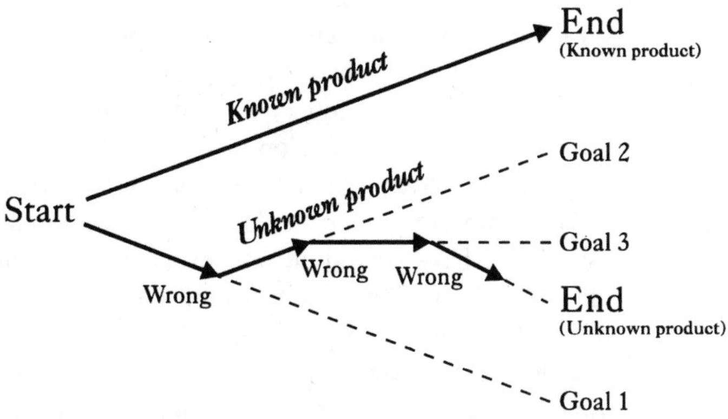


**Figure 4.8** We are not well suited to work in a deterministic way with something unfamiliar. We prefer to try something and then iterate making the solution better and better.

The method we use should allow us to work in such an iterative way. Note that it is not a question of using a method or not. We *always use some method* when we work. If we are fully aware of the method we use, we can write it down on paper and document it. If we do not understand it very well, it is just a set of more or less well-defined rules of thumb that guide us when we work.

## Partitioning

When we iterate, we do not want to be concerned with too many details at a given moment. We want to view a restricted piece of the total. This need is a basic reason for partitioning.

To minimize the damage that the iterative way of working causes to the system structure, we must divide the system into smaller isolated parts, within which we can make changes without affecting other parts. Each part should be totally independent of all other parts in a system, except for some well-defined communication between them, the interface. If we make such a partitioning, an error in one part will not have an impact on the rest of the system. The only thing that can cause problems will then be changes to the interfaces between the parts.

Ideally, a complex problem is reduced to something less complex when we use partitioning because we develop concepts (objects) that deal with parts of the original complex problem. We thus solve one part of the problem at a time. For each part problem we develop or modify one object or a few objects. When we have solved all part problems and integrated them, we have our system. This approach is facilitated by the object-oriented approach, because the objects are isolated from each other. For example, there need not be a central object with which we must always deal. Instead, an object is an isolated world to which we have delegated some responsibilities. Thus, the object does not interfere much with the rest of the system, and consequently it is possible to solve a part of the problem at a time. This is the way we typically program in a small to medium project when we use a language such as Smalltalk. However, experience shows that this paradigm can also be true when we develop large systems in other object-oriented languages. This characteristic of object-oriented system development can also be felt during the maintenance. New needs can often be handled by developing new concepts (objects). Changed needs can be dealt with by changing an existing (fairly isolated) object. With a system developed in a more traditional way, the structure of the system instead has a tendency to deteriorate and become more and more complex with each change.

The difference between a large and a small object-oriented system is, apart from having more objects, that in the large object-oriented system, we tend to solve problems by using already developed concepts (objects). This is similar to saying that we enlarge the language with new high-level constructs—our objects—that can be used to solve more and more complex problems.

The studies mentioned in the preface of this book confirm that the most important factor for successful development of a large system is that it is partitioned in an appropriate way. This partitioning must support parallel development of the parts that make up the system. This, in turn, calls for a clear separation of implementation and specification in each object. Such a separation makes it possible to develop an object in the system even if other objects are not yet implemented. Thus if the separation exists, the object being developed needs only the specification(s) of other object(s). This is an extremely important point because the difficulty with software development is not in the development of the parts but in making them work together. The integration is hard, because it is difficult to develop clear and complete interfaces between the parts. In object-oriented development we are helped because the early focus on the interfaces helps us. Summarizing, we find several aspects of the object-oriented technique that help us develop software:

- Its natural use of different abstraction techniques helps us handle complexity (for example, the way the class keeps attributes (data) and methods (functions) together).
- Its natural way of expressing things. Talking about objects comes natural to most customers. (This statement is less valid in technical software development).
- The support for an iterative way of working.
- The object idea makes us focus early on interfaces and helps us partition a system.

We have already dealt in detail with the three first points (abstraction techniques, how the object is a natural way of modeling, and the iterative way of working). In the section, "Selecting Good Interfaces," later in this chapter, we discuss the interface aspect.

## ADAPTING THE PHASE MODEL

> *Our ideas are only intellectual instruments which we use to break into phenomena; we must change them when they have served their purpose, as we change a blunt lancet that we have used long enough.*
>
> —Claude Bernard

### New Type of Phase

Sticking to the experience we have gained since the 1950s does not mean that the phase model will remain unchanged when we use it during

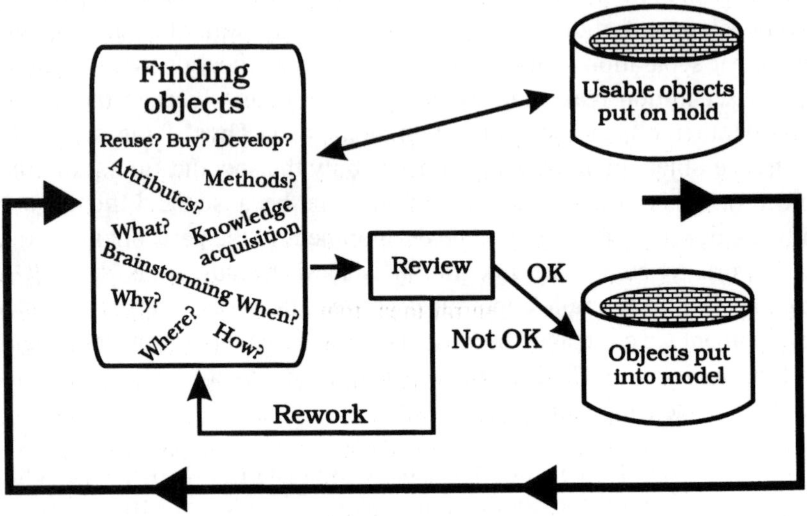


**Figure 4.9** An object-oriented phase.

object-oriented development. The key is to keep good ideas but to change the phase model to fit the object-oriented development process. The first change involves the idea of the phase. In Figure 4.9 we illustrate the changed phase. In each phase we now find objects, attributes, and methods. The main difference between the phases is that we tend to find "bigger" objects in earlier phases. If we find objects that agree with our purpose but are not usable in the current phase, we remember them, putting them on hold. We bring the other objects into our model if they agree with our purpose. (Note that relevant documents and classes must, of course, also be stored.) A picture such as the one in Figure 4.9 cannot capture all details. For example, how to handle different versions of a model simultaneously is not shown.

Finding objects but putting them on hold instead of putting them directly into the model shows that object-oriented development is not a true top-down development but also incorporates bottom-up elements. This is so because often the objects we find, but cannot use immediately are low-level objects that we put into the model when we reach lower levels. Often this approach is called the *build approach.* *

*The build approach was first suggested by Michael Deutsch in his book, *Software Verification and Validation* [13]. With this approach the functionality of a system is implemented in increments called builds. Each build represents a significant subset of the system's capability an-dadds to the functionality implemented by earlier builds. Each build, when it is implemented,

Phases tend to be less strictly separated. In the beginning, analysis dominates and at the end, coding dominates. The activities, however, exist more or less during the whole development process. This means that, at a certain point in time, we typically have some objects that have finished analysis while other objects have been designed. Still other objects may even be implemented. We thus tend to view a phase, during object-oriented software development, more as a certain set of activities than something that moves a project from one baseline to the next baseline.

Instead of having the processing of documents as the central idea of the phase, we have, as the central idea, that we are searching for objects. The paradigm is now not only one of "What shall we build?" but one of "Is there a class we can use?" and, if no class exists to instantiate the object we need, "Is there a class similar to the one we need?" Objects that we need in a certain phase we thus put into the model whereas other objects are discarded or put aside for possible later inclusion in the model. In this way we build hierarchical object structures, where in the beginning we try to find high-level objects. As the development proceeds, we include more and more detailed subobjects in our model. The number of levels we get in our object structure depends on the complexity of the system. Note that the choice of the number of levels should be left to us and not be restricted in any way by the object-oriented modeling technique we use. The work flow will not be a strict one from analysis to design to coding. Rather, the work flow will go back and forth between analysis, design, and coding activities. We illustrate how the relation between phases is changed in Figure 4.10. This is such a radical departure from how the phase is used in the traditional phase model that we ought to avoid the word phase in object-oriented modeling. However, the term is convenient to use and is well-established, so as long as we are aware that objects need not be in the same state of completion, no harm should be done. Base-lining, CM, etc. are also needed in object-oriented modeling, and the similarities are more important than the differences. We thus keep the term phase rather than invent a new term but enlarge the concept a bit.

---

incorporates parts of the system from both high and low levels. One advantage of the build approach is that some functionality will be available early. If the first functionality to be implemented is the most critical one, another advantage becomes apparent; the critical functionality will be the one most tested (because it will also be tested with each subsequent build). The process is driven by a tool called an SVD (System Verification Diagram). The SVD consists of stimulus/response elements (threads) that are directly linked to the requirements of the system. Each thread is allocated to a specific build. The SVD is typically created directly from the requirements specification before the software architecture is defined. Later each thread is connected to the parts of the software architecture that implements the thread. A detailed description of this method is not intended for this book.

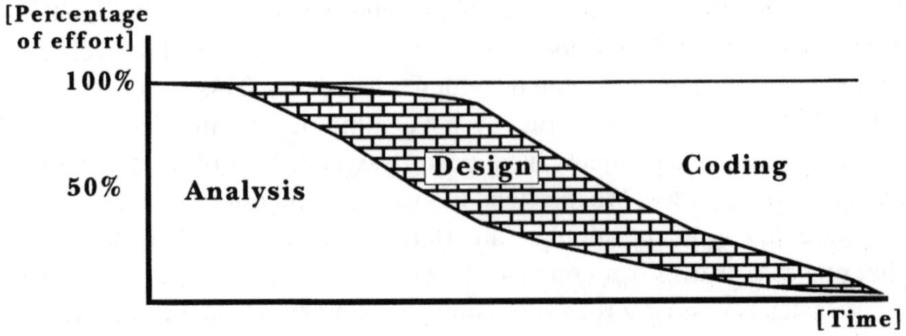


**Figure 4.10** Effort spent on analysis, design, and coding during object-oriented software development (example).

**Definition.** A *phase* is a set of activities performed with the purpose of refining an object or a set of objects (including concerned document(s), class(es), etc.) to a new well-defined state of completion.

If we are referring to a set of objects, we are actually referring to the creation of a baseline, and our new definition can thus encompass the more traditional view of a phase. (However, a traditional phase would demand all objects be more or less in the same state of completion, such as analyzed, designed, or implemented.)

As mentioned, a *baseline* represents a set of documents and/or products that we have formally, in a defined and described way, reviewed and approved. (A baseline can also consist of one specification document or product). Baselines then serve as a basis for further development, and they can be changed only by a formal change control procedure. A *milestone* is a scheduled event for which someone is held responsible, and it is used to measure progress. We need milestones and baselines in object-oriented development, too, in order to measure progress and get some structure into our efforts. Baselines and milestones should include the estimated extent and degree of completion for both class and object structures at different points in time.

Note, Figure 4.10 leaves out some important details, such as (1) testing, (2) the integration phase, and (3) baselines and milestones.

The actual relation between analysis, design, coding, testing, and integration activities may vary from application to application. An old rule is the 40-20-40 rule. This rule states that about 40% of the effort is spent on analysis and design, 20% on low-level design and coding and 40% on integration and test. Object-oriented techniques will typically decrease the testing effort, whereas the first part, involving analysis and design, will increase.

***What and How***

Usually we say that analysis is the process of defining the needs a system will satisfy. We specify *what* the system must do to satisfy our customer, but we do not say anything about *how* the system will do this. Design, on the other hand, is often taken to imply the "how" part. The danger here is to think that analysis equals "what," whereas design equals "how." This is not true, as illustrated by the following discussion.

A system has a sensor. Part of a specification for the system could be "The sensor is used to make temperature measurements." This would be the "what" part. The next question we ask ourselves is "how" this is going to be implemented. We could end up with an implementation like the following sketch:

```
What: "Make a temperature measurement"
IF Sensor_exists THEN      //Beginning of the How
                          //part, the implementation
   Initialize_the_sensor;
   Get_ten_measurements;
   Calculate_the_mean_value;
   Compensate_the_mean_value;
   Convert_mean_value_to_temperature_in_Celsius;
   Return_temperature;
ELSE
   Return_error;
END_IF;
```

The problem with the simple what and how explanation for analysis and design, respectively, is seen when we consider that each step in this "how" *really* is a new "what." For example, the Get_ten_measurements could be implemented as

```
What: "Get_ten_measurements"
// The How part begins here
WHILE "Still_measurements_to_do" DO
   Get_one_measurement;
   Store_measurement;
END_WHILE;
```

or something more complicated.

Thus, each "what" is implemented by a "how," which is actually a set of new "whats":

```
What - level i
  {What1 - level i+1
  What2 - level i+1
  .
  .
  Whatn -level i+1
  }
```

We should regard the "what-how" idea as a tool for building a system in several levels of abstraction. Thus, we do not insist on two levels of abstraction (what and how) but repeat the process, getting as many levels as we need for the system we are building.

A "how" is thus best viewed as a tool for revealing the next layer of objects and their methods. The idea is illustrated in Figure 4.11. To the left

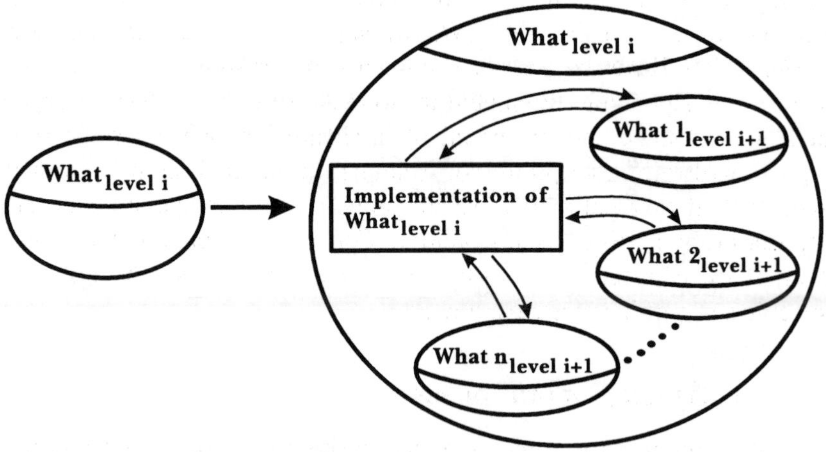


**Figure 4.11** A "how" can be viewed as a tool for revealing the next layer of objects.

in this figure we show an object with a method called $What_{level\ i}$. The implementation of this method is sketched to the right. Note that a method can be implemented in different ways. The only restriction we put on the implementation is that only methods at the same level and/or at the next lower level should be used when we implement the method. In particular, we put no restriction on the sequence in which the implementation will use (call) methods at the next level.

We can view data in the same way. Consider, for example, an invoice; that is, the *what* is an invoice and the *how* would be the parts of it. The conclusion we can draw from this discussion is that taking the analysis-design distinction for a what-how distinction is an oversimplified truth. Instead we should regard the development process from analysis to design as a nested process, where we go from high abstractions to low-level abstractions. The process is thus repeated, enabling us to divide the subobjects we find into new subobjects until we feel no more need to define smaller objects. At this stage, coding begins. (If we code the object structure, we start coding earlier.)

It is thus very natural to find high-level objects (analysis) as well as low-level objects (top-level design, low-level design). This agrees with experience. The only real distinction we can make between object-oriented analysis, design, and coding is the purpose of the activity (phase). *Analysis* is (more) user centered and *design* is (more) centered around the actual implementation details. For example, in design we probably discuss what hardware we are going to use. Unfortunately, even this rule of thumb often tends to blur, because it is very common to be given a set of specified hardware from the start. (We are supposed to use *some* hardware *Period.*) This hardware will then influence the analysis. If we find ourselves in this position, we should try to make sure the analysis is dependent not on some specific brand of hardware but only on some more logical hardware description. For example, in the analysis it is probably acceptable if we mention that we are going to have a temperature measuring sensor giving us the temperature in Celsius. It is not acceptable, however, if we connect the analysis with a particular sensor having some specific setup of hardware parameters.

## The Development Process

It is important that the architecture (high-level object structure) of an application is defined early and that enough effort is put into this. The architecture should be defined by a small team involving the best analysts. Most important to these individuals is the ability of abstract thinking. It is common in object-oriented development to use the build approach or some variant of it. When the architecture has been specified, the main effort should remain a top-down effort regarding the object structure. The development is, as mentioned, also one of bottom-up: We define objects and develop them, probably also combining them with other objects. When an object has been developed, we can unit test it. When we combine it with other objects we can integration test it. Using this approach, we can thus perform some of the integration testing early. If we consider these facts, we get the relations between phases shown in Figure 4.12. The graphs should not be regarded as absolute truths but rather as indications

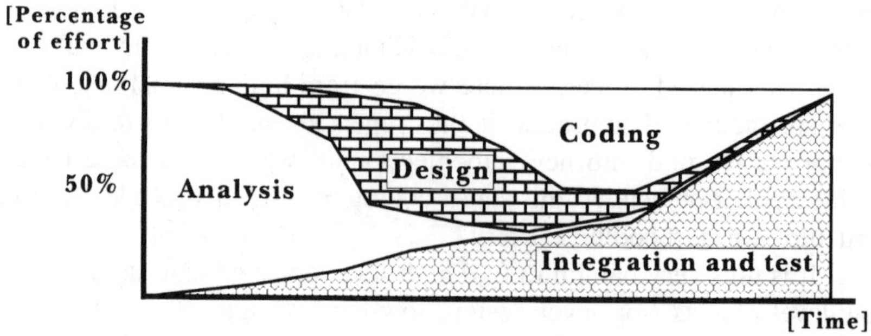


**Figure 4.12** Effort spent on different activities during object-oriented software development (example).

of how efforts are distributed in a typical project. See also the section "System Architecture" in Chapter 5.

The preceding discussion is about the development of one or several applications. Parallel to this we should have another activity going on in the company: the production and enhancement of available reusable components. If we consider this, we can draw a general picture of the development process in a company such as the one in Figure 4.13. This figure shows two applications being developed. At the very top of the figure we have indicated some class structures that are used when we implement the applications. They represent the continuing development and refinement of reusable components in a company. The applications are represented by the groups of circles below the class structures, which contain an increasing number of objects as time goes on (from the left to the right in the figure). In the end, such a group will represent a completed application. It is probable that the objects represent parts of the system from a high logical level as well as lower levels closer to the actual hardware.

The strict separation of class structures and object structures in Figure 4.13 may also help to explain why it is possible to implement an object structure in a language without the class construct, such as in Ada. However, if the implementation language lacks a class construction, we will run into some problems. For example, because we cannot keep similar objects together with a class construct, we cannot implement a change in one place (the class) but have to implement the change in all concerned objects, multiplying the change effort with the number of objects created from the class. Also, variations of similar objects will be more difficult to implement (because we cannot subclass a base class) and manage (because we do not have a class structure to connect related classes).

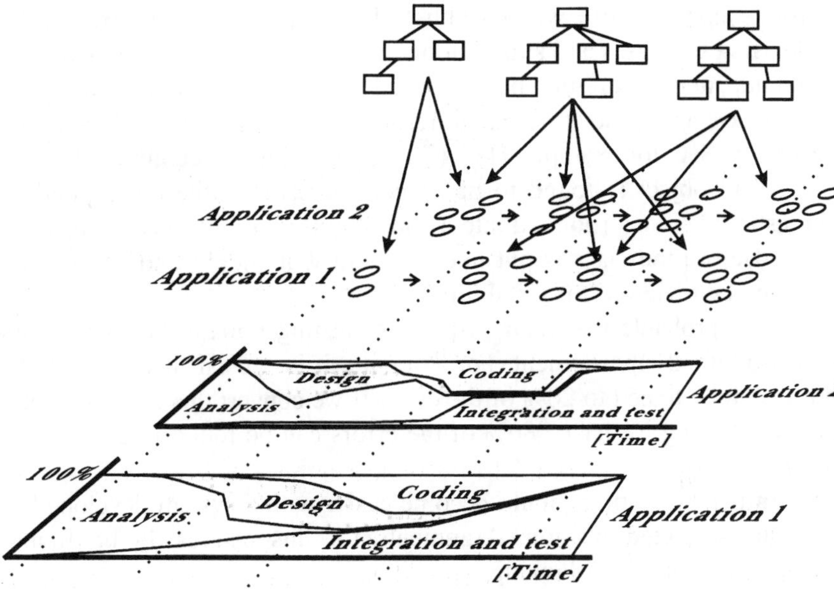


**Figure 4.13** The development process.

At the bottom of the figure we show how the effort spent could be distributed among different activities (phases): analysis, design, coding, and integration and test.

The integration and test phase consists basically of two types of testing, unit testing and integration testing. There are other names for testing, such as performance test, acceptance test, ergonomic test, and so on, but unit and integration tests are the main ones. For an in-depth discussion, see [11], [12], [23], or some similar type of work. *Unit testing* simply means that we test a single unit. However, because a unit in our case is an object and an object can have subobjects, a unit test can involve several objects. The purpose of *integration testing* is to test how objects work together. The normal manner for integration testing is to add one object (or group of objects) to an already-tested object structure. Objects that we add should have been unit tested before being added.

We can also divide testing into what is often referred to as *static* and *dynamic* testing. Static testing implies that no computer is used to run the code. Static testing techniques include *code inspections* and *walk-throughs*. Descriptions of these techniques vary, but in essence they imply that a senior programmer and/or a group of programmers read the source code together with the author(s) of the code. Static testing should follow a step-by-step procedure, with checklists. In dynamic testing we execute the code using test cases and similar tools. Static testing is an underestimated technique, and it can often be very efficient. However static and dynamic testing have a tendency to reveal different kinds of errors, so both types are necessary. See, for example, [11]. (This book is highly recommended.)

If an object is found to be of general interest, the corresponding class should be incorporated into a company's library of reusable components. Before the class is put into the library, it should undergo further tests and be reviewed for suitability.

It is probable that many aspects of testing remain the same in an object-oriented environment. For example, it is typical that 80% of the errors can be traced to 20% of the code. If we convert this rule to object-oriented testing we have "80% of the errors can be found in 20% of the objects."

In theory, testing should become easier with a system developed in an object-oriented fashion. Arguments for this can easily be found. Among them are the following:

- Objects are encapsulated microworlds that can be tested in isolation.
- Often objects are created from existing classes that have already been extensively tested.
- The object-oriented model has a better and more correct structure because of better communication with the customer and because of the powerful modeling structures available with object-oriented development.

However, experience indicates that testing does not become easier. At the moment too few data have been collected to say how true this statement is true and, if true, why testing is not easier. However, this author suspects that it is true and that the situation is due to an immature understanding of the object-oriented paradigm. That is, developers concentrate too much on the class structure and too little on the object structure. If we think too little about the object structure, we will, for example, not get clearly separated parts that can be tested separately. Note also that C++ is often used to implement the system. C++ is not a simple language to understand nor a language that helps us when we are going to test. Experience from systems developed in Ada is more encouraging.

Before we leave our discussion of the phase model, it should be noted that, in the past, few projects have been able to follow a strict phase model. Most projects have had one official model—the phase model—but, in practice, worked the phases more or less as we indicate they can be worked with object-oriented modeling. Thus, the big value with an object-oriented approach is, perhaps, that we now have a tool that fits how we need to work. Next we turn to a discussion of interfaces.

## SELECTING GOOD INTERFACES

Well-chosen interfaces are extremely valuable during the integration of software units. The interface is also a basic part of the object. Good interfaces are elusive, so it is appropriate to discuss interfaces in detail.

### Big Bang

The integration phase is sometimes called the Big Bang phase. The nickname is taken from the way software development is often done. First, more or less isolated programmers or teams of programmers develop their modules. Then all these modules are put together in the integration phase. Then we wait for the result, which is often close to total havoc. When the disaster is final, we try to put the pieces together in order to understand what really happened. Unfortunately this Big Bang development keeps reappearing in new forms.

One aspect of integration is how the objects that we create when integrating are formed. We have already partly dealt with this when we discussed how an aggregation of objects should result in something new. We made the following definitions:

**Definition.** *Aggregation* is the act of collecting together in a way that the collection, when it is made, forms a new idea. The aggregation should also hide details of its parts. This means that new details should appear, whereas other details should be hidden when we form the aggregate.

**Definition.** An *aggregate* is a collection of parts that together forms something new that is more than just the sum of its parts. It introduces new characteristics belonging to the whole rather than the parts. It is an abstraction that helps us ignore details and thus helps us conquer complexity.

In the integration phase the objects of a system start interacting via their interfaces. An object might be an aggregate in itself, but the integration phase is also an aggregation activity. We thus find a repeating pattern. We integrate smaller parts into bigger parts, which we then integrate again. The pattern of aggregation is repeated.

Our success in making the integration will depend on the interfaces. That is, *the important point to keep in mind is that the success of the integration is governed mainly by how well we made the interfaces fit together.* So, let us discuss what an interface is and how to define it.

## What Is an Interface?

Using the entries *interface* and *interface requirement* [IEEE], we formulate this description.

The *interface* is a shared boundary, across which information is passed ...constraints on formats, timing, or other factors caused by such an interaction.

Or, we make the following definition.

**Definition.** The *interface* is *everything* we must agree upon, in order to be able to communicate with, handle, use, and understand something (such as an object) properly. If we draw a circle around something (or a sphere because we cannot enclose a three-dimensional item using a two-dimensional circle), we can say that the interface is everything that goes through this circle *and* everything else we must agree upon to properly communicate with, handle, use, and understand that something.

Figure 4.14 illustrates the definition. The *and* in the definition is very important. For example, it is not enough to say that a measuring device can give us a distance. We must also decide whether we should measure the distance in centimeters, feet, or something else.

The interface can be likened to a *contract*, where the object agrees to deliver a set of services under some precisely stipulated conditions.

This is simple—but only on the surface. Finding the *everything else* is not an easily accomplished task. Defining the interface is very difficult, because it must be complete without including any unnecessary details. A guide is that the amount of communication between different objects in a system should be minimized. A second guideline is that there should be no ambiguity as to how the communication is made. Another very important characteristic of a good interface is that it does not change over time, but is stable.

Summarizing and adding a few thoughts, we arrive at the following guidelines for the interfaces:*

---

*The first three guidelines and the last guideline are discussed in more detail by Meyer in his book, *Object-Oriented Software Constructions* [6].

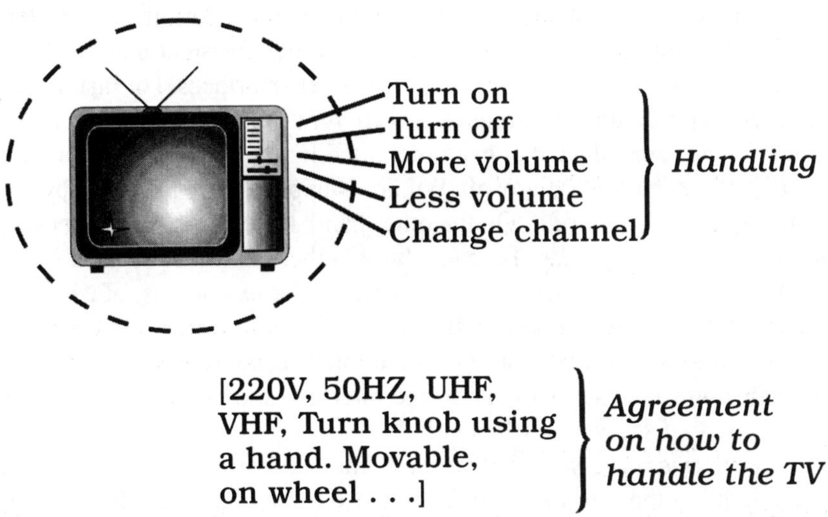


**Figure 4.14** The interface includes all the details we need to define exactly in order to handle something.

- Few interfaces
- Small interfaces
- Explicit interfaces
- Consistent interfaces
- Coherent interfaces
- Low semantic gap in interfaces
- Stable interfaces
- Support of information hiding

*Few interfaces* simply imply that an object should communicate with as few other objects as possible. *Small interfaces* gives us the rule that if an object communicates with another object, it should exchange as little information as possible. (Few and small interfaces are aspects of low coupling that are discussed in Chapter 2). With an *explicit interface,* it is easy to determine how the exchange of information is done. A good example of an interface that is *not* explicit is when subroutines in a Fortran program exchange data via a large common block of data.

*Consistent interfaces* imply that the way the interfaces are designed should be similar between different objects. For example, if several objects have a method that uses the same parameter, this parameter should not be first in one parameter list and last in another parameter list. If a set of parameters have the same function, the names for the parameters should be the same or at least similar. The rule of consistent interfaces can also be applied to, for example, Graphical User Interfaces. For instance, if the same type of menus are used in different applications, they should appear in the same place. For example, the File menu is usually located at the upper left part in Microsoft Windows applications followed by the Edit menu to the right of it. On the other hand, I use Ctrl-R in my desktop program to get a preview of a page, but another command is used in my word processor for preview of a page. (This latter example is, of course, a breach of the rule of consistent interfaces).

*Coherent interfaces* imply that the interface should deliver a set of logically connected services. Thus, the interface should display the cohesion property discussed in Chapter 2.

*Low semantic gap* in an interface implies that the concepts we use when defining the interface should be close to how the user thinks. (The semantic gap is discussed in Chapter 1).

*Stable interfaces* are important because they make it easier for us to develop a system. Knowing that an interface of an object will not change with time gives us a point of reference. Handling changes is always a difficult problem in systems development, and thus such points of references are very valuable.

The methods are the natural starting point for an object interface because they represent the "handling of the object." But that does not cover the whole situation. The key word is *using*. We want to achieve our aim, and the object is there to help us. To do so, the object must include the methods we need, but it must also be a good abstraction to relieve us of details that the object should manage for us. The interface should thus support *information hiding*. This means that we should have the least possible number of methods and the maximum abstraction (leaving out) of implementational details. An effort to make the object more reusable might change this a bit, because the interface must then be complete for a whole set of applications and not only for the application under development.

To summarize, the interface is the shared boundary between objects. When we define the interface, we must define two parts: The first part is the messages supplied and the other part is the agreement on the format for the use of these messages.

We could sum up these guidelines in the following "energy" rule: Interfaces should give rise to a *minimum amount of energy spent,* either when executing them (few and small interfaces) or when understanding them (explicit, consistent, coherent, low semantic gap, stable interfaces, and support for information hiding).

Apart from the guidelines for the interface mentioned previously, we give the following recommendations:

- The interface should define a *complete* set of messages but nothing more. The messages should be usable and not too detailed or too simple.
- The supplied interface will be used by a user/customer, and it is *the need of that user* that must be the center of attention. We should not include anything just because *we* think it is usable. On the other hand, we should not leave out anything just because *we* think that it is an obvious detail; the detail could be much less obvious to the user.

## Examples

Experience shows that in practice it is difficult to select a proper interface. In particular it is often difficult to decide how many details the object should manage by itself—that is, what level of responsibility it should have. Therefore let us look at a few simple examples.

Please note that we have used the words *defined need* instead of *specification* or *description* and the word *service* instead of the more correct *method*. We do this in the following examples because these words better capture the nature of our aim.

### *A Simple Radio*

**Defined need:** Listen to a simple FM/AM radio (see Figure 4.15).

We need to define the services of a radio in a way that it can be of use to us. If the color, size, or another part of the format is not important, then we can disregard this detail (for example, if we will use the radio despite color).

A good interface specification could contain parts as follows:

**Services:** Radio on–Radio off; Increase volume–Decrease volume; Increase frequency–Decrease frequency; Select FM or AM.

**Format:** FM: 88–108 MHz; AM 52–160 KHz; In: 220 V, 50 Hz, max. 30 W; Out: max. 10 W; European-style power cord connection; Portable; Battery-operated option.

How detailed the specification should be depends on the need for details. Maybe the preceding description is enough, or maybe we need to specify it further:

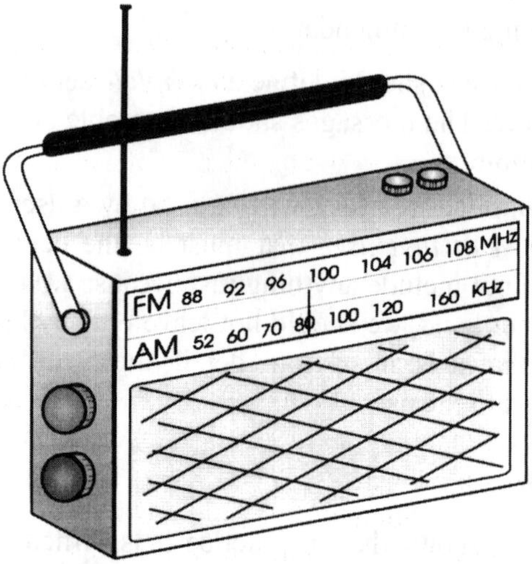


**Figure 4.15** We need to define the interface if we want to use a radio.

**Format:** FM: 88–108 MHz; AM 52–160 KHz; In: 220 V, 50Hz, max. 30 W; Out: max. 10 W; European-style power cord connection; Weight: max. 2 kg; Size: max. 10 × 20 × 30 cm; Portable; Radio should be fitted with a handle; Battery-operated option, 9 V.

The format could also include other things. For example, it could include the rule that the service "Radio on" must be applied before any of the other services can be requested. Unfortunately, there is no simple rule to follow. Too many details might tie up the next development phase, as they will probably put unnecessary constraints on it. On the other hand, lack of details could make our integration harder.

---

**Example**

The specification Size: max. 10 × 20 × 30 cm could cause problems for the implementors if, for example, they lack a standard transformer that will fit a radio of this size. They will then have to order a nonstandard transformer, perhaps increasing the price significantly. Another specification, such as Size: max. 12 × 20 × 30 cm, might have been just as suitable for our customer while allowing a standard transformer. It is not uncommon to specify too much. This will cause problems for the implementors and thereby increase the price. On the other hand, a specification such as Size: max. 10 × 20 × 30 cm may be too inexact if the radio is supposed to fit exactly a box of a certain size.

---

### *A Hardware Measurement Sensor*

**Defined need:** A camera designer needs to include a sensor that can measure the distance between a camera and the object we are photographing (see Figure 4.16).

It is important that we take on the role of a camera designer when we decide about the interface: The designer needs something in the camera that can function as a measuring device.

When this problem is solved in my seminars, suggestions are often made that we should state whether IR light should be used to do the measurement or if some other technique should be used. But such implementation details are best left to the maker of the sensor, because it is enough for the designer of the camera to know that the sensor can deliver measurements of a certain accuracy.

Discussions also often start about the sensor's way of making measurements: on command or continuously, always having an updated measurement to deliver when we want the service "Measure distance" performed. But the way of measuring is something we can also leave to the designer of the sensor. When *we* want to use the sensor, we are interested only in questions such as, "Will it fit our camera?" and, "Will it give us correct measurements?", aspects that the following specification addresses.

**Services:** Measure distance; Reset.

**Format:** Measuring range 0.6 m–infinity, Accuracy 5%, Measurement not older than 0.1 s; Size see Figure; Weight: max. 0.015 kg; Type of hardware connection, see Figure; Electrical protocol details, see figure; Power requirements: 3V ±10%, max. 0.02 A. (Figures are not shown.)

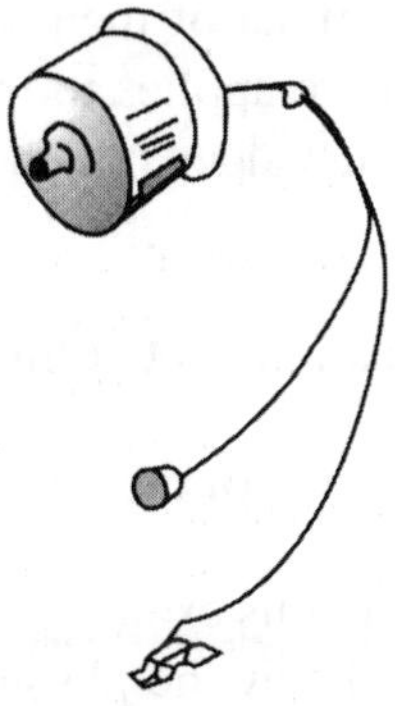

**Figure 4.16** A sensor.

*Software for the Measurement Sensor*

We consider the same example as above but with a different type of user in mind. We are no longer dealing with the designer of the camera. Instead, we are dealing with the needs of the software developer who is developing the software that will encapsulate the actual hardware-measurement device.

**Defined need:** We have a computer in the camera with a main program that sometimes needs a measurement. That is, we have a main program that needs a simple interface to the measurement sensor mentioned in the previous example.

This example illustrates how we can hide hardware details from a main program by introducing special software for the hardware, called a driver. Details such as understanding the electrical protocol are best left to some other code than to the main program. If we change the actual hardware, all we should have to do is to change the implementation of the driver for the sensor. The main program could then call the changed driver in exactly the same way as before the change of hardware.

The services and part of the format are the same as for the actual hardware device, because we are talking about the same defined needs (measurement of the distance).

**Services:** Measure distance; Reset.

**Format:** Measuring range 0.6 m–infinity, Accuracy 5%, Measurement not older than 0.1 s; Call made in C++.

*A Simple Database*

**Defined need.** We need to store verifications.

A good interface should not bother us with details. Instead it should present us with the minimum set of methods we need, but still be complete. (The solution given here applies to the bookkeeping done in Sweden. For example, Swedish law does not allow us to update a verification or to delete a verification).

**Services:** Store verification; Get verification.

**Format:** The actual format of the verification; Call made in C++.

An interesting aspect on this example is that it points out why earlier databases, where we had to know the physical location of the records on the disk, presented bad solutions; They did not hide a sufficient number of details. If we want to use a database in a bookkeeping program, we are interested in the services just mentioned, but not in where on a hard disk the verifications are stored.

## BASIC OBJECT TYPES

*Form follows function.*

—Louis Henri Sullivan

Strictly speaking, all objects are created as equals because all objects must have attributes, methods, and an identity, but in reality we find that objects often appear in different roles or flavors.

In this section we will review some basic categories of objects that we find when we model systems.

### Information and System Objects

Traditionally, we built one model of our information (data) and one model of the behavior (the functions we want to act on the data) during analysis. This approach changed when the object was introduced. Today we model the information and the behavior with the same concept, the object. We illustrate this fact by showing Figure 2.20 again (as Figure 4.17).

We have already touched this important property of the object, but let us now look at it in detail.

Whereas the data (information) model plays an important role in the data processing community, behavior models are the stars in the technical

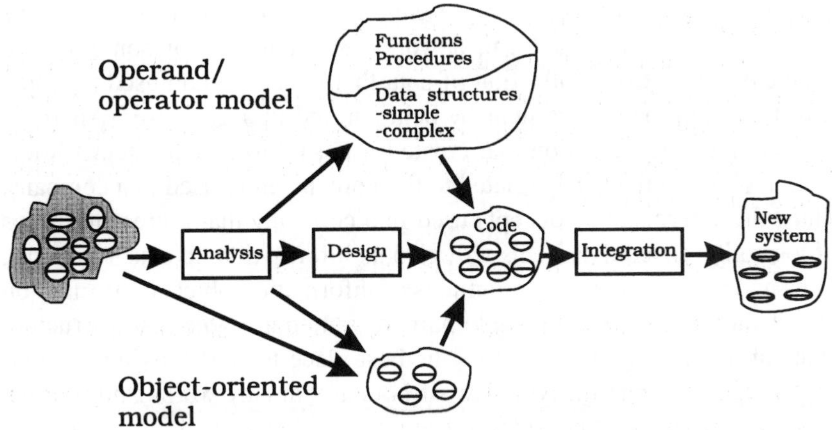


**Figure 4.17** The object models both data and functions.

section of the software-development community. This is quite natural considering the different characteristics of these two different fields of business.

The strong need to model the information in the data processing community and the equally strong need to model behavior (dynamics) in the technical field remain, even if we use object-oriented modeling. These two needs explain why we often encounter objects that are dominated by either the information or the behavior aspect. This is nothing but a natural parallel to the earlier division of software development into data-intensive and function-intensive software development, respectively.

Typical data-intensive systems are systems developed for the data processing market, often using COBOL. The functions in these systems are relatively simple, whereas the amount of data is overwhelming. On the other hand, systems developed for the technical market contain very complex functionality, whereas the data often come second. With these systems, most of the energy is spent on describing and implementing the behavior of the system. Two typical representatives of these two fields are banking systems and defense systems, respectively.

In the object-oriented world, these aspects, information and behavior, have been united in the object idea. However, because the old difference lingers, we often see two different types of objects. Let us call these two types of objects *information objects* and *system objects*, respectively. Both are needed and both are real objects with information (attributes) and behavior (methods).

Information objects are thus used for holding information, whereas system objects to a larger extent deal with the behavior of a system. Note the *larger extent* in the previous sentence. Our information objects are not without behavior and our system objects are not without data, because both are real objects.

An information object represents a *data carrier*. It can often be derived from a paper, a form, a worksheet, a report, or some similar source of data. It is a collection of data that is needed and used together, and it is often made persistent by being stored in a database. (Anything that survives the execution that created it is said to be persistent.) Information objects are closely related to the nomenclature used in a company. Thus, those terms and concepts used in a company that represent groups of logically related data items will give us information objects. Accounts, bills, and invoices are good examples of information objects. Information objects are often the most stable parts of a model. (Note that a structure chart of a company might not be the best place to start looking for concepts, data, etc. The official view of how a company works and the real way it works may be very different.)

A system object is a handler of information objects. For example, it is typically a system object that is responsible for acquiring an information object at a certain point in time and also a system object that is responsible for discarding the information object when it is no longer of use to the company. A system object can often be given a certain role in a system. A typical role for a system object in a technical application is to handle a sensor or another hardware device. See also the following discussion in the section "Object-Oriented Thinking." The structure of an information object is typically simpler than the structure of a system object. For example, an information object often contains mostly attributes, whereas a system object typically contains subobjects as well.

---

**Example**

Invoice and driver: An invoice represents several attributes but usually has simple methods, and we call it an information object. A driver for a hardware device, on the other hand, might use very complex algorithms for digital filtering or something equally complex and is thus to be regarded as a system object.

---

Note that there is no absolute borderline between these categories of objects. Thus, it is easy to get a mix where the borders are not clearly drawn. It should perhaps be emphasized that it is neither the amount of data nor the complexity of the functionality that determines whether we ought to think about an object as an information object or a system object. The question is, rather, "What is the important aspect of an object?" Is the object responsible for some well-defined data or is the object handling/managing other objects? (Note, an information object may manage subobjects, but if it manages other objects it is probably best to view it as a system object.) Then, of course, if an object is responsible for data, it is probable that it has more data than functionality—and vice versa.

Finally, it should be noted that it is a good idea to track down the owner of an information object. If we cannot find someone responsible for the data contained in an information object, we should appoint one. If someone is given the responsibility for an information object, it suddenly becomes much more important to have a clear definition of it.

### *Object-Oriented Thinking*

Whether systems development starts from a manual situation or not, it is always helpful to start by viewing all activities as if they were performed by hand. The idea is to form a picture of the system, where system objects are the actors playing more or less important roles and information objects are the things acted upon by system objects. Each object should be responsible for a well-defined part in the play.

We can also view the software system as a company or part of a company with its own employees, departments, and so on, where everything works together to achieve the end result of a company/system.

A similar approach to systems development has been mentioned in the book *Modeling the World with Objects* by Phil Sully [24]. In this book, Sully mentions that theoreticians in eighteenth-century medicine often described physiological processes as being carried out by little folk called homunculi. For example, the process of seeing was considered to be the result of homunculi operating just behind the eyes. These little folk somehow converted what someone saw into messages that other homunculi, the "brain" homonuculus, could interpret and operate upon. Thus, this approach also results in a picture of the system where objects manually perform their activities.

If we use this approach and model a system as something manual, we should be aware that outdated technological solutions might creep into the model. Such solutions should be deleted from the final model.

BPR (Business Process Reengineering) is a way to make radical changes in an organization to make it more efficient. In a BPR project we model the user's business processes, so that everyone can see which ones are redundant, which ones can be removed, which ones can be redesigned, etc. This modeling effort is often carried out with the use of traditional structured analysis methods, such as data flow diagrams. However, the preceding illustrations clearly indicate that object-oriented modeling is eminently suitable as a technique for describing an organization and thus can be used for BPR. Object-oriented techniques will of course not guide us explicitly when we try to decide what we want to remove, change, or add, but we will be able to describe things in a way that can easily be understood from management and down. There is no fundamental difference in how we apply the ideas in this book if we model an organization to use the model for BPR. We define actors, use-cases, mini-uses, subsystems, system objects, information objects, etc. and introduce them in the same order as if we were to model a (computer) system. (Use-cases, mini-uses, actors, and subsystems are discussed in the following paragraphs and in Chapter 5.) The only real difference is that much of the model we build is not and will not be implemented on a computer. (However, there is nothing to stop us if we think that something hitherto manual should be implemented on a computer.)

***Building with System Objects in Layers***

Some system objects are easy to find, such as system objects directly connected with the hardware. It is very common that parts of hardware give reason for having objects in a model. For example, an input or output device might be modeled with a hardware driver. This hardware driver is then one of our system objects.

In fact, reflecting hardware parts as objects in our model is a good principle for the design. It is in full agreement with the close (1:1:1) mapping idea. System objects directly related to hardware are also easy to find, making it a good way to start the modeling.

We can thus find a first layer of system objects by looking at the hardware (see Figure 4.18). It is good practice to make this mapping as close as possible.

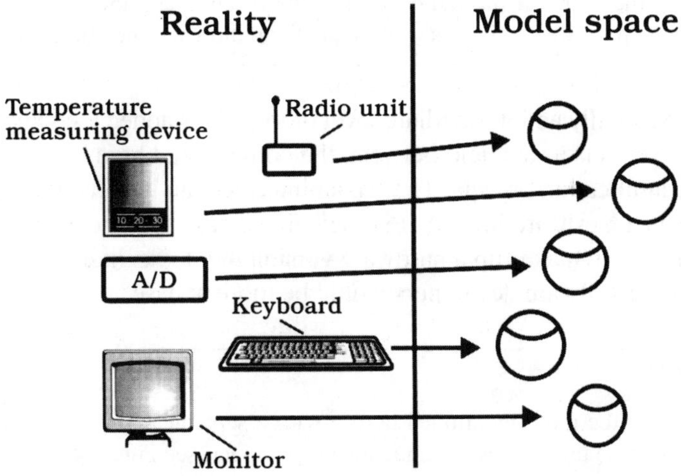


**Figure 4.18** Hardware items can be modeled with objects.

---

**Example**

A radio unit has a transmitter and a receiver as separate parts. If we are going to have a one-to-one mapping, we should reflect this in our model by having two objects, one object for the receiver and one object for the transmitter. If one of these parts changes, then we have to change only the corresponding object in our model.

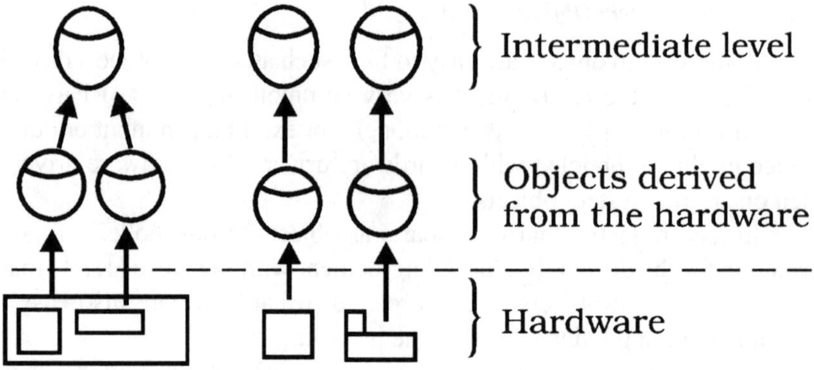


**Figure 4.19** Objects derived from hardware, managed by an intermediate layer of objects.

On the other hand, if the radio unit has the receiver and the transmitter as one integrated part, we can just as well model the radio with one object in our model.

---

Normally an intermediate level of objects is added (see Figure 4.19). This layer acts as a shield between the complicated hardware and the rest of the application objects. That is, an intermediate level is introduced that presents a hardware level that is logical and easy to handle. We could say that this level makes up a hardware version that looks like something with which the software developers would be more at ease.

---

**Example**

If we have the radio mentioned before with a separate receiver and transmitter, we could hide this fact by introducing a new object (see Figure 4.20 (a)). An even better solution would be to aggregate the receiver and the transmitter (see Figure 4.20 (b)). This aggregate could then present the rest of the system with just one object. If we change the radio hardware to another unit that has the transmitter and the receiver integrated, we need only substitute this object.

---

Having one object instead of two is an example that illustrates how we can make the interface for the hardware easier to handle. This is so because we hide some details (the fact that the radio unit is made up of two different hardware parts).

We summarize: Mapping hardware parts into (system) objects is a good starting point because

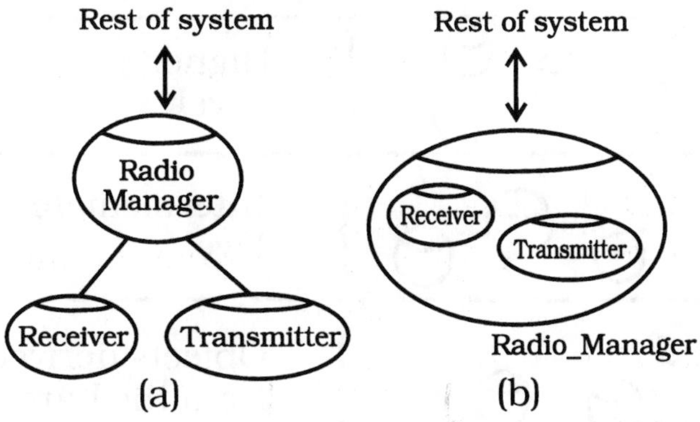


**Figure 4.20** Two ways to model the objects corresponding to receiver and transmitter in a radio.

- If a hardware part changes, it is easy to locate the corresponding software that needs to be changed.
- This approach makes modeling easy, because each hardware part prompts us to put one object into our model.

However, this simple scheme of mapping hardware parts directly to system objects is seldom enough. We also need to model more of the behavior of the system. When the design continues and we try to build a conceptual model of what the system will do, we can design a set of objects that use the intermediate objects to achieve what the system is supposed to achieve. We can use system objects for this too, and we then get a three-layer model, as seen in Figure 4.21. In the figure we have a lower layer, consisting of the system objects that are directly derived from our hardware. This layer is normally also used to hide low-level hardware details. A second layer is introduced to hide more hardware idiosyncrasies. The third layer of objects carries out the main logic of the system. That is, these "high-level" objects constitute the main logic, making the system do what we want the system to do. The lower levels of objects concentrate on encapsulating hardware idiosyncrasies, giving the higher-level objects a less complex interface to the hardware. The third layer can also be layered if needed, giving us a system with four, five, or more levels.

Information objects typically appear in connection with the data of the system.

---

### Example

If we want to keep track of hardware parts in an inventory system, we will get information objects. With this purpose (keeping track of hardware parts), we will

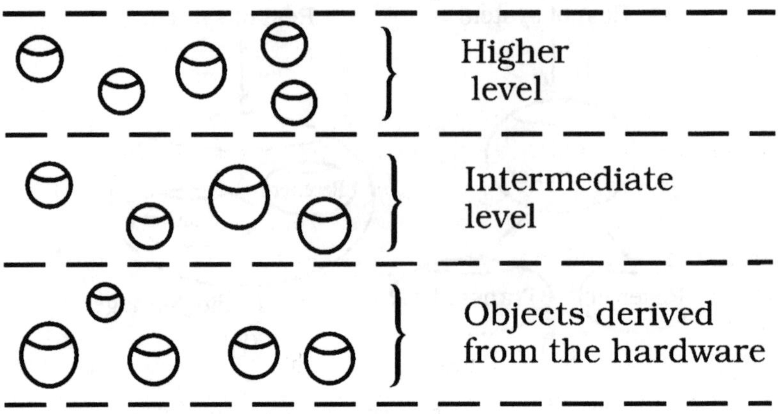


**Figure 4.21** A system is typically built in several layers of abstraction.

get objects where the important aspect is data (inventory number, price, type, etc.), and we call them information objects. In Figure 4.22 we exemplify the discussion with a sensor. If the sensor were an integrated part of a system, the important aspect of the sensor would be its behavior, and we would refer to the corresponding object in our model as a system object.

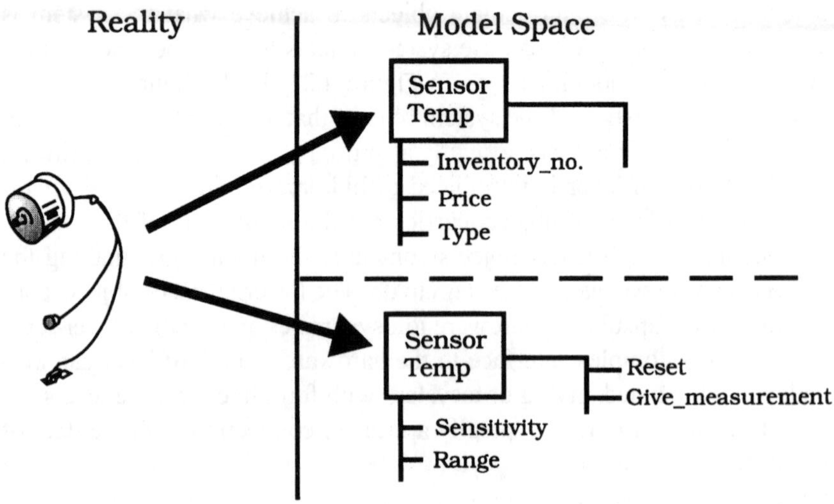


**Figure 4.22** A sensor modeled as an information object (top) and a system object, respectively. (Only class descriptions for the objects are shown.)

We thus conclude that the same hardware part can generate a system object *and/or* an information object in a model. Different purposes yield different objects.

At first, when a system is being built, the lower level(s) of hardware-derived objects tend to dominate. It is natural to find them, and they are easily found. Strictly speaking, this need not be true, however. If those who make the model are good at making abstractions, we might instead tend to find objects dealing with the logic of the system first. This latter case is unusual because of the scarcity of people who are good at abstracting.

When the design continues, new thoughts occur, and ideas for new and "better" objects emerge. When the design has been going on for some time, it is common to find many objects that are not easily associated with the hardware or with ideas that existed before the modeling activity began. However, one important solution to the software crisis is to have a direct correlation between reality, the model, and the implementation of the system. The design process should not be allowed to deviate too much from this solution.

***Summary—Information and System Objects***

In a model we often find two different categories of objects:

- One category is the group of objects where the data are the stars. They are often composed of many important—typically complex—attributes, whereas the methods can be few and/or simple. They normally do not occur in one single instance.
- Another category is the group of objects, where behavior is the primary aspect. The objects in this group often have few and/or simple attributes but complex methods. In many cases they occur in one single instance.

We call these two categories of objects information objects and system objects, respectively. It is good design to keep these two types of objects apart, because of their radically different nature. Information objects such as invoices and bank accounts are objects that are often created and deleted during execution time, and when we need to make them persistent, it is likely that we will store them in an object-oriented database. The more "technical" algorithm-intensive objects will typically exist during the execution of a system. We will probably not need to store these in a database; instead they will be created when a system starts to run and cease to exist when the system stops running. They represent the main logic in a system.

## Actor/Agent/Server

It is often wise to classify (system) objects further. A classifying scheme is the actor, agent, and server scheme (see Figure 4.23). This is a way of classifying objects according to the way they call other objects. That is, an actor object is never called but calls other objects, whereas a server object never tries to call another object. The agent is a sort of go-between object that can call other objects as well as be called.

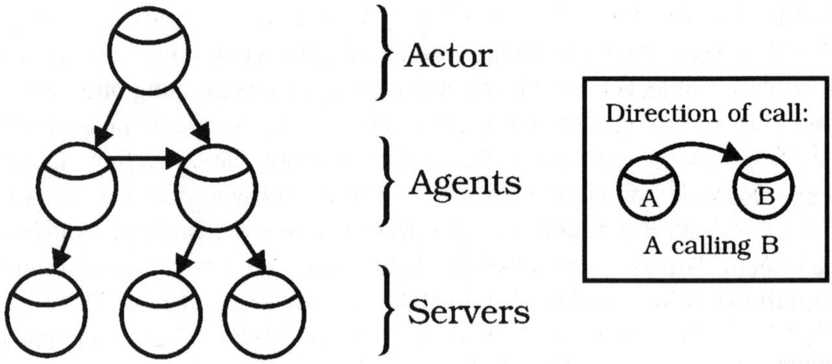


**Figure 4.23** Actor/Agent/Server.

## Active/Passive

Another classification scheme is the active/passive scheme. If an object is *active* it has a task* and can thus execute parallel to other active objects. If an object does not have a task, it is *passive*. In our opinion, an active object is the same as a process.

Unfortunately, active and passive are sometimes thought to be equivalent to actor and server, respectively, but this is a misunderstanding. For example, an active object need not be an actor object. In the same way, a server object is often passive, but it need not be.

---

### Example

An example of an object that is active but not an actor is a hardware manager object with a task. Let the active object regularly collect values from some sensors and calculate updated average values. The values would then be available to other objects when they make a call to this hardware manager object. If the sen-

*A task is an independent thread of control in a system. If we have several such threads of control executing in parallel in an interleaved manner, we call it *multitasking*.

sors are encapsulated by their own objects, our manager object is an agent. (The manager calls the sensor objects and is called when other objects need updated average values.) If the sensors are not handled by special sensor objects of their own, but are handled directly by the manager, the manager object is a server, because it is only called by other objects. In both cases it is active, because it has a task inside.

---

### Client/Server

Object-oriented ideas are a natural fit for client/server technology. With the client/server technology we can spread out the logic of an application so that it better relates to the business needs of a company. The client/server technology exists in some variations, but normally the server manages physical data on disk and arbitrates between clients requesting the data. The client provides an interface between a user's application and the server. It manages a logical view of the data.

The client/server system can be viewed as a mix of active/agent/passive and actor/server ideas. We have two parts executing in parallel. The client is often called the front-end, and the server often is called the back-end. The client is an agent, because it is between the application and the server, but it is also doing independent processing on its own, thereby being active. The server is also doing processing on its own, thus being active as well. If the roles can be exchanged, both the client and the server should be called agents. The client/server arrangement matches the way many companies operate. The client/server idea is thus less exact but maybe of more practical use than active/passive and actor/agent/server classification.

### Actor-User Role

Ivar Jacobson in his book *Object-Oriented Software Engineering* [27] introduces the concept *actor* as representing a role played by a user. An actor is not a particular user but represents the role a user or a group of users typically perform when they use a system.

This is not the same use of the concept actor as in the previous section. The context will make it clear whether we are referring to a user's role or an actor as described in the previous section.

When we refer to an actor as a user, we mean a role that is played by a person when using a system. We do not include the use of a system by another system. Such "user roles" will be modeled with interface objects, which is the topic of next section.

## Interface Objects

We define an interface object in the following way.

**Definition.** An *interface object* encapsulates aspects dealing with communication.

The communication can be to and from a system or can occur between parts of a system. The interface object should encapsulate in such a way that if the communication paradigm is changed, only the interface object has to change, leaving the rest of the system unchanged. The better an interface object is at doing this, the higher is its quality.

One reason we need high-quality interface objects is that if we separate the interface from purer application-oriented parts of our model, it will be easier to reuse the application parts. Another reason why we should make this separation is that we can then develop interface parts in parallel with (more) application-oriented parts.

Interface objects should display the characteristics of a good interface discussed in the section "Selecting Good Interfaces." In the following we first look at some examples of interface objects. We then look at the situation from a more general point of view.

## Examples of Interface Objects

Our first example is the *wrapper object* term that we borrow from the book *Object-Oriented Software Development* by Mark Lorenz [26]. This object encapsulates a non-object-oriented system or a part of a non-object-oriented system. A wrapper object functions as an interpreter, allowing an object-oriented system to communicate easily with a non-object-oriented (sub)system.

The object paradigm can be used to build object-oriented, knowledge-based systems. This concept is outside the scope of this book; the reader is referred to a work such as *Object-Oriented Conceptual Modeling* by Dillon and Tan [25]. However, an interesting idea is to encapsulate an expert system with a wrapper object. We then get an object that we can call a *logical object*. This object can be passive, available to other objects when they have questions to ask, or active, monitoring something. If the logical object is an active object, we can let it take intelligent action when certain criteria or events occur.

Probably the most important type of interface object is the type of object that handles communication and interaction between a user and a system. This type of interface object is often very complex and has a complicated object structure. As mentioned before, it is a good idea to separate this type of object from the purer application related parts of a model. An example of this is found in Chapter 7, "A Distribution System," where two alternative solutions for a small hand-held computer are mentioned. One alternative involves using a windowing system, and the other alternative involves using a button interface. In both these alternatives the application part of the model remains the same if we successfully separate the interface part of the system from the rest of the system.

We sometimes refer to objects dealing with application-related parts of a model as *application objects,* to contrast them with interface objects. It is not always easy to separate interface objects from purer application objects. This is especially true if we are to implement the system in a particular environment, as some programming, for example, in Smalltalk soon shows. However, it is beyond all doubt that such a separation is a good idea. It makes it easier to move a system to a new platform and to reuse application objects in a similar application, and it supports parallel development, where one group develops interface objects and another group develops application objects.

An object that encapsulates hardware idiosyncrasies of some hardware device by providing well-specified high-level services to other objects is also an example of an interface object. In this book we often refer to this type of object as *driver objects*. Sometimes we will also name them by giving them the suffix *driver*—for example, "Sensor_driver." However, because we want to keep the names short, we add this suffix only if we feel it is necessary. An object managing several driver objects can also be viewed as an example of an interface object because it encapsulates low-level details concerning the communication with driver objects during the management of the sensors. We will often add the suffix *manager* to this type of objects, called *manager objects*. For example, a system object controlling and coordinating measurements made by several sensors could be called a "Sensor_manager."

In the following section, we will look at three communication cases and at how we can model high-quality interface objects for them.

### Modeling Interface Objects

When an object calls a method belonging to another object, we have the situation depicted in Figure 4.24. The figure shows how object A is calling B.B_method. The problem is that this situation is simple only when the objects are in the same computer. In Figure 4.25 (a) we show this situation. (We use the broken line to enclose objects that are in the same computer or process.)

Situation (a) is thus trivial, but (b) and (c) in Figure 4.25 are not.

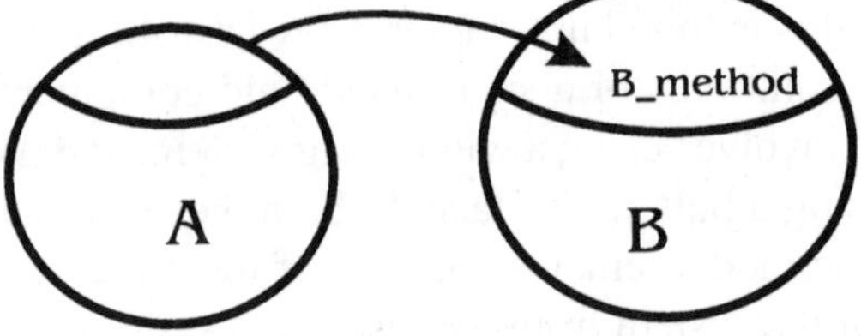


**Figure 4.24** The starting point for our discussion.

In (b) we have two objects and they are in different computers. This is equal to having two subsystems executing in parallel in different computers.

Situation (c), when A is an individual trying to use the system, is equal to a user—an actor—using facilities supplied by a system—for example, an operator registering an order.

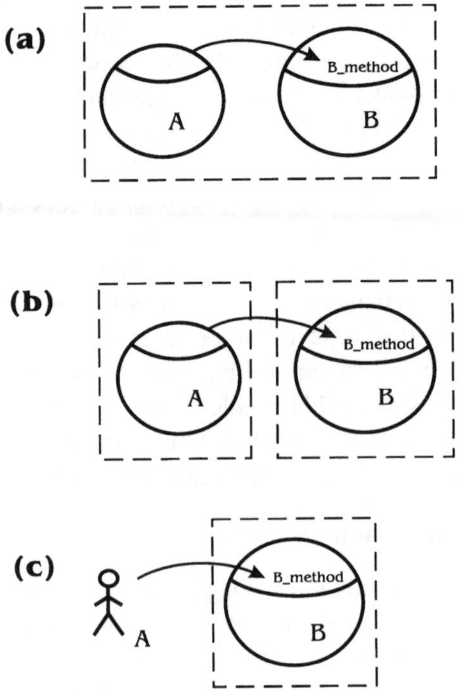


**Figure 4.25** Three fundamentally different cases of communication.

In this book we will call an interface object that handles methods applied by an actor a *dialog object.* Objects handling the interface between subsystems will be called *connection objects*.

We will look into (b) and (c) in some more detail in the next two sections.

***A and B as Objects in Different Computers***

If A and B are located in different computers, it is not possible for them to call each other directly. Referring to our earlier discussion of modeling, we remember that we can look at our hardware as a source of possible objects. When systems communicate, they do so by using hardware. If they are communicating via radio or satellite, they must use transmitters and receivers. If they communicate via a telephone line, they must use modems. Subsystems could be communicating via some type of network, which would also suggest some hardware. All these cases can be modeled as in Figure 4.26 Here we have introduced the objects B_connect and A_connect. They. represent the hardware *and* hide its idiosyncrasies.

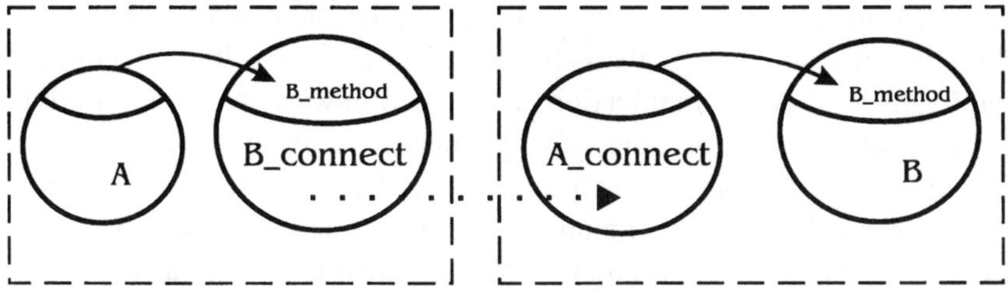


**Figure 4.26** A calling B, when they execute on different computers

Note that we have two options in regard to where to put a new object like A_connect. We can place A_connect outside B but in the same computer, which is the situation shown in the figure. The other option is to put A_connect inside B (and in the same computer as B). We discuss this latter option shortly.

What happens when object A calls B_connect.B_method? Well, B_connect takes care of whatever is necessary to order A_connect to call B.B_method. In this way we simulate a call from A to B.B_method. The abstraction B_connect can easily be augmented to make it do more. For example, we could let B_connect distribute calls to more than one object. A solution could be:

```
{
// Send to several objects:
B_connect.Broadcast_b_method;
}
```

The advantage of putting A_connect outside B is that B retains the interface, as described in Figure 4.24. If we regard this initial figure as a high-level specification, the solution gives us the advantage of preserving the initial interface. That is, this is a solution where we *preserve* the initial interface and visibility, something that will probably make testing simpler. The disadvantages are several: We solve simple communication problems but nothing else. We do not solve complex bidirectional communication problems, where A_connect needs to communicate with subobjects of B. Methods such as B.B_method will often be very simple and not do more than forward a call to a subobject where most of the logic belonging to the method is found. We will discuss such *empty methods*—methods dominated by message forwarding logic—last in this section.

***When A Is a Person***

If object A models a human being, he or she cannot communicate directly with the code, methods belonging to B. In real life a person uses hardware for this communication, so let us follow the reasoning outlined earlier and introduce an object for this hardware. Alternatively, we could introduce several objects. Each object would then correspond to a hardware part needed in the communication process between user and system. Let us, for the sake of simplicity, instead select a level of abstraction in order to hide all this in one object and call that object A_dialog. This object may then contain drivers and logic for a display, a keyboard, a mouse, and the like.

We again have two basic options: to put A_dialog outside or inside B. Figure 4.27 shows putting A_dialog outside B. The advantage is, as in the previous example, that we retain the initial interface and visibility of B. This solution will probably soon present us with problems, however. The problems derive from the high-level character of methods applied by actors. In the following we will call these high-level methods for mini-uses. (Mini-uses are discussed in detail in Chapter 5).

To illustrate, we look at a slightly adapted mini-use called Update_parameters taken from Chapter 6. The pseudocode for this mini-use is

```
{
// Find out what types of sensors the
// Weather_station has.
```

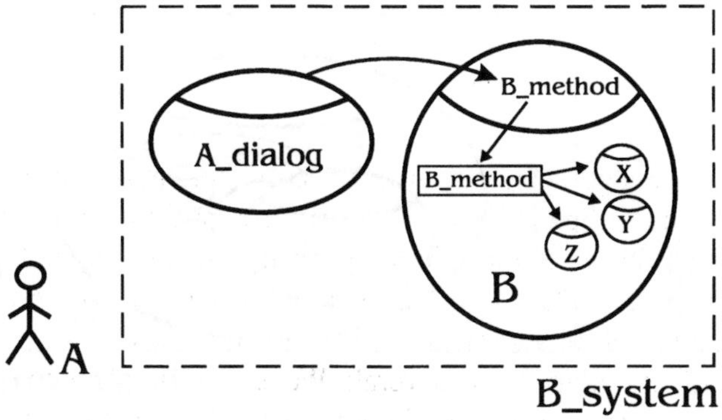


**Figure 4.27** Actor A communicating via A_dialog with B.

```
// Display these
// Ask user what sensor(s) he or she wants to
// update
the_values := // Get parameter values from user
Some_sensor_manager_object.Update_parameters(the_
values);
//
}
```

If B is our Weather_station and calling Update_parameters corresponds to calling B.B_method, we would get a rather complex logic. This complex logic results because the execution of the pseudocode representing our Update_parameters can be carried out only in an interactive way. For example, to find out what sensors A_dialog is supposed to show our user, A_dialog must ask B what sensors are attached to this particular B (Weather_station). To ask this question, we would have to add a method to B that could give this information to a caller, keep this information in A_dialog, or augment B_method so that it can supply this information. If we choose to augment B_method in a way that it could take care of all necessary communication, it would become very complex and specialized.

Thus we see that a mini-use is not ordinarily of a character that yields a simple method call. Instead, it often tends to involve complex interactions. We could add necessary methods to B, but they would only carry out a message-forwarding bureaucracy. If we are willing to sacrifice the interface of B and implement our mini-use in another way, everything becomes much simpler. That is, if we put A_dialog inside B, we move A_dialog to a lower abstraction level (see Figure 4.28). A_dialog can now see subobjects such as X, Y, and Z. (Note, A_dialog cannot see any

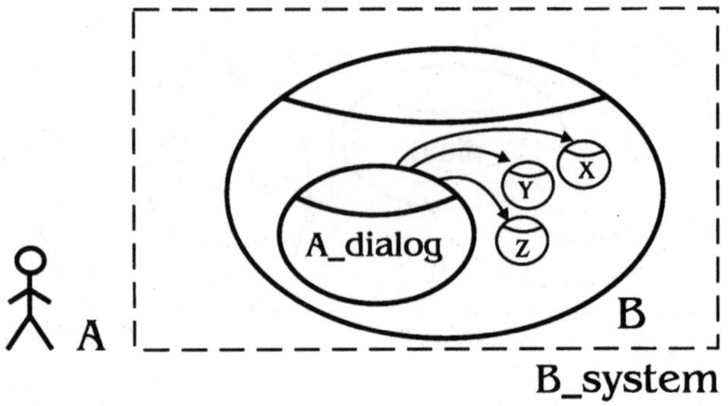


**Figure 4.28** Same case as in Figure 4.27, except A_dialog put inside B.

possible subobjects *inside* them.) With the increased degree to which A_dialog can see details, A_dialog can ask direct questions to relevant subobjects of B. This makes way for a fairly straightforward implementation of our pseudocode. It is thus a matter of putting the objects on their correct level of abstraction.

If B is left without any methods and attributes of its own, we should model the situation as in Figure 4.29. The enclosing object is not necessary if we have no methods or attributes needed to attach to it.

With the two last solutions, we have not preserved the initial interface, but this need not be serious. If we take a closer look at the situation, we realize that there is a fundamental difference between an actor calling a method and an (executing) object calling a method. A human being can-

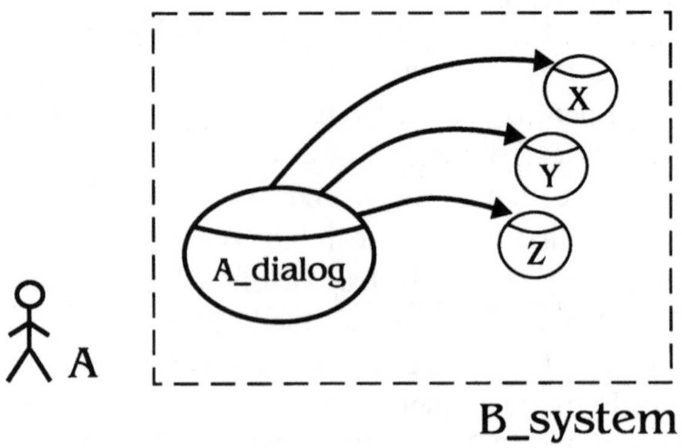


**Figure 4.29** Same case as in Figure 4.28, except B has been removed.

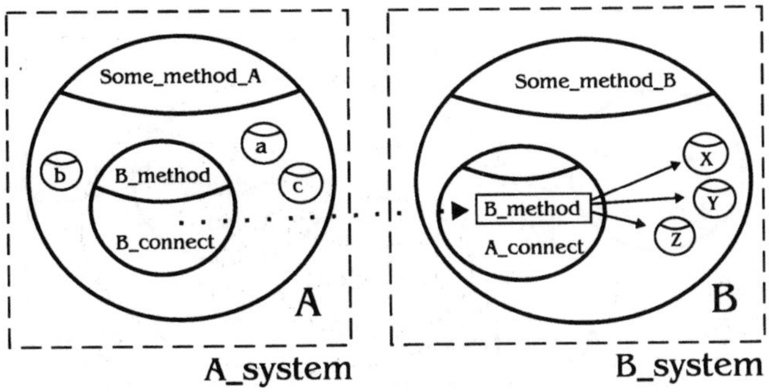


**Figure 4.30** Communication between objects on different computers.

not send a message directly to a system, activating a method. A normal method, on the other hand, can be executed by sending a message to an object. Thus it is just natural that we experience some type of transformation when we move from a high-level view to a more low-level view, where we are closer to the implementation. This difference is one reason we introduced the concept of mini-use, which we discuss further in Chapter 5.

Finally, we model the situation in Figure 4.25 (b), where two communicating objects are on different computers, and their interface objects are inside their respective objects (see Figure 4.30). Note that although we have put both B_connect and A_connect inside their respective objects, it is not necessary to do so. We could have put A_connect inside B but B_connect outside A, for example.

If A and B are without methods when we have done this, we should model the situation as in Figure 4.31. With the solutions shown in Figure 4.30 and 4.31, we do not preserve the initial interface, because B_method no longer belongs to B in the first solution, whereas in the second solution, B does not even exist.

The use of dialog and connection interface objects is further illustrated in our two example chapters, Chapters 6 and 7.

### *Empty Methods*

We called methods dominated by message-forwarding logic *empty methods*.

**Definition.** An *empty method* is a method in which the body is without code, or in which the code in the body only implements some simple message-forwarding logic.

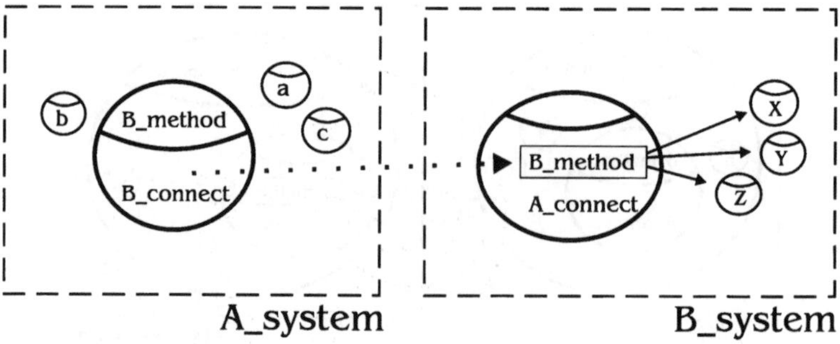


**Figure 4.31** Same case as in Figure 4.30, except enclosing objects are removed.

When we put interface objects outside the object with which we want to communicate, we often get empty methods. A typical situation is sketched in Figure 4.32. That is, A_dialog calls methods of B, but these methods do not contain much of the logic, because most of the implementation of the methods is located in the subobjects to B. For example, most of the code executed when Method_1 is called is found in subobject 1. If we have several such methods—which is not uncommon—we find that the interface of B often acts as a forwarding agency for message calls coming to B. The problem with this is that we get methods that are without logic except for message-forwarding logic thereby giving us an extra level of abstraction but not really contributing anything to the implemen-

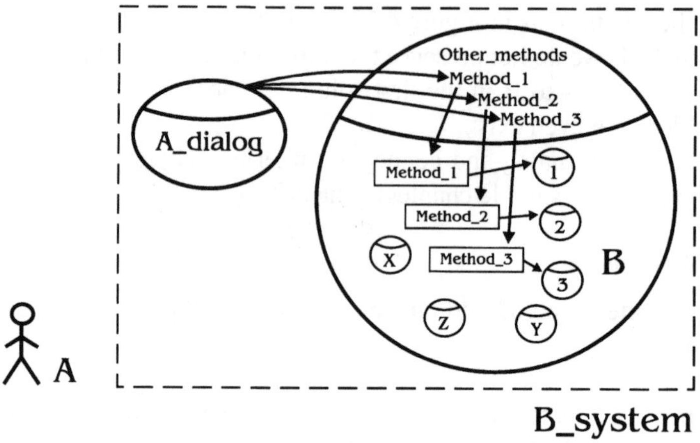


**Figure 4.32** B with empty methods.

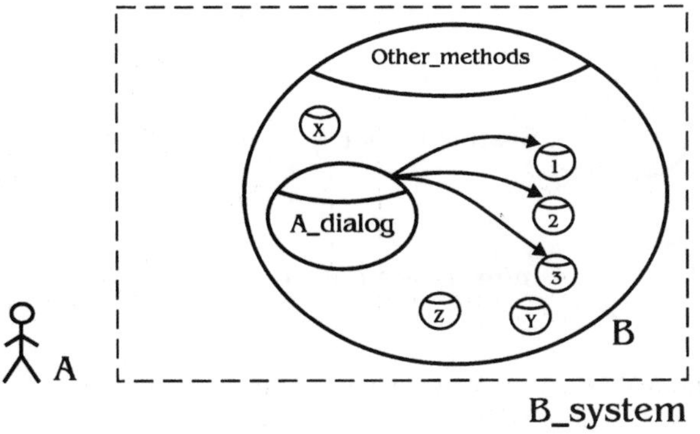


**Figure 4.33** Same case as Figure 4.32, except empty methods are removed

tation of the method. We find the real logic in other objects. A solution to this problem is illustrated in Figure 4.33. For example, if most of the logic belonging to Method_1 is carried out in object 1, A_dialog could call it directly if we put A_dialog inside B. The difference is that putting an object inside another object enables it to see the subobjects of the object. The advantage of putting A_dialog inside B is that we can simplify the logic of the system.

If B is without other methods, when we have taken away message-forwarding logic, we should draw the model as in Figure 4.34.) In this figure we have taken away the enclosing object B. (If an object does not have any methods or attributes of its own, we should omit it.

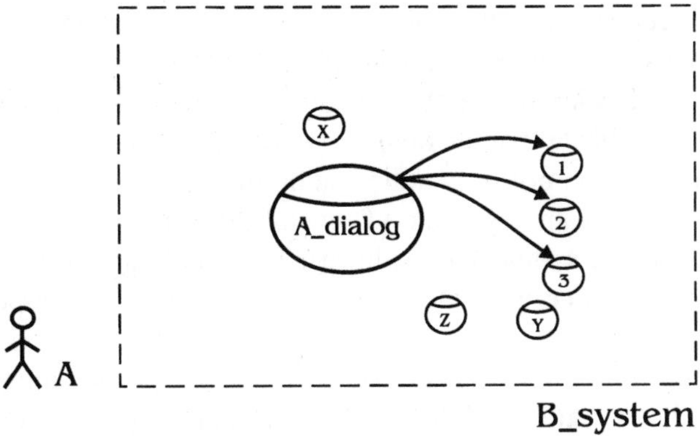


**Figure 4.34** Same case as Figure 4.33, except enclosing object is removed.

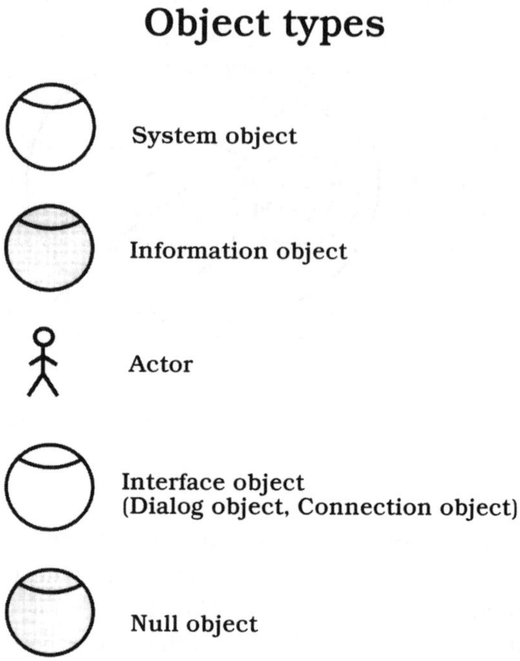


**Figure 4.35** Drawing objects. Note that no special notation is introduced for interface objects or null objects.

## Drawing Objects

Figure 4.35 shows how we indicate the type of an object. If we have a system object, we draw the object as suggested in Chapter 2. This symbol is then used, whether the object is actor/agent/server/client and/or active/passive. If such information is important, a word can be put inside the symbol to indicate that the object is actor, agent, or whatever.

An information object is indicated by filling the object symbol with gray. If an object is an aggregate of several information objects, we normally give only the symbols at the lowest level this shading with gray.

A user with a certain role, an actor, is indicated with a person-like symbol.

Interface objects are system objects, and we do not introduce any special symbol for them. However, we can add "dialog," "connect," or "connection" to the object name if we want to indicate that an object is an interface object. Two examples of this are Weather_station_connection and Local_serviceperson_dialog. (These objects are used in Chapter 6.)

A special type of information object is the *null object*. A null object does not contain any information but is nevertheless drawn as an information object because it is used like an information object. For example, it is common that we have a list or a set of information objects. The null object is then useful when we want to indicate that we have reached the last information object in this list or set. We do this by giving the information objects a method Is_null, which returns the value TRUE if the object is a null object and the value FALSE if the information object contains information.

The following example is adapted from Chapter 7 and illustrates the use of a null object:

```
// Get an information object:
a_picking_object:=
Picking_manager.Get_a_picking_object("First");
WHILE NOT a_picking_object.Is_null DO
// Do something
a_picking_object:=
Picking_manager.Get_a_picking_object("Next");
END_WHILE;
```

## STATE TRANSITION DIAGRAMS

The problem with state transition diagrams is that they become complicated when a system grows from a small system to a medium or large system. This is true especially if there are more than a few different states in the model. If state transition diagrams are to be used, then each diagram should be restricted to one object. The object should be a true independent microworld. We send it a message asking it to do something, and the behavior of the object is then modeled with a state transition diagram. We recommend the simple approaches to state transition diagram notation advocated by Coad and Yourdon [4] or Grady Booch [21] rather than the more complete (and complicated) type found, for example, in *Object-Oriented Modeling and Design* [9]. The notation used by Coad and Yourdon is shown in Figure 4.36.

State transition diagrams can be used in object-oriented modeling. However, using state transition diagrams and object-oriented analysis and design techniques yields different results. To illustrate this we will model an elevator first with state transition diagrams and then using a pure, object-oriented modeling approach (see Figure 4.37). Note that the purpose of this example is *not* to prove that object-oriented modeling is

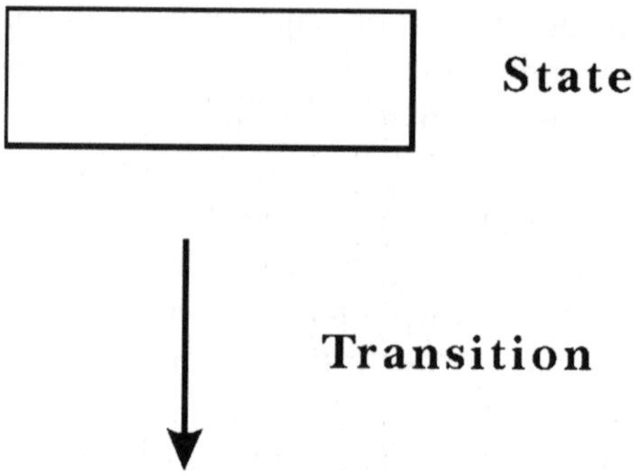


**Figure 4.36** Typical symbols used in state transition diagrams.

always superior to using state transition diagrams but to indicate the fundamentally different approaches used with these two techniques.

The idea with state transition diagrams is basically to select logical parts (such as a valve, a cabin, or a door) and then group events around them. An *event* is something that happens at a point in time, and a *state* is an abstraction of the attribute values of an object. The logical parts should be as independent as possible. It should thus be possible to take away one state transition diagram without having to do much remodeling of other state transition diagrams. The events we use should be external events. That is, we should not include events occurring inside a system. Such

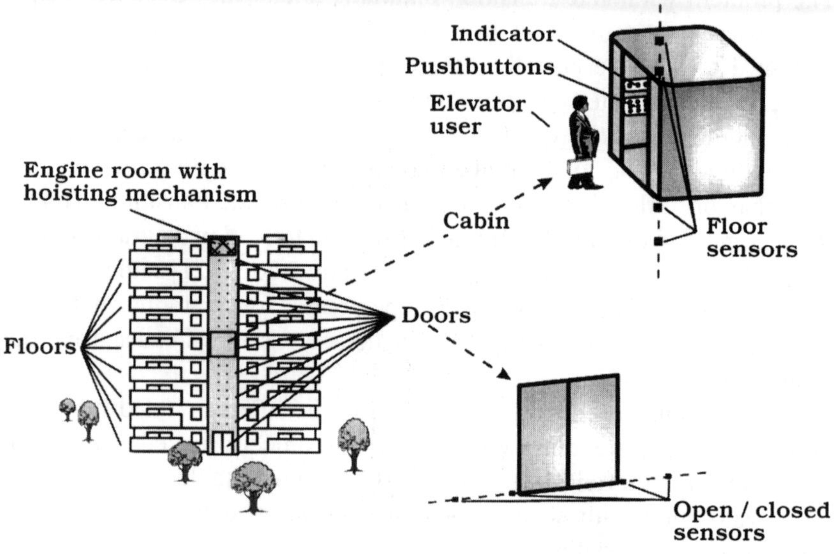


**Figure 4.37** An elevator example.

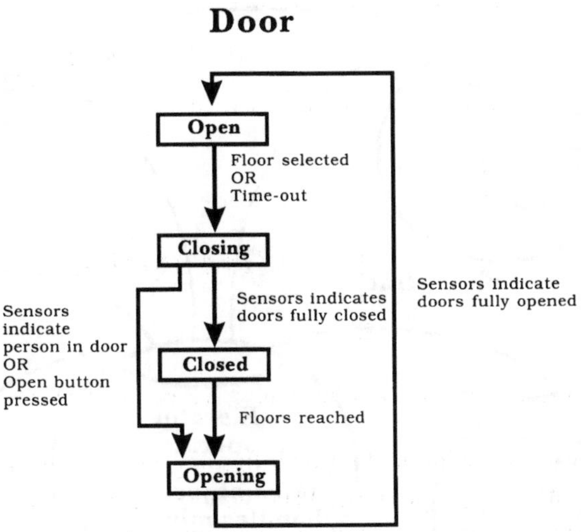


**Figure 4.38** State diagram: Cabin.

internal events are responses to external events and need not be included in the model. In Figures 4.38 and 4.39 we have drawn a state diagram for the door belonging to the cabin and a state diagram for the cabin itself, respectively.

Text inside a rectangle names a state, and text close to an arrow describes the conditions needed to go from one state to another. For example, in the state diagram describing the door, we can see that the

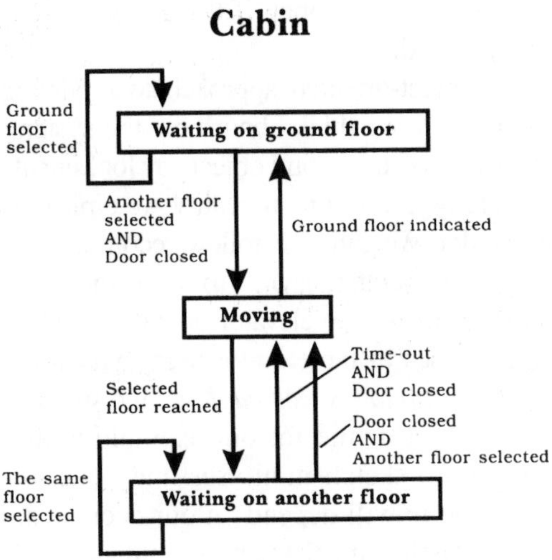


**Figure 4.39** State diagram: Door.

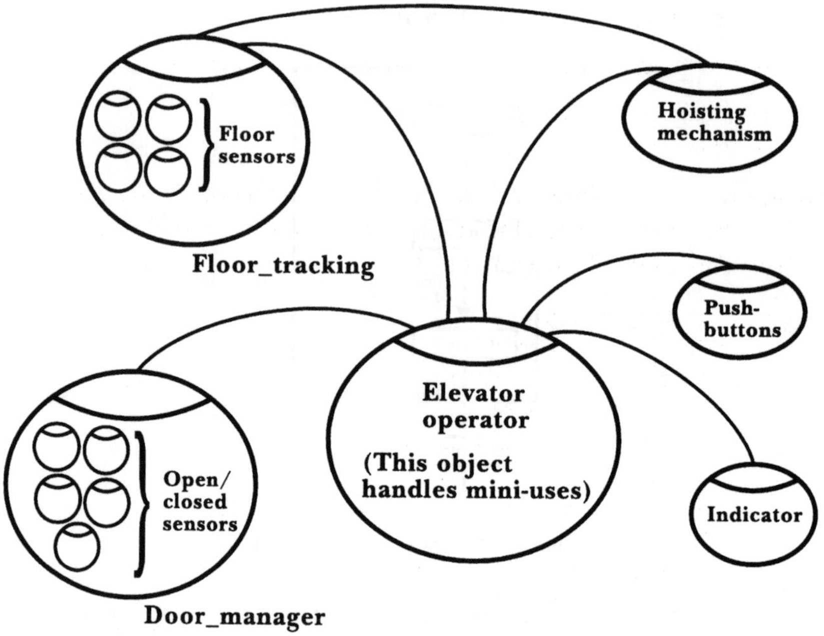


**Figure 4.40** A possible object structure for the elevator example.

door will start to close when a floor has been selected or a time-out has occurred. This state diagram also tells us, among other things, that a door that is closing will reverse and open if there is a person in the door or if the open button is pressed.

If we take an object-oriented approach to modeling, we do not use events and states. Instead, we think about how the system will be used (by defining mini-uses), and we try to find objects by looking at reality. For example, for each hardware object we find in reality, we typically put a corresponding object in our model. We can also follow recommendations given earlier and invent an elevator operator, trying to view the model as if we were describing a manual process. The elevator operator would be responsible for carrying out the mini-uses of the elevator user. Typical mini-uses would be *close doors, open doors, go to a specified floor*, and so on.

A possible object structure for our example is illustrated in Figure 4.40.The next step is to sketch mini-uses and code, using pseudocode. The pseudocode we write will depend on our decisions. For example, we must decide if the hoisting mechanism should be intelligent enough to accept and understand calls such as

```
Hoisting_mechanism.Go_to_floor(2);
```

or if it should only understand simple calls such as

```
Hoisting_mechanism.Go_up;
Hoisting_mechanism.Go_down;
```

leaving the responsibility of finding the correct floor to someone else, such as the Elevator_operator. In the sketch of a main loop, shown here, we have chosen the former solution:

```
// Initiate system
IF "Everything OK" THEN
WHILE TRUE DO // Main loop for Elevator_operator
   selected_floor:= Push_buttons.Pressed_a_button;
   // Go to another floor?
   IF (NOT selected_floor.Is_null) AND
   selected_floor<>Floor_tracking.Current_floor
   THEN
   Door_manager.Close_doors;
   // Wait here until doors closed
   Hoisting_mechanism.Go_to_floor(selected_floor);
   no_of_iterations := 0;
      WHILE TRUE DO
      // Check if we have reached the selected
      // floor.
      Our_current_floor :=
      Floor_tracking.Current_floor;
      Indicator.Indicate(our_current_floor);
         IF (our_current_floor = selected_floor)
         AND
         Hoisting_mechanism.Has_stopped_at_floor
         THEN
         EXIT; // WHILE TRUE DO loop
         ELSE
         no_of_iterations := no_of_iterations + 1;
         // Wait "some small time"
         IF no_of_iterations > some_big_number
         THEN Error;
         END_IF; // Error
         END_IF; // Stopped at floor
      END_WHILE; // Check reached floor
      Door_manager.Open_doors;
   END_IF; // Go to another floor.
END_WHILE; // Main loop
END_IF; // Everything OK
```

The need for state transition diagrams is small in object-oriented modeling. However, we sometimes need to model a state. We use attributes for this. In a sense, it is true that the state of an object is described by all the values of its attributes. This was the description we gave of state earlier, and it is also one of the possible definitions we find in [IEEE] (2).

**Definition.** State: (1) A condition or mode of existence that a system, component, or simulation may be in—for example, the preflight state of an aircraft navigation program or the input state of given channel. (2) The values assumed at a given instant by the variables that define the characteristics of a system, component, or simulation. [IEEE]

To distinguish between the rather uninteresting state (2) and the more interesting modeling state information (1), we refer to (2) as the mathematical state of an object. State information that tells us something interesting about an object's behavior and that, from a modeling viewpoint, we need to keep track of, we call behavioral state. We call an attribute modeling some behavioral state (=1) a state attribute.

If we feel the need to use state transition diagrams, we can do so. However, if we find ourselves using a lot of state transition diagrams, we should be warned: We are probably not thinking in an object-oriented way.

Note that it is possible to give an object, a subobject, or a whole system behavioral states. Remember, though, that the purpose of a behavioral state is to aid in our modeling effort—not to describe some more mathematical state (defined by all the values of our attributes).

State can also be modeled by encapsulating all state specific behavior in special state objects rather than letting state attributes directly model the state. Each object encapsulates the behavior associated with one particular state and the objects are instantiated from classes having the same interface, thereby being interchangeable. When the state needs to be altered, the state object is exchanged for another state object. Typically, a state object is a subobject of another object using it. Thus the state-specific behavior is localized to the state subobject leaving the main object free from state considerations. In the state pattern described in *Design Patterns* [35] all state objects are instantiated from subclasses to the same abstract class which defines a common interface. In this way, the common interface for the state objects is defined in one place.

It is the experience of this author and others that using state transition diagrams will not aid much in object-oriented modeling. This is so because we attack a problem in two fundamentally different ways when using state transition diagrams and object-oriented modeling techniques, respectively.

We did not develop the elevator system in full because the idea with this section was only to illustrate the different approaches used with state transition diagram modeling techniques and object-oriented modeling techniques: Thus, with object-oriented modeling we start by finding objects, give them methods, find mini-uses and implementations of mini-uses, etc. With state transition diagrams, we primarily model around events and states.

## SUMMARY

We began this chapter by introducing the phase model commonly used when developing software.

Today, it is popular to declare the phase model dead, but the phase model is the result of experience gained in earlier software projects and is still to a large extent viable today. We must still make a good requirements specification, give the system good architecture, and prepare for testing early. These activities and advice on how to implement them are the soul of the phase model. The code and fix model is a major reason for failing projects. However, the phase model is changed by object-oriented technology. For example, the distinction between analysis and design blurs.

We then continued by discussing several important points:

- The interface is the key to successful software development. It should encompass all that is needed to understand an object and nothing more. We can divide it into two parts: The actual services that the object can perform and the agreement (or the format) under which these are performed.
- Objects often come in different flavors, and we found that it is a good idea to categorize them in different ways:
  - Data aspects dominate information objects, whereas system objects are dominated by behavioral aspects.
  - A system should be built using several levels of system objects.
  - Actor objects are objects that call other objects but are never called themselves. Server objects are their opposites, and agent objects can call other objects and can themselves be called.

- We also use the concept "actor" to represent a user role.
- An active object contains a task,whereas a passive object does not.
- We also briefly discussed client/server objects.
- Interface objects encapsulate aspects dealing with communication.

■ State transition diagrams can be used but yields a result very different from object-oriented modeling.

# 5

# Subsystems

## *Partitioning of Systems*

*Divide et impera.*

—Divide and rule.
Ancient political maxim cited by Niccolò Machiavelli

## INTRODUCTION

In the investigations mentioned in the preface, one factor kept emerging as *the* factor for successful development of large systems. That vital factor is the ability to partition a system into subsystems.

This chapter begins with a presentation of two types of subsystems essential when we build large systems. The first type of subsystems we discuss deals with the partitioning of an application into smaller parts, whereas the second type of subsystem is concerned with the managing of class libraries.

The second half of this chapter discusses how we can describe behavior of a system. We start by taking the users (external) viewpoint, discussing mini-uses and use-cases, which are ways of defining what a system shall do in user-friendly terms. We then show how to implement these mini-uses and introduce other concepts such as message traces. Finally, we look at how we can make time estimations. The basic reason to include this topic is that it is a convenient way to show how behavior can be distributed among objects.

## SUBSYSTEMS

We gave this definition of a subsystem in Chapter 4.

**Definition.** A *subsystem* is a secondary or subordinate system within a larger system. [IEEE]

In this chapter we develop the idea of a subsystem. The most important purpose of a subsystem is to help in the parallel development of the parts that make up the system. This implies that it should be possible to develop a subsystem in a separate and independent subproject. Such a parallel development of subsystems can be accomplished only if the development activity in one subproject does not interfere with the activity in any other subproject. If a subsystem is to follow this rule, it is necessary that dependencies between subsystems be minimized. We soon realize that the argument for employing subsystems is very close to the argument for using aggregation techniques. Thus, one of the two types of subsystems we judge to be essential is such a grouping of objects.

Our working definition of a subsystem will be the following.

**Definition.** A *subsystem* is a grouping of objects *or* classes with the purpose of supporting the distributed and parallel development of these groupings. The single most important property of such a grouping is that it be made as independent as possible of other groupings (subsystems). A subsystem should display low coupling and high cohesion.

Thus the two types of subsystems that we judge to be essential are as follows:

- *Groupings of objects* (instances): These groupings form the applications we build. That is, here we find nested object structures, which we design using aggregation.
- *Groupings of classes*: This is an administrative way of grouping classes that logically belong together.

Note that the basic idea behind subsystems is to group things together, but that the *purpose* of both types is to support parallel development in a project. Accordingly, we must minimize the dependencies between subsystems. Thus, the main point with a subsystem is that it be as independent as possible. A few synonyms for the word independent may make this important idea clearer. A subsystem is

- Self-reliant, free from the control or influence from other subsystems
- Self-determining, self-governing
- Separate, unconnected with other subsystems.

Sometimes a system such as an operating system is called a subsystem, but such a subsystem does *not* satisfy the requirements stated in our definition. Such a "subsystem" is of a distributed character, rather than a nested character. That is, its resources are available in the whole system. Such a system represents a third kind of subsystem, a false subsystem.

A final point before we start the discussion: If we can give a subsystem a meaningful name, we probably have a good subsystem. The names we give to classes, methods, subsystems, and so on, are very important. Well-chosen names are essential for a good understanding of a model.

## GROUPINGS OF OBJECTS

We have already discussed essential properties needed for this type of subsystem, groupings of objects, in connection with aggregation. In particular, a subsystem as part of a larger application must be its own independent microworld, forming something new, something usable, and something more than the sum of its parts.

A subsystem should interact with the rest of the system only through a well-defined interface. It is a part—a building block—like a circuit board, a roof on a house, or a supporting beam of a bridge. It is there supporting the rest of the system but not interfering with it, except through its well-defined interface. The interface idea has been discussed earlier. It defines the possible handling of something *and* the format needed for this handling. Examples of subsystems are the following:

- A *circuit board* has a certain size, certain levels of voltage for communicating with the bus, etc.
- A *roof of a house* has a certain size and other properties, making it suitable as a roof.
- A *beam of a bridge* has a certain strength and is connected with the rest of the bridge via some kind of joining.

### Aggregation Revisited

A group of objects, an aggregate, can be viewed as a new object. The main arguments for this are as follows:

- The aggregate should model an idea, just as an object does.
- The aggregate should have its own attributes and methods. These attributes and methods need not be directly related to the subobjects of the aggregate.

An example of an attribute that is better connected to an aggregate as such rather than to its parts (subobjects) is error status. A value for such an attribute is the result of some intelligent checking algorithm rather than just a copy of some value found in an attribute belonging to a subobject. Other examples are the attributes *color* and *price* of an object Car_xyz1. What subobject should be responsible for those attributes? One or several parts—but hardly all—of the car might have the same color. It is probably not possible to calculate the price of the car using the prices of the individual parts. Because attributes such as *price* appear in connection with the assembling of the larger object Car_xyz1, they should also be connected with the aggregate rather than with a part of it. We can apply the same argument to the methods of an aggregate, as illustrated in the following example.

---

**Example**

There are 1002 sensors in a plant. Of these, 475 sensors are supposed to be regularly updated with the same 12 parameter values. The updating is done by an operator operating via slow telephone line from his or her home every 5 to 20 minutes. We now have the option either of sending 475 messages via that slow telephone line or making the system smarter. Why not aggregate these 475 sensors and distribute the parameters to the aggregate? That is, the operator would send *one* message with 12 parameter values to a method attached to the aggregate. This method would then distribute the values locally to the subobjects of the aggregate. (If we form such an aggregate, it is evident we can give it other managing responsibilities, too.)

---

The method in the example is clearly related to the aggregate as such rather then to any of the sensors.

A trivial example is the following order to a fleet: Go_to_coordinates X:Y. Because we are used to thinking about our fleet as one unit, we prefer to send one message to our fleet rather than one message to each ship in that fleet.

Another important point in good object-oriented modeling is that objects should be simple to map to our reality. If this is to be the case, our aggregates must not be designed in an ad hoc way, for example, just because we have too many details and want to hide details. Instead, the aggregate must be a usable idea of its own.

---

**Example**

A table is a grouping of its parts, but it is also an idea usable on its own. In the same way the idea Car is more than just the sum of its details.

---

## From Bits to Ideas to Subsystems

*To call forth a concept a word is needed; to portray a phenomenon, a concept is needed. All three mirror one and the same reality.*

—Antoine Laurent Lavoisier

How do we select subsystems for an application? We have already discussed how to find objects, to some extent, in connection with our discussion about the importance of having a clear purpose. Because subsystems are objects, the same principles apply to them. In this section, let us approach the subject from a different angle.

At the bottom of any computer software we find bits. (A bit is a digit taking one of the binary values, zero or one.) Today, no computer language is restricted to building systems using only bits. A few languages, such as C and C++, still have powerful means of manipulating these bits. However it should be evident by now that very few of us are interested in designing complex systems using such low-level ideas. What we want to do instead is to build our application using abstractions as close as possible to the ideas we use when we talk about our business. If we are going to build a system for bookkeeping, we do not want to reason about bits or records or some other idea related to the current computer language. Instead, we want to talk about our verifications, closing of accounts, balance sheet, or something else we are used to thinking about. Object-oriented modeling gives us this ability. Using object-oriented modeling, we can construct objects that represent these ideas. Using aggregation, we can use ideas to develop new high-level concepts. Let us look at a simple example illustrating this discussion. In the example, illustrated in Figure 5.1, we have controllers A, B, and C, which are used to control sensors X,

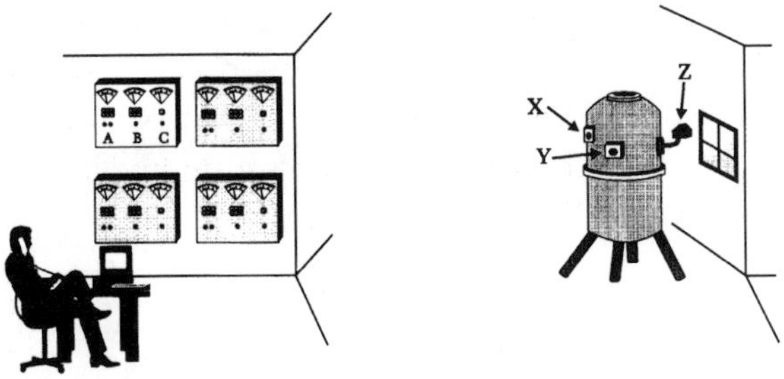


**Figure 5.1** Controllers A, B, and C used to manage sensors X, Y, and Z.

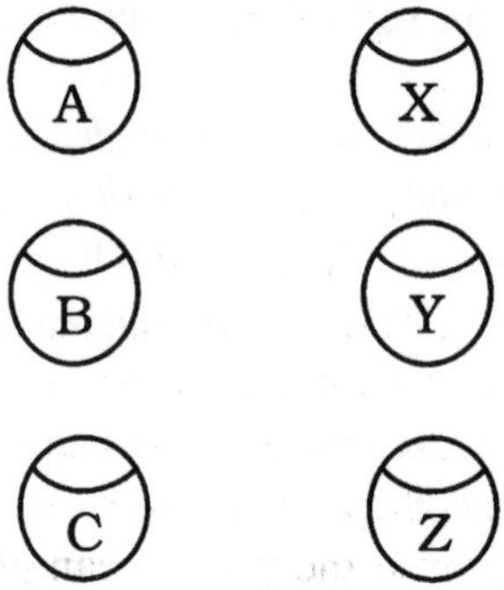


**Figure 5.2** A first model.

Y, and Z. We limit our model to these controllers and sensors in the following. Note that talking and thinking about controllers and sensors is close to a user's view if that user is the person managing the system.

As a rule we get one object in our model for each part we find in reality when we make the model using object-oriented techniques. Using a more traditional method, we would instead have talked about records, functions and so on, ideas that would not have been as close to the ideas used by our user. Thus we get the model shown in Figure 5.2. Next we might realize that we have connections between our controllers and our sensors: A controller can turn off and turn on a sensor, for example. The controller might also be able to change the parameters of the sensors. We can model this as shown in Figure 5.3. But is this a good model? Remember that models are usually much larger than this one. Although this model is simple, we can still realize that we also need to use objects on a

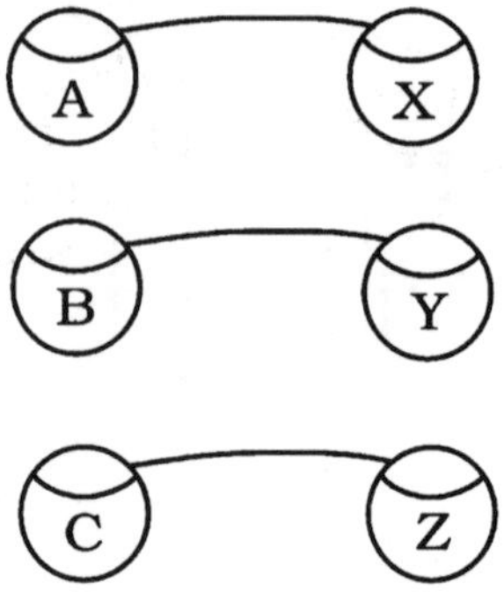


**Figure 5.3** Model slightly improved.

"higher" level—thereby hiding details. This is the basic idea behind one of the subsystem types, groupings of objects.

If we look at Figure 5.1, with our operator controlling the machinery through a control panel, it should not be too hard to see that we already have two high-level ideas available in this figure, the control panel and the machinery. Thus, we could draw a model such as the one shown in Figure 5.4. In this model we have added two objects: Controller and Sensor_manager. These objects manage the objects A, B, C and X, Y, Z, respectively. These two groups of objects are good candidates for subsystems because the groups can probably be developed in parallel.

When Controller talks with Sensor_manager, it should not refer directly to a managed object but use a logical name for it instead, where physical details have been abstracted away. For example, if the Controller wants to turn off sensor X, it should simply send the message

```
Sensor_manager.Turn_off("x_sensor");
```

where x_sensor is a logical reference and not a hard-wired physical reference.

An even better way to model is shown in Figure 5.5. In this figure we have made A, B, C and X, Y, Z into subobjects of Controller and Sensor_manager, respectively. Controller manages its subobjects and

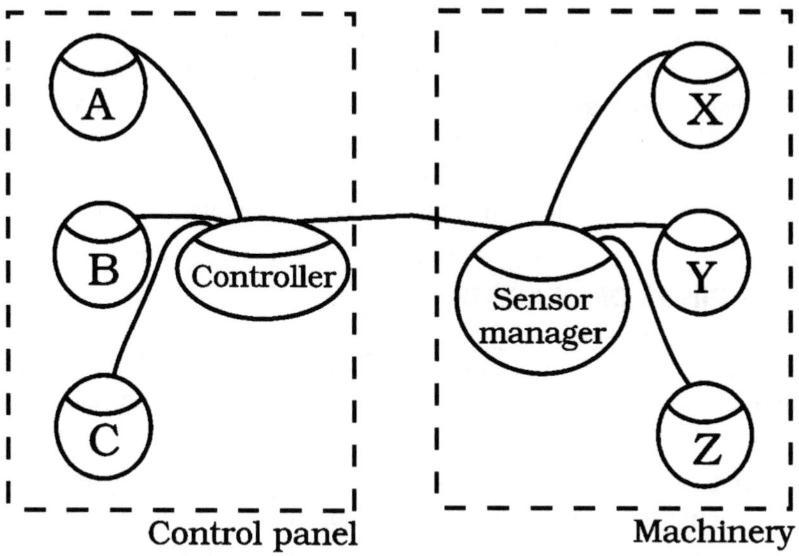


**Figure 5.4** Model augmented with "managing" objects.

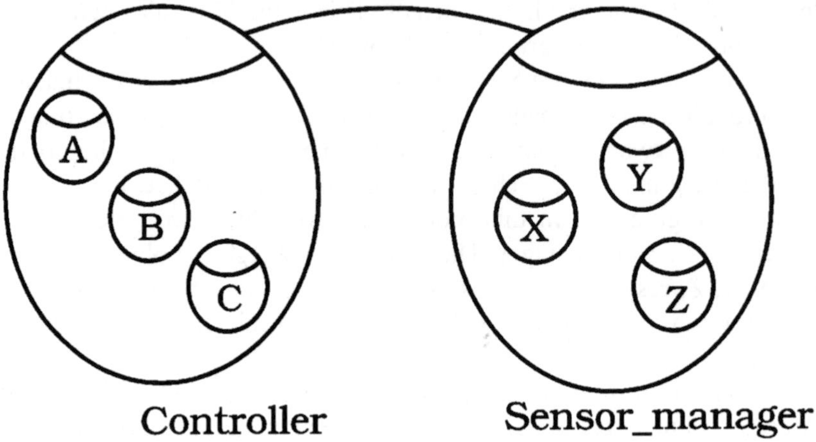


**Figure 5.5** Final model.

Sensor_manager has a similar function for its subobjects. With this design it is impossible for X, Y, and Z to call A, B, or C directly, and vice versa.

We thus understand that with object-oriented modeling, we can build a model using ideas close to a user's own vocabulary. We also realize that if there is a need to build a system in a nested manner, the levels of nesting are often already there, invented by the user. They have been invented simply because human beings need to structure a system in a nested way if they are to grasp it and be able to handle it properly. The important conclusion is that we can often find small objects as well as large objects (often subsystems) by understanding the concepts (vocabulary) that the user uses when referring to his or her system. If we are to develop, instead, a system representing something totally new, the lesson is that we have to invent a practical set of abstraction layers (levels) and that we should pay great attention to the concepts (vocabulary) we introduce.

## GROUPINGS OF CLASSES

The second type of subsystem we judged to be necessary [2] was grouping of classes. Reasons for grouping classes differ. Examples include the following:

- Classes are kept together because we use them together. They might make up a package of related classes dealing with a graphical user interface, a mathematics package, or something else that is distributed simultaneously.

- Classes are kept together because a development team has some particular expertise or simply because the members of the team are located at the same place.

There should be no inheritance between such groupings of classes. In the following we discuss how our two types of subsystems can be layered. We also discuss possible connections between groupings of classes and groupings of objects, why to keep them separate, and some other aspects.

## LAYERING OF GROUPS

Looking at Figure 5.6 we see two ellipses. The two ellipses might represent two major subsystems of a system. If we are looking at a particular application, we are looking at objects. The inner ellipse in each subsystem then represents a group of objects that supplies some basic functionality.

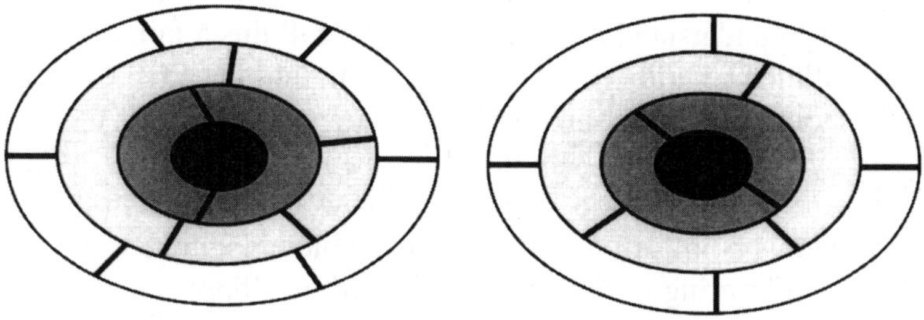

**Figure 5.6** Two ellipses representing two subsystems.

Let us assume that the system is a system used to supervise alarms coming from sensors in a building. Let us also assume that we want to trace what happens if we need the function: Make an updated report of the status of the sensors. (We call the function A1.) Figure 5.7 illustrates our example. Function A1 is implemented using functions supplied by the exterior layer. This layer should supply our operator with high-level, easy-to-use functions. The high-level functions are then implemented by using the functions on the next level. This continues until we reach low-level functions, probably close to our hardware. Note that even if we illustrate a message flow from a very high level to a low level here, it does not invalidate the point made earlier about the necessity of dividing an implementation into levels of abstraction. That is, a method should be implemented

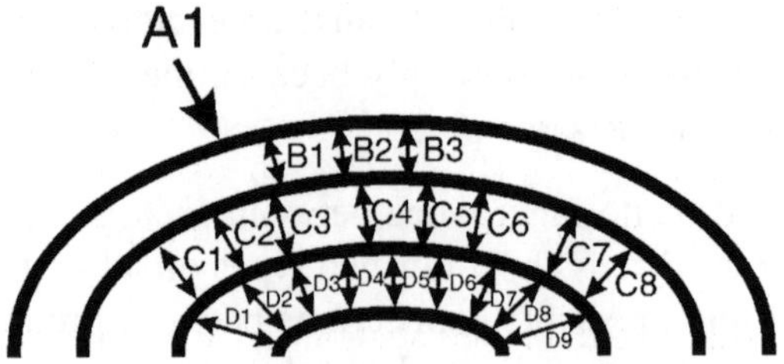


**Figure 5.7** A function, A1, implemented by calls to lower levels.

using only methods from the same level, methods from the next lower layer of subobjects, and/or other logic particular to the method. For example, when we reason about the implementation of A1, we should need to concern ourselves only with B1, B2, and B3. If we want to reason about, for example, B1, we should need to involve only C1 through C8 and possibly B2 or B3, but not any of D1 through D9. See also the discussion about message traces later in this chapter.

We might fail and need to involve C1 through C8 and D1 through D9 in order to understand A1. The reason we call this a failure is that we have not fulfilled solution A, using abstraction, introduced in Chapter 1.

The point here is that an object structure represented by the ellipses in Figure 5.7 must be built with this layering aspect in mind. Doing so in an intelligent way makes it easier to build new applications in the future. To illustrate this point, let us look at the example in Figure 5.8. In this figure we have a layering of objects, represented by ellipses and three functions A1, A2, and A3.

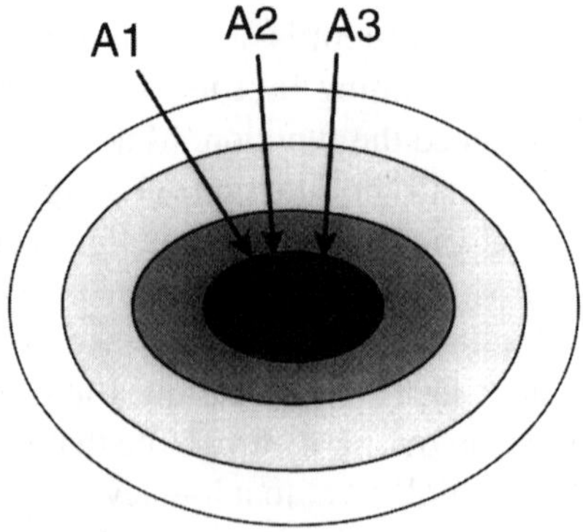


**Figure 5.8** Three functions implemented using low-level functions.

The figure illustrates that, to implement these functions, we have to define how the functions in one layer will use the functions in the next inner layer, all the way to the innermost ellipse. This is a typical situation where we are reinventing the wheel because all we have as a base, when we start implementing our functions, is the inner ellipse, representing basic functions.

If we are successful in our abstraction of company-specific functions, we might succeed in building a platform with some basic functions often used in our company. If this platform is available when we set out to implement the functions A1, A2, and A3, the situation would be like the one illustrated in Figure 5.9. This figure illustrates how the implementation becomes easier to make because we have more high-level functions available from the start. This is an advantageous situation because the implementation of the system will be speeded. (We can implement A1, A2, and A3 faster if we can skip implementing one level of ellipses.)

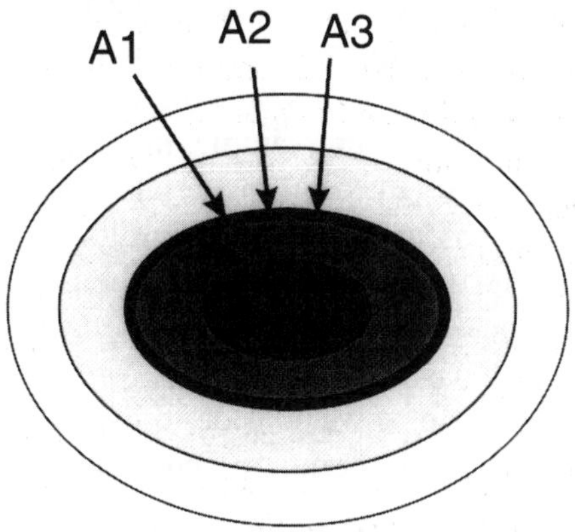


**Figure 5.9** Implementing A1, A2 and A3 using more high level functions.

We could also illustrate the layering of classes with ellipses. However, classes represent reusable components rather than object structures. Hence, we replace the ellipses in our illustrations by rectangles.

The innermost rectangle could represent the class structures supplied along with the compiler (see Figure 5.10). The next layer could represent class structures bought by the company from another supplier than the compiler vendor, etc. Again the basic idea is that a layer uses items, here classes, available in the closest inner layer. A good layering will make it possible to design new classes by using only the closest inner

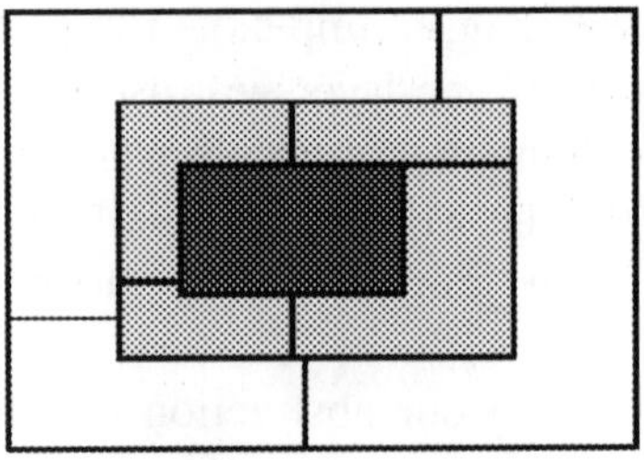

**Figure 5.10** Layering of classes.

layer of classes. If a class design needs access to something supplied by a layer that is closer to the center, the class should not access that layer directly but through the in-between layers. The reason for this is again solution A, introduced in Chapter 1. Classes in an inner layer should not use classes in an exterior layer. This layering of classes is something we find in other industrial fields. For example, modern house-building techniques do not start from scratch with materials such as nails and boards but with larger subsystems such as complete walls.

Let us further illustrate this point by looking at how we have succeeded in the electronics field in layering components. In Figure 5.11 we see class structures with basic electronic parts. We have various integrated circuits, resistors, and so on. If we consider this particular group, we find that they have many things in common and that we can easily describe

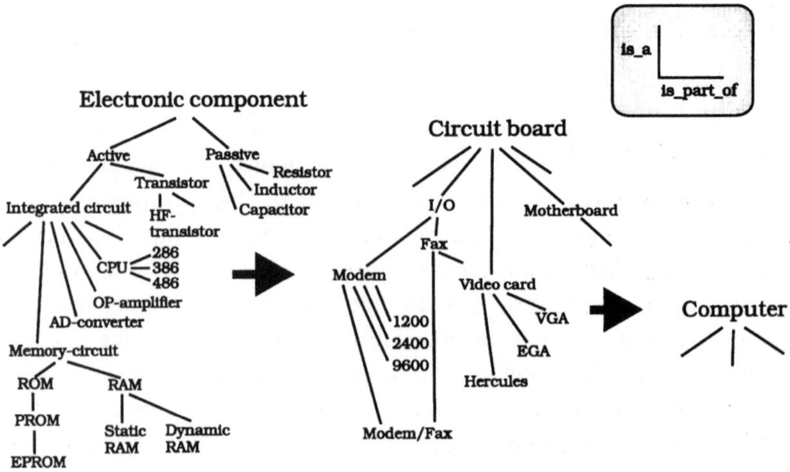


**Figure 5.11** Electronic components put into class structures.

them with a class structure, as we have done to the left in the figure. If we use this class structure when instantiating objects to build object structures, we can build video boards, sound boards, modems, motherboards, and so on. When we have built several different types of boards, we get a group of things that can actually better be described with a new class structure, (the middle class structure in the figure). Putting these higher-level items together will give us computers and other electronic equipment. When we have built several different types of computers, we might decide to describe them with a new class structure, too. Electronics has used this type of classification to good advantage. We continue this discussion in our last chapter, "The Future."

The point is that it is very natural to group classes (components) in class structures, but it is also natural to introduce a layering where "lower-level" class structures are used to implement higher-level types of class structures.

The actual layering of these components is not a simple issue, but a few rules are as follows:

- In each layer, the components belonging to the layer should be on the same level, having a similar character. For example, computers should not be mixed with resistors.
- The components should be usable together, easily joined to form larger things. This demands some type of standard for a common interface so that the components can talk with each other.

---

**Example**

TTL components have a common defined set of voltage levels, etc.

---

---

**Example**

The product, *New World Infrastructure*™ (Integrated Objects, Inc.), is a system with a set of objects. The objects can communicate with each other via a common dictionary. We can see the objects on a screen, and when we move an object on top of another object, the moved object can drop information into the other object using this common dictionary. This is a trivial example, but it illustrates nicely how the problem of "talking with each other" can be solved.

---

As our understanding of what really forms a set of workable components grows, we will see more examples of such groups of components.

### Connections Between Groupings

Look again at the figures with layers of objects and classes, respectively. Doing so might lead us to the conclusion that inner ellipses of object structures contain objects created by instantiating classes found in the inner rectangle. For example, it is probable that basic low-level functions, supplied by the object structure represented by the innermost ellipse, originate from one or several classes found in an innermost rectangle. Although such a connection is probable and is also a good idea, we cannot state it as a rule. There may, for example, be objects in outer layers of the ellipses that have been created from classes found in the innermost rectangle.

---

**Example**

A computer is assembled using circuit boards, but we probably also use lower-level components such as resistors and/or capacitors.

---

## TWO STRUCTURES—TWO MODELS

Grouping both objects and classes together is considered a poor idea because of experiences gained in [2]. There are many arguments for keeping object structures and class structures in separate models. We saw one important argument when we discussed the need for having two different types of subsystems, one type of subsystem for the groupings of objects and another type for the grouping of classes. Here are some other reasons:

- The building of our application and the building and improvement of our component storage have goals that are in conflict. A component (class) should be well-defined and well-documented, with a "wide"—complete—functionality. On the other hand, in a project building an application, we do not want to implement more functionality than is absolutely necessary for our application. In a project, we are often understaffed and unable to document our work enough.
- Separating the model we make of our application, the object structure, and the class structures facilitates our understanding of the application we try to build. The application should be the center of attention in a project, and connecting it too closely to our storage of components, our class structure(s), makes things more

complicated. Often we hear comments such as, "When we separated the is_a and the is_part_of information, things suddenly became clear to us."

- Separating object structures and class structures reduces the risk of simulating aggregation with multiple inheritance.

How can we implement an object-oriented organization? In Figure 5.12 we see one suggestion. We divide the responsibilities between those building the applications in projects and those building our storage of components. We put programmers who enhance current components and add new components in a product organization. The organization of a company in an object-oriented fashion is further discussed in Chapter 8.

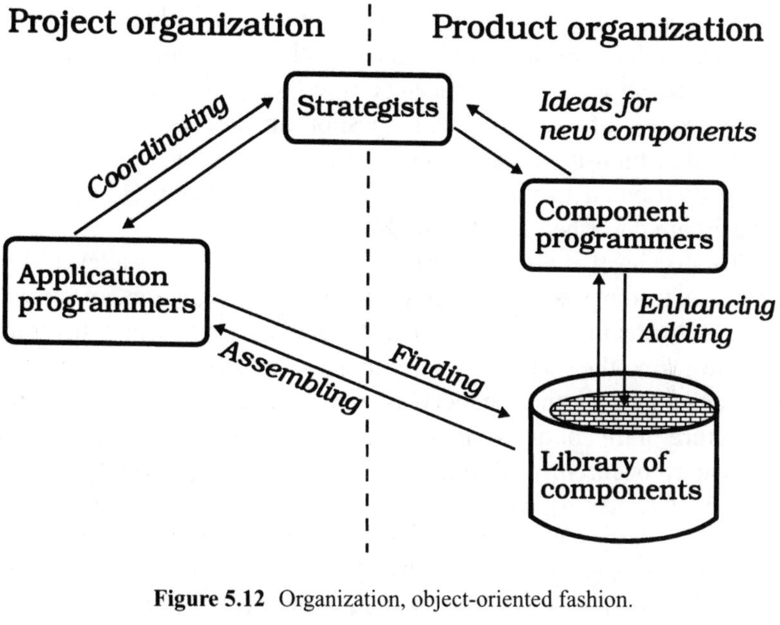


**Figure 5.12** Organization, object-oriented fashion.

## System Architecture

We mentioned in the beginning of this chapter that the most important factor for successful development of large systems was the ability to partition a system into subsystems. This is closely related to defining an architecture for a system, a vital step.

**Definition.** *Architecture* is the organizational structure of a system or component. [IEEE]

**Definition.** *Architectural design:* (1) The process of defining a collection of hardware and software components and their interfaces to establish the framework for the development of a computer system. (2) The result of the process in (1). [IEEE]

In the following, we restrict the discussion to groupings of objects. Defining a good architecture for a system is thus a most important factor, but how do we go about doing it? The architecture should be defined by a small team that is extremely good at doing abstractions. The top part of the architecture should be defined early. Thus, in the analysis phase we define the first subsystems and probably one more level of the architecture. If the system is very large, we have to develop one or possibly a few more levels. The architectural design is thus started in the analysis phase. The major consideration is how to divide our problem domain into part problem domains that can be understood and developed in parallel by different project groups. Interfaces between the subsystems we find during the process of answering this question are always in focus. If use-cases (and/or mini-uses) have been defined at the system level, they must now be distributed to the subsystems we have defined. (Mini-uses and use-cases are described in detail in the next section.)

The top level is thus the system, and the next level is a level of subsystems. A leading principle must be established for the rest of the architecture by the team doing the initial architectural description. This leading principle forms the rest of the layered structure of objects, the architecture. Basically, only three concepts have been introduced to describe an architecture in this book: system, subsystem, and system object. (System objects may occur in different variants, as described in "Basic Object Types" in Chapter 4). When we formulate a leading principle for the architectural design, it is a good idea to introduce names for the layers and the type of objects used in these layers. Because systems vary in usage and complexity and because company cultures vary between companies, no standard exists for this naming. Typical names for levels and objects, such as system level, system block, design block, and function block, are often not very revealing. The word block is often replaced with object if it refers to objects, such as function object. Better names are helpful for clarity. Note that the process is not strictly top-down, because it is often necessary to go down a couple of levels to gain in understanding. With the new understanding we get by doing this, we then go back up and refine our architectural design. For example, it is common that a trade-off between hardware and software must occur, which influences lower layers of our architectural design. See also, "Building with System Objects in Layers" in Chapter 4.

## DESCRIBING BEHAVIOR

In the first part of this chapter we discussed how to partition a system. In the rest of this chapter we will concentrate on how to describe and distribute the behavior of a system.

### Distributing Behavior

The behavior of a well-designed object should be evident from the methods belonging to the object. The key point is that *a method should be fully self-explanatory.* That is, the name of the method, its parameter list, and its context should be enough to explain what the method is all about and how it can be used. No further explanation should be necessary. This is admittedly an ideal situation, but it should be our goal, and it can often be achieved. This implies that we should be able to understand a method without knowledge about its implementation. Let us start our discussion by looking at the function/subfunction technique, which is a well-known abstraction technique. For example, a function with the name Measure_temperature can easily be comprehended without any other details than its name. We take the example one step further in Figure 5.13, where we show a general implementation of this function. Again, we can understand the steps done when the function is run without referring to any low-level details. We can understand it because Measure_temperature is partitioned into a well chosen set of subfunctions. The point is a simple

```
Function Measure_temperature(a_selected_sensor);
   Begin
   Init_sensor(a_selected_sensor);
   a_value := Get_sensor_value(a_selected_sensor);
   the_temperature :=
   Convert_value_to_Celsius(a_value, C1, C2, C3);
   Update_Coefficients(C1, C2, C3);
   Return the_temperature;
   End;
```

**Figure 5.13** A function is an example of an abstraction.

one but is repeatedly broken because the principle is hard to apply. Finding good abstractions takes time—something of which we are always short in a project.

We can apply this subfunction technique when we implement methods, too. If the object in question is a nested object, the method might be carried out by several subobjects contained in the object. That is, each subobject does a part of the implementation needed to make up the total implementation of the method.

When we distribute the behavior we should be *lazy*, which means that if something can be done at a lower level, we let the lower level do it. We thus always try to push away as much of the work as possible to lower levels. For example, if a method Method $_{\text{level } i}$ can transfer some part of its implementation to the next lower level, we design the method that way (see Figure 5.14). Thus, if something can be delegated, we delegate it.

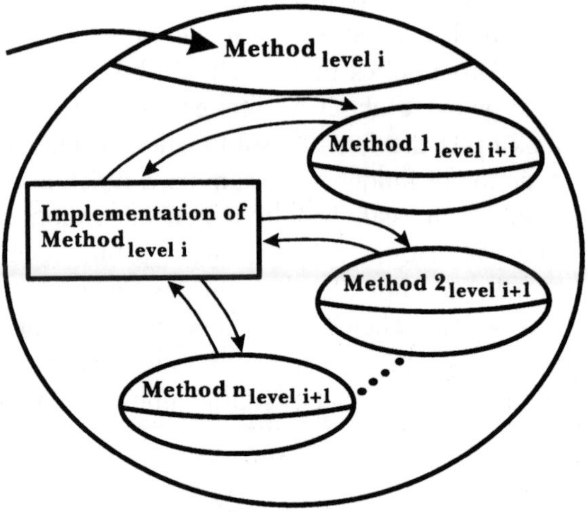


**Figure 5.14** We transfer as much as possible of an implementation to lower levels.

Note that if the behavior is one conceptual unit but is distributed among several objects, we might get a situation where making changes to this behavior is difficult. That is, if the behavior is one conceptual unit, it should probably be managed by one object and not be scattered all over the system. Such scattering is not atypical for object-oriented systems built by beginners, however. The idea of distribution of behavior in a system is good design, but it does *not* mean that the *responsibility* for carrying out a well-defined task must—or should be—distributed over a system.

---

**Example**

A weather reporting unit has several measurement sensors. The task of *collecting values* regularly from these sensors should then be given to a managing object rather than distributed among different objects, such as the drivers for the individual sensors.

---

The key is—as always—to formulate a well-defined purpose for each object.

The highest level on which we can describe the behavior of a system is when we describe how a user can use a system. We will next look at how we can do this.

## Taking the Viewpoint of the User

Why is the viewpoint of the user so important? Simply stated, it is important because in the final analysis, the business is what the user says it is. Viewing the system from the user's perspective and using his or her words, definitions and understandings of the meaning of those words significantly increase our chances of building the system the user needs.

A system may have only one main object but more commonly a system can be divided into a few main objects. The first methods that we find are different ways of using the system and/or its main subsystems. The term we use for one of these high-level methods is *mini-use* (see Figure 5.15).

It should be possible to reason about these high-level methods without going into any details concerning the objects of the system. In Figure 5.16 we illustrate this idea. Mini-use 1 is thus carried out by using

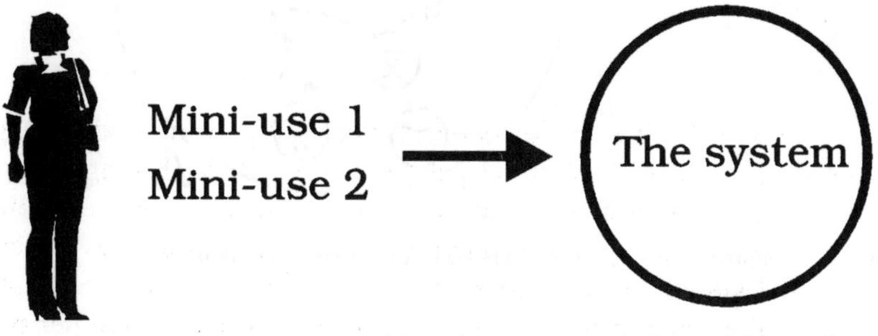


**Figure 5.15** A mini-use is one well-defined way of using a system.

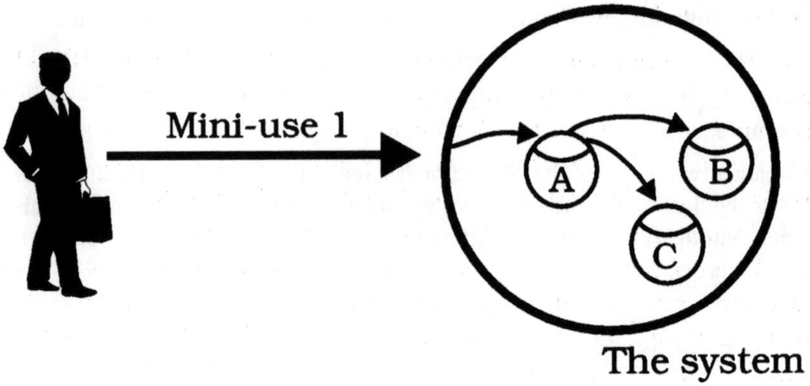


**Figure 5.16** A mini-use is implemented by objects.

methods supplied by subsystems (or objects) A, B, and C only. The subsystem character implies that when we start to implement A that implementation can be done in parallel with the implementation of B, and C.

A can probably be divided into objects too (see Figure 5.17), such as X, Y, Z, and W, which then represent smaller subsystems (or objects). Note that it should be possible to reason about the method A_method_1 without referring to details found inside X, Y, Z, and/or W. (The preceding discussion presupposes that subsystems (objects) are encapsulated.)

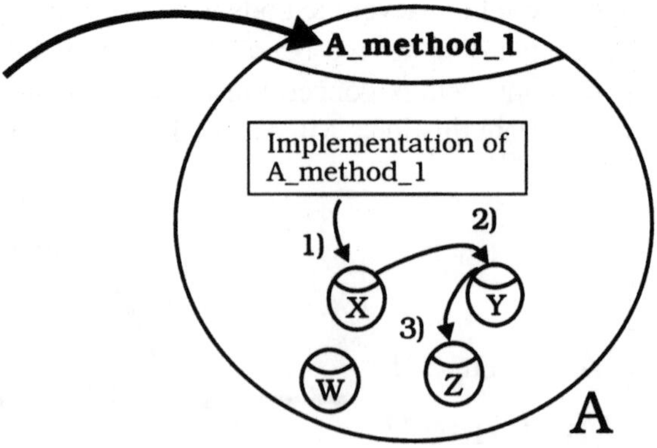


**Figure 5.17** On lower levels we refer to methods and not to mini-uses.

***Mini-uses and Use-cases***

A mini-use is one well-defined way of using a system described in a user-friendly way. An example of a mini-use is pressing the Play button on a videocassette recorder. Other examples of mini-uses are those we see when we start a Windows program. In Figure 5.18 we see a menu bar with words such as File, Edit, and Tools. These words represent mini-uses.

Figure 5.19 illustrates that it is common that we can expand a mini-use. In the figure the mini-use File has the sub-mini-uses, New, Open, Save, etc. That is, a mini-use is often made up of a group of smaller mini-uses, sub-mini-uses. We seldom use the term sub-mini-use; instead, we refer to a sub-mini-use as a mini-use. Drawing windows with menus is in fact a good way of getting a grip on how use-cases should be implemented. If we describe the system's interface with menus, our mini-uses will simply be the commands we put in the menus. We update our description of a mini-use and give the following definition.

**Definition.** A *mini-use* is one well-defined way, or set of ways, of using a system that is delivered to the customer and is described in user-friendly terms. When an application is delivered, the mini-use is available in the user interface.

A mini-use is like a method, except that it can be requested by a user outside the system, whereas a method is a service that can be called only

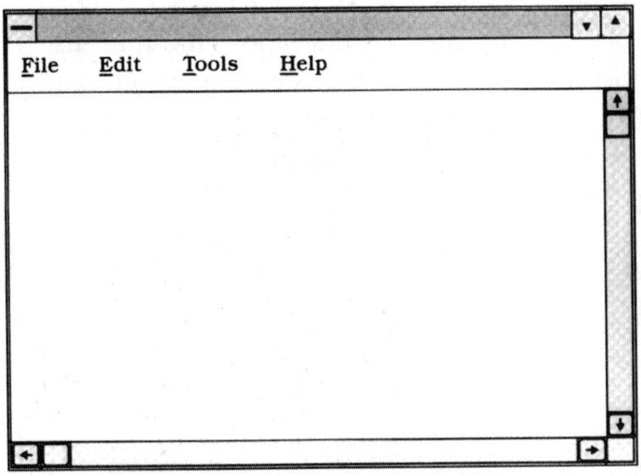


**Figure 5.18** Examples of mini-uses.

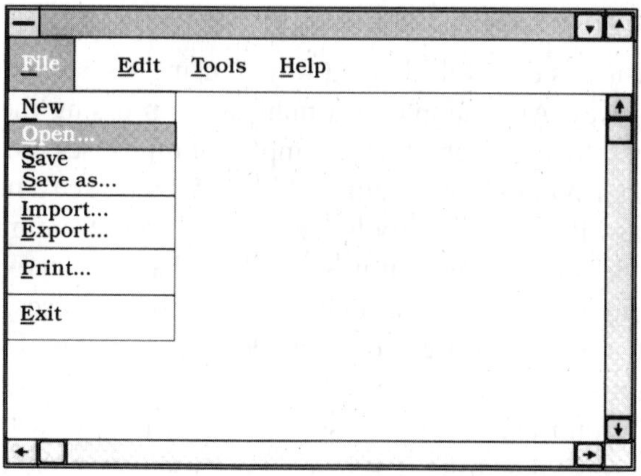


**Figure 5.19** A mini-use can represent a group of smaller mini-uses.

from another executing object. Main differences between a mini-use and a function found in a non-object-oriented requirements specification are that the mini-use is always connected to a specific actor and that the mini-use can always be found in the user interface. (The concept actor was described in Chapter 4 as a well-defined role for a user or a group of users.)

A *use-case* specifies the interactions that take place between a user and a system in order to accomplish some well-defined, typical work. We implement a use-case by calling one or several mini-uses (the same ones or different ones). We call them in sequence, and when we have called them, we have accomplished a well-defined work. For example, if we want to Edit an existing file, we first apply the mini-use Open file. We then call mini-uses such as Copy, Paste, and so on. A use-case such as "Edit an existing file" is typically ended by calling a mini-use such as Save or Exit. A mini-use is a use-case, but typically a simple one. We give the following definition.

**Definition.** A *use-case* is a sequence of mini-uses performed to achieve some typical work. A special case of a use-case is the carrying out of one mini-use.

To involve a user in the process of defining what a system will do is not a new idea. The interesting aspect of the mini-use, the actor, and the use-case concepts is that they give us tools for involving the user in a concrete way. It is one thing to talk about involving the user and quite another to have well-established concepts and procedures for how to do this.

The relation between mini-uses, use-cases, and the total functionality of a system is illustrated in Figure 5.20. In the figure we let each dot represent a mini-use. Basically, all the dots together make up the total functionality of a system that is delivered to a customer. In the figure, we also see examples of use-cases. A use-case is made up of calling a set of mini-uses. Note that some use-cases might use the same mini-uses and that not all mini-uses need be included in a use-case (as we have defined use-cases). When we describe use-cases we should begin with normal examples rather than unusual examples.

The difference between a mini-use and a use-case lies both in their purpose and in their normal complexity. The purpose of a mini-use is to describe a single service that a system can deliver *directly* to a user. The set of all mini-uses defines the functionality of a system. The purpose of a use-case is to drive the software development process. In particular they are central to finding the mini-uses of a system. Use-cases are also the starting point for defining test-cases used later in the development process. A mini-use is directly connected to some service that the system delivers, for example, by pushing a button. This is seldom true for a use-case because it typically involves the use of several mini-uses. A use-case is thus also regularly more complex than a mini-use. Both mini-uses and use-cases are descriptions of how a system is used, in terms the end user can understand. Our definition of the concept of use-case is very close to how Ivar Jacobson defines it in his book *Object-Oriented Software Engineering* [27]. However, we use the idea mainly for finding mini-uses and as a basis for constructing test cases. Note also that we let the set of all

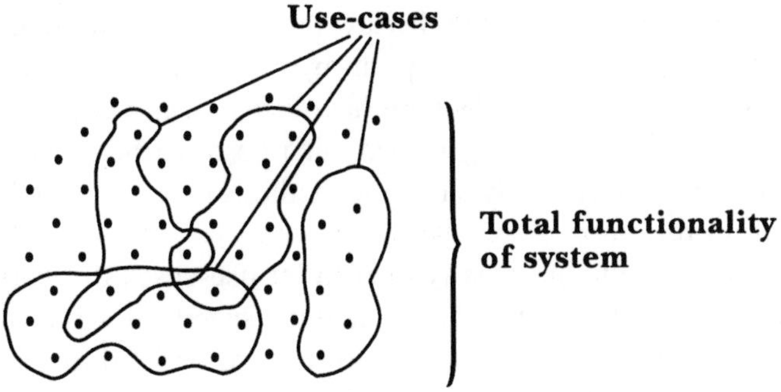


**Figure 5.20** Relation between a systems total functionality, mini-uses and use-cases.

mini-uses define the total functionality of the system and not the set of all use-cases, as Ivar Jacobson suggests [27]. We only need to include use-cases (in a requirements specification) if their functionality is not clear from the mini-uses. Mini-uses could be said to make the software process more requirements-oriented because they help us relate use-cases to a requirements specification.

When we start to describe a mini-use or a use-case, it is a good idea to describe it using ordinary text. The text should be written so that it can easily be understood by a user. A user preferably writes the first draft of a *usage scenario* himself or herself. Often a (usage) scenario is a description of the specific interactions we have with a machine in order to do something such as insert a card, type in a secret code, type in an amount of money, and so on. In this case we can view a usage scenario to be the same thing as a use-case. However, if we look at the literature, it is evident that usage scenario is a less well-defined concept than use-case. We thus make the following more general definition of this concept.

**Definition.** A *usage scenario* is a user-friendly text describing how a system is used by a user or a group of similar users. A use-case is a special case of a usage scenario.

A usage scenario is thus normally less exact than a use-case and may leave out details or explain things in a less sequential way than a use-case. A usage scenario may also be a text that summarizes several different ways of using a system. Writing a usage scenario is often the first step when we want to define use-case(s), but it can also (as in Chapters 6 and 7) be used as an alternative to use-cases.

The next step is to develop the text into something more structured, such as pseudocode or text in a point-by-point fashion. A use-case is described with pseudocode, showing how different mini-uses are called. The implementation of a mini-use can also be described using pseudocode. In this case we typically show the methods that are called to implement the mini-use.

Finally, even though it is typical to let use-cases drive an object-oriented development process, there is nothing specifically object-oriented about use-cases as such. That is, use-cases could be used to drive a non-object-oriented development process too. However, use-cases work very well with an object-oriented approach, which is the reason we have discussed them in some detail here.

## Example: A Videocassette Recorder

We meet mini-uses every day. For example, when we buy a VCR (Videocassette Recorder), we are presented with several mini-uses (see Figure 5.21):

- Play
- Fast forward (Fwd)
- Fast rewind (Rw)
- Record
- Stop
- Pause
- Program
- Change the channel

When we start to sketch a model of the VCR, we look for parts of the VCR that display a fully self-contained character. We might end up with parts like these:

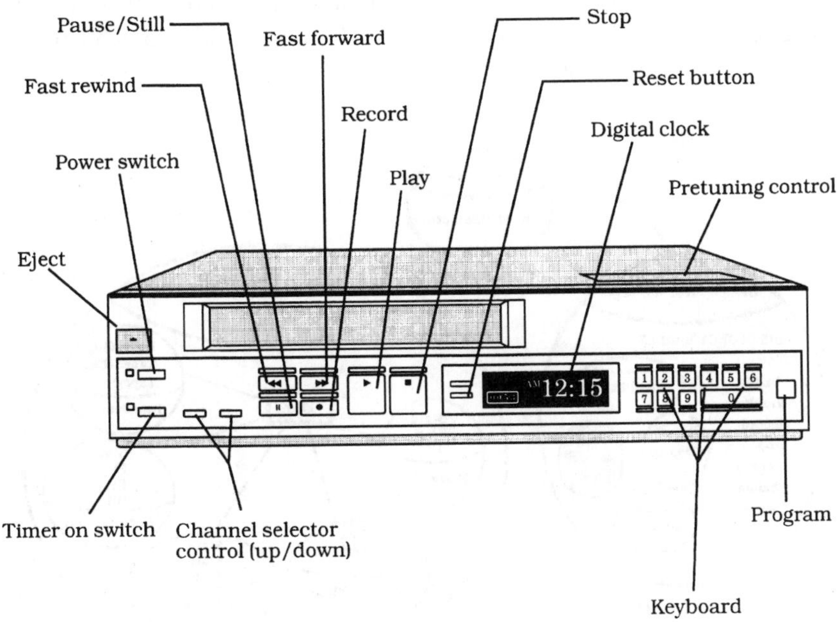


**Figure 5.21** A VCR.

- Display
- Keyboard
- VideoButtons
- TapeController
- HeadOnRelay
- TapeSensor
- PlayMotor
- FwdWindingMotor
- RwWindingMotor
- RecordData
- ChannelSelector

Objects such as Display, Keyboard, Videobuttons, TapeSensor, PlayMotor, FwdWindingMotor, RwWindingMotor, and ChannelSelector were found because they are directly related to hardware parts (see Figure 5.22).

TapeController and HeadOnRelay are objects designed to manage the VCR and the VCR heads, respectively. When the VCR is in automatic recording mode, the information regulating starting and stopping the recording is stored in RecordData. Note that we have chosen these objects to be self-contained microworlds. Each such microworld is capable of ful-

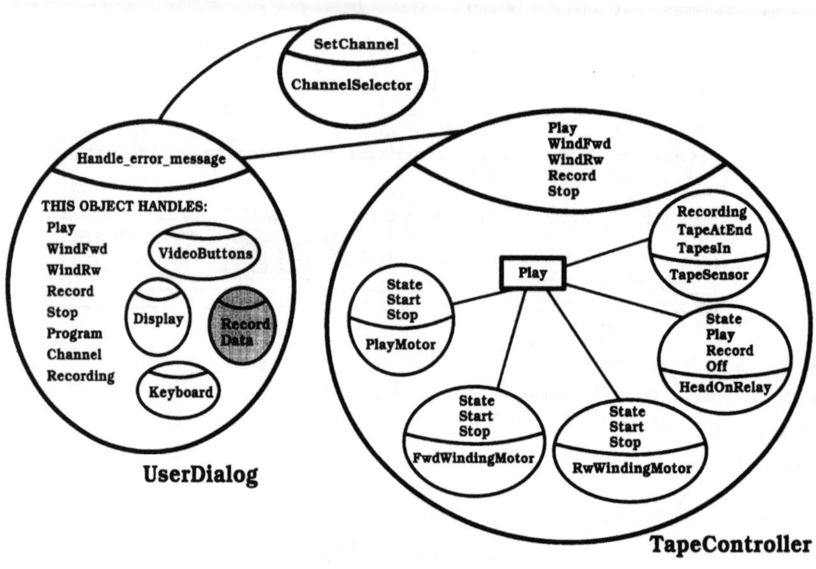


**Figure 5.22** Sketch of possible objects for a video system.

filling its role and purpose. This self-contained, self-explanatory character is found in all well-chosen methods, objects, and subsystems. It is their most important property if they are to be independent of each other. For example, we can grasp the intention of the mini-use Play without knowing anything about its implementation details.

The ChannelSelector, UserDialog, and TapeController could be our subsystems. It is a good idea to design the system using subsystems even if we do not need to divide the software into smaller subsystems for parallel implementation.

The UserDialog handles the dialog with the user. The method Handle_error_message is called by ChannelSelector or TapeController if they need to show a message to the user.

An example of a use-case is

- Rewind (to beginning of tape)
- Play
- Stop

Another example of a use-case is to use the mini-use Program to program the time and channel for a recording. We sketch this use-case:

- Program (pressing the Program button)
- Press numerical keys (Keyboard) to enter time for start of recording
- Program
- Press numerical keys to enter time for end of recording
- Program
- Press numerical keys to select channel
- Program

Implementing a method or a mini-use should be possible simply by using the next level of (sub)objects. For example, the method

```
TapeController.Play;
```

can be implemented by using the subobjects of TapeController.

To illustrate this fundamental idea, let us sketch how the method could be implemented with text in a point-by-point fashion for TapeController.Play:

- Check that TapeSensor.TapesIn = TRUE
- Check that HeadOnRelay.State = Idle
- Check that FwdWindingMotor.State = Off

- Check that RwWindingMotor.State = Off
- IF the conditions above are satisfied, then call HeadOnRelay.Play and PlayMotor.Start ELSE do nothing.
- Continue with play until we reach the end of the tape (TapeSensor.TapeAtEnd = TRUE) or TapeController.Stop is called.

The same principle applies to the next level of objects:

- The methods supplied by subobjects can themselves be understood without their internal details being referred to. For example, the method HeadOnRelay.Play is understood to set the heads in the VCR so that Play can be started. We understand this method without knowing the exact setup of heads in the VCR or how they are supposed to move.
- When we want to implement a method, it is enough to use the next level of subobjects. We need "explode" an object only one level at a time.

Of course, when a high-level mini-use is being run, it will involve methods at both high and low levels. The point is that we as designers should need to concern ourselves only with one level of objects at each stage of the design.

### Message Traces

A message often starts other messages. We are sometimes interested in following these messages through a system. The drawing made of this is sometimes called a *message trace* [25] or a *message thread* [24]. The process may also be referred to as drawing an *interaction diagram* [27]. When we try to set up such a message trace, it is a good idea to use a base case that corresponds to the normal effect of the initial message. When the base case is understood, we can try to trace messages considering more unusual cases.

Using this technique, we draw vertical lines to represent the objects. Horizontal lines are then drawn to show how the objects call each other.

If we employ abstraction techniques in which parts of the interaction sequences are grouped together, we get a figure like Figure 5.23. That is, using the technique of building a function using subfunctions, we summarize what occurs between (1) and (2), not showing every detail. This approach is much better than the approach shown in Figure 5.24, which is an example of a situation where we have shown too many details. The first message trace is better because it adheres to solution A, introduced in

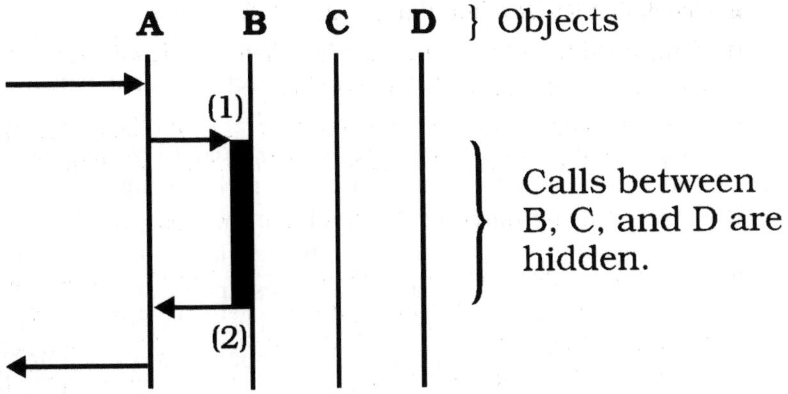


**Figure 5.23** A message trace.

Chapter 1. Solution A states that we should use abstraction to reduce the number of things we have to deal with simultaneously. This is exactly what we do in the first message trace. If we accept solution A in Chapter 1, we would not want to or need to show the complete calling sequence. Instead, our primary ambition would be to hide details. Note that the examples are small and only illustrate the principle. In real projects the message traces could be much larger than the ones shown in our figures.

In the extreme case a method can be understood only by using a message trace showing low level details. Unfortunately, this "extreme case" is more the rule than an exception with many object-oriented

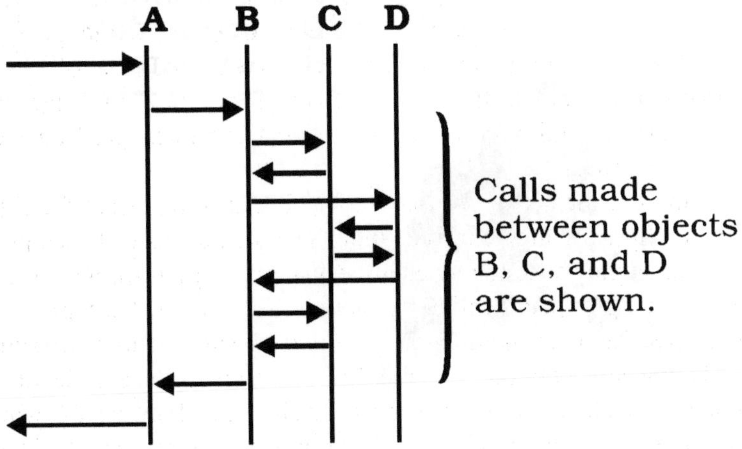


**Figure 5.24** A message trace showing too many details.

modeling techniques. This situation arises when methods belonging to sub-objects can be understood only by referring to their implementation—a typical mistake. It is not easy to select pertinent names for methods or a suitable level of abstraction that reveals appropriate details but hides what is irrelevant. That is, the need to look at low-level details arises because we cannot understand what is happening when the method is called, using only the top-level information (method name and parameter list) plus context. We have then failed to give methods a proper level of responsibility, making it necessary to show details at high and low levels *simultaneously.* The advantage, however, of applying abstraction is so significant that great effort should always be put into designing a proper leveling. The starting point for finding this leveling of methods is to give each object a well-defined role with a prescribed level of responsibility.

If we look at typical everyday situations, we often find that responsibilities are divided in a leveled way. An example that illustrates how leveling of details makes it possible for someone to understand and handle an everyday situation is the case of a person who wants to book a ticket (see Figure 5.25). All the customer needs to know about the complex reality that will eventually get him or her where he or she wants to go are where to start the trip, the destination, the departure and return times, and the

**Figure 5.25** Buying a ticket.

maximum price he or she wants to pay. The booking agent has to deal with these details as well as with some more information.

However, none of the persons involved must ever know *every* detail of what is happening on the lowest (most detailed) level. The same principle must be applied to the complex systems we build today if we are to be able to handle them successfully.

Software development methods that need detailed message traces are deficient simply because they do not use adequate abstraction techniques when deciding the interface/responsibilities of objects. Or, if we have tried to use good abstraction techniques but got message traces that can be understood or used only if they include several levels of objects, then we have simply failed to find good interfaces. (See earlier chapters for a discussion of interfaces.)

### Making Time Estimations

This topic is included as an illustration of how behavior can be distributed in a system. If a system is modeled and implemented in an object-oriented way, as outlined in this book, then making time estimations is simple—at least in theory. A common way to make time estimations is to use a message trace. In Figure 5.26 we see an example. Method_1 is implemented by some code in the system. This code probably calls methods in other objects. Let us say that three objects are called when Method_1 executes: A, B, and C. That is, when Method_1 executes, it makes one call each to, for example, A.A2_method, C.C1_method, and B.B2_method. The time needed to execute Method_1 can then be calculated as the sum of the following:

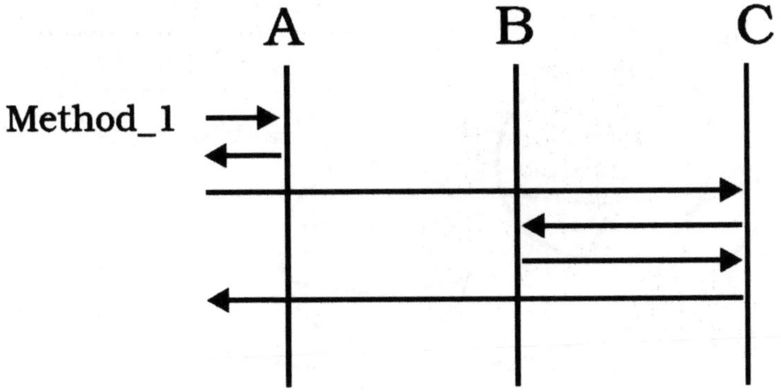


**Figure 5.26** Message traces can be of help when we make time estimations.

$T_{logic}$ = Time needed to execute the main logic of the method itself
$T_{call\ a}$ = Time needed to handle the call to A
$T_{call\ b}$ = Time needed to handle the call to B
$T_{call\ c}$ = Time needed to handle the call to C
$T_{a2}$, $T_{b2}$, and $T_{c1}$ = Time needed to execute the methods in our objects A, B, and C, respectively

If we have a very efficient implementation of message calls, the times $T_{call\ a}$, $T_{call\ b}$ and $T_{call\ c}$ might be insignificant. If this is not the case, we get the following equation:

$$T_{method\_1} = T_{logic} + T_{call\ a} + T_{call\ b} + T_{call\ c} + T_{a2} + T_{b2} + T_{c1}$$

If we use a figure of an object-oriented model, the calculation is even easier to understand (see Figure 5.27).

To trace message-passing in a system can be very difficult if we do not force a nested structure on our object structure. In short, this nested structure should ensure that to understand the implementation of a method, we need only look at the subobjects of an object and not the subsubobjects, etc. Note that we are here referring to the implementation. The *use* of a method should be understood without looking at the implementation. This is a very important design goal.

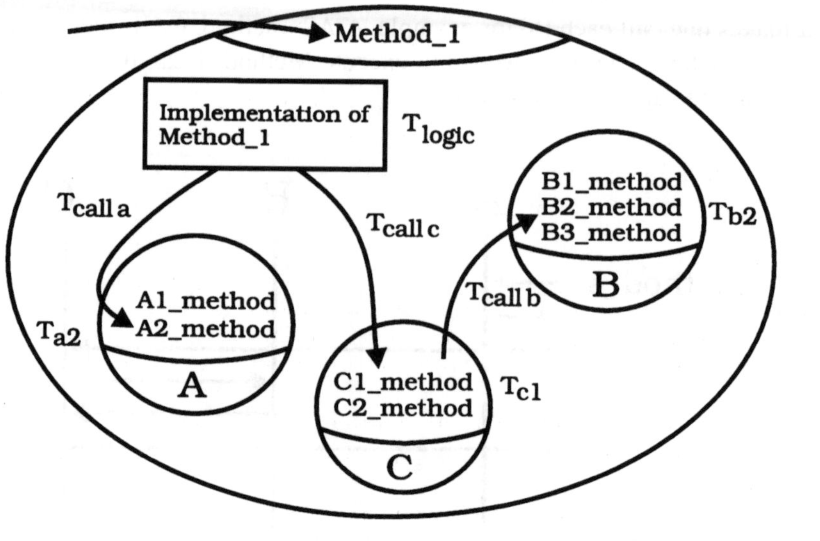


**Figure 5.27** Making time estimations is reduced to adding the time needed to perform each activity.

If we want to estimate the time a certain method or (mini-use) will need, we can simply trace its execution through the system, adding times as we follow the execution (see Figure 5.27). In the figure we assume that a mini-use or method is possible to comprehend by going down *one* level in the object structure. Thus, we must add only the time needed to perform each thing done when Method_1 executes to compute the total time Method_1 takes when it executes.

Instead of showing all the details of the control flow, we thus summarize it by ignoring what happens at lower levels (that is, the control flow inside the subobjects). In this way the message hierarchy and the control flow are tightly connected with the object hierarchy (the nested object structure). In the author's opinion this is a good way to design, although it might lead to complications. One complication is that we might get a slow system. A possible way to remedy this is given later in this subchapter.

If objects A, B, and C contain one task each, we get a system with objects executing in parallel. A detailed discussion of real-time[*] issues is beyond the scope of this book, but we will point out a few details:

- The object-oriented paradigm is very natural for modeling concurrent systems.[†]Processes in distributed systems communicate by sending messages.[‡] The object-oriented paradigm can be used directly to map this communication. Note that the notion of object-oriented message passing combines information transfer into a single construct, whereas other models of concurrency, such as semaphores do not.[§]
- Objects can be specified as asynchronous or synchronous,[‖] that is, in terms of whether the object may continue processing after it has sent or received a message.

---

*Consider a system composed of two processes, one process inside the computer and the other one outside the computer. Real-time systems are systems in which there are time requirements on the processing inside the computer. That is, if the processing inside the computer is unable to give a correct reaction inside the time requirement, then the processing outside the computer fails.

†A concurrent system has two or more processes executing in parallel.

‡Note that this "message" is a real message and not the object-oriented message. However, the analogy between them is very strong.

§A semaphore is a shared variable used to synchronize concurrent processes by indicating whether an action has been completed or an event has occurred. [IEEE]

‖No special notation is given in this book for this concept, but it can be indicated by writing the word synchronous or asynchronous in the object.

Returning to the preceding equation and generalizing the discussion, we get the equation

$$T_{\text{method\_X}} = T_{\text{logic}} + \text{Sum of } (T_{\text{first method}} \text{ to } T_{\text{last method}}) + T_{\text{adm calls}}$$

where

$T_{\text{method\_X}}$ = time needed to execute the method "X"
$T_{\text{logic}}$ = time needed for carrying out the main logic not done in subobjects
$T_{\text{first method}}$ = time to execute the first method called
$T_{\text{last method}}$ = time to execute the last method called
$T_{\text{adm calls}}$ = time for administrating all calls to methods

If the times for $T_{\text{first method}}$ to $T_{\text{last method}}$ have not already been calculated, we can repeat the process in a recursive way. That is, when we want to compute the time needed to execute, for example, A2_method, we open the object, A, find its subobjects, and repeat the process just outlined.

If the time needed to execute a method of a certain object depends on the workload of other objects, we get a much trickier situation. If objects A, B, and C are active—that is, with a task—we cannot compute the time their methods will need unless we can be sure they will be given a prescribed part of available resources. It would be easiest to give them top-priority. This would ensure that objects A, B, and C always got 100% of the available resources when a method of theirs was called. However, this guarantee might be impossible. The second best thing is to make sure they will get at least some known minimum percentage of the available resources, for example, by using some time-sharing algorithm. However, time-sharing introduces an administrative load, reducing the total sum of available resources. We get the following equation:

$$R_a = (R_{tot} - R_{adm})P_{\%}$$

where

$R_a$ = resources available for an object
$R_{tot}$ = total amounts of resources
$R_{adm}$ = resources used for administrating the time sharing
$P_{\%}$ = percentage of resources made available for the object executing the method

The new compensated times for the execution of methods are then found using the following equation:

$$T_{\text{new}} = T_{100\%} * R_a/R_{tot}$$

where

$T_{new}$ = the new compensated time needed to use the method
$T_{100\%}$ = time needed to execute the method if its object has 100% of the available resources ($R_a = R_{tot}$)

If $R_a$ is a minimum of available resources, $T_{new}$ is a worst-case estimation.

If an object B has methods that are too slow, we can break up object B into its parts. Figure 5.28 shows the idea. In part (a) we find a caller invoking the method B.Slow_method. If this method is too slow, we study how it is implemented. The next level of objects is illustrated in part (b). With the knowledge we gain in this study, we can probably implement a faster method. For example, we might find that the method invocation of the method attached to Z is unnecessary. We can then either implement a new method, Not_so_slow_method, that does not call Z (and attach this to B), or we can break up B. Depending on the program logic, it might be

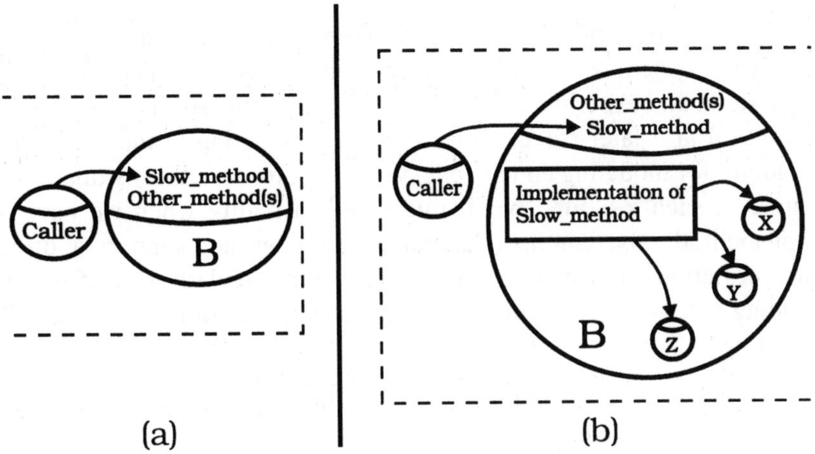


**Figure 5.28** To speed up a method, we need to study its implementation.

possible to speed up the execution even more. For example, if the main task of the logic of Slow_method is to call the objects in a certain order, it is easy to put this logic in the caller instead. That is, an advantage of breaking up B is that we can skip some administrative message-forwarding logic (see Figure 5.29). We gain a little time by letting the caller call the relevant objects directly. Our caller also has a better control of the situation, which might be an advantage if we are doing something that is part of a critical real-time system.

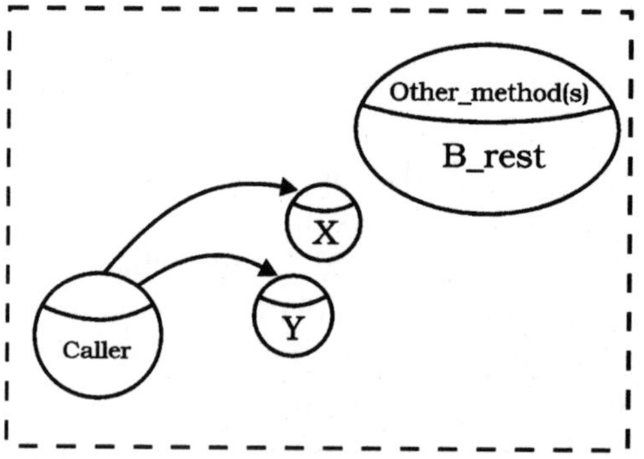


**Figure 5.29** Calling objects directly is one way to make a method execute faster.

Using a pure object-oriented modeling approach as a first attempt to model a system is often a good idea. It increases our understanding of the system, and experience shows that the real-time aspects can often be dealt with at a later stage. Object-oriented modeling is thus a natural paradigm for modeling concurrent systems. In theory, time estimation is simple in such a model, but it might fail in reality when we have to implement the system in a language that does not support a direct transformation from model to code. This is particularly true if we are building a real-time system where our demands on timing are high. To sum it up:

- It is fairly easy in theory to make time estimations in an object-oriented model.
- One way of speeding up a method is to break up an object into its subobjects and use the knowledge of how methods call each other to implement a faster method.

## SUMMARY

- We need two types of subsystems when we develop applications: groupings of objects and groupings of classes. The main reason for a subsystem is that it helps us develop parts of a system in a parallel fashion.
- Groupings of objects represent our applications.
- Groupings of classes represent our library of reusable components.
- Object structures and class structures should be kept in separate models.
- Objects, methods, and subsystems should display a self-explanatory and self-contained character.
- Mini-uses and use-cases are descriptions of how a system can be used expressed in user-friendly terms.
- A mini-use is a service that a system delivers. A mini-use may also represent a group of (sub)mini-uses. The total sum of all mini-uses is basically equal to the functionality a system can deliver.
- Use-cases are examples of how one or several mini-uses are applied to carry out some typical work.
- A usage scenario is a description of how a user or a group of similar users use a system. It may be less exact than a use-case, may describe several use-cases, and does not have to include all details, such as what mini-uses will be involved.
- Object-oriented modeling is a natural paradigm for modeling concurrent systems. Time estimation is simple in such a model, but it might fail in reality when we have to implement the system in a language that does not support a direct transformation from model to code.

# 6

# A Weather Data Acquisition System

## *Example One*

> *Even when the laws have been written down, they ought not always to remain unaltered.*
>
> —Aristotle

## INTRODUCTION

In order to sense the ideas outlined in this book, we sketch how a system used for collecting and processing weather data can be modeled. Note that it is impossible to describe a system such as the one outlined in this chapter in all its details, which is also not the intention of this chapter. The idea with this and Chapter 7 is to apply object-oriented concepts introduced in this book and to train the reader in object-oriented thinking. Implementation details are left out whenever possible.

The system was modeled in one of the investigations [3] mentioned in the preface. The idea with this investigation was to evaluate the ease with which Ada and C++, respectively, could be used to implement an object-oriented model.

First we describe the system in general terms; then we add more details to our model until we reach pseudocode for some main mini-uses and methods. As we continue, we discuss various points about our model; in the end we add a few words concerning the implementation of a system in Ada or C++. The notation we use is described in Appendix 2, and the object-oriented modeling approach we use is described in Appendix 3. Thus, reading Appendices 2 and 3 before reading this chapter is recommended. Note, however, that we do not strictly follow the approach described in Appendix 3.

### Naming Conventions

We have adopted the following practices in Chapters 6 and 7:

- The context determines whether a name refers to a class or an object.
- However, when modeling, we normally prefix the name of a class with a C. If we are referring to some object created from this class, we leave out the prefix. If we want to point out that we are referring to an object, we prefix the name with an A_, a_, An_, an_, The_, or the_. Names starting with a_, an_, and the_ may also indicate normal variables.

For example, CError_report is a class name but Error_report and An_Error_report refer to objects created from class CError_report.

Note also that we have not implemented any initializing methods or constructors in Chapters 6 and 7 because they are viewed as a coding issue. Attributes and objects are thus assumed to be properly initialized, even if the pseudocode does not indicate this explicitly.

## PROBLEM DESCRIPTION

### Context Picture

The system consists of two basic parts, the main (central) part that stores and processes data about the weather and several weather data collecting units. We call these two parts Main_central and Weather_station(s). The system is illustrated in Figure 6.1.

### Usage Scenario

Weather_stations report measured data via radio, satellite, or telephone to the Main_central, where the data are processed. Weather_stations collect measurements concerning

- Air temperature and pressure
- Sun hours per day
- Wind speed and direction

A Weather_station need not contain sensors for all these types of measurements and consequently need not report data for the same types of measurements as another Weather_station. The measurements are stored in the Weather_stations in some simple form, and they are reported periodically to the Main_central. Measurements can also be sent to the Main_central if the Main_central requests this or initiated manually by a local serviceperson at a Weather_station. A Weather_station will also send

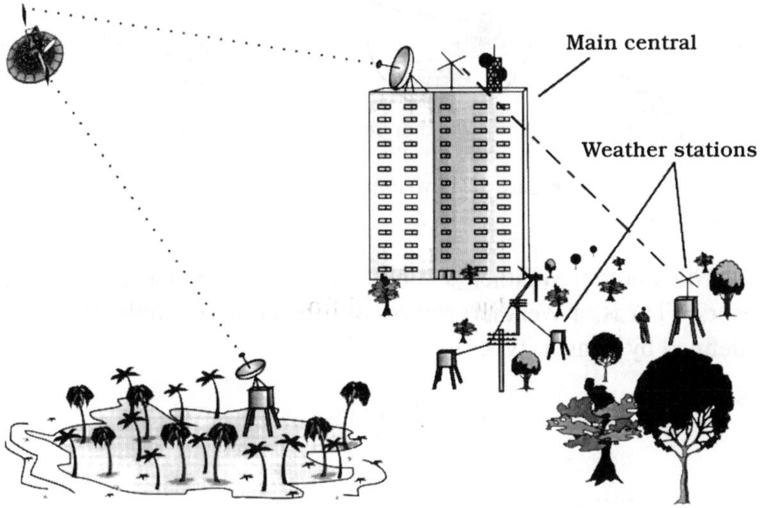


**Figure 6.1** The system we model in this chapter shown in the form of a context picture.

error reports to the Main_central on request from the Main_central or a local serviceperson. The local serviceperson must also be able to update parameters for the sensors via a simple user interface available at the Weather_station. Note that in the rest of this chapter we normally use the singular for Weather_station even though the system contains many weather stations.

This is the main outline of the system. We should, perhaps, also mention that a local serviceperson is not stationed at a Weather_station. He or she will just be there when needed.

## Two Important Information Objects

The information transmitted from a Weather_station to the Main_central is modeled with two classes: CWeather_report and CError_report. Two examples of objects from these classes are shown in Figure 6.2. An object of class CWeather_report contains CSample objects. A Sample is a list of measurements. Each CSample object contains measurements for each sensor at a Weather_station. Because we may equip a Weather_station with different sets of sensors, a Sample from one Weather_station need not contain the same set of measurements as a

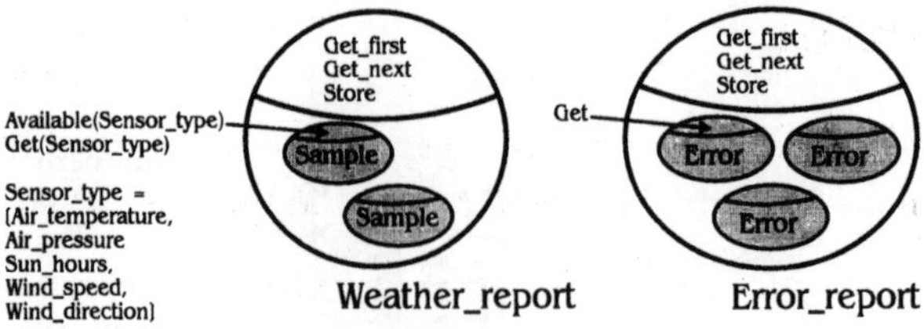


**Figure 6.2** Two information objects.

Sample from another Weather_station. Sensor_type defines allowed types of sensors. That is, a Weather_station may be equipped only with sensor types defined by Sensor_type:

```
Sensor_type =
        [Air_temperature,
        Air_pressure,
        Sun_hours,
        Wind_speed,
        Wind_direction];
```

We use Sensor_type to extract a measurement from a particular sensor. For example,

```
A_sample.Get(Sun_hours);
```

returns the measurement for sun hours from the sample A_sample. At this stage the actual structure of the measurement is not defined, but it could be an array of measurements collected during the last 24 hours. If we want to know if a Sample contains a particular type of measurement, we can make the following call:

```
A_sample.Available(//Sensor_type);
```

For example:

```
A_sample.Available(Sun_hours);
```

will return one of the following values:

```
[Is_available, Is_not_available, Is_not_installed]
```

These values tell us whether measurements for the sun hour sensor are available, measurements are not available, or the sensor has not even been installed.

An object of class CError_report object contains a set of CError objects. A CError object describes one error. The classes CWeather_report and CError_report have much design in common.

## A FIRST MODEL

One advantage of modeling in an object-oriented fashion is that it is easier to run in an iterative way. We can, even at this early point, sketch the basic outlines of the system (see Figure 6.3).

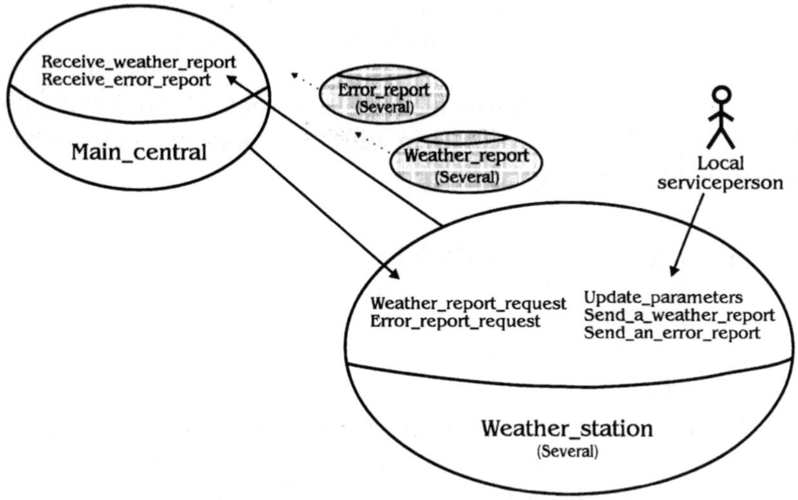


**Figure 6.3** A draft context drawing of our system.

As we go on, we will see that it is easy to add details. For example, we will open the high-level objects Main_central and Weather_station and add subobjects to them.

We have shown the information object character of the Error_report and Weather_report by making them gray. Main_central and Weather_station are to be regarded as system objects, and we indicate this by leaving them white.

The local serviceperson is also an object, but as he or she represents a user role, we draw a simplified sketch of a person representing an actor. We name this person Local_serviceperson and show what mini-uses of the Weather_station he or she is interested in. The mini-uses

```
Update_parameters
Send_a_weather_report
Send_an_error_report
```

have been derived from the initial description of the system found before. They represent various services that the Weather_station shall supply. Thus, these mini-uses are methods, albeit somewhat special. For example, it is not possible for the Local_serviceperson to call Update_parameters *directly* because he or she is not an object executing in the same system as the object Weather_station. This is a basic modeling problem, and it was discussed in the section "Interface Objects" in Chapter 4.

### About Null Objects

Null objects are information objects that are "empty." All information objects are assumed to have a method Is_null, whether we show it explicitly or not. We use this method to check whether an object is empty. We typically need null objects when we want to operate on a sequence of information objects. A typical loop is

```
{
an_object:= // Get a first information object
WHILE NOT an_object.Is_null THEN
// Do something
an_object:= // Get next information object
END_WHILE;
}
```

It is possible to operate on null objects with the set of methods available, but they will not change the object or return any usable information except, possibly, a comment line that the object is empty. For example, if we call a Display method for a null object,

```
some_null_object.Display(. . .);
```

no information will be shown except, possibly, a comment indicating that this is an empty object.

Storing a null object in another object results in nothing. The state of a null object cannot be changed. Note also that the Null object idea is similar—but not identical—to the use of nil. For example, in Smalltalk, nil is the sole instance of the Smalltalk class UndefinedObject, whereas a Null object is an instance of respective class and may exist in several instances. The concept "null" as used here has nothing to do with the special ASCII null control character (NUL). Null objects are also discussed in Chapter 4.

## CONTEXT DRAWING

As we continue discussing our weather data reporting system, we find that it must do much more than in our first sketch. For example, we will probably find other user roles, actors, such as a Meteorologist and a System supervisor. These users need mini-uses too. We will also find that a Weather_station must supply several more mini-uses. In Figure 6.4 we show our final context drawing of the system. (An asterisk (*) indicates that a more detailed figure (an exploded view) for the subsystem (or object) in question is available.)

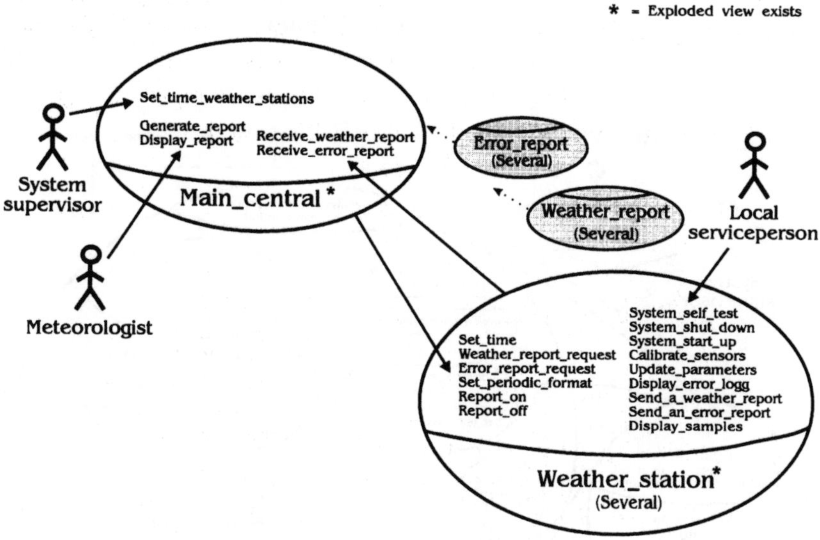


**Figure 6.4** Our final context drawing.

In the drawing we have added a System_supervisor, a Meteorologist, and some possible mini-uses for them. We have also added the following mini-uses to Weather_station:

- Set_time
- Set_periodic_format
- Report_on
- Report_off

These mini-uses are services the Main_central needs the Weather_station to supply. The Local_serviceperson also needs some more mini-uses:

- System_self_test
- System_shut_down

- System_start_up
- Calibrate_sensors
- Display_error_logg
- Display_samples

## SUBSYSTEM MAIN_CENTRAL_SYSTEM

Figure 6.5 shows a detailed figure of Main_central_system.

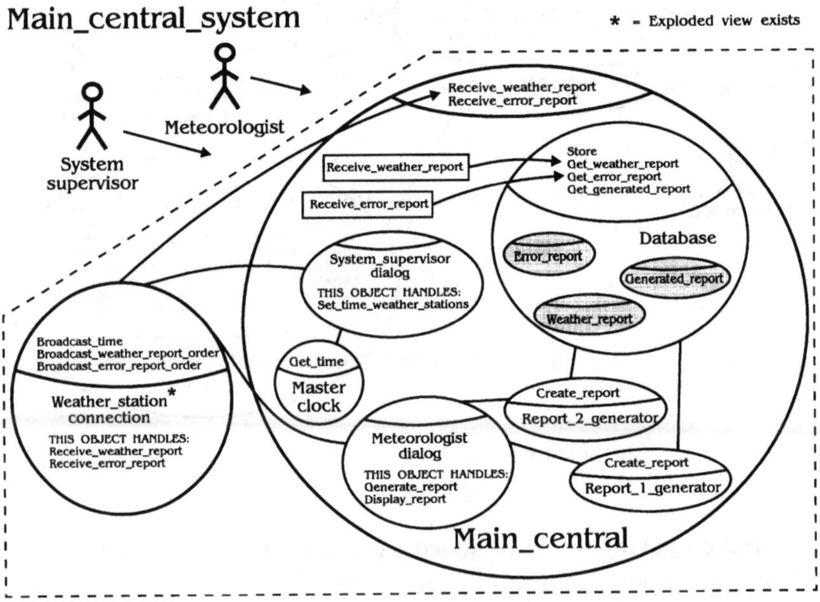


**Figure 6.5** Main_central_system.

### Main_central

We choose to put the communication object, Weather_station_connection, outside the object concerned, preserving some of the initial interface of Main_central. This is a good solution because the communications are straightforward and not bidirectional. Note also that we have shown the interface of Main_central (the methods Receive_weather_report and Receive_error_report) as well as some of their logic (the rectangles with their attached arrows).

Main_central is not developed in detail. For example, our model has only a simple report-generating mechanism, where two types of reports can be generated by Report_1_generator and Report_2_generator, respectively.

*Actors*

Mini-uses belonging to the actors System_supervisor and the Meteorologist are handled by two objects: System_supervisor_dialog and Meteorologist_dialog, respectively. (Mini-uses for the Meteorologist are discussed in connection with the corresponding dialog object.) That an object handles mini-uses is indicated by the words "THIS OBJECT HANDLES:" in the object. These two objects incorporate all that is necessary to communicate with the two types of users (actors). We choose to put these interface objects inside Main_central because we need interactions with different subobjects to simplify their logic.

***Methods: Main_central***

**.Receive_weather_report(a_weather_report)**

```
{
Database.Store(a_weather_report);
}
```

**.Receive_error_report(an_error_report)**

```
{
Database.Store(an_error_report);
}
```

## Weather_station_connection

Main_central uses Weather_station_connection when it needs to send a message to one or several Weather_station(s). In Figure 6.6 we sketch an exploded view of the Weather_station_connection. This interface object also takes care of messages coming from the Weather_station. Thus, this system object handles mini-uses needed by the Weather_station.

***Mini-uses: Weather_station_connection***

There are two mini-uses for Weather_station_connection: Receive_weather_report and Receive_error_report. They are implemented by calling the corresponding methods in Main_central: Receive_weather_report and Receive_error_report, respectively.

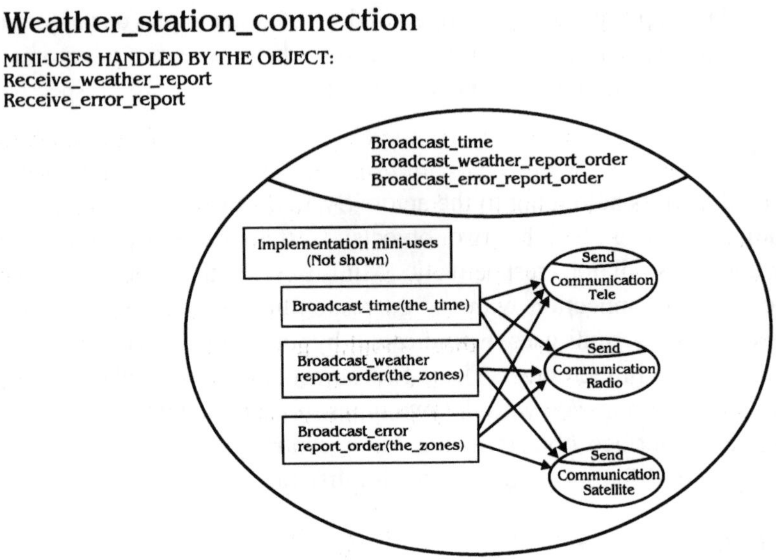


**Figure 6.6** Weather_station_connection.

### *Methods: Weather_station_connection*

**.Broadcast_time(the_time)**

```
{
Communication_Tele.Send(the_time);
Communication_Radio.Send(the_time);
Communication_Satellite.Send(the_time);
}
```

**.Broadcast_weather_report_order(the_zones)**

```
{
transmit_this := weather_report_please +
the_zones;
Communication_Tele.Send(transmit_this);
Communication_Radio.Send(transmit_this);
Communication_Satellite.Send(transmit_this);
}
```

**.Broadcast_error_report_order(the_zones)**

```
{
transmit_this := error_report_please +
the_zones;
Communication_Tele.Send(transmit_this);
```

```
Communication_Radio.Send(transmit_this);
Communication_Satellite.Send(transmit_this);
}
```

Whereas the objects Communication_Radio and Communication_Satellite can simply broadcast information, the object Communication_Tele has to be more intelligent. If Communication_Tele would call all weather stations that communicate via telephone lines, it would probably soon overload available telephone lines. It must thus know the weather stations that get their orders by telephone lines and it must be able to decide which of these that should get a message. If we let Communication_Tele keep track of the locations of the weather stations, it can use the information available in the_zones to decide which weather stations to call.

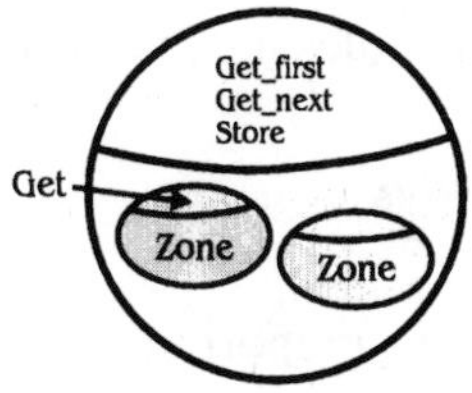


**Figure 6.7** A CPlacement object.

The object the_zones is a CPlacement object (see Figure 6.7). A CPlacement object contains one or several CZone objects. A CZone object may represent a single spot (longitude and latitude) or one or several area(s). The areas may overlap each other. A Weather_station can belong to a single spot and/or one or several areas. In our model, each Weather_station is aware of its location. (Implementation of this only partly shown). This fact is used by a Weather_station to check if a message concerns it or not before it responds.

In the following we discuss some aspects of the subobjects of Main_central, concentrating on the Meteorologist_dialog.

## Database

### *Methods: Database*

**.Store(an_object)**

The method Store is overloaded and can thus store objects of several different classes such as CWeather_report, CError_report, and CGenerated_report.

**.Get_xxx_report**

A Get method returns an object as indicated by the name of the method.

## System_supervisor_dialog

This interface object handles the interface for the actor System_ supervisor.

## Master_clock

This system object keeps track of the time.

## Meteorologist_dialog

This interface object handles the interface for the actor Meteorologist.

***Mini-uses: Meteorologist_dialog***

**Generate_report**

This mini-use generates a report in the form of a CGenerated_report object and stores it in the Database. The report is generated roughly in the following way:

```
{
// Error reporting not implemented
report_type := // Ask the user what type of
// report he or she wants to generate.
given_report_identity := // Ask the user to give
// an identity for the report.
// Check that the given_report_identity is
// unique for the user or else get another one.
in_identity :=
user_identity + given_report_identity;
update_database := // Ask the user if we shall
// update the measurements in the database.
IF update_database THEN
   the_zones := // Determine what geographical
   // areas shall report their weather data.
   Weather_station_connection.Broadcast_weather_r
   eport_order(the_zones);
   // Wait until the database is updated.
END_IF;
CASE report_type
```

```
'1': the_report :=
Report_1_generator.Create_report(in_identity);
'2' :the_report :=
Report_2_generator.Create_report(in_identity);
END_CASE;
Database.Store(the_report);
}
```

The report, the_report, is contained in an object of class CGenerated_report (see Figure 6.8).

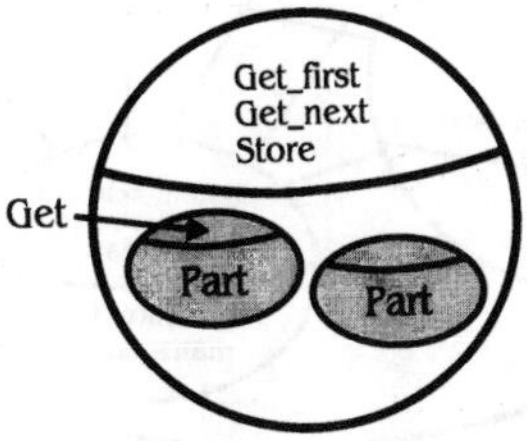


**Figure 6.8** An object of class CGenerated_report.

**Display_report**
This mini-use selects a report, fetches it from Database and displays the contents of it.

### Report_1/2_generator

**.Create_report**
This method generates a report and returns it to the caller in the form of an object of class CGenerated_report.

## SUBSYSTEM WEATHER_STATION

Next we "explode" the Weather_station, showing the subobjects of Weather_station (see Figure 6.9). We will discuss the subobjects one by one.

### Actor Local_serviceperson

Mini-uses for this actor are discussed in connection with Local_serviceperson_dialog.

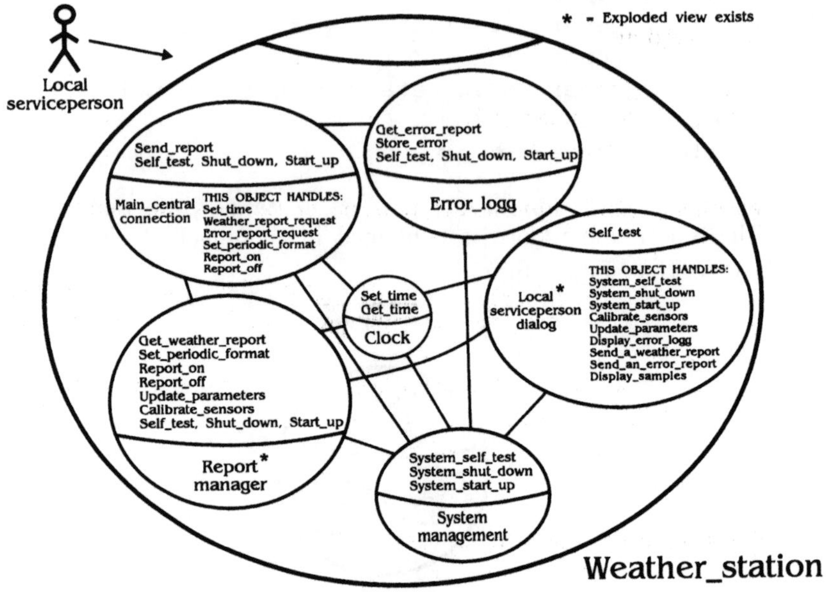


**Figure 6.9** Weather_station.

## Main_central_connection

Main_central_connection is the communication connection to the Main_central_system. For example,

```
{
Main_central_connection.Send_report
(A_weather_report_object);
}
```

will send a CWeather_report object to the Main_central.

When Main_central orders a mini-use, it transfers this information to a Weather_station via some hardware. The hardware implements the radio, tele, or satellite connection. Main_central_connection hides these hardware details (at the Weather_station), leaving a simple interface to the other subobjects.

This object implements several mini-uses. Parameters to a mini-use indicate supplementary information, which is transferred at the same time as the mini-use. Let us sketch the mini-uses of Main_central_connection.

***Mini-uses: Main_central_connection***

**Set_time(time)**

```
{
Clock.Set_time(time);
}
```

**Weather_report_request(start_time, no_of_samples, the_zones)**

```
{
// Check that this Weather_station is concerned.
// If it is inside the_zones then act in this way:
the_weather :=
Report_manager.Get_weather_report(start_time,
no_of_samples);
Send_report(the_weather); // Send the report
}
```

**Error_report_request(the_zones)**

```
{
// Check that this Weather_station is concerned.
// If it is inside the_zones then act in this way:
the_errors := Error_logg.Get_error_report;
Send_report(the_errors);
}
```

**Set_periodic_format(time_period, no_of_samples, the zones)**

```
{
// Check that this Weather_station is concerned.
// If it is inside the_zones then act in this way:
Report_manager.Set_periodic_format(time_period,
no_of_samples);
}
```

**Report_on(the_zones)**
This method turns on the periodic reporting of Weather_reports.

```
{
// Check that this Weather_station is concerned.
// If it is inside the_zones then act in this way:
Report_manager.Report_on;
}
```

**Report_off(the_zones)**

```
{
// Check that this Weather_station is concerned.
// If it is inside the_zones then act in this way:
Report_manager.Report_off;
}
```

***Methods: Main_central_connection***

**.Send_report(an_object)**

This method sends the information contained in an_object. The method can handle objects of several classes, such as CError_report and CWeather_report.

**.Self_test, Shut_down, Start_up**

These methods correspond to the same methods supplied by Report_manager. Please see this object.

## Error_logg and Clock

The CError_logg object stores CError objects. CError objects may be stored in the Error_logg by any subobject to Weather_station. Clock manages the local time.

## System_management

This object starts and shuts down subobjects to Weather_station. It also tests subobjects (Main_central_connection, Local_serviceperson_dialog, Report_manager, Error_logg, Clock) and makes an internal self test. The Self_test method available in most objects returns a CTest_result information object. Such an object contains a set of CResult objects (see Figure 6.10). Each CResult object is the result of a test.

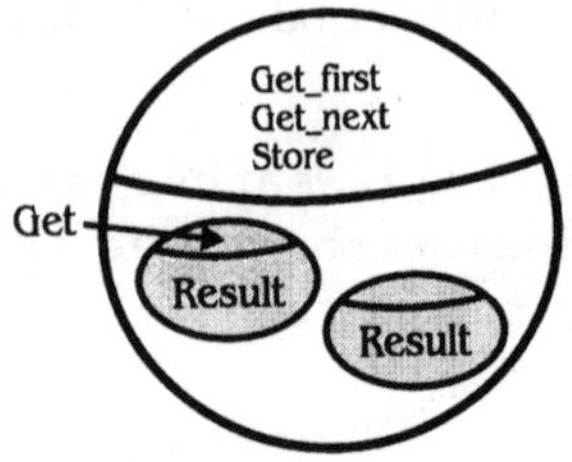


**Figure 6.10** A CTest_result information object.

## Local_serviceperson_dialog

In Figure 6.11 we see an exploded view of our Local_serviceperson_dialog.

Local_serviceperson_dialog is the interface to the Local_serviceperson. It contains some simple drivers and logic for interfacing via a keyboard and a simple display. It also has the logic necessary to carry out the mini-uses for Local_serviceperson. Let us sketch these mini-uses.

***Mini-uses: Local_serviceperson_dialog***

**System_self_test**

```
{
the_test_result :=
System_management.System_self_test;
a_test := the_test_result.Get_first;
WHILE NOT a_test.Is_null DO
  Display.Show(a_test.Get);
  a_test := the_test_result.Get_next:
END_WHILE;
}
```

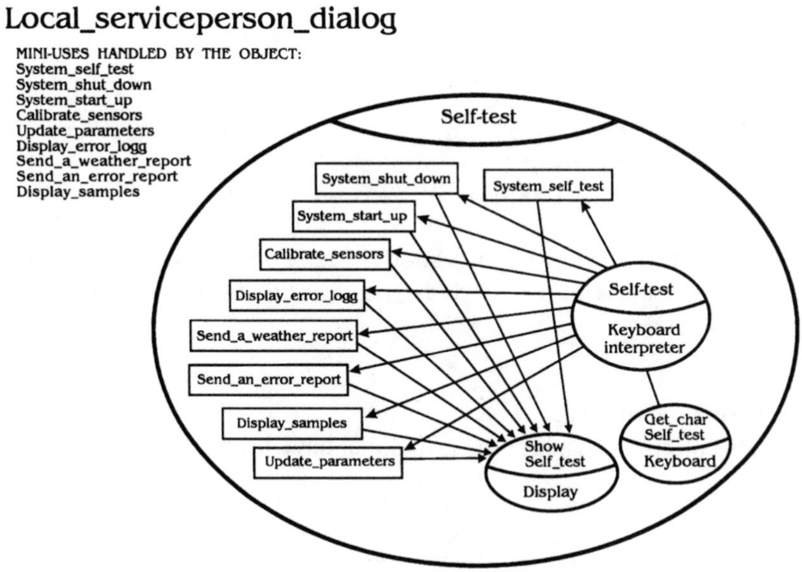


**Figure 6.11** Local_serviceperson_dialog.

**System_shut_down**

```
{
the_shut_down_result :=
System_management.System_shut_down;
// Rest see: System_self_test
}
```

**System_start_up**

```
{
the_start_up_result :=
System_management.System_start_up;
// Rest see: System_self_test
}
```

**Calibrate_sensors**

```
{
Report_manager.Calibrate_sensors;
}
```

**Update_parameters**

```
{
// Find out what types of sensors the
// Weather_station has:
the_current_parameters :=
Report_manager.Update_parameters(// A null
// object);
// Display these
// Ask the Local_serviceperson what sensor(s) he
// or she wants to update.
// Get new parameter values for those:
the_values :=
// Get parameter values from Local_ serviceperson
Report_manager.Update_parameters(the_values);
//
}
```

**Display_error_logg**

This mini-use displays the errors that have been stored.

```
{
the_errors := Error_logg.Get_error_report;
// Rest see: System_self_test
}
```

**Send_a_weather_report**

This mini-use sends a Weather_report on request from a Local_serviceperson.

```
{
time := // Enter specifications for time
samples := // Enter no of samples
the_weather :=
Report_manager.Get_weather_report(time, samples);
Main_central_connection.Send_report(the_weather);
}
```

**Send_an_error_report**

This mini-use sends an Error_report on request from a Local_serviceperson.

```
{
the_errors := Error_logg.Get_error_report;
Main_central_connection.Send_report(the_errors);
}
```

**Display_samples**

This mini-use displays weather measurement data on request from a Local_serviceperson.

```
{
time := // Enter specifications for time
samples := // Enter no of samples
a_weather_report :=
Report_manager.Get_weather_report(time, samples);
a_sample := a_weather_report.Get_first;
go_on := TRUE;
WHILE go_on AND NOT a_sample.Is_null DO
// Display measurements for the sensors:
IF a_sample.Available(Sun_hours) = Is_available
THEN
Display.Show("Measurements for sun hours: ");
Display.Show(a_sample.Get(Sun_hours));
ELSE
Display.Show("No measurements for sun hours.");
END_IF;
// The same type of code for
// the rest of the sensors
// .
IF // Display more? THEN
a_sample := a_weather_report.Get_next;
```

```
ELSE
go_on:= FALSE;
END_IF;
END_WHILE;
}
```

***Methods: Local_serviceperson_dialog***

**.Self_test**

This method makes a self-test of all subobjects to Local_serviceperson_dialog.

```
{
FOR "each subobject belonging to Local_service-
person_dialog" DO
// Test the subobject
// Store one Result object:
the_test_result.Store(a_result);
END_FOR;
// Return a CTest_result object:
Return the_test_result;
}
```

## Report_manager

We display an exploded view of Report_manager in Figure 6.12. This object handles the periodic reporting of Weather_reports to the Main_central. This is done by calling the Main_central_connection periodically, which could be achieved by having a task inside Report_manager that implements the following logic:

```
{
// When weather report is due:
a_weather_report :=
// Make a weather report
Main_central_connection.Send_report(a_weather_
report);
}
```

The Report_manager contains an information object of class CParameter_values called Current_parameter_values. A CParameter_values object contains a set of CValue objects (see Figure 6.13). Each CValue object contains the parameter(s) needed to calibrate one sensor. A CParameter_values object does not contain more CValue objects than the number of possible sensors at a Weather_station.

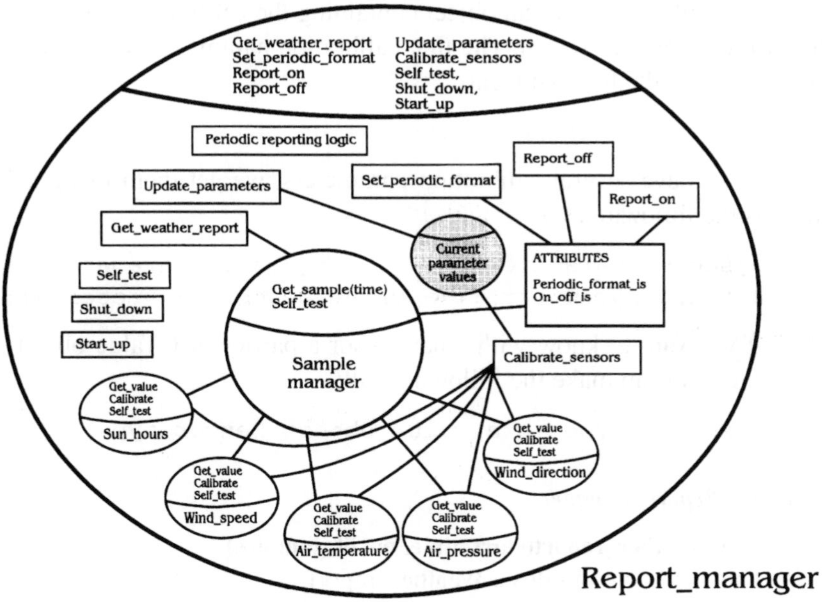


**Figure 6.12** Report_manager.

When a CValue object is stored in a CParameter_values object, a check is made: If an old CValue object exists for a particular sensor, it is overwritten by the new CValue object. If no CValue object for a particular sensor exists, a new CValue object is created and stored in the CParameter_values object (Current_parameter_values).

A calibration value, a CValue object, for a certain sensor is acquired by a call, for example,

```
a_value_object :=
Current_parameter_values.Get(Air_temperature);
```

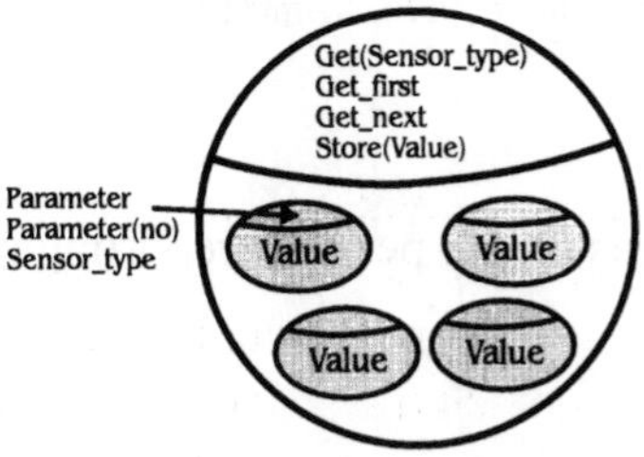


**Figure 6.13** An object of class CParameter_values.

This call will return an object containing the calibration value(s) for the Air_temperature sensor. The first calibration parameter for this sensor is acquired by the following call:

```
the_first_parameter := a_value_object.Parameter;
```

If we have several calibration parameters, we get them using calls such as the following:

```
a_second_parameter := a_value_object.Parameter(2);
a_third_parameter := a_value_object.Parameter(3);
```

If we want to know with what sensor a particular CValue object is connected, we can make the following call:

```
a_sensor_type := a_value_object.Sensor_type;
```

***Methods: Report_manager***

**.Get_weather_report(start_time, no_of_samples)**
This method compiles a Weather_report.

```
{
FOR the_time := start_time TO (start_time +
"no_of_samples") DO
a_weather_report.Store(Sample_manager.Get_sample
(the_time));
END_FOR;
Return a_weather_report;
}
```

**.Set_periodic_format(time_period, no_of_samples)**
This method places new settings in the Periodic_format_is attribute.

```
{
// Time for periodic reporting:

Periodic_format_is.time := time_period;
Periodic_format_is.samples := no_of_samples;
}
```

**.Report_on**
This method turns on the periodic reporting of Weather_reports.

```
{
On_off_is := ON;
}
```

**.Report_off**

```
{
On_off_is := OFF;
}
```

**.Update_parameters(new_parameter_values)**

This method substitutes old calibration values with new ones. If new calibration values for a sensor are not supplied, we keep the old values. The current set of parameter values is always returned to the caller. Thus, this method can also be used to retrieve the current set of parameter values (by calling it with new_parameter_values set to a null object).

```
{
IF NOT new_parameter_values.Is_null THEN
   a_parameter_value :=
   new_parameter_values.Get_first;
   WHILE NOT a_parameter_value.Is_null DO
      // Substitute a calibration value:
      Current_parameter_values.Store(
      a_parameter_value);
      a_parameter_value :=
      new_parameter_values.Get_next;
   END_WHILE;
END_IF;
Return Current_parameter_values;
}
```

**.Calibrate_sensors**

This method calibrates each sensor using the calibration values available in Current_parameter_values.

```
{
Air_temperature.Calibrate(Current_parameter_
values.Get(Air_temperature));

Air_pressure.Calibrate(Current_parameter_values.
Get(Air_pressure));

Sun_hours.Calibrate(Current_parameter_values.
Get(Sun_hours));

Wind_speed.Calibrate(Current_parameter_values.
Get(Wind_speed));
```

```
Wind_direction.Calibrate(Current_parameter_
values.Get(Wind_direction));}
```

**.Self_test**

This method makes a self test of all subobjects of Report_manager.

```
{
FOR "each subobject belonging to Report_manager"
DO
// Test a subobject
// Store one CResult object:
the_test_result.Store(a_result);
END_FOR;
// Return a CTest_result object:
Return the_test_result;
}
```

**.Shut_down**

```
{
// No special shut down mechanism is imple-
// mented. Instead each object is tested.
FOR "each subobject belonging to Report_manager"
DO
// Test a subobject
// Store one CResult object:
the_shut_down_result.Store(a_result);
END_FOR;
// Return a CTest_ result object:
Return the_shut_down_result;
}
```

**.Start_up**

```
{
// Give Current_parameter_values default values
FOR "each subobject handling a sensor" DO
// Calibrate the sensor
// Test the sensor
// Store one CResult object:
the_start_up_result.Store(a_result);
END_FOR;
// Test the Sample_manager:
the_start_up_result.Store(Sample_manager.
Self_test);
// Return a CTest_result object:
```

```
Return the_start_up_result;
}
```

This concludes our discussion of the object structure for our weather data acquisition and reporting system. Next we continue discussing class structures that could be designed to support the object structures we need to implement the system.

## CLASS STRUCTURES

### Introduction

A class structure is a modeling tool allowing us to keep similar classes together, needed when we design an object structure. This helps us beat complexity. It is also a tool for reusing code.

If we had used a class library such as one of those available in Smalltalk, Visual C++, or Borland C++, it would have influenced our class structures and probably our object structures as well. Having such an existing class library is an asset, because it supplies us with ready-made components that can be incorporated into our object structure either directly or after some minor changes. However, it is also a problem because such a class structure will influence our object structure, making us focus less on it. This does not necessarily increase the chances for a well-designed application. The main purpose with a class structure should thus be to model similarities between classes and not to reuse code, even though these two uses of a class structure are intermixed. It is very important for the modeling purpose to govern the reuse aspect, or we will get an unorganized reuse of code, resulting in bad object structures—that is, an application with a bad architecture.

This system was built without having a ready-made library with class structures from the beginning, so our object structure was created without any influence from other class structures. We thus concentrated our attention on the object structure—not the class structure, following the principles laid out in this book. We "forget" the class structure when we build our object structure because of the experiences gathered in [1,2]. These showed clearly that the object structure will be better if we do not let existing class structures dominate our work.

A drawback to this approach is that possible class structures are often not immediately apparent. Another drawback is that we do not reuse classes as much as if we had used an existing class library. In the future, when class libraries become larger and we get more experience in using them, class libraries will play a more central role than in this example. However, the focus should always be on the needed object structure of the application.

Next, we sketch some possible class structures. Our starting point then is the object structure, describing our application, and a knowledge of what the objects contained in that structure are supposed to do. Our task is in essence very simple: What classes do we need to instantiate these objects? and Can we design classes preserving a good object structure while reusing code? The class structures suggested should not be regarded as final.

### Sensors

We have several sensors that deliver different measurement values. When we look at the exploded view of the Report_manager, we see that these sensors have a lot in common. It is thus probable that these sensors can be instantiated from similar classes. Without knowing the exact implementation details of the sensors, it is not possible to say if all sensors can be instantiated from one class or if we should keep similar parts of the design in an abstract class. This latter solution is shown in Figure 6.14, where we have the abstract class CSensor and a unique subclass for each sensor. (Sun_hours is instantiated using CSun_hours, etc.)

### Interface Objects

Interface objects communicate with users and with each other in very different ways. We use the Local_serviceperson_dialog object in a

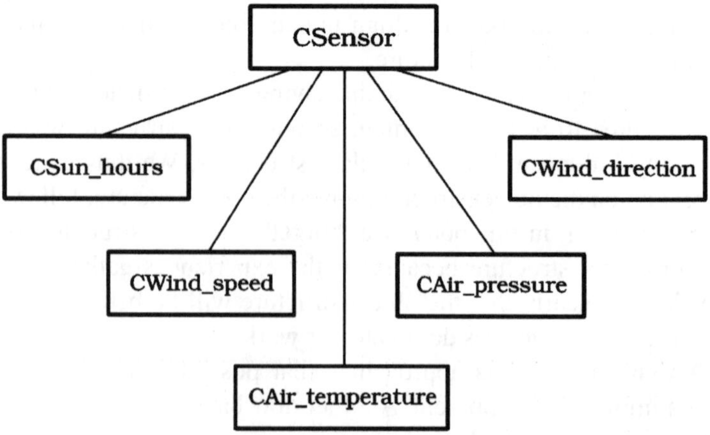


**Figure 6.14** Sensor classes.

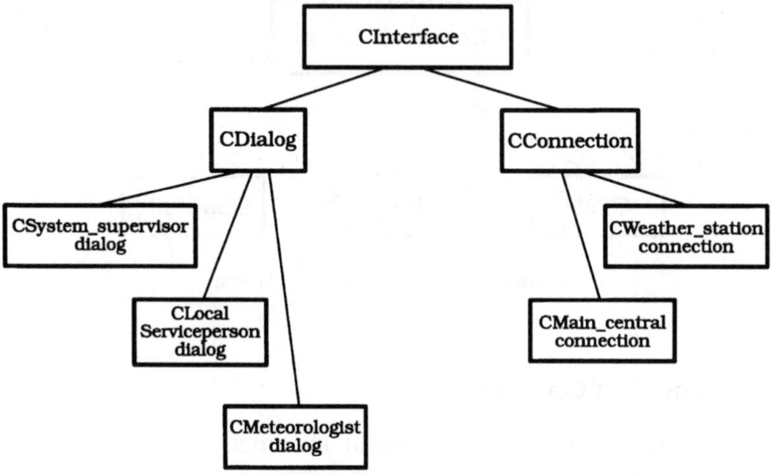


**Figure 6.15** Interface classes.

very different way than we use Main_central_connection, for example. Nevertheless, it is possible that these objects have some parts in common, which we can place in an abstract class, CInterface (see Figure 6.15). CDialog objects and CConnection objects are probably different. Thus, we introduce two other abstract classes below CInterface to reflect this.

## Two Class Structures

The class structures shown in Figures 6.16 and 6.17 illustrate how we can create abstract classes to reuse design.

For example, the abstract class CCommunication contains design used by classes CTele, CRadio, and CSatellite. This could be a good idea because the objects instantiated from these classes probably have a lot of design in common.

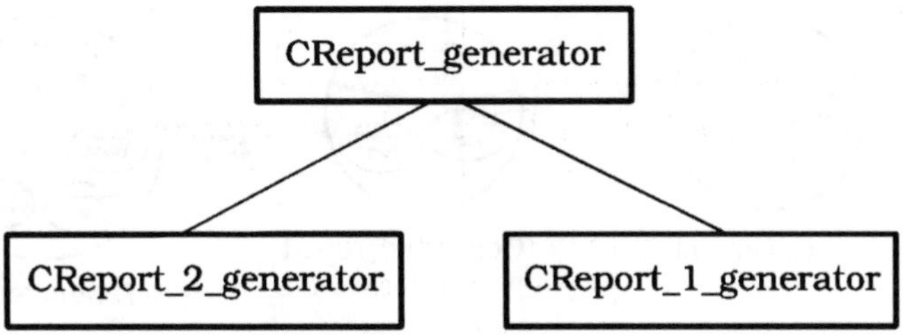


**Figure 6.16** Report classes.

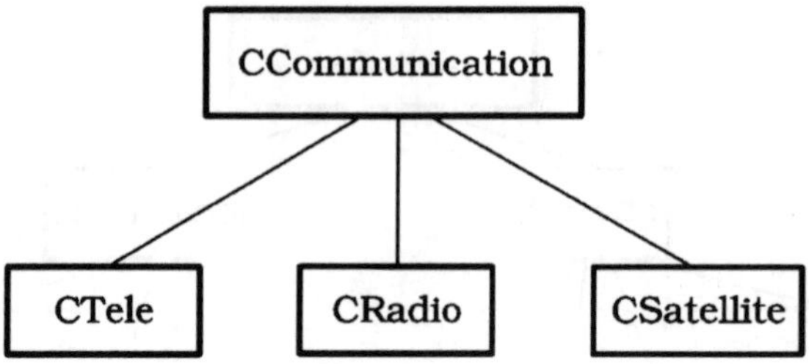


**Figure 6.17** Communication classes.

## Information Objects

We have several different types of information objects, but if we look at the examples displayed in Figure 6.18, we soon realize that some of them have a lot of design in common.

It is thus probable that these objects can be created from classes that have a lot in common. One such solution is illustrated in Figure 6.19. We have an abstract class, CInformation, containing the design that subclasses, such as CWeather_report, CError_report, have in common.

Figure 6.20 illustrates an alternative solution, in which we have considered that some objects are very similar. Thus the objects Error_report, Test_result, Placement, and Generated_report are with this solution created from the same class, CInfo. It is conceivable that it would also be

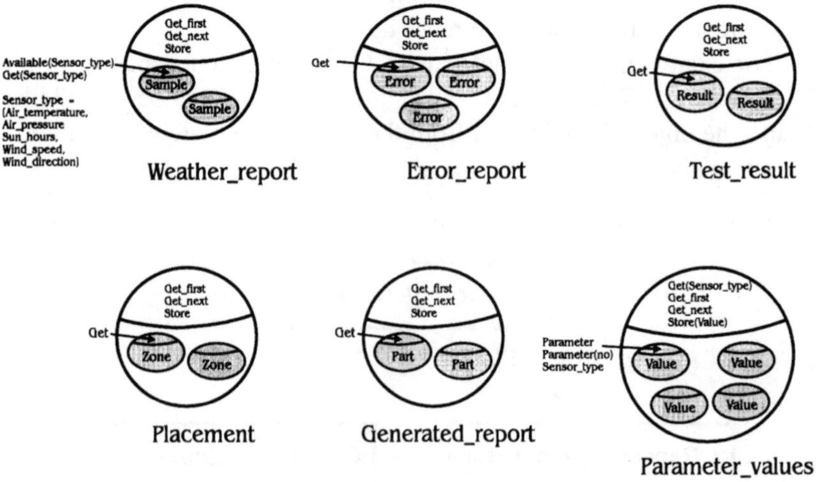


**Figure 6.18** Typical information objects used in the system.

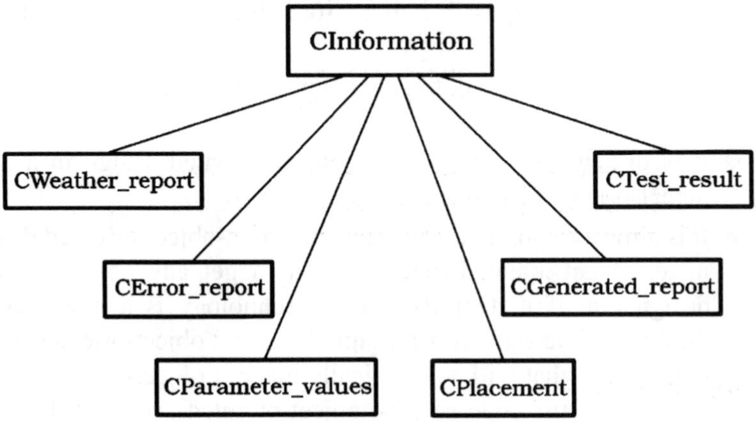


**Figure 6.19** Information classes, alternative one.

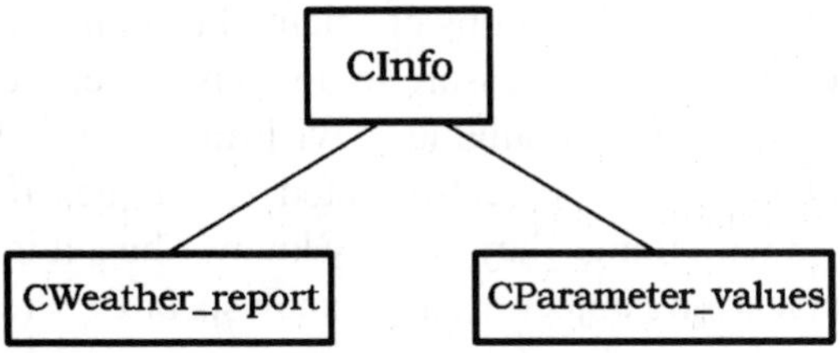


**Figure 6.20** Information classes, alternative two.

possible to create CWeather_report objects from CInfo, but we have kept the subclasses CWeather_report (and CParameter_values) that were introduced in our first solution alternative. Note that there is no abstract class with this solution.

The next step would be to design class structures for classes such as CSample and CError, but that is left to the interested reader as an exercise.

## IMPLEMENTING THE MODEL

Meyer [6] has pointed out that modules should correspond to syntactic language units. He calls this principle "the principle of the linguistic modular unit." Experience shows that this observation is very relevant and that we can apply it to objects too. In particular, experience shows that

- It is difficult, but possible, to go from object-oriented analysis to a non-object-oriented design.
- It is extremely difficult to go from non-object-oriented analysis to an object-oriented design.
- It is difficult to implement an object-oriented design in a non-object-oriented language.
- It is almost impossible to implement a non-object-oriented design in an object-oriented language and to get any object-oriented design out of it. Object-oriented technology is a new way of thinking. If we start with a design that is not object-oriented, there is no magic that will automatically make it object-oriented when we code. If the code is to be object-oriented, we must design it that way.

Figure 6.21 sums it up. We sometimes hear that we should make an analysis using SA (Structured Analysis) but make an object-oriented design, or that we should do an object-oriented design but do the coding using C or Pascal or Fortran. Pressure to do so is sometimes exercised by management, which is then indulging in wishful thinking. It is not possible to save money through object-oriented techniques if programmers continue working with things they already know. Thus, it is not a waste to spend money on learning object-oriented analysis or C++ (even if the programmers already know SA or C).

A rule when considering an object-oriented design is that the closer a programming language corresponds to object-oriented concepts, the easier it will be to implement the design. The most important language construction, when implementing an object structure, is a construction suitable for implementing objects—not necessarily a class construct. Thus

| | | | |
|---|---|---|---|
| OO Analysis | → | Design | Possible but difficult |
| Analysis | → | OO Design | Extremely difficult |
| OO Design | → | Code | Difficult |
| Design | → | OO Code | Why bother? |

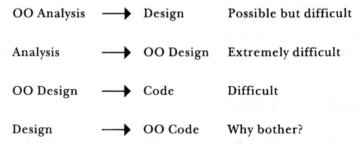

**Figure 6.21** (Analysis, Design, and Code imply non-object-oriented ditto).

implementing an object structure in, for example, Ada is not impossible. We next discuss this aspect in more detail.

### Implementing in Ada and C++

Ada does not have any constructions (directly) suitable for implementing classes or class structures, but the object structure can be mapped to the Ada package construct. As an example, we show a possible body for Error_logg in Weather_station:

```
with Clock;

package body Error_logg is
--Parameter lists are not shown.
   function Get_error_report . . .
   procedure Store_error . . .
   function Self_test . . .
   function Shut_down . . .
   function Start_up . . .
end Error_logg;
```

Note that the visibility is regulated by the "with clause" in the above example. Thus, with this solution, Error_logg can access the Clock object but no other subobjects of Weather_station. We here encounter a major problem that must be solved when we go from design to implementation, namely, what subobjects will access which subobjects? In a model such as the one shown in Figure 6.9 of Weather_station, we have put no restrictions on how the subobjects may access each other. Thus, the model in Figure 6.9 allows the Error_logg to access all other subobjects. This total freedom cannot easily be directly transferred to an implementation in Ada or C++. A model such as the one displayed in Figure 6.9 must be made more explicit concerning how subobjects need to call upon each other or it will be very difficult to implement it. The way to do this is to remove all unnecessary lines and arrows. When we have removed unnecessary lines and arrows, we should try to transform double dependencies (lines without arrows or lines with double arrows) into one-directed dependencies (lines with one arrow). The dependencies that are left will decide the implementation.

Implementing classes and class structures in Ada is another matter. A class for some set of information objects can often be implemented as an abstract data type using generic packages. It is also possible to simulate a class structure, but that is beyond the scope of this book. The arrival of Ada 9X will ease the effort of mapping from an object-oriented model into an implementation done using Ada.

The object structure has no direct construction in C++ that can be associated with it in the same way as we associated packages and objects in Ada. It is, however, quite possible to use the class construction to represent the object structure, as we show here. A problem with the use of the class construct to define object structures is that we mix two structures that we, from a modeling point of view, would like to separate. Next we sketch a possible C++ implementation for a Weather_Station:

```
#include "reportma.h" // Including files:
#include "clock.h"
#include "mcconnec.h"
#include "errorlog.h"
#include "locsrman.h"
#include "systmang.h"

class CWeather_station
{
public:
   CWeather_station(// Setting up input and
   // output);

private:
   CReport_manager Report_manager;
   CMain_central_connection
   Main_central_connection;
   CError_log Error_log;
   CClock Clock;
   CLocal_serviceperson_dialog
   Local_serviceperson_dialog;
   CSystem_management System_management;
};
```

The same recommendations apply for this solution: Remove as many of the dependencies allowed in the design model as possible before commencing the implementation. From this C++ code we cannot directly determine how subobjects may call other subobjects. For example, to determine if Report_manager may call Main_central_connection, we must look into the reportma.h file and check whether Main_central_connection has been made available to Report_manager. Generally speaking, it is often easier to implement the object structure in C++ than in Ada because of the more flexible structure in C++. For example, in Ada, double dependencies often lead to compilation problems.

Implementing classes and class structures in C++ is simple. However, we have a slight naming problem. Are we going to give a name like "Report_manager" to the class or to the corresponding object? In the preceding example we let the object keep the name, while the class is given the same name but prefixed with C, following the practice we established in the beginning of this chapter—for example, Report_manager (object) and CReport_manager (class). (If we create more than one object from a class, this simple naming paradigm must be augmented.)

## SUMMARY

In this chapter we modeled a technical system where data collecting units—called weather stations—periodically sends weather data to a main central. The idea was not to develop the system in full but to demonstrate how the principles and concepts described in this book can be used to model and—to some extent—to implement a system. In particular, the principles outlined in Chapter 1 were applied. For example, principle B, the close mapping principle, was supported by the use of mini-uses, actors, information objects, and system objects because these concepts directly relate to the way a user perceives a situation: An actor represents a typical user role and mini-uses directly relate to how the user uses the system. Information objects and system objects relate to two fundamental types of objects that occur when we model. Principle A, the principle of abstraction was applied, for example, when partitioning the system into layers: system, subsystems, objects, subobjects, etc. This principle was also applied when high-level "methods"—mini-uses—were implemented in layers of abstraction using methods.

Throughout the chapter we tried to name items with names that were natural and intuitive, following principle D in Chapter 1. Principle C, using structures, was followed when, for example, the aggregation structure was used to group subobjects into objects and when the class structure was used to structure classes into class hierarchies.

We also introduced some new concepts that support these principles, such as the context picture and the context drawing. The context picture was used to describe the problem in a way that is close to how the user perceives the situation. The parts shown in the context picture are easy to trace to corresponding parts in a context drawing. Exploding parts in the context drawing in the nested way we used in this chapter again supported the close mapping rule.

The iterative aspect of systems development is difficult to demonstrate, but in part we showed it by first introducing a draft context picture followed by a final context picture. Support for an iterative approach when modeling a system was also demonstrated by the fact that we could develop the system in stages. First, we concentrated on the user's view; this was followed by stages closer and closer to the implementation of the system.

We concentrated on the object structure for the application—rather than the class structure—simply because the process of defining the objects of an application is what must first be understood. To reuse objects, a class library must be available, and a working knowledge of this library must exist. We did not have this advantage when modeling our system. However, the difference between designing a system as outlined in this chapter compared to a situation where we have a working knowledge of an available class library is only this: When, during the definition of the application structure, an object is found to exist in a class library, it need not be implemented but can be taken directly from the class library (possibly after some minor modifications).

# 7

# A Distribution System

## *Example Two*

*Practice is the best of all instructors.*

—Publilius Syrus

## PROBLEM DESCRIPTION

The system presented in this chapter is based on an existing system that has been simplified and adapted to fit as an example in a book.

### Context Picture

The system is made up of two main parts, distribution unit(s) that supplies articles and shops that sell the articles. We call these two parts Shop and DU (Distribution Unit), respectively. The system is illustrated in Figure 7.1. A shop needs a simple and straightforward way of communicating with distribution units. For instance, it should be possible to order articles by calling a distribution unit, via mail or by uploading the order via modem directly to the distribution unit.

A distribution unit should be as automated as possible. For instance, no manual work should be involved at a distribution unit when an order is received via modem. A shop can order articles from any existing distribution unit.

### Context Drawing

A final context drawing of the system is shown in Figure 7.2. Actors, their mini-uses, objects, and their methods are described in the following text. The idea is to give a feeling for the modeling activity rather than to give a complete and detailed implementation. Note in particular that many objects have incomplete sets of methods and/or methods that are not fully developed. Thus, some parts are more developed than other parts

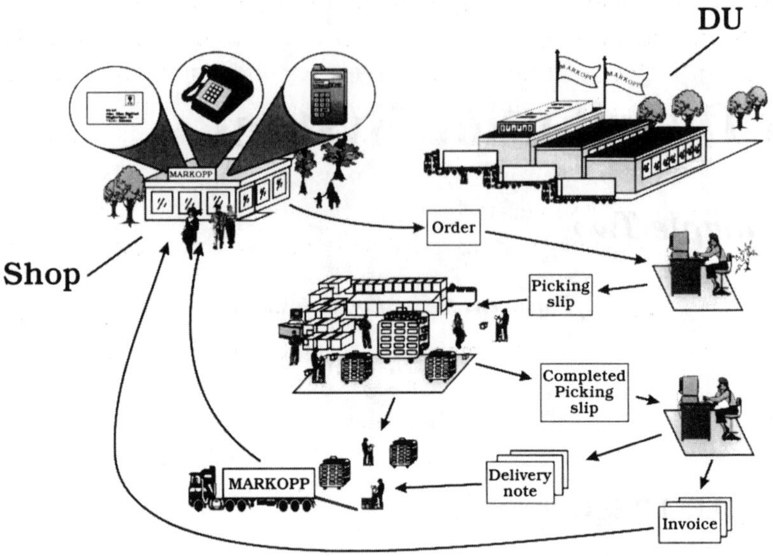


**Figure 7.1** Context picture of the system we model in this chapter.

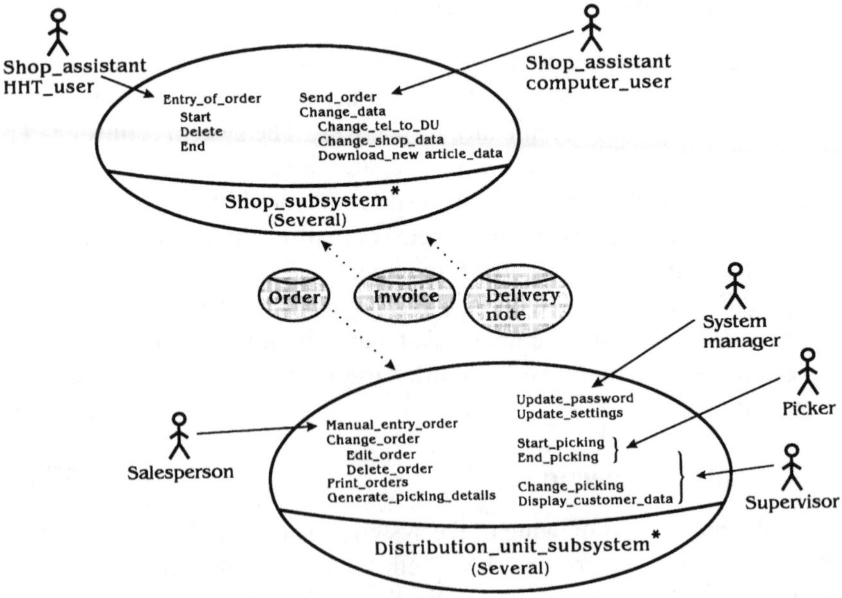


**Figure 7.2** Context drawing for our distribution system.

in the following text. This illustrates the typical situation, when doing object-oriented development, of having some objects in the analysis phase, other objects in the design phase, and still other objects close to implementation. The mini-uses most fully developed are Start_picking, End_picking, and Change_picking, which give the reader the most complete picture of how we can trace a mini-use to its implementation.

Objects are assumed to be properly initialized with default values for attributes. This is viewed as a coding issue and is not dealt with in this (analysis/design) chapter.

A few low-level details are taken for granted. For example, pressing the F8 key (Function key number 8) is the accepted way of exiting many commands at terminals at distribution units. We view such details as unavoidable customer requirements. A symbol table could have been built for such keys, but to keep things simple, we have not done so.

If you have not already read Appendices 2 and 3, describing the notation and the methods summary, respectively, we strongly suggest that you read them before reading this chapter. Note, however, that we have not strictly followed the approach suggested in Appendix 3.

## SUBSYSTEM SHOP_SUBSYSTEM

Figure 7.3 shows the objects in the shop subsystem.

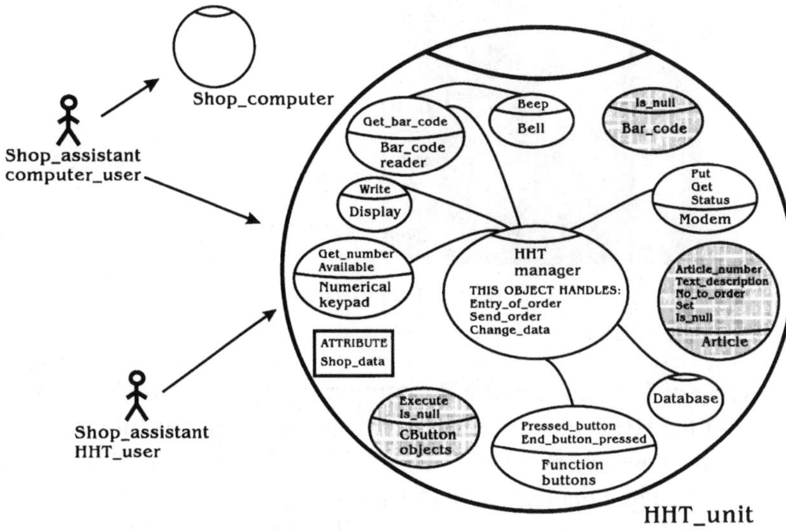


**Figure 7.3** The shop subsystem.

## Shop_computer

This part of the system is not implemented.

## Actor Shop_assistant_HHT_user

*Usage Scenario*

Each day a shop assistant walks through the shop, checking whether any articles need to be ordered. If there is a need to order an article, the bar-code of the article is read into an HHT unit (Hand-Held Terminal unit). The bar-code is available on a bar-code label close to the article. The HHT unit is a hand-held unit used in a shop when registering articles to be ordered. The HHT unit is illustrated in Figure 7.4.

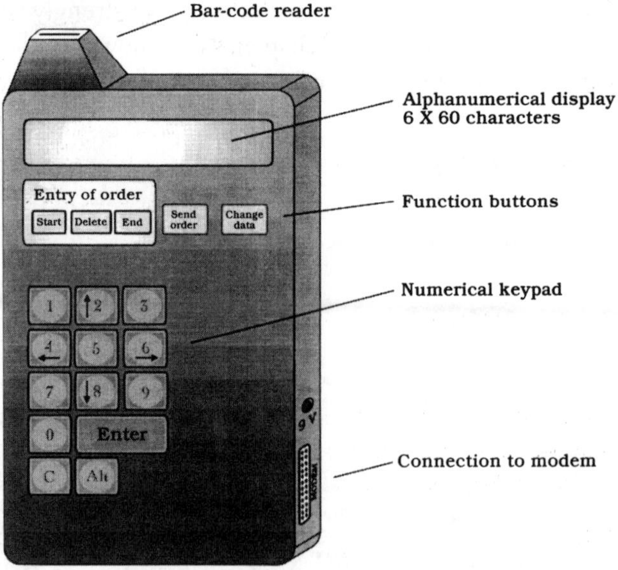


**Figure 7.4** An HHT unit.

The article number and a description of the article is shown on the display of the HHT unit when a bar-code has been successfully read. The display can show several lines of text. The number of items to be ordered is then entered into the HHT unit. This process is repeated until all articles to be ordered have been stored in the HHT unit. The HHT unit is then given to the Shop_assistant_computer_user.

There is a manual procedure corresponding to the one just outlined that is used when an HHT unit is not available and the order is sent via mail or telephone to the DU.

The following mini-uses are described assuming an HHT unit is used, but they could be implemented on a portable PC using, for example, a Windows system. The mini-uses are activated with function buttons found on the HHT unit. For instance, the mini-use Start is called when the Start button on the HHT unit is pressed.

### *Mini-uses: Shop_assistant_HHT_user*

**Entry_of_order**

This mini-use consists of three (sub)mini-uses: Start, Delete, and End.

**Start**

This mini-use starts the process of entering article numbers and number of articles. First, a text is displayed asking whether the articles are to be added to the ones already stored in the HHT unit or whether all stored articles are to be deleted before the process starts. The bar-code reader is then used. When a bar-code has been successfully read, a descriptive text of the article is displayed on the HHT unit's display. The number of items to be ordered is then entered into the HHT unit. The article number and the number of items to be ordered are stored.

**Delete**

An article is deleted. When this mini-use is activated, a text describing the last entered article and a text asking whether the article shall be deleted is displayed. A simple press of the ENTER button deletes the displayed article. The numerical keypad can be used to step through the articles entered into the HHT unit in case the last entered article is not the one to be deleted.

When the numerical keypad is used to step through the stored articles, the display always shows the article number and a description of the article that will be deleted by pressing the ENTER button. Pressing End before an article has been deleted (by pressing ENTER) ends this mini-use without deleting an article.

**End**

The process started with the mini-use Start (or Delete) is ended with this mini-use.

## Actor Shop_assistant_computer_user

The personnel responsible for managing the computer at a shop also use the HHT unit. The HHT unit can be connected to a modem and, through this, it can communicate with a DU. The current set of ordered articles stored in the HHT unit can be uploaded to DU, and new data (article number and description of articles) can be downloaded to the HHT unit.

***Mini-uses: Shop_assistant_computer_user***

**Send_order**

This mini-use will send stored articles to a DU via a modem. If the modem is not connected to the HHT unit or if some other error occurs, a text describing the error is displayed. The user is also informed about a successful upload.

**Change_data**

This mini-use consists of three (sub)mini-uses: Change_tel_to_DU, Change_shop_data and Download_new_article_data.

**Change_tel_to_DU**

This mini-use sets a new telephone number used when calling DU via a modem.

**Change_shop_data**

This mini-use stores new data about the shop (address and other data). The data are needed when calling DU via a modem. The text is entered on the numerical keypad following some scheme.

**Download_new_article_data**

This mini-use downloads new article number data and text description for articles from DU via a modem.

## Display

This system object is the interface to the display. Text scrolls upward as text is entered in a normal fashion.

**.Write**

A new line of text is written on the display with a call like this:

```
Display.Write("The text-line to display");
```

### Numerical_keypad

This system object interfaces to the keypad.

**.Get_number**

A number is read from the Numerical_keypad with this method—for instance;

```
a_number := Numerical_keypad.Get_number;
```

The call is not returned until the ENTER button has been pressed. If the ENTER button is pressed without entering a number first, the returned value is a carriage return.

**.Available**

This method is used to check if a number is available. If the ENTER button has been pressed, a TRUE value is returned when calling this method; otherwise a FALSE value is returned.

### Function_buttons

This system object interfaces to all function buttons on the HHT unit.

**.Pressed_button**

The last pressed function button is read from the Function_buttons with this method—for instance,

```
a_button_object := Function_buttons.Pressed_button;
```

A CButton object of one of the following classes is returned: CStart, CDelete, CEnd, CSend_order, or CChange_data.

The call is returned when a function button has been pressed.

**.End_button_pressed**

This method returns the value TRUE if the End button has been pressed (otherwise it will return the value FALSE). After having been called, the method returns the value FALSE until the End button is pressed again.

### CButton Objects

CButton is an abstract class with the subclasses CStart, CDelete, CEnd, CSend_order and CChange_data. These subclasses are described shortly.

These objects are a good example of a border case between information objects and system objects. If we had considered their behavior as the important aspect, we would have called them system objects. However, the important aspect of these objects is that they give us the information that a button has been pressed and information about which button was pressed. We thus choose to call them information objects.

**.Execute**

Each CButton object has a method Execute, which is called when the corresponding mini-use is executed.

**.Is_null**

This method returns TRUE if the object does not contain any interesting information, that is, it is a null object. If the object contains relevant information, the method returns the value FALSE. (All information objects are assumed to have an Is_null method whether we state it explicitly—as here—or not. More information about the use of null objects is available in Chapters 6 and 4).

### *CStart Objects*

**.Execute**

```
{
Display.Write("1 = Delete currently stored
articles before adding new ones");
Display.Write("2 = Exit");
Display.Write("Any other selection = Add articles
to currently stored ones");
Display.Write("Your selection: ");
a_selection := Numerical_keypad.Get_number;
IF a_selection = 2 THEN
EXIT; // Exit method
END_IF;
IF a_selection = 1 THEN
// Delete articles
END_IF;
a_bar_code_object := Bar_code_reader.Get_bar_code;
WHILE NOT a_bar_code_object.Is_null DO
    // Display text description of article
    Display.Write("Please enter number of articles
    to order");
    a_number := Numerical_keypad.Get_number;
    // Store the order for this article
```

```
    a_bar_code_object :=
    Bar_code_reader.Get_bar_code;
END_WHILE;
}
```

*CDelete Objects*

**.Execute**

```
// Delete an article
```

*CEnd Objects*

**.Execute**

```
// Do nothing
```

*CSend_order Objects*

**.Execute**

```
// Upload data to DU
```

*CChange_data Objects*

**.Execute**

```
{
Display.Write("Select one of:");
Display.Write("1 = Change telephone number");
Display.Write("2 = Enter new shop data");
Display.Write("3 = Download new data from DU");
Display.Write("Your selection: ");
CASE Numerical_keypad.Get_number;
'1': // Change telephone number
'2': // Enter new shop data
'3': // Download new data from DU
ELSE:// Display.Write("You entered an invalid
// number!");
END_CASE;
}
```

## Bar_code_reader

This system object interfaces to the bar-code reader.

**.Get_bar_code**

When a bar-code is successfully read, by the bar-code reader, a CBar_code object is returned. If a bar-code is unsuccessfully read, a signal is issued by the HHT unit (by calling Bell.Beep). If the End button is pressed, a null object (an empty CBar_code object) is returned.

### *CBar_Code Objects*

The information obtained by reading a bar-code is contained in a CBar_code object, which is operated upon to get the information. The methods for this object are not implemented.

## Bell

This system object interfaces to a simple sound device.

**.Beep**

Issues a beep sound from the sound device.

## Modem

This system object interfaces via a modem connection port with a modem.

**.Put**

This method outputs one character to the Modem.

**.Get**

This method reads one character from the Modem.

**.Status**

This method is used to get the (error) state from the Modem.

## Attribute: Shop_data

This complex attribute contains the address of the shop, the telephone number to DU, and other data needed by the software in the HHT unit.

## Database

No special way of managing the data has been selected for the HHT unit. However, the solution outlined in the following could be used: Let the Database manage information objects of class CArticle using the methods outlined next.

**.Clear_orders**

This method sets all numbers to order to zero for all CArticle objects in the Database. (The Database is emptied of orders.) Calling this method is equivalent to calling all CArticle objects in Database like this:

```
an_article_object.Set(0);
```

**.Store**

This method stores one CArticle object in Database like this:

```
Database.Store(an_article_object);
```

**.Get(an_article_number)**

This method returns a CArticle object corresponding to the article number.

**.Get_First**

This method returns a first CArticle object. See also the method Get_next.

**.Get_next**

This method returns a next CArticle object. These two last methods can be used to cycle through all CArticle objects in Database:

```
an_article_object := Database.Get_first;
WHILE NOT an_article_object.Is_null DO
// Do something
an_article_object := Database.Get_next;
END_WHILE;
```

***CArticle Objects***

A CArticle object has the methods Article_number, Text_description, No_to_order, and Set. The three first methods return the corresponding data. For instance, the following call returns the article number:

```
an_article_object.Article_number;
```

The Set method is overloaded, so the following calls set the article number, text description of the article, and the number of articles to order, respectively:

```
some_article_object.Set(an_article_number);
some_article_object.Set(a_text_string);
some_article_object.Set(a_number_to_order);
```

(This presumes different types for the parameter types. For example, the type of an article number should not equal the type used for a_number_to_order.)

### HHT_manager

This is the central system object of the HHT manager. The main logic of the HHT_manager is as follows:

```
WHILE TRUE DO
Display.Write("Please select function.");
a_button_object := Function_buttons.Pressed_button;
a_button_object.Execute;
END_WHILE; //TRUE
```

## SUBSYSTEM DISTRIBUTION UNIT

Figure 7.5 displays a detailed drawing of the objects used in the distribution unit subsystem. Some of the subobjects in this figure are large and would probably be handled as (sub)subsystems of their own in a project.

### Actor Salesperson

Those orders that are not registered automatically in the Order database via an upload from HHT units are registered manually by a Salesperson. Manual orders may come via letter or via telephone. The contents of an order is shown in Figure 7.6. Note the distinction between customer data and article data, as specified in the figure.

The Salesperson also has other tasks, which are described in connection with the mini-uses outlined here.

#### *Mini-uses: Salesperson*

The following mini-uses are implemented by Salesperson_dialog.

**Manual_entry_order**

This mini-use is used to register an order that has arrived via letter or telephone. When the customer number is entered, the rest of the customer specific data is retrieved and displayed. The Salesperson then registers other customer data. When customer data have been entered, the Salesperson enters data for each article.

When the order has been correctly entered, it is managed by the Order_manager.

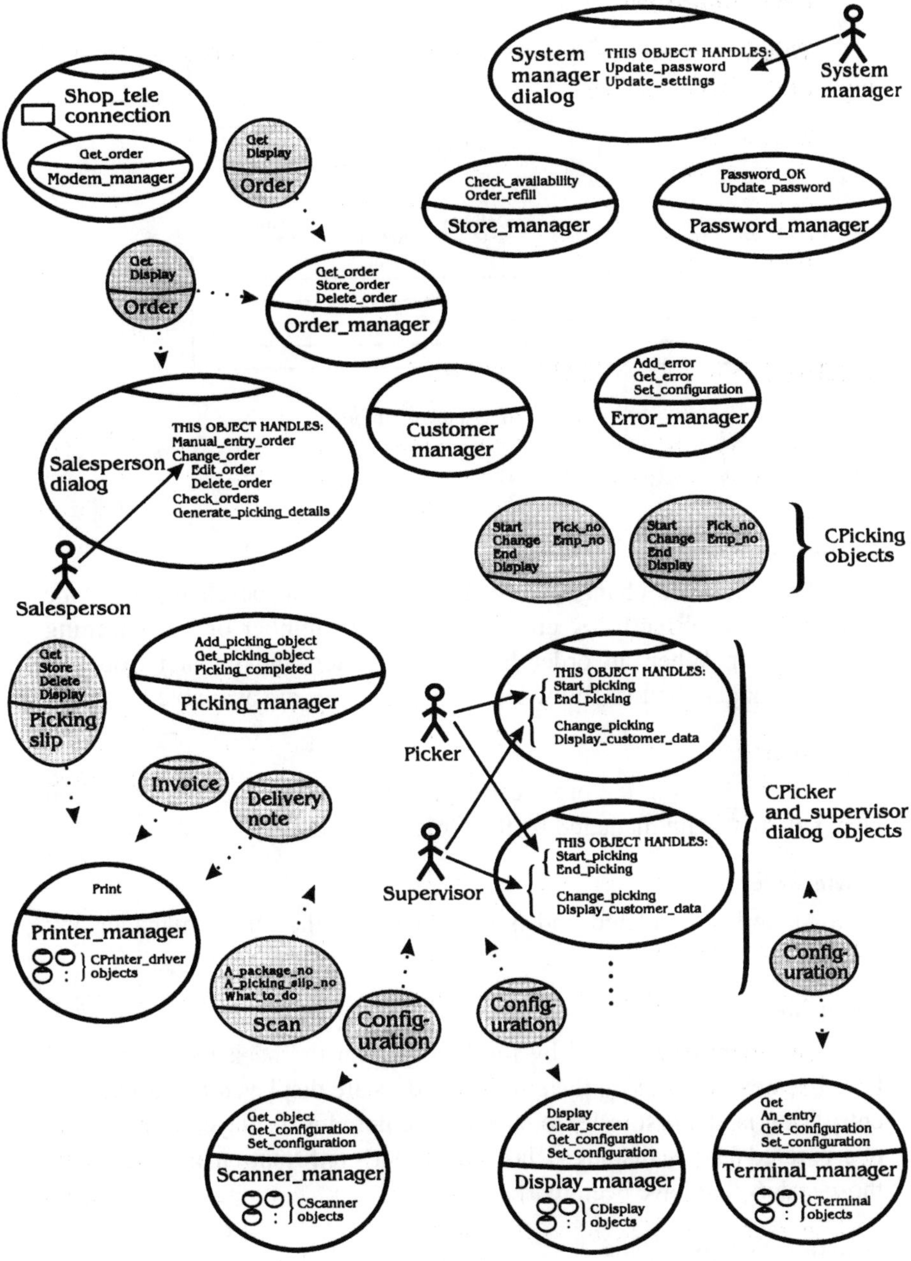


**Figure 7.5** The distribution unit subsystem.

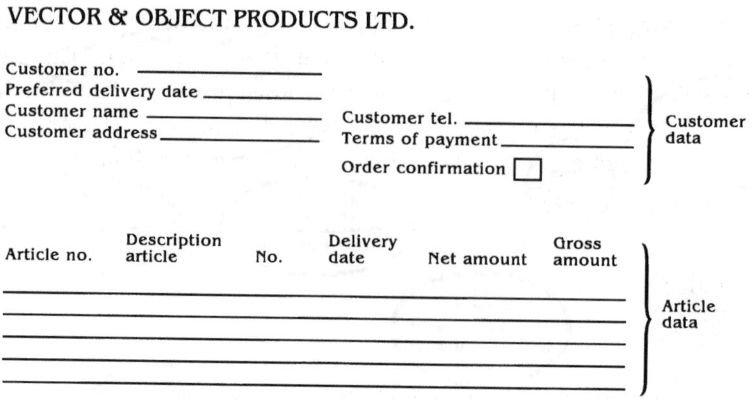


**Figure 7.6** Sketch of an order.

**Change_order**

This mini-use changes an order. The order to be changed can be selected either directly by entering the order number or by searching for the order. When an order has been selected and fetched from the Order_manager, the two following (sub) mini-uses are available.

**Edit_order**

All the fields in the order can be changed. When the order has been changed, it is again managed by the Order_manager.

**Delete_order**

An order is deleted and not managed by the Order_manager any longer.

**Check_orders**

This mini-use is used by the Salesperson to check the orders that have been entered during the day. The orders are displayed in the order of entry. That is, the first order to have been entered is displayed first and the one entered last is displayed last. An order confirmation is printed for those orders that have been marked for this.

**Generate_picking_details**

This mini-use generates a CPicking object. The CPicking object is given the initial state "unassigned." The Salesperson selects the orders to be part of a particular picking and decides the delivery date and the sequence of deliveries to the shops concerned.

A picking slip with packaging labels (including a start label and an end label) are also printed as a result of calling this method. The Salesperson selects the appropriate printer for this printing. The CPicking object is given to the Picking_manager and is then available for further processing. A picking slip is placed manually in a pigeonhole, where it is then fetched by a picker.

## Actor Picker

***Usage Scenario***

The Picker is using a picking slip to tell him or her what packages to pick. Each Picker has a pigeonhole where the picking slips are stored. A picking slip consists of a start label, package labels, and an end label. The start label contains general information, such as total number of packages, picking list number, and so on. There is a package label for each package to be picked. The end label indicates end of picking. An example of a picking slip is shown in Figure 7.7.

The procedure for the picking is outlined to give a better understanding of the work for the Picker: The Picker takes a picking slip and walks to a terminal, where he or she enters employment number and, if no picking is assigned to the Picker, a picking slip number. Entering a picking slip number can be done either by using a scanner (bar-code reader) or by using a terminal. This starts the picking process. The Picker then uses a truck with little wagons where packages are placed. Package labels contain information about where packages can be found, and they are sorted in such a way as to minimize the route of the Picker. The Picker picks a package for each package label and pastes the package label on the package. If a package is missing the corresponding package label is left on the picking slip. The picking is ended when all available packages have been picked. The Picker then goes to a terminal where he or she enters his employment number and (possibly) records missing packages.

***Mini-uses: Picker***

These mini-uses are implemented by CPicker_and_supervisor_dialog objects.

**Start_picking**

This mini-use is called when a Picker is starting to pick packages. He or she enters an employment number and, if no picking is assigned to the Picker, a picking slip number at a terminal.

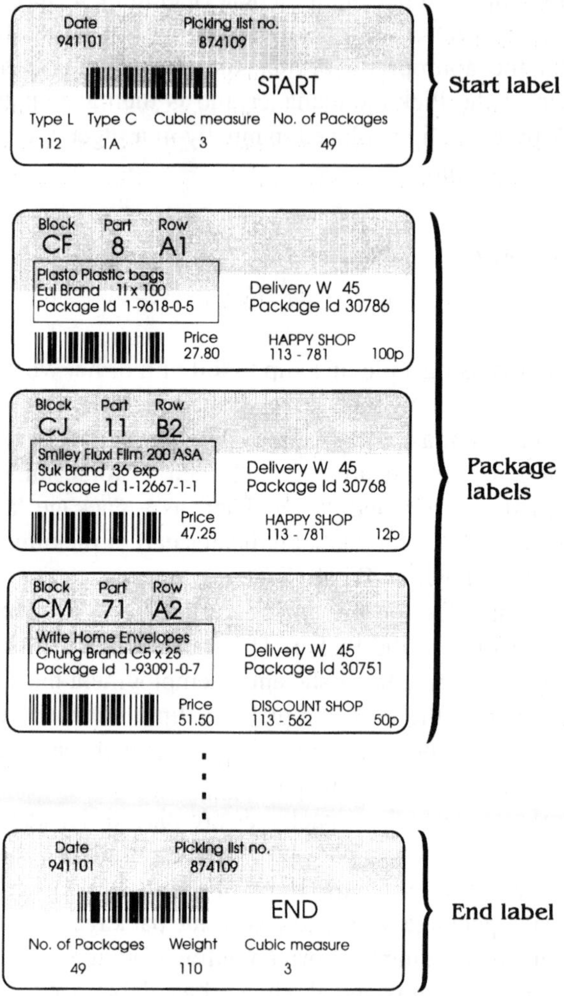


**Figure 7.7** A picking slip.

**End_picking**

This mini-use is called when a Picker ends the picking. He or she enters an employment number at a terminal. If packages were missing, he or she also enters the corresponding package numbers and number of missing packages.

A completed picking results in the printing of delivery note and invoice. (If no packages are missing, the picking is completed.)

## Actor Supervisor

The Supervisor is in charge of completing or changing those orders that could not be fully completed because of shortages of one or more packages. One way of completing the order is to find the missing packages in some other stock. The Supervisor can also call the customer in order to discuss substitute packages or deletions from the order.

### *Mini-uses: Supervisor*

These mini-uses are implemented by CPicker_and_Supervisor_dialog objects.

**End_picking**

See also the mini-use End_picking for the Picker. This mini-use can also be called by the Supervisor when he or she has been able to fill the order or changed it so that the order no longer contains any missing packages and the order thus can be ended. He or she enters an employment number and a picking slip number.

A completed picking results in the printing of delivery note and invoice. (If no packages are missing, the picking is considered to be completed).

**Change_picking**

This mini-use is used by the Supervisor to change a picking list. This is normally only done if a picking cannot be completed unless the order quantity for some packages are changed, for example, by setting the order quantity for one or several packages to zero.

**Display_customer_data**

This mini-use gives the Supervisor information about the customer, such as telephone number, name of person to contact concerning the order, etc.

## Actor System_manager

See system object System_manager_dialog, which implements the mini-uses of the System_manager.

## Shop_tele_connection

This object accepts calls from shops coming in via modem. A shop thus communicates with the Shop_tele_connection when uploading an order. When a call from a shop is made via modem, resulting in an order, the order is given to the Order_manager in the form of a COrder object.

Shop_tele_connection is the interface via modem to the shops. A Modem_manager subobject takes care of hardware idiosyncrasies. This subobject manages several modems, if more than one modem is used, leaving a simple interface to Shop_tele_connection.

The main loop in Shop_tele_connection is

```
{
WHILE TRUE DO
   an_order_object := Modem_manager.Get_order;
   IF an_order_object.Is_null THEN
   // Wait some time
   ELSE
   Order_manager.Store_order(an_order_object);
   END_IF;
END_WHILE; // TRUE
}
```

### Customer_manager

This object manages a list of customers with their names, addresses, etc. Note that this object is only indicated.

### Order_manager

This object manages orders. Note that COrder objects need not actually be stored in the Order_manager. This is a design issue that we can decide when we have selected our type of database. The reader is referred to the parts of this book discussing databases. However, conceptually it is best to view it as if we are storing COrder objects in Order_manager.

Note, in a more complete implementation of the system, we would have more options of how to process an order. For example, setting the state of an order to Deleted but keeping its information until the order had been fully processed (paid, for instance).

**.Get_order(an_order_no)**

This method returns a COrder object corresponding to an_order_no.

**.Get_order(a_date, search_criterion)**

The Get_order method is overloaded. This version of the method is used to return an order according to a given search_criterion.

**.Get_order(a_date, search_criterion, sequence_Id)**

This version of the method is used to iterate over orders for a particular date. When the method is called with search_criterion set to First, the sequence_Id is initiated by the system to a unique sequence identifier. This sequence identifier is used by the system, when search_criterion is set to Next, to keep track of consequent calls of Get_order.

For example, the following pseudocode does something to all orders entered on a particular date, starting with the first order that date.

```
{
the_date := // Enter a date
an_order_object := Order_manager.Get_order(
the_date, First, an_Id);
WHILE NOT an_order_object.Is_null DO
// Do something
an_order_object := Order_manager.Get_order(
the_date, Next, an_Id);
END_WHILE;
}
```

The sequence identifier makes it possible to have several parallel iterations going on. This solution is more complex than the one we used in the Shop subsystem but is necessary because we have more than one user in the DU. If no order is found with a Get_order call, a special null COrder object is returned containing no information (except that it is a null object).

**.Store_order(an_order_object)**

This method stores an order. If an order with the same order number exists, it is overwritten and an error message is stored in the Error_manager. Thus, if an order is retrieved, changed, and stored again by Order_manager—without the old version first having been deleted—this fact is registered in Error_manager.

**.Delete_order(an_order_no)**

An order with the an_order_no number is deleted. If no order with that number is managed by Order_manager, nothing happens except that an error message is stored in the Error_manager.

***COrder Objects***

Each object of this class contains the information found in one order.

**.Get**

This method is used to retrieve information stored in a COrder object. It is overloaded and can thus be used to retrieve different types of information.

**.Display**

This method returns the contents of an order in the form of ASCII strings, which can then be sent to a screen or a printer for output.

**.Is_null**

Returns TRUE if the object does not contain any interesting information. If the object contains relevant information and can be used, the method returns the value FALSE.

## Salesperson_dialog

This is the interface for the Salesperson to the computer system, and this object is thus responsible for handling the mini-uses of the Salesperson. These mini-uses have not been developed in any detail to keep down the length of this chapter. If you want to study in detail how a mini-use is converted into method calls, see the mini-uses handled by CPicker_and_supervisor_dialog object(s).

**Manual_entry_order**

```
{
an_order_object := // Enter customer specific data
// and article data
// When customer number is entered display all
// customer data
Order_manager.Store_order(an_order_object);
}
```

**Change_order**

```
{
// Enter order number or search?
IF // Order number entered THEN
an_order_object :=
Order_manager.Get_order(// Order number)
ELSE
WHILE // Not found DO
// Enter date and search criteria
an_order_object :=
Order_manager.Get_order(// a date, // a search
// criterion);
END_WHILE;
END_IF;
```

```
// Make local copy of order
IF NOT an_order_object.Is_null THEN
// Delete order:
Order_manager.Delete_order(an_order_object);
IF // Edit order THEN
// Edit/change local copy of an_order_object
Order_manager.Store_order(an_order_object);
END_IF;
END_IF;
}
```

**Check_orders**

```
{
an_order_object := Order_manager.Get_order(
// today, First, a_sequence_Id);
WHILE NOT an_order_object.Is_null DO
   // On current screen show:
   an_order_object.Display;
   // Do something
   // Print order confirmation if order is marked
   // for this
   an_order_object := Order_manager.Get_order(
   // today, Next, a_sequence_Id);
END_WHILE;
}
```

**Generate_picking_details**

```
{
// Select orders, delivery date and sequence of
// delivery
// Create a CPicking object for this and set its
// state to unassigned
Picking_manager.Add_picking_object(
a_picking_object);
// Select printers
// Print picking slip:
Printer_manager.Print(// A printer for labels,
a_picking_slip_object);
}
```

## System_manager_dialog

This object handles the mini-uses of a system manager. Again, note that mini-uses have not been implemented in any detail to keep down the length of this chapter. We thus briefly describe only two mini-uses. In a fully implemented system, many other mini-uses would be necessary to manage the system properly.

**Update_password**

This mini-use updates the passwords used in the system, especially the passwords necessary for those permitted to change data available in CPicking objects. Most of the logic is carried out by the Password_manager:

```
{
Password_manager.Update_password;
}
```

**Update_settings**

This mini-use is used to display and/or change the configuration of scanners, displays, terminals, etc. Items can be added or deleted. New hardware I/O addresses can be set, and so on.

The main work is carried out by calling the Get_configuration and Set_configuration methods available in objects such as Scanner_manager, Display_manager, and Terminal_manager.

## Store_manager

This object keeps an inventory of the articles. This object is also called when placing requests for refill of packages.

**.Check_availability(a_picking_object)**

This method returns an object (of class CPicking) containing packages, listed in a_picking_object, that are not in stock. If no packages are missing, a null object (of class CPicking) is returned.

**.Order_refill(a_picking_object, a_priority)**

This method orders refill of the packages contained in a_picking_object with priority a_priority.

## Password_manager

**.Password_OK(a_password, emp_no)**

This method returns TRUE if a_password is acceptable for a user with employment number emp_no, otherwise, FALSE is returned.

**.Update_password**

This method is used to update lists of passwords used in the system.

## Error_manager

The Error_manager collects errors as they are reported to it by Add_error calls. At regular intervals, errors are printed on a printer. Errors stored in the Error_manager can also be read by calling the Get_error method. The method Set_configuration is used to assign a printer to the Error_manager and for other things.

## CPicker_and_supervisor_dialog Objects

For each Terminal (with attached scanner) and Display pair used, a CPicker_and_supervisor_dialog object is created. These objects implement the mini-uses for Picker and Supervisor.

**Main loop**

```
{
display_Id :=
// A unique code identifying a display.
terminal_Id :=
// A unique code identifying a
// terminal and its attached scanner.
   Display_manager.Clear_screen(display_Id);
   WHILE TRUE DO // Main loop
   Display_manager.Display(display_Id, "Select one
   of :");
   Display_manager.Display(display_Id, "'1' :
   Start, change or end a picking");
   Display_manager.Display(display_Id, "'2':
   Display customer data");
   Display_manager.Display(display_Id, "   ");
   Display_manager.Display(display_Id, "==>>");

   CASE     Terminal_manager.Get(terminal_Id)
   '1':    Work_with_a_picking(display-Id, terminal-Id);
   '2':     Display_customer_data;
   ELSE Display_manager.Display(display_Id, "No
   existing option selected!");
   END_CASE;
END_WHILE; // Main loop
}
```

**Procedure Work_with_a_picking (display-Id, terminal-Id);**

Note that an employee can work with only one picking at the same time. If a Picker is not assigned a picking, a Picker selects a picking list by entering a picking number via terminal or via scanner (a bar-code reader).

A Picker starts a picking. A Supervisor is authorized to change a picking, and a Picker or a Supervisor ends a picking when the picking is completed.

```
{
Display_manager.Clear_screen(display_Id);
Display_manager.Display(display_Id, "Please enter
your employment number:");
// Check if the employee is assigned a CPicking
// object:
an_emp_no:= Terminal_manager.Get(terminal_Id);
a_picking_object :=
Picking_manager.Get_picking_object(an_emp_no);
//
// If no CPicking object was assigned to the
// employee, try the following:
WHILE a_picking_object.Is_null DO
   Display_manager.Display(display_Id, "Please
   enter picking slip no");
   Display_manager.Display(display_Id, "==>>");
   // Read from scanner (or terminal):
   a_scan_object :=
   Scanner_manager.Get_object(terminal_Id);
   IF a_scan_object.Is_null THEN
   EXIT Work_with_a_picking // Exit procedure
   ELSE
   a_picking_slip_no :=
   a_scan_object.A_picking_slip_no;
   a_picking_object :=
   Picking_manager.Get_picking_object(
   a_picking_slip_no);
   END_IF;

   IF a_picking_object.Is_null THEN
   Display_manager.Display(display_Id, "No picking
   slip found!");
   Display_manager.Display(display_Id, "Enter F8
   to Exit");
   END_IF;
END_WHILE; // Null object
// If we get here we must have a_picking_object <>
// null
Display_manager.Display(display_Id, "Please use
scanner or terminal to continue");
```

```
a_scan_object :=
Scanner_manager.Get_object(terminal_Id);
IF a_scan_object.Is_null THEN
EXIT Work_with_a_picking // Exit procedure
ELSE
CASE a_scan_object.What_to_do
'Start'      : a_picking_object.Start(display_Id,
               terminal_Id, an_emp_no);
'Change'     : a_picking_object.Change(display_Id,
               terminal_Id, an_emp_no);
'End'        : a_picking_object.End(display_Id,
               terminal_Id);
ELSE Display_manager.Display(display_Id, "Error");
END_CASE;
END_IF;
} // End of Procedure Work_with_a_picking
```

**Procedure Display_customer_data;**

This procedure displays data about a customer.

```
// Not implemented
```

## CPicking Objects—An Introduction

CPicking objects are created by a Salesperson via Salesperson_dialog. Each CPicking object corresponds to a picking slip. A null CPicking object exists that is returned when a method cannot return an existing CPicking object.

A CPicking_slip object contains CPackage objects (see Figure 7.8).

### *Persistence*

CPicking objects are made persistent using a pure object-oriented database. Thus, there is no need in our model for a database with special store/retrieve methods. Whether some data—such as our CPicking objects—are in volatile RAM or persistent is thus transparent, and the code does not differ (much), depending on whether some data—such as our CPicking objects— is stored in volatile RAM or are persistent. For a further discussion of this the reader is referred to the text about object-oriented databases found at the end of Appendix 1.

### *COrder_data Object*

Each CPicking object contains one subobject of class COrder_data called Order_data. This subobject contains data about the orders that

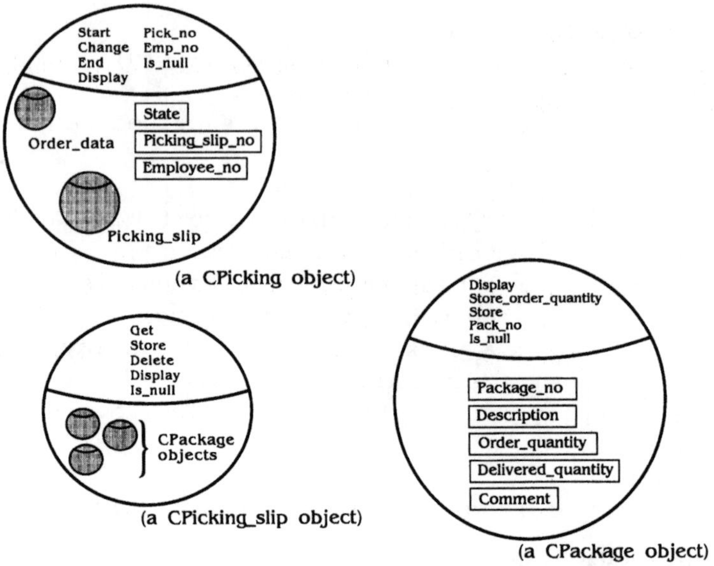


**Figure 7.8** A CPicking object contains a picking slip object which contains CPackage objects.

correspond to the CPicking object. It is generated in connection with the mini-use Generate_picking_details.

*CPicking_slip Object*

Each CPicking object contains one subobject of class CPicking_slip called Picking_slip. This object contains CPackage objects.

*Methods: CPicking_slip Object*

**.Get(package_no)**

This method returns the CPackage object that corresponds to package_no. If no CPackage object corresponds to the package number, a special null CPackage object is returned containing nothing except a comment that no package corresponding to this package number exists.

**.Store(package_object)**

This method stores a CPackage object. If a CPackage object with the same package number exists it is overwritten.

**.Delete(package_no)**

This method deletes a CPackage object corresponding to the package_no.

**.Display(package_no)**

This method returns information about a package, corresponding to the package_no, in the form of a set of ASCII strings.

*CPackage Objects*

Each CPackage object corresponds to a package label, which in turn corresponds to a package with articles that has been ordered. Most of the information items in a CPackage object can be read and changed individually. However, here we list only methods basic to our partly implemented system. Note, that a CPackage object contains information that corresponds to a label (start-, package-, or end-label).

*Attributes: CPackage Objects*

A CPackage object contains the attributes Package_no, Description, Order_quantity, Delivered_quantity, and Comment. Description is a complex attribute containing label information not found in other attributes.

*Methods: CPackage Objects*

**.Display**

This method returns the following information: package number, a description of the package, order quantity, delivered quantity, and a comment. Comment may be empty. Information is returned in the form of an ASCII string.

**.Store_order_quantity(an_integer)**

This method stores the value in an_integer as the (new) order quantity.

**.Store(an_integer)**

This method stores the value in an_integer as the (new) delivered quantity.

**.Store(a_text_string)**

This method stores a_text_string as the new comment. (Store is thus overloaded.)

**.Pack_no**

This method returns the package number.

**.Is_null**

This method returns TRUE if the object does not contain any information, is a null object. If the object has information about a package label, the method returns the value FALSE.

### *Attributes: CPicking Objects*

A CPicking object contains the following attributes:

```
State : [unassigned, assigned];
Picking_slip_no : Picking_slip_no_type;
Employee_no : Employee_no_type;
```

### *Methods: CPicking Objects*

**.Start(disp_Id, term_Id, emp_no)**

This method initiates a picking. If packages are missing, the missing packages are displayed to help the employee avoid unnecessary work by skipping these packages. New articles are ordered automatically.

```
{
Display_manager.Clear_screen(disp_Id);
If State = assigned THEN
   Display_manager.Display(disp_Id, "This Picking
   already started");
   ELSE // OK to start
   State := assigned;
   Employee_no := emp_no;
   Display_manager.Display(disp_Id, "Picking
   initiated for picking");
   Display_manager.Display(disp_Id, "slip no: ",
   Picking_slip_no);
   missing_packages_object :=
   Store_manager.Check_availability(// This
   // object);
   // Tell Picker what packages are missing:
   Display_manager.Display(disp_Id,
   missing_packages_object.Display);
   IF NOT missing_packages_object.Is_null
   THEN // Refill
   a_priority := 2;
   Store_manager.Order_refill(
   missing_packages_object, a_priority);
   END_IF;
```

```
    END_IF;
} // End of Start
```

**.Change(disp_Id, term_Id, emp_no)**

This method is used by the Supervisor to change a picking list. If the picking is not completed, the Supervisor typically makes changes to the order quantity of a package or finds the missing articles elsewhere so that the picking can be completed. After such a change of a picking list or supplementary picking, the Supervisor (or the Picker) uses the mini-use End_picking to end the picking.

```
{
Display_manager.Clear_screen(disp_Id);
Display_manager.Display(disp_Id, "Please enter
password.");
Display_manager.Display(disp_Id, "Password: ");
a_password := Terminal_manager.Get(term_Id);
IF Password_manager.Password_OK(a_password, emp_no)
THEN
Display_manager.Display(disp_Id, "Make authorized
changes OK. End with F8.");
WHILE // Make changes to packages DO
// Make changes:
// The Supervisor selects a package and changes
// one or several of the attributes:
// - Order_quantity
// - Delivered_quantity
// - Comment
END_WHILE;
ELSE
Display_manager.Display(disp_Id,
"Password illegal ");
END_IF;
} // End of Change
```

**.End(disp_Id, term_Id)**

This method ends a picking when a picking has been completed. If packages are missing, the Picker should not end the picking but enter the deviations made from the picking slip.

```
{
Display_manager.Clear_screen(disp_Id);
Display_manager.Display(disp_Id, "Please record
missing packages. ");
```

```
Display_manager.Display(disp_Id, "Please enter
package no:");
Display_manager.Display(disp_Id, "If no
deviations, please enter F8");
a_scan_object :=
Scanner_manager.Get_object(term_Id);
IF NOT a_scan_object.Is_null THEN // Is null if F8
// key pressed
a_package_no := a_scan_object.A_package_no;
a_package_object :=
Picking_slip.Get(a_package_no);
WHILE TRUE DO
   Display_manager.Display(disp_Id,
   a_package_object.Display);
   Display_manager.Display(disp_Id, "Enter text
   string to enter comment");
   Display_manager.Display(disp_Id, "Enter integer
   to change delivered quantity");
   Display_manager.Display(disp_Id, "Enter F7 for
   a new package number");
   Display_manager.Display(disp_Id, "Enter F8 to
   Exit");
   something_entered :=
   Terminal_manager.Get(term_Id);


   CASE something_entered
   'F8': EXIT End // Exit this method (End)
   'F7':{
      Display_manager.Display(disp_Id, "Enter
      new package number:");
      a_scan_object :=
      Scanner_manager.Get_object(term_Id);
      IF a_scan_object.Is_null THEN
      EXIT End // Exit this method
      ELSE
      a_package_no := a_scan_object.A_package_no;
      a_package_object:=
      Picking_slip.Get(a_package_no);
      END_IF;
      }
   ELSE: {
      IF a_package_object.Is_null THEN
```

```
        Display_manager(disp_Id, "Package number in
        Error, no update done!");
        ELSE
        // Store update:
        a_package_object.Store(something_entered);
        Picking_slip.Store(a_package_object);
        END_IF;
        }
    END_CASE;
END_WHILE; // WHILE TRUE DO LOOP
END_IF;
IF // Picking ended THEN
Picking_manager.Picking_completed (// This
// CPicking object);
END_IF;
} // End of End
```

**.Display(disp_Id, term_Id)**

This method displays the packages contained in Picking_slip. Packages are displayed on the screen, indicated by disp_Id, one screenful at a time, until all packages have been displayed. The process of displaying package information is regulated from the terminal identified by term_Id.

**.Pick_no**

This method returns the picking slip number.

**.Emp_no**

This method returns the employment number.

**.Is_null**

This method returns TRUE if the CPicking object does not contain any relevant information, is a null object. If the CPicking object contains information about a picking slip, and so on, the method returns the value FALSE.

## Picking_manager

An employee can work with only one picking at the same time. Picking_manager checks that an employee is assigned only one CPicking object at a time. Picking_manager keeps track of the CPicking object that belongs to a particular employee and that only one user (Picker or Supervisor) tries to change a CPicking object at the same time.

A Supervisor has access to all CPicking objects except those currently being accessed by someone else.

CPicking objects are not stored in the Picking_manager. The Picking_manager only keeps track of them and is used to stop illegal uses of CPicking objects. The Picking_manager can thus be said to implement a simple locking mechanism. Methods Picking_manager:

**.Add_picking_object(a_picking_object)**

A CPicking object is added to the list of CPicking objects managed by the Picking_manager.

**.Get_picking_object(an_emp_no)**

This method returns a CPicking object, which has been assigned to an employee, corresponding to an_emp_no. If no CPicking object is assigned to an_emp_no a null CPicking object is returned.

**.Get_picking_object(a_picking_slip_number)**

This method returns a CPicking object corresponding to a_picking_slip_number. If no such object exists, a null object (of class CPicking) is returned. Note that this method is thus overloaded. (The type of the parameter an_emp_no is different from the type of the parameter a_picking_slip_number.)

**.Picking_completed(a_picking_object)**

The CPicking object denoted by a_picking_object is deleted from the list of CPicking objects managed by the Picking_manager. Invoices and delivery notes are printed for the orders involved in the picking. The orders now completed are also deleted from the Order_manager.

### Printer_manager

This object is the interface to available printers and the manager of those. If an attempt is made to use a nonexisting printer, the error is reported to the Error_manager.

**.Print(a_printer, an_object)**

This method prints an_object on the printer defined by a_printer.

### Scanner_manager

This object manages CScanner objects. Each CScanner object functions as a driver for an assigned scanner. If an attempt is made to use a nonexisting scanner, the error is reported to the Error_manager.

**.Get_object(term_Id)**

This method returns a CScan object from the scanner attached to the terminal with identity term_Id.

If the scanner does not pick up a correctly read label within a short time, the Scanner_manager checks to see if something has been entered at the terminal.

```
an_entry := Terminal_manager.An_entry(term_Id);
```

Note that this call does not wait until something has been entered as the call

```
an_entry := Terminal_manager.Get(Term_Id);
```

would have done. This process is then repeated until either a label has been correctly read or something has been correctly entered at the terminal.

If something is entered at a terminal it is used to construct a CScan object. However, only one information item is then assigned to an attribute of a CScan object according to some scheme. (For example, it could be that picking slip numbers and package label numbers start with different alphanumerical characters.) Those attributes that are not explicitly set to any values are given default values representing nonexisting values for the attribute in question—for example, a nonexisting package number.

If function key F8 is pressed, a null object is returned.

**.Get_configuration**

This method returns an object describing the scanners handled by the Scanner_manager.

**.Set_configuration(a_config_object)**

This method updates the Scanner_manager settings.

### *CScan Object*

A CScan object contains the information that is read from a label. In our partly implemented system, it contains only a picking slip number, a package number, and/or the information Start if a start label, Change if a package label, or End if an end label. In a fully developed system, a CScan object would contain more information and methods.

**.A_package_no**

This method returns the package number contained in the CScan object. If the attribute is not set, a value representing a nonexisting package is returned.

**.A_picking_slip_no**

This method returns the picking slip number contained in the CScan object. If the attribute is not set, a value representing a nonexisting picking slip is returned.

**.What_to_do**

This method returns the value Start, Change, or End, depending on the label read or the number entered at the terminal. If nothing could be read, the value Error, is returned.

## Display_manager

This object manages CDisplay objects. Each CDisplay object functions as a driver for an assigned screen. If an attempt is made to use a nonexisting display, the error is reported to the Error_manager.

**.Display(a_disp_Id, $param_1$, $param_2$, , , $param_n$)**

This method displays a row of text on the appropriate screen. $Param_1$, $param_2$, , , $param_n$ can be either text strings or integers. This method needs at least one parameter apart from the parameter a_disp_Id.

**.Clear_screen(a_disp_Id)**

This method clears the screen that corresponds to the given a_disp_Id.

**.Get_configuration**

This method returns an object with information about the displays handled by the Display_manager.

**.Set_configuration(a_config_object)**

This method updates the Display_manager settings with the settings contained in a CConfiguration object.

## Terminal_manager

This object manages CTerminal objects. Each CTerminal object functions as a driver for an assigned terminal. If an attempt is made to use a nonexisting terminal, the error is reported to the Error_manager.

**.Get(term_Id)**

This method will return a value when a function key is pressed or a sequence of alphanumerical keys has been pressed, ending with ENTER. The value returned is the function key or a value corresponding to the sequence of alphanumerical keys entered. A call is not returned until a function key, a correct sequence of keys ending with ENTER, or ENTER has been entered. (Note that a value may thus contain characters other than digits.)

When the method has been called, the current value is erased and a new function key, a sequence of alphanumerical keys ending with ENTER, or ENTER must be entered before the method will return a value. (Simply entering ENTER returns the value *Carriage return*.)

**.An_entry(term_Id)**

This method returns a value as the method Get, but if ENTER (or a function key) has not yet been entered, the returned value is <ESC>. A call is thus returned more or less immediately.

The current value is *not* erased when this method has been called.

**.Get_configuration**

This method returns an object describing the terminals handled by the Terminal_manager.

**.Set_configuration(a_config_object)**

This method updates the Terminal_manager settings with the settings contained in a CConfiguration object.

## Summary—Information Objects: Distribution Unit

Also see the discussion about the shop subsystem.

**COrder objects**

See section Order_manager.

**CInvoice objects**

This is not implemented in any detail.

**CDelivery_note objects**

This is not implemented in any detail.

**CPicking objects**

See section CPicking objects—An Introduction.

**CPicking_slip objects**

See section CPicking objects—An Introduction.

**COrder_data objects**

See section CPicking objects—An Introduction.

**CPackage objects**

See section CPicking objects—An Introduction.

**CScan objects**

See section Scanner_manager.

**CConfiguration objects**

This information object contains information necessary to set and read settings for Scanner_manager, Terminal_manager, Display_manager, Error_manager, etc.

## CLASS STRUCTURES

### Introduction

Also see the introduction to the section, "Class Structures" in Chapter 6. We again stress the point that the intention with these example chapters is to help the reader think about objects and object structures—not classes. In a real situation, we would probably take a more active interest in possible class structures during analysis and design than we have shown in Chapters 6 and 7.

After some study of the object-oriented structures for this system, the following class structures should appear as reasonable.

### CObject_manager

The Order_manager and the Picking_manager objects have a lot in common. They both manage objects, and their responsibilities often coincide. For example, they both have to implement a simple locking mechanism for the objects they manage.

The Customer_manager and—to some extent—the Store_manager, the Password_manager, and the Error_manager also resemble the Order_Manager and the Picking_manager. Figure 7.9 shows a possible class structure. The abstract class CXObject_manager has been introduced to reflect that its three subclasses have some particular things (design) in common.

In our implementation Customer_manager is without methods, and among the rest of the objects we do not find many common method names. This does not, however, stop us from putting similar classes in the same class structure when it is clear that they have a lot of modeling aspects in common. When we continue with our implementation we can rename methods so that methods having the same behavior get the same

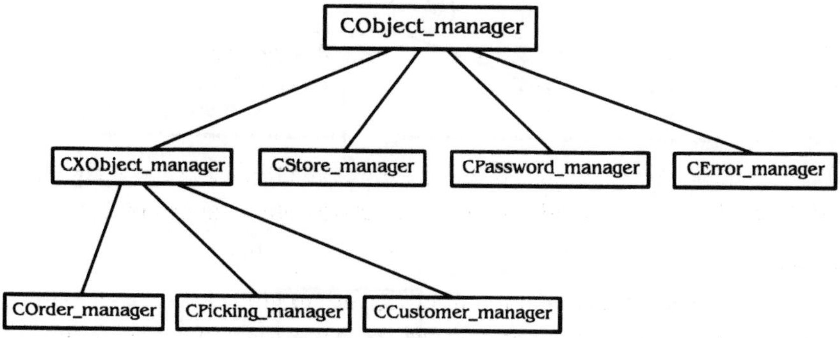


**Figure 7.9** CObject_manager.

name or we can implement a general method—available to subclasses—and use it to implement the methods. An example of the former solution would be to give the method Store_order in Order_manager and the method Add_picking_object in Picking_manager the same name. An example of the latter implementation strategy would be to design a general method for the class CXObject_manager, let it be inherited by COrder_manager and CPicking_manager, and use it in these classes to implement the Store_order and Add_picking methods, respectively.

It is also not clear yet whether subclasses should inherit methods or whether we should use delegation to implement methods. However, it is not unlikely that, for example, COrder_manager could best be implemented by adding a subobject supplying necessary methods for management of objects. Thus, some of the methods of this class would not be inherited. Instead, they would be implemented using the methods of the added subobject, which is the basic idea of delegation. (Delegation is explained in Chapter 3.)

The preceding discussion is also applicable to the rest of this section.

## CDialog and CManager

There are several modeling similarities between the System_manager_dialog and Salesperson_dialog, and it is possible that they could be derived from the same class. There are also modeling similarities between Scanner_manager, Display_manager, and Terminal_manager. Possible class structures are shown in Figure 7.10. Again, we have introduced an abstract class, CXManager, to reflect that two subclasses have more modeling similarities (design) in common than the rest of the classes.

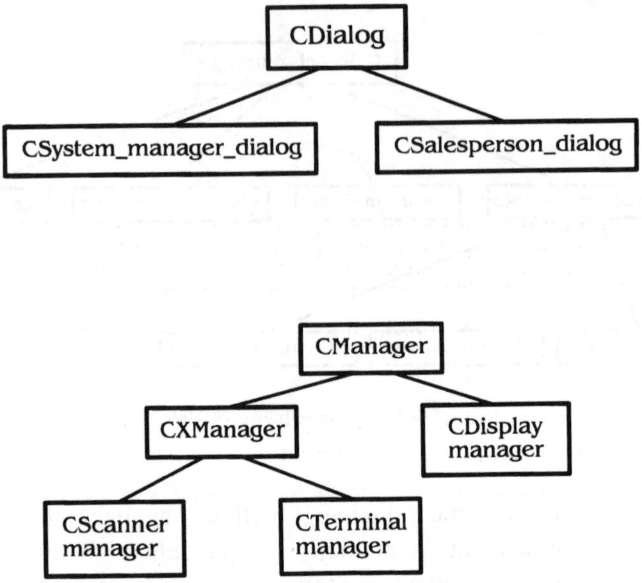


**Figure 7.10** CDialog and CManager.

## Information Objects

The CButton objects used in the HHT unit give us a straightforward class structure, which is shown in Figure 7.11. Our information objects used in DU also have common modeling details, such as the method Is_null. However, the details are less similar than for the CButton objects used in the HHT unit and the information objects used in Chapter 6. It is thus difficult to see obvious modeling possibilities for the information

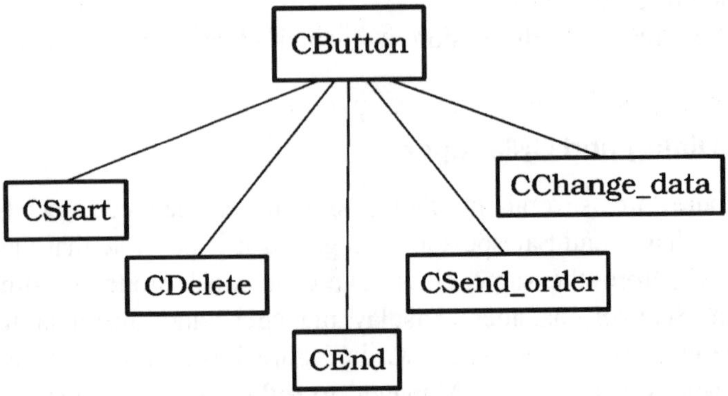


**Figure 7.11** CButton.

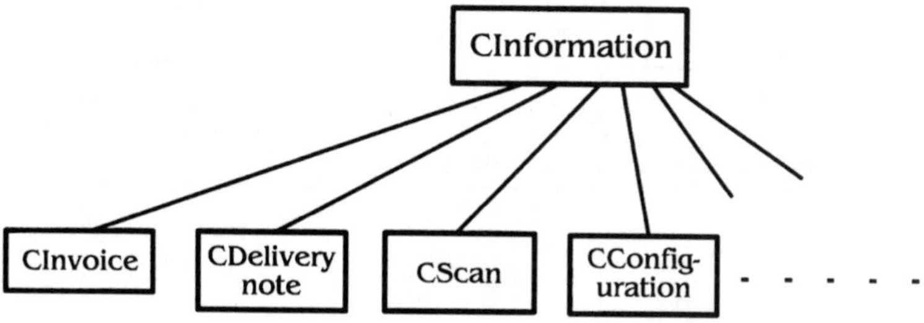


**Figure 7.12** CInformation.

objects we use in the DU. For example, even though both Order_manager and Picking_manager manage objects—COrder and CPicking objects, respectively—these information objects are very dissimilar.

The only true similarity between our information objects in the DU is that they are information objects. Thus a possible way to model this is indicated in Figure 7.12. However, it must be agreed that this class structure is a bit artificial.

### A Few Other Possible Class Structures

More likely possibilities are found if we look at Shop_subsystem and the Distribution_unit_subsystem at the same time. Thus, it is probable that the CScanner objects in the Distribution_unit and the CBar_code_reader object in the Shop_subsystem are similar. In the same way, it is probable that the Modem object (Shop_subsystem) has a counterpart used by the Modem_manager (DU). The CBar_code object (Shop_subsystem) and the CScan object (DU) and the CArticle object (Shop_subsystem) and the CPackage object (DU) could also have modeling similarities. Either we then create similar objects from the same class or create objects from subclasses having the same superclass. These latter solutions are illustrated in Figure 7.13.

Other possible modeling scenarios are left to the interested reader.

## SUMMARY

In this chapter, we modeled a data processing system in which shops order merchandise from distributing units. We did not develop the system in full but concentrated on selected parts. For example, some mini-uses were more fully developed than other mini-uses. The chapter demonstrated how we can apply object-oriented concepts and principles to

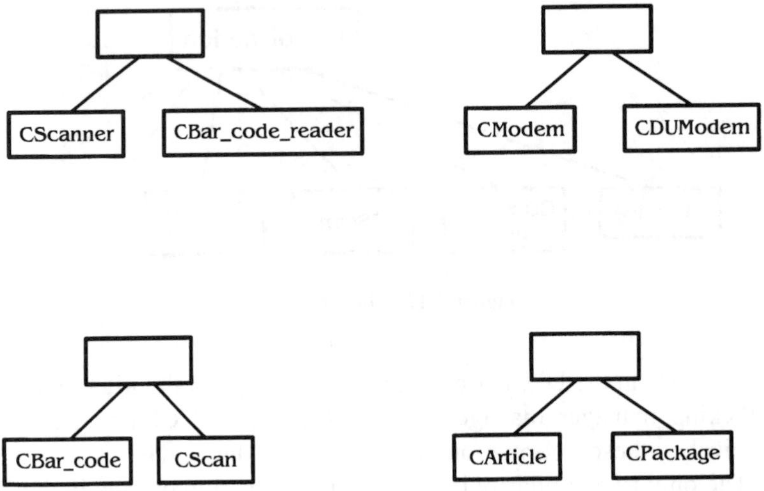


**Figure 7.13** A few possible class structures.

model a system. It was shown that we could model this data processing system with the same concepts as those used in Chapter 6, which modeled a more technically oriented system. We thus used concepts such as actors, mini-uses, information objects, system objects, subsystems, context picture, context drawing, etc. It is interesting to note how general these concepts are. See also the summary for Chapter 6.

# 8

# Soft Factors

## *Some Social Issues*

> *There is nothing more difficult to take in hand, more perilous to conduct, or more uncertain in its success, than to take the lead in the introduction of a new order of things.*
>
> —Niccolò Machiavelli

## INTRODUCTION

It is natural for professional engineers to concentrate on technical factors. This is also the basic approach we have followed in this book, although we started out by discussing in Chapter 1 some fundamental limits to the human mind when dealing with complexity. The problem with this technical approach is that, in real life, purely technical issues are sometimes of less importance than other factors. When management makes decisions or when projects fail or succeed, those other factors often play the major role. These other factors include market factors and soft factors.

Examples of market factors are availability and quality of development tools, databases, software for interfacing to databases, communication standards, and graphical user interfaces.

Soft factors are harder to define. However, examples include aspects of software development, such as: How well does a team of software developers work together? Do we have an adequate organization of the software development effort? What about the company culture? Are the development methods and other supporting factors, such as computer facilities, good enough?

In this chapter we discuss some questions concerning these soft factors. We start by discussing the importance of being able to find good abstractions and how a method and a notation can support this. We continue with a discussion about how an organization should be changed to achieve the full potential of the object-oriented paradigm. Finally, we give some recommendations concerning the introduction and the management of object-oriented software development.

## ABSTRACT THINKING

A main theme of this book is, without any doubt, the importance of making good abstractions. A main argument is that proper abstractions are a key factor in successful object-oriented software development. We need a well-developed ability to make good abstractions if we are to find relevant objects and classes. Because we have already stressed its importance, we shall here only mention a few points concerning it. The complexity of modern systems is overwhelming, and if we are to conquer complexity we must have

- Methods that simplify complexity by applying techniques for finding and designing good abstractions.
- Notation that supports the use of methods without introducing any new unnecessary details.
- Project members who are good at making abstractions.

Let us look at these three points, starting with the first two: methods and notation.

### Methods and Notation

Some people feel that if we are given a good notation, the solution will follow. However, a notation will not automatically give us a solution, but an intelligent set of symbols might guide us.

If we look at successful attempts at notation, we find that they have several qualities in common:

- They are *self-explaining* and do not need much decoding effort.
- They encourage a *close mapping* between model and the application we are constructing.
- The notation *guides us* when we search for a solution.
- The notation does *not introduce any new details* when we design a model unless they are necessary.

Looking at the example in Figure 8.1, we see that the symbols used are *self-explaining* to a large degree. For example, the symbol used for a capacitor reveals a little about the basic construction of capacitors, and the symbol indicates that DC current will have difficulty passing this type of component. The symbol used for transistors shows the direction of the main current, and so on.

The electronic symbols also encourage a *close mapping* between model and the circuit we are designing, because each symbol represents a

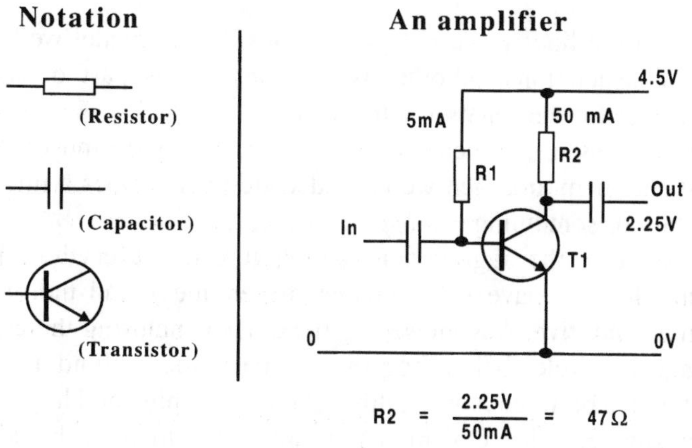


**Figure 8.1** A notation must fit its usage.

corresponding hardware part. The third quality mentioned is also found because the symbols *guide us* in finding a solution. A transistor can indeed amplify current and/or voltage.

Finally, the last quality is also found, because it is *difficult to omit any of the details* found in the model of the amplifier without making the model more difficult to understand or incomplete.

If we turn to software, we find that the notations used there seldom meet the qualities mentioned. For instance, a common way of describing aggregation is neither self-explaining nor without unnecessary details. In Figure 8.2 we see how aggregation is often modeled. The circles represent

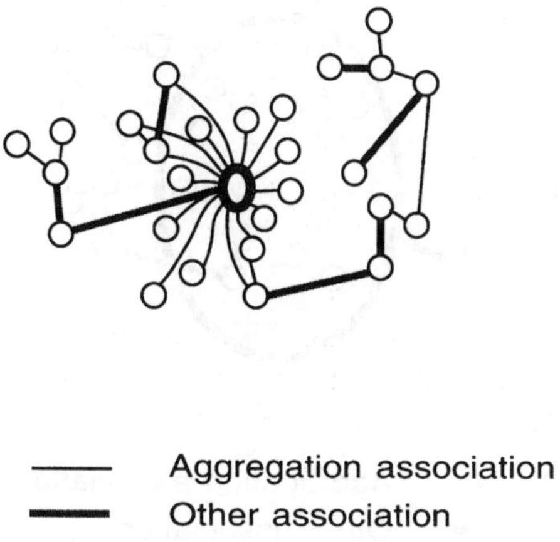


**Figure 8.2** A drawing of an aggregation

objects, and the lines represent associations. In the model we have both is_part_of associations and other associations. The is_part_of association lines make up the aggregation information.

These lines are, in themselves, information that we must grasp. First we must see them and then we must decode them. (Does a line indicate aggregation or something else?)

If we draw the aggregation as in Figure 8.3, everything becomes much simpler. We have fewer details (fewer lines), and the drawing is much more intuitive. Anyone seeing the ellipse enclosing the circles can guess that the circles belong together—a basic idea behind aggregation. The difference between how we think about something and how we model it is now smaller—the semantic gap is smaller. A method should support simplifications like this, because we should need to invest energy only in the search for a solution to our problem. All energy used for other things, such as decoding a notation, is wasted energy.

In Figure 8.4 we see an even better illustration of this point. Some of us may remember the "good old days" when we programmed our computers directly with zeros and ones which were read into the computer by setting toggles on the front. The three lines with zeros and ones, in the figure can represent the instruction of adding five to a variable x. It could be fun to program a computer with toggles, but those of us who are mainly interested in executing the statement x:= x + 5 will prefer the second solution in the figure to the first one, because the second solution involves less energy spent on decoding. An even better solution would be if we could

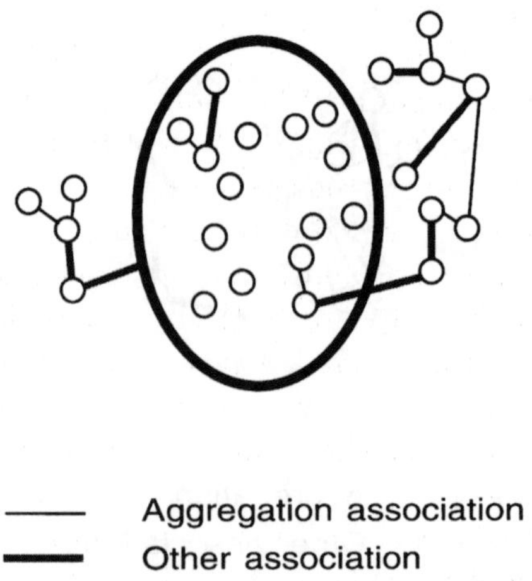


**Figure 8.3** Figure 8.2 simplified.

**A solution:**

```
11011011 11101101
11110011 00000101
00110111 11101101
```

**A second solution:**

```
MOVEA, X;
ADDA, 5;
MOVE, X;
```

**Figure 8.4** Expressing addition of a number in two different ways.

simply write the statement x:= x + 5; directly, which explains some of the success behind high-level languages. This point is not always well understood, as anyone who looks at today's different notation schemes will soon see. The problem of x:=x + 5 might be considered trivial, so why bother about a natural notation? Perhaps thinking about the following equation can clarify the point:

$$y := x^5 + sin(2x)/2^{1/2} * 5x + 17;$$

The problems with notation, as indicated, seldom occur when we model small systems. The problems occur when a model grows, something that happens in real life but seldom happens in a three-day seminar or the equivalent.

If we are to fulfill the quality of having a close mapping between our model and what we construct, then there should be a simple mapping between the symbols in our model and the code. Each symbol should be easily traceable to something in the code. Unfortunately, this quality is often lacking. There are also other problems related to notation. One of them is illustrated in Figure 8.5. Having read this book, your first guess concerning the figure is probably that it shows a class structure. Looking closer at it, we find this to be wrong. The figure describes an algorithm for updating records in a file using a popular notation. The problem is that, when we try to read a notation, we also have to put energy into decoding it, and if we are used to decoding it in a particular way, we can easily read it in an incorrect way.

Object-oriented modeling is basically the idea of taking ideas used by a customer, turning them into objects, adding some new objects, and then grouping the objects—probably in several layers—into an application. If

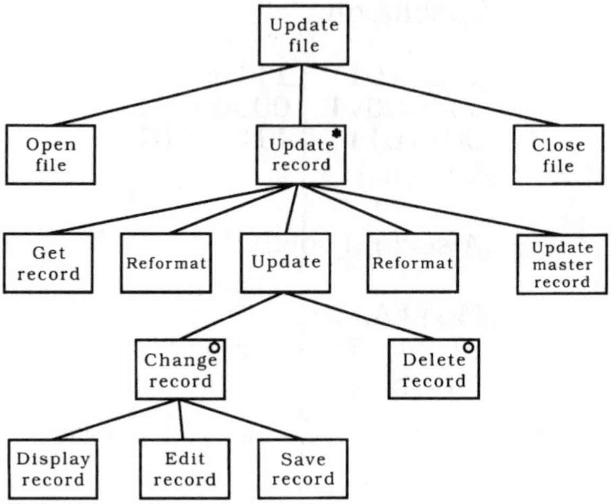


**Figure 8.5** A class structure?

the developer is too focused on technical details he or she will probably not find the proper objects. A good method and notation should help the developer to forget technical details related to computers, communication protocols, etc. It appears that those involved with administrative software development usually are more inclined to speak to the customer on his or her own terms than those involved with technical programming.

Let us formulate the preceding discussion as our first two laws about software development:

1. A method and its notation should simplify the modeling activity by (a) hiding irrelevant facts, by (b) not introducing any new unnecessary details, and by (c) simplifying communication between customer and developer.
2. A notation should mirror the method being used and, in an intuitive fashion, help explain what a model is all about, thereby making the model easy to understand.

## People

As we have noted in this book, we need an ability to make proper abstractions to define good class structures and object structures. Well-chosen class structures are one of the keys to reuse, and a good object structure (architecture) is a key to success when implementing an application.

Unfortunately people are often not put where their abilities are best used. There is a principle called the Peter principle. It states that people are

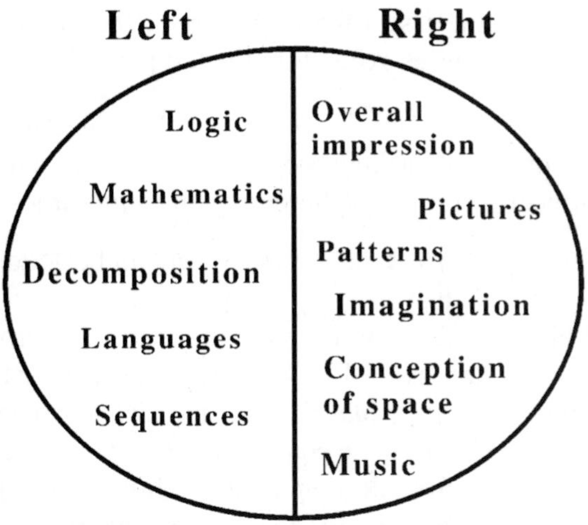


**Figure 8.6** Left and right parts of the brain.

promoted to their level of incompetence. The Peter principle often seems to be at work in teams doing object-oriented development, because people who show a good ability at coding in, for instance, C or C++ are often promoted in the next project. This promotion might then involve the responsibility of dividing the work of developing software between groups of people. However, someone good at handling the details involved while programming is not necessarily good at partitioning a system.

If we map intellectual abilities in the right and left parts of our brain, respectively, we arrive at two different sets of capabilities. We illustrate this in Figure 8.6. We can use this knowledge to explain why people have varying capabilities to make good abstractions and why they are thus more or less fitted to work with analysis and design or coding, respectively.

An analyst needs a good ability for abstracting, and if we look at what is needed for that we find a need for characteristics such as the following:

- Building a good class structure requires an ability to find similar *patterns* in various classes.
- Making a good object structure requires an ability to disregard details in favor of a *whole*.
- A good *imagination* will make it easier to try out solutions and combine objects and classes and thus find the optimal solution among many possible solutions.
- To think in *pictures* is a useful ability when we try to figure out a good object structure.

We find these abilities in the right part of the brain. On the other hand, programming requires skills from the left part of the brain:

- Ability to observe and *decompose* details into *sequences*.
- Ability for logical thinking because programming is writing in a *language* that is very *logical*, bordering on *mathematics*.

We thus conclude that a good programmer need not be good at object-oriented analysis and design at all.

It might also be the case that good programmers, programming in low-level languages, are skillful at keeping many facts current in their minds simultaneously. This means they do not have to depend on an ability to make abstractions to handle complexity. This then hinders them—or at least some of them—from developing an ability to make good abstractions. There are those who are very good at keeping many details current simultaneously. Still, they will eventually meet their limit. Thus, our third law can be stated as follows:

3. The most important key to efficient object-oriented software development is to assign tasks to people according to their abilities to think abstractly.

For example, the basic key to successfully developing an application using object-oriented technology lies in finding the very few who are good at making abstractions and in placing them in charge of the definition of object structures and class structures.

## ORGANIZATION

### Components

Object-oriented programming is an opportunity, but we will not achieve its full potential unless an organization is adapted to its needs. One such need is the need to focus the development process on reuse. If a phase model is used, a special phase could be inserted where the possibility of reuse is evaluated. The object should be regarded as a building block used when developing software. Because building blocks might be found in any phase, it is better to include this reuse evaluation in all phases.

In the following we use the word *component* as a synonym for building block. A component has been put through extensive testing and reviewing, making it reusable under many different circumstances. It is thus a class with a low error rate, high-quality documentation, and complete functionality. Note that the component must have high quality or it should not be made available because an error in a component will be multiplied by the number of projects using it. By *complete functionality* we mean that a component has enough functionality to make it usable in many projects, as opposed to being usable in one or a few projects. A component has been categorized and put in a reuse library. We summarize with the following definition:

**Definition.** A *component* is a class that has been previously developed, is of high quality, has complete functionality, and is meant to be reused in several applications.

Note that the word component is not standardized, and the concept is thus also sometimes used in a more general sense.

**Definition.** A *component* is one of the parts that make up a system. A component may be hardware or software and may be subdivided into other components. *Note:* The terms module, component, and unit are often used interchangeably or defined to be subelements of one another in different ways, depending upon the context. The relationship of these terms is not yet standardized. [IEEE]

Figure 8.7 illustrates how a company can organize its software development. We divide the software development effort in a company into two parallel activities. To the left we find a project organization, and to the right we find a product organization.

The project organization is used for the projects that develop applications. A project organization and a product organization exist in two radically different environments or cultures. A project culture is centered around short-term goals, such as making an application as fast as possible, meeting deadlines, or showing a big profit *this* year. It involves time schedules and tight budgets and is often under great pressure to meet these requirements. This is not a good environment for developing components, our reusable software objects. Instead, we need a product organization where the goal is to build products to be reused. A product culture brings out more long-term goals. Here, we are interested in making software components, and we can often view an application that takes a little longer time than planned as an investment rather than as a failure, if we can just get some components in the process. In a product culture, we can also emphasize what is good for the company as a whole rather than what is good for a particular project.

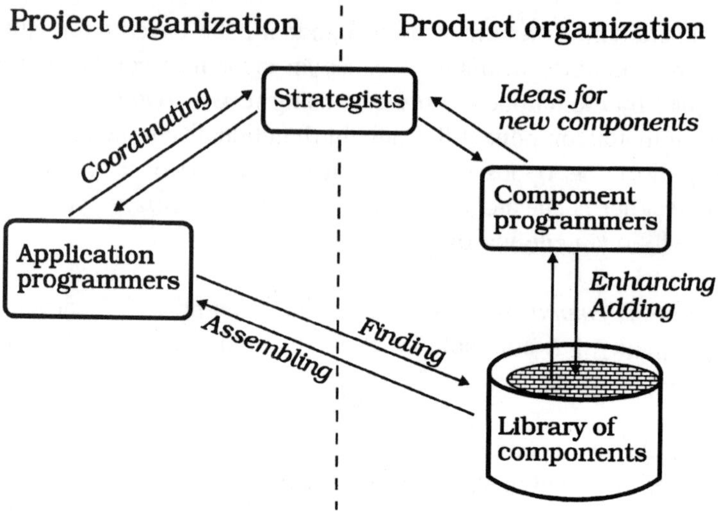


**Figure 8.7** A recommended object-oriented organization for a company.

If the components are to be reused, they must satisfy several criteria:

- They must be easy to find and understand or they will not be (re)used.
- They must be of high quality. That is, they must be well-documented, and be very stable and without errors, or a project will refuse to (re)use them.
- They must incorporate more functions than needed in one project, or they will not be used in more than that project.

All these criteria are in stark conflict with the environment we usually find in a project. Giving a project more resources for it to meet these goals simply will not work. If a project gets more resources, the resources will be used to meet the most pressing need that exists at the moment—whatever it might be.

If components are to be easy to understand, they must not only be well-documented, but they must also be well thought out. Items (objects, variables, etc.) must be named in a thoughtful way. The structure must be easy to follow. For example, there should not be much use of recursion. All these factors will decrease the cost of (re)using a component but will certainly raise the price of developing it compared with a quick and dirty solution. (A solution that will, by default, be chosen in a project under pressure).

People are not objective but will automatically perceive whatever they are doing as much better than anything not developed by themselves.

Thus, if the "not invented here" attitude is to be overruled, a potential component must, for example, have much higher stability than a project-developed object. Again, we find that a component will cost more. It all boils down to one question: Do we believe in the idea of the component or not? If we believe it is a good idea, we can accept higher initial costs.

## Project Member Roles

In Figure 8.7 we indicated three roles for project members:

- Application programmers
- Component programmers
- Strategists

If we use an object-oriented programming language, application programmers, of course, develop classes, too. The separation into application programmers and component programmers in Figure 8.7 then only implies that those classes-components that are to be used in more than one application is the responsibility of the product organization.

Application programmers should be good at making abstractions, because that will make them more likely to reuse components. Their task is to focus not on the details of a component, but on its usage. They should display an interest in thinking about the "whole," the component, rather than about implementation details of the component. If they can do this, they will be more able to visualize what objects to group together when they build an application. Building an application object by object should be their paradigm.

Component programmers should also have an ability to think abstractly, but they should be more interested in the details of the components. Their main task is to make each component as easy to use as possible and as stable as possible. A component programmer can also take part in a project. Usually, he or she participates only at the start of the project, when bringing in detailed knowledge about existing classes relating to one or more areas. For example, he or she could give information about the use of interface components. In this way a component programmer can help give a project a quick start.

Strategists are coordinators and mentors. They should have extensive experience about software reuse, especially as it applies to the company where they work. In particular, they must have a good knowledge of available components and experience about building applications. This makes it possible for them to act as go-betweens and give ideas both to application programmers and component programmers. The application programmers need advice as to what objects to use. The component programmers need advice about the way they should augment the functions of their components, what components to add to the library of reusable components, and where to optimize. A complete view of both applications and components is needed to make accurate decisions about optimizing. Consequently, this job is not ideally suited to either application programmers or component programmers. Instead the strategists should make such decisions.

Strategists should be responsible for evaluating nonsuccessful library searches because they give valuable information about needed components. They should also take the main responsibility for eliminating the "not invented here" attitude. Symptoms of this attitude are, for example, feeling safest when personally writing the code, feeling productive when writing code rather than reusing code, and measuring productivity in lines of code.

We can imagine other roles, too. For example, we could have library managers, tool programmers, user interface designers, and other types of roles. A library manager is responsible for managing the reuse library, and a tool programmer specializes in building tools to support object-oriented development. These types of roles are secondary; the primary ones are application programmers, component programmers, and strategists. An important question in connection with these roles is how to assign people to them. We are not all created alike. Some of us may be good at creating abstractions and at finding objects, and others may be good at implementing classes. Some of us will thrive in a project culture trying to meet deadlines, whereas others will just develop ulcers and feel miserable. We thus need a mix of people, and we need to assign them appropriately. Some of the characteristics needed for various roles have been outlined previously. Two additional recommendations are

- If you hate meeting deadlines, you should probably be a component programmer.
- If you have experience both with building components and building applications, if you like to manage people, and if you are able to delegate responsibilities, then you are well suited for a role as a strategist.

Note that the assignment of project members into different roles does not necessarily mean that this assignment is static. Thus, we can well imagine that someone starts as a component programmer, works as an application programmer for a while, works as component programmer again, and in the end takes on the role of a strategist. We state a fourth law:

4. One of the keys to get reuse in a company is to set up an organization that explicitly supports two independent and separate activities: developing applications and developing reusable classes (components).

It is difficult to set up such an object-oriented organization when the company is learning the basics of object-oriented software development. More about the introduction of object-oriented technology is found in the section "Recommendations" in this chapter.

## OBJECT-ORIENTED TECHNOLOGY

*Minds are like parachutes. They only function when they are open.*

— Sir James Dewar (Attributed)

The typical approach employed by companies is to adapt one or several object-oriented development methods and create a company-specific method. The main reason for this is that existing methods are not complete. For example, sufficient support for hard real-time systems is something that is frequently missing.

A problem is that object-oriented methods often do not support established standards. A requirements specification might, for example, have a certain predetermined layout and content. With an object-oriented approach, we might get another type of requirements specification altogether.

An object-oriented approach often involves a close connection between language, component libraries, and tools. This might involve changes in the way an application is developed, something that might also disagree with established standards.

Today many tools are marketed as object-oriented. Unfortunately, they are often insufficiently adapted to object-oriented ideas. That object-oriented programming languages often fail regarding many software engineering aspects has already been mentioned. For example, C++ is very difficult to read unless we exert great effort to make it readable (see Appendix 4). Often the pointers used in C++ play havoc with the application, making it crash, and so on. However, generally speaking, object-oriented software engineering should produce software of higher quality. Reasons for this are that objects are well-defined parts accepting only a specified set of messages, objects may not access (interfere with) data in other objects, messages can often replace branching statements, the number of unique code lines in a system is often decreased because of inheritance, and so on.

## The Cost of Introducing Object-Oriented Technology

Object-oriented engineering will initially increase the price of software development because it involves a great educational effort and because building components is expensive. Presently, few class libraries are available that can be bought and easily incorporated with other class libraries. This will change, but today often only a few class libraries are readily available to the developers. Thus, the big payoff will come when a company has developed its own class libraries; however, these class libraries are not available in a first project. In the long run object-oriented software development should decrease the costs.

### *Decreased Costs During Software Development*

Costs should decrease for reasons such as the following:

- An object-oriented requirements specification is easier to understand for a customer than a functional requirements specification. It is thus probable that an object-oriented requirements specification will be closer to the real needs of a customer than a non-object-oriented requirements specification. This means fewer corrections, which translates into lower costs.
- A large part of a system is built object by object rather than line by source code line.
- Less unit testing is needed because components have already been tested. This also implies that reliability (quality) will improve steadily.
- The integration testing will be easier because of the early focus on the interfaces implied by the object-oriented paradigm.

### *Decreased Costs During Maintenance*

During maintenance, costs should decrease because

- A requirements specification closer to the real needs of a customer means fewer errors during maintenance.
- Understanding where a change in reality should change the implementation is easier because of the close mapping between reality, model, and implementation.
- It is easier to understand what changes the customer really needs, because we talk about objects rather than data plus functions.

## Where Is Object-Oriented Technology?

Most new technologies pass through several stages of development. This is also true for a new technology such as object-oriented engineering (see Figure 8.8). The first stage is an exploratory stage, where various

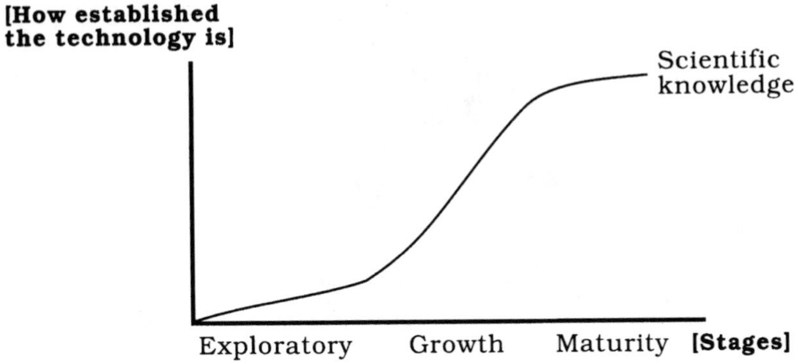


**Figure 8.8** Stages of a new technology.

ways of using the technology are tried. Pilot projects are started, etc. Then comes a stage with rapid and often uncontrolled growth. This stage is characterized by confusion, because the technology is not yet properly understood. This stage is followed by a last stage, where the technology matures and eventually becomes scientific knowledge. Today most companies appear to be in the exploratory stage, whereas object-oriented technology as such is in the growth stage. However, the situation is a bit more complex than this because object-oriented technology entails a radical paradigm shift in the way we think. Thus it is also relevant to apply Kuhn's paradigm shift, introduced in Chapter 1, to object-oriented technology (see Figure 8.9).

## Who Will Be Affected by Object-Oriented Technology?

If Kuhn's paradigm shift is applicable to object-oriented technology, as many believe, we will eventually see a revolution with long-lasting and radical effects on the way we develop software. This means that everyone in a company will be affected by object-oriented technologies. Referring to Robert Anthony's organizational pyramid, introduced in the preface, we can say that it would be a mistake to leave the introduction and implementation of object-oriented technologies in a company just to the managerial and/or

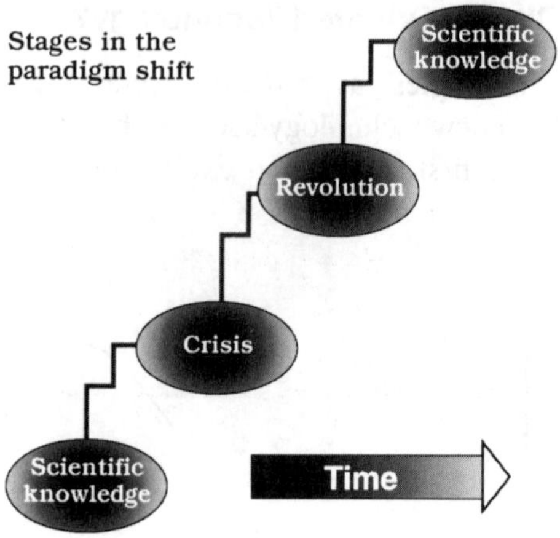


**Figure 8.9** Kuhn's paradigm shift.

**Figure 8.10** Robert Anthony's organizational pyramid.

operational levels (see Figure 8.10). A basic understanding of the technology and a clear commitment to this new technology at the strategic level is essential. Unless we have this, a successful introduction of object-oriented engineering in a company will not occur.

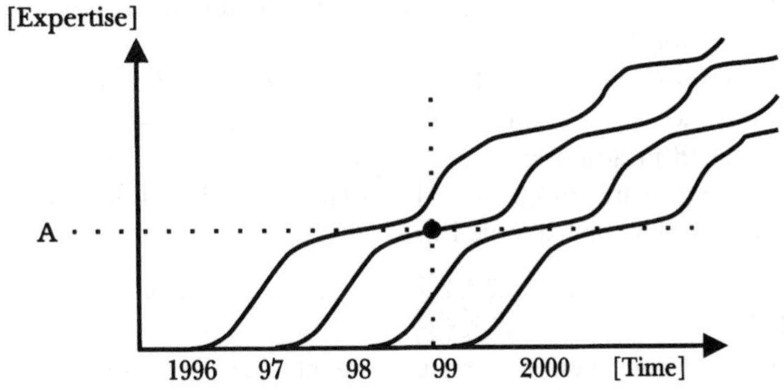


**Figure 8.11** Learning process for object-oriented thinking.

## RECOMMENDATIONS

### Introducing Object-Oriented Technology

*One of the greatest pains to human nature is the pain of a new idea.*

— Walter Bagehot

There is a learning process involved that we cannot avoid. As illustrated in Figure 8.11, the effect of introducing object-oriented techniques is not an instant one. It takes time in an organization for the ideas to mature into something that can influence the software development efforts. The later we start the learning process, the lower our expertise will be. For example, if we want to reach expertise level A in 1999, the learning process must have started no later than 1997.

It must be stressed that object-oriented technology demands a very serious commitment from every person in a company. In particular, it must be endorsed by management, as a true use of the technology will cost more at first compared to continuing with older techniques. The learning period is often longer than anticipated. The cost of introducing object-oriented technology is repeatedly underestimated because we tend to include only the clearly visible costs in our estimations. The cost and time spent on trial and error is simply forgotten, even though this cost makes up a large part of the total cost. For example, the cost for a compiler or another tool is noted, but we ignore the time we spend on understanding a chosen method, although this latter cost is much higher than the cost for the tool.

A major difficulty with class libraries is the sheer difficulty in learning them. However, learning and using them are essential ingredients in object-oriented programming. *Objects may be reusable, but this is only their potential.* Time invested in learning about class libraries is well spent, as the following example shows.

---

**Example**

A beginner had been coding a component during a couple of weeks. He had a question concerning a detail and asked another developer about it. This latter developer had been using object-oriented techniques for some time, and she had also spent time learning about available class structures. When the problem and the use of the component had been explained, she could suggest a solution that (re)used some already existing components. That is, in less than 30 minutes she could present a finished solution. Compare this to the weeks the beginner had already spent designing a solution which was not even finished. [1]

---

Working in groups and having group reviews is an excellent way of spreading knowledge about available classes. Some other recommendations are as follows:

- The best way of introducing object-oriented technology is by giving the personnel abundant time for education and training. If object-oriented ideas are first applied to an area not too close to the normal area of work, it is often easier to accept them. When the object-oriented ideas have been understood, they can be applied to a system that is typical for the company where the personnel works.
- Management must be trained in object-oriented technology or they will not be able to manage the new technology properly. Put another way: A basic understanding of object-oriented technology cannot be delegated.
- Start out on a small scale. First object-oriented ideas must be taught. Next, a pilot project should be completed, where a small low-risk but relevant application is developed. A pilot project works as a test of how object-oriented techniques will work in your environment. A pilot project should be controlled. The idea of the pilot project must be sold to all involved, and all involved must be willing to participate. The project should involve an important but not critical application. Recommended

length for a pilot project is three to five months with three to five of the best people doing the job. Experience from other projects, as available in seminars, books, reports, etc., should be compiled and used. Proper training of the group and availability of object-oriented modeling and language gurus are critical success factors. The project should be tracked precisely and a report and presentation of the results made. Problems and success should be described. Finally, a plan for proceeding should be identified. A secondary (pilot) project should involve an important nontrivial application and three to seven people, and it should last five to twelve months. Its purpose is to validate technology and augment object-oriented methods before mission critical projects are started.

- It is a good idea to set up a metric system and start collecting statistics. This way it will be possible to measure improvements in the software development process. Productivity will be highest with small teams of six people or less.
- Object-oriented techniques do not merge painlessly with techniques such as structured analysis. It must thus be understood that the thinking and the communication between users and analysts are fundamentally different with object-oriented analysis than with other methods, such as structured analysis. Although the basic ideas behind object-oriented technology are simple, it is quite clear that some people have great difficulty in grasping the ideas. People will thus adapt to the object-oriented paradigm with different speed. When planning a project, it is important to be observant of this and assign responsibilities appropriately. Some will spend a lot of time trying to go from a function-oriented way of thinking to an object-oriented way of thinking. Others, whom we might call gurus, will have trouble seeing the world in any other way than in an object-oriented way. The time it takes for someone to go from the stage of beginner to the stage of guru depends on the talents and the motivation of that person but is also proportional to the time spent together with people that think in an object-oriented fashion. There appears to be a percentage, perhaps 10–20%, who cannot adapt to the object-oriented paradigm. There is no point in forcing someone who has great problems with object-oriented ideas to work with tasks such as finding objects or designing a system architecture. Instead, he or she should be given the task of developing some well-defined object, such as a driver for some device.

- Availability of expertise and frequent access to a mentor are crucial for success. It is not probable that a company starting object-oriented software development has this, so outside help must be brought into the company early.
- Clear senior-management commitment is vital. This commitment must be reflected in clear objectives, a generous budget, and letting skilled people do the job, not just those who happen to be available. We must not underestimate the "not invented here" syndrome. We repeat: It takes a definite, honest, and clear commitment from management to successfully launch and implement an object-oriented organization. Thus, if senior management doesn't actively support the introduction and use of object-oriented technology, it won't succeed.
- C++ is a popular language for implementing object-oriented systems but it is in no way a simple language to learn or to use. It is wrong altogether to start object-oriented education with a course in C++. Instead, we should first teach the basic ideas behind object-oriented modeling. The ability to make good abstractions should be exercised. This done, it is time to introduce an object-oriented language. It is better to start with a true object-oriented language such as Smalltalk than C++. In Smalltalk, "everything" is an object, which forces the developers to think in terms of objects. The terminology in Smalltalk and C++ differs. Thus, to avoid confusion it is vital that the terminology be defined early. The terminology used should be the one available in object-oriented analysis and design—not some subset of it available in, for example, an object-oriented language. If C++ is later chosen as the programming language, remember that it is a very complicated language. For a further discussion of C++, see Appendix 4.
- It is very difficult to launch a new organization when the organization learns object-oriented modeling techniques.
- A reuse library should be planned. Note that it is a good idea to plan a reuse library at this stage, but the payoff from using a reuse library will come much later than in the first project. It takes time to establish a library of reusable classes because it is not immediately apparent what classes we need in a typical project. Such understanding grows gradually from experience.
- Select a good method. A method will make or break the efforts of a project. Usually a chosen method must be adapted and allowed to evolve with time and the changing needs of a company. At the

end of this section, we present a list that can be used to evaluate methods. Often, the informal analysis and design method used in a pilot project does not scale up well. Thus, a method used in a pilot project must often be changed and augmented before it can be used in larger projects.

- Support the pioneers. Enthusiasts are worth their weight in gold. Do not delay object-oriented technology by ignoring enthusiasts who can spread goodwill in the organization.

## Managing Object-Oriented Technology

> *Plans fail for lack of counsel, but with many advisers they succeed.*
>
> —Proverbs 15:22

Try to find a working compromise between the need for a more creative and chaotic software development process and the equal need of an orderly systematic way of developing a system (see Figure 8.12). Too little chaos, and good solutions will not be found. Too little discipline in the software development process, and everyone will soon be close to a total nervous breakdown. The degree to which we need discipline depends on the type of project we are working on. The scale goes from extremely rigorous software engineering for the software in a passenger airplane to no or little discipline if we are to program a macro for a word processor to be used on our PC at home.

The following are additional recommendations:

- In a project it is very important to identify key users and domain experts. Interviews with them must be planned in advance and

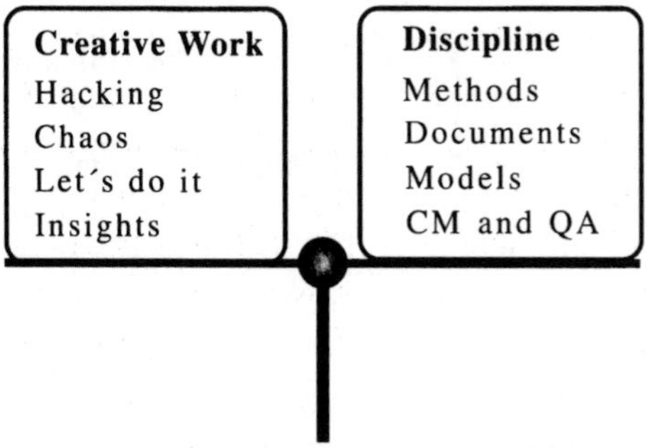


**Figure 8.12** Find the optimal balance!

have clear objectives. Interviewing is a key skill. Interviewing is discussed more in Appendix 3.

- The ability to make good abstractions is essential if any good object-oriented development is to occur. Let those who are proficient at creating abstractions do the analysis and the design and decide about class structures.
- A prototype is always a good way to gain a better understanding of what the system is supposed to do. A prototype should be thrown away when it has fulfilled its role.
- Using lines of code to measure progress is meaningless. A much better way to measure progress is to count classes that have been accepted and to monitor the stabilization of the interfaces. The interfaces should stabilize over time, or something is very wrong in the project.
- It is difficult to go from non-object-oriented activities to object-oriented activities. The idea is outlined in Figure 8.13, where an activity name without a preceding "OO" refers to a non-object-oriented activity. The figure is further discussed at the end of Chapter 6.
- The organization of a company should be changed and adapted to include component programmers, application programmers, and strategists. The organization should thus support two parallel activities in a company, building applications and making reusable components, in order to reap the full benefits of the object-oriented technique. Changing the organization can be planned early but is hard to do at the same time as learning the basic ideas. The project organization for an application should reflect the object structure of the application. The product organization should, on the other hand, reflect the structure of the reuse library.

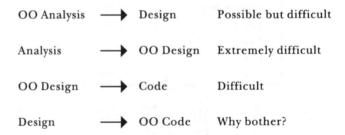

| | | | |
|---|---|---|---|
| OO Analysis | → | Design | Possible but difficult |
| Analysis | → | OO Design | Extremely difficult |
| OO Design | → | Code | Difficult |
| Design | → | OO Code | Why bother? |

**Figure 8.13** Mixing object-oriented technology with non-object-oriented technology is seldom easy.

- The idea of reuse of components is fundamental to an increase in productivity in the long run. Ideas such as polymorphism and inheritance are only details in something much bigger. A well-planned reuse library is thus an important profit center for a company. Managing object-oriented software development is basically synonymous to centering the organization with application programmers, component programmers, and strategists around a reuse library. The reuse library should be updated, monitored, and cared for in all ways so that it can realize the full potential of supplying components to projects. If we are to monitor this process, we have to set up metrics and collect statistics. (This topic is outside the scope of this book, and the reader is referred to works such as *Object-Oriented Software Development* by Mark Lorenz [26] or to trade journals [33].) Note that if we do not continually augment the reuse library, we will reach a productivity plateau. This idea is illustrated in Figure 8.14.
- If those who reuse are compensated when they do so, reuse will come more frequently. A good idea is to give rewards both to those who use components and to those who suggest new, interesting components. Money is a strong incentive. The opposite is

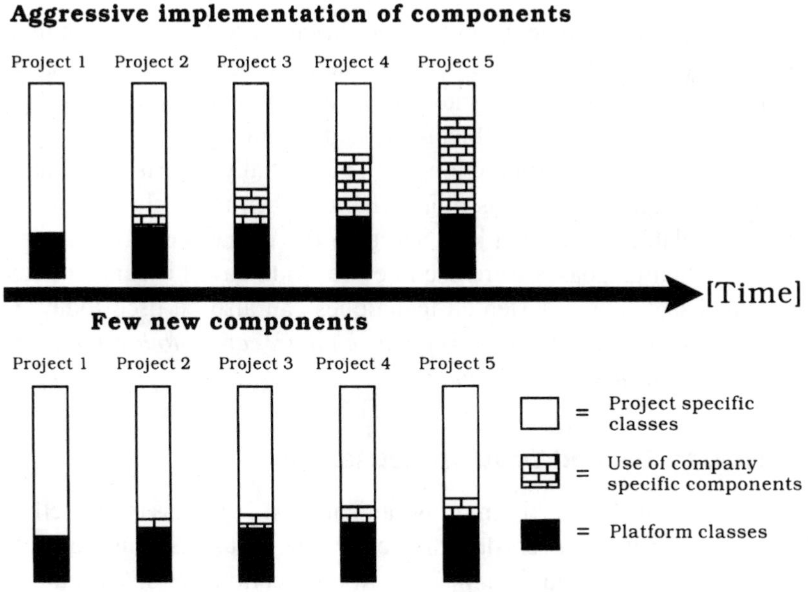


**Figure 8.14** Components increase reuse—but only if they are available.

also true: If a project has to pay when it reuses, projects will tend to develop their own classes, and less reuse will occur.

- The quality of a component can be increased if someone is assigned the ownership of it. People tend to take pride in what is theirs, which can be used to increase the quality of components.
- Reading code is much more important in a reuse environment. Thus, well-structured code with high quality names and good documentation for components are important. A documentation standard is helpful. (More information about documentation can be found in Appendix 3.) It is important that a component is easy to understand, but it is equally important that it is easy to find. If components are easily found, reuse will increase. Thus, tools should be bought or built to support searching for components in the reuse library.
- Everything does not change with object-oriented techniques. For example, a defined software process, precisely specified requirements, well-defined software architecture for the application (done early) and an integrated tool set that works well are still crucial factors governing success or failure.
- Tools supporting a selected method make it much easier for users of the method to accept the method.

There are still problems with object-oriented software development, as with other types of software development. Problems include no established standards, poor tools, and complicated programming languages. Do not expect any miracle. Object-oriented technology may be essential for a company to survive in the long run, but initially it costs more than it returns (see Figure 8.15). This might change when more class structures become available on the market. See also the discussion in Chapter 9. Remember that databases were used before Codd gave his rules for relational databases. Object-oriented techniques can also be used today. *Do not overestimate what object-oriented technology can do today, but do not underestimate what it can do tomorrow.*

### How to Sell and Develop Reusability

Because of the inertia in an organization it is necessary to sell the idea of reusability to everyone in a company. Reuse is thus not automatic. We must plan and design for it. In this section, we discuss how to introduce a reuse project and also, but to a lesser extent, how to develop reusability.

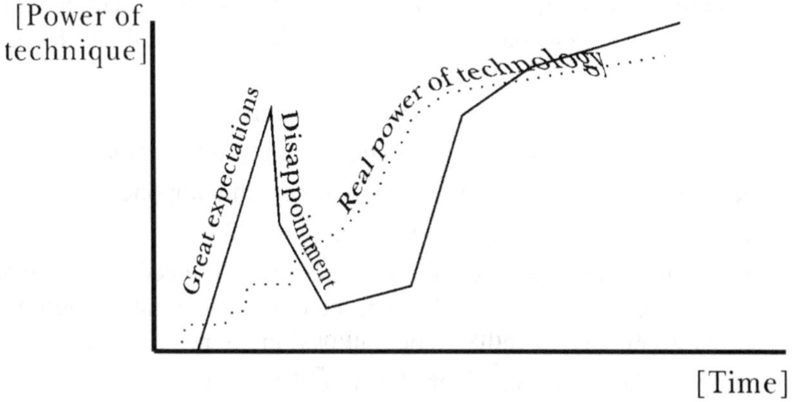


**Figure 8.15** When a technology is introduced, users expect too much of it. This technology is then met with disappointment, and the power of the technology is underestimated. In reality, the power of the technology increases continuously.

The importance of training has already been mentioned. The training should start with a short seminar, taking from half a day to one full day. This seminar should present the reuse project and the goals involved. The seminar should show the components available in the reuse library and the components soon to be available. Characteristics of a high-quality reusable class should be discussed, and what a user should do to suggest a class to become a component should be demonstrated. Apart from this short training seminar, we also need specialized courses in the selected programming language, database, tools, etc. However, the most important characteristic that must be trained early is the ability to think in objects. This training includes modeling using object-oriented structures, abstract thinking, and more.

It can be a good idea to start a magazine containing varied information about the reuse project. The first issue could contain an interview with the management, where a clear commitment to the reusability project is shown. When successful reuse has been accomplished, interviews should be published about those having done the reuse. New components can be presented in the magazine, along with summaries of discussions and articles dealing with reuse. The idea of the magazine is to show the long-range commitment to the reuse project and to act as a forum for discussion. The magazine can be four to eight pages, with three to four issues during the first year.

Management should be given regular 30 minute presentations of the status of the reuse project. Success stories should be reported and problem areas discussed. Feedback loops must be set up to collect experience. Experience must be systematically collected about the following:

- How should the reuse library be used and enhanced?
- What are the basic characteristics of a reusable component?
- How do we recognize a class as a potential component?
- What components does the company need?
- What complementary additions are typically needed for a class, developed in a project, if it is to be transformed into a high quality component suitable to be included in the reuse library?
- How should a component be described and classified so that it can easily be found by a user?

## About CASE

A first round of analysis can be done using pen and paper. Involving CASE too early in a discussion with a customer might backfire. Pen and paper are very underestimated tools. Using little cards of paper to note down the objects and classes as they are found is very flexible. Such an approach encourages creativity more than something "finished" drawn on a computer. There is a danger with nicely drawn analysis documents: That they have been produced on a laser printer and look very nice does not mean they are correct.

It is crucial that the analysis process has strong support among all involved. It is easier to achieve this using informal pen and paper techniques than more sophisticated tools that are only available on computers and that, perhaps, produce output that is only easily understood by experts and enthusiasts. CASE tools become more important the closer we get to the coding of a system.

Good tools are more essential with object-oriented programming than with earlier techniques. We need good class browsers, symbolic debuggers, version management systems, etc. Unfortunately it was found in our study [2] that tools promise much more than they deliver. In particular, they are weak in multi-user support and version control. It is our opinion that this will change drastically in the future and that good tools will give a significant competitive edge to those who know how to use them. Stated in another way: *Not* the language but the richness of the software development environment will be a key factor to efficient software development in the future.

## EVALUATION CRITERIA

*Nothing quite new is perfect.*

— Marcus Tullius Cicero

We used the following criteria in one of the studies [2] mentioned in the beginning of the book. They can be used when a company tries to evaluate a method to be used in their software development efforts. Generally speaking, a positive answer to a question below is to be regarded as a point in favor of the method. The importance of a positive answer is left to the judgment of the reader.

**Basic facts**

Basic facts should include: Who has developed the method? How available is support for it (training, consulting, books, etc.)? How common is the method? Is it used in existing projects? Is it based on actual experience? Is it good software engineering?

**Maturity and stability**

Have the developers of the method stopped changing it? How long has the method been around? Does the method relate to earlier experience? Will it still exist in 10 years? What is the size of the company developing the method? Has the method been used successfully?

**Areas of use**

Is the method general? (Or is it targeted to some specific software development area such as administrative development, real-time applications, etc.) Is it targeted to small, medium, and large systems? Is the method independent of programming languages?

**The object-oriented paradigm**

Does an object have attributes, methods, and an identity? Are the attributes in the object encapsulated? Does the method separate class structures and object structures? Are the class structures built in a normal way? (That is, does the method use the standard type of inheritance as explained in this book or have the developers of the method invented something more "advanced"?) Do the object structures support the idea of nested objects (that is, the idea that objects can be aggregated to new objects that can in their turn be aggregated)? Is the method truly object-oriented? (Or is it, for example, just a mix of old techniques?)

**Notation**

Is the notation easy to use and understand? Does the notation mirror the method?

**Tools**

Are there any tools that support the method and notation? Are they easy to use? Do they include support for version and change control?

**Phases**

Is the phase model adapted to object-oriented ideas? (For example, with object-oriented modeling, the phases tend to become more similar. The difficult transformations of representations of the model between phases so typical for other methods become much less evident). Is it possible to run the phases in parallel? (Or must, for example, the analysis be entirely finished before the design can start?)

**Complexity issues**

Will the method help in beating complexity? That is, does the method give us good abstraction techniques to handle the complexity of an application? Will the method support different views of an application (that is, for example, easily give an overall view of the system while still being able to expose low-level details for those who need to see it)? Does the method support the partitioning of a system into subsystems (as described in this book)?

**Maintenance**

For the most part, the time during which a system is maintained is much longer than the time it took to develop the system. It is thus a good idea to check if the method includes any support for maintenance.

**Using the method**

Is the method simple? Does it only include necessary ideas? (Or are there many variations of different types of associations, classes, and so on?) Is it possible to grasp the basics of the method in two or three days?

**Applicability of method**

All the factors already mentioned are important, but the key questions are always: Does the method meet your needs? Can *you* use the method?

## SUMMARY

- Nontechnical factors are often more important than purely technical factors when determining the success of a project.

- A key ingredient in object-oriented development is the ability of abstract thinking. Some people will never learn to apply the object-oriented paradigm, whereas others will understand quickly. Those who excel should design system architecture(s) and plan and design class structures.
- A successful use of object-oriented development in a company needs a total commitment from everyone involved—especially the management—and a change of the organization.
- There are still problems with object-oriented technology and weak tool support. This does not mean, however, that we cannot use object-oriented technology today. Do not overestimate what object-oriented technology can do today, but do not underestimate what it can do tomorrow!
- This chapter also provided several recommendations concerning the introduction and management of object-oriented technology, how to sell reuse, and several criteria for evaluating a software development method.

# 9

# The Future

## *A Few Thoughts*

*Revolutions never go backward.*

— Wendell Phillips

## INTRODUCTION

To make predictions about the future we should look into the past, as history is a good teacher. Let us thus review some examples of how theories have evolved in the past.

The first well-authenticated expression that the fundamental character of matter is discrete rather than continuous is accredited to Leucippus and his disciple Democritus, two Greek philosophers of the fifth century BC. Modern atomic theory is ascribed to the English chemist and physicist John Dalton (1766–1844). He was studying how different substances react to each other, and these experiments persuaded him that each chemical element is made up of small, indivisible particles—atoms. He was interested in metaphysics and had the idea that we should explain things in an intellectual and "beautiful" way. He therefore suggested that atoms should be represented with circles of different sizes, empty or filled with different details. We should combine them in a way that would give the resulting construction a geometrical balance. In Figure 9.1 we see some examples of these designs.

The Swede Jöns Jacob Berzelius probably had the idea that something was beautiful if it was easy to use, so he instead suggested that

1. We should represent an atom by the first one or two letters in the Latin name. For example, oxygen should be represented by O, from oxygenium and gold by AU, from the Latin name aurum.

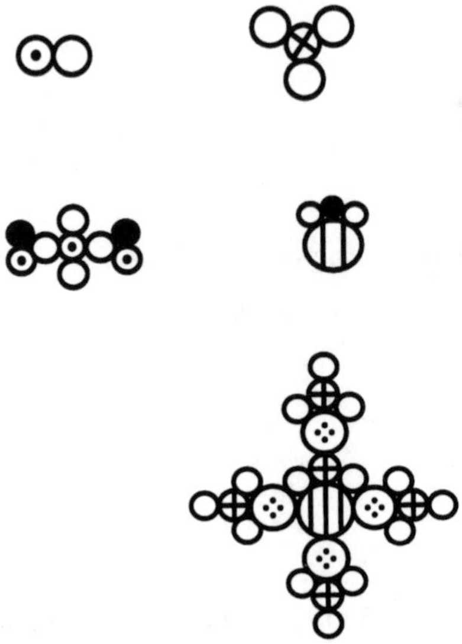

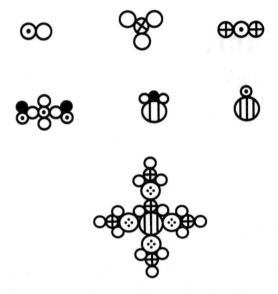

**Figure 9.1** A "beautiful" way to describe groupings of atoms according to John Dalton.

2. To indicate the presence of more than one atom, we should add an index number to the abbreviation. For example, two oxygen atoms should be written $O_2$.

Today, we all know that of these two theories, the one that was more *practical* survived.

Before we had modern astronomy, there were theories that used complex ways of describing the movement of stars and planets. A geo-centric (earth-centered) planetary system was founded in the Hellenistic age through the work of Hipparchus of Rhodes (second century BC). It was completed by the Alexandrian astronomer Ptolemy (second century BC) and described in his Almagest. This astronomical classic remained authoritative for at least 1400 years. According to this Ptolemaic system, each planet moved in a small circle (the epicycle), the center of which was carried around upon another larger circle (the deferent), that carried the planet around the earth (see Figure 9.2). Because this did not quite explain the movements, other ideas, such as the equant, were introduced to explain observations. With the set of ideas he developed, Ptolemy could describe accurately the movements of the stars and planets. The theory was very complicated to use, however.

The Polish astronomer Nicolaus Copernicus (1473–1543) initiated the modern age in astronomy. He disposed of much of the complexity of

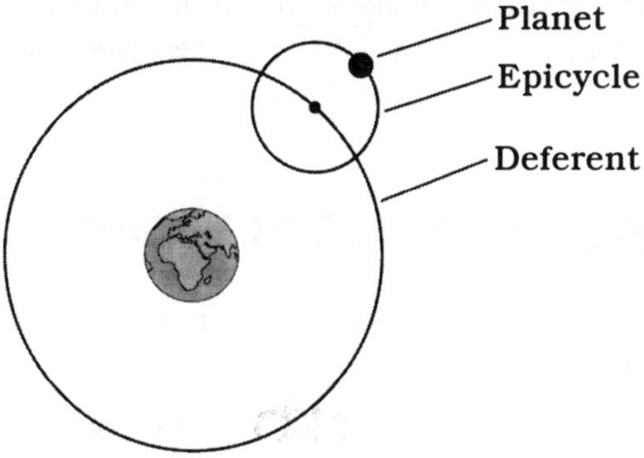


**Figure 9.2** An early way of describing the movement of a planet.

the Ptolemaic system by assigning the central position to the sun. He said all planets revolved around the sun and, among them, the earth also rotated daily on its axis. There were at this time no physical grounds to prefer this theory to the Ptolemaic system, but it *simplified the practical work* of designing planetary tables. The same practical reason for preferring a theory occurred for Johan Kepler, a German astronomer (1571–1630). After many months of fruitless attempts to fit an old-time epicyclic system to the motion of Mars, he discovered that each planet revolves in an ellipse, with the sun in one of the foci. His work did much to establish the Copernican theory, but he failed in formulating a physical explanation for his planetary laws because he still accepted Aristotelian mechanics. Eventually, through the work of such scientists as Galileo Galilei and Newton, we got the theories that we still largely use today.

Roughly the same type of development took place in the field of physics. The Greek philosopher Aristotle (384–322 BC) put forward the theory that any physical substance is composed of four elements (earth, water, air, and fire) in combination with four "qualities" (heat, coldness, dryness, and moisture). This theory was easy to understand, but it also failed the test of time. The theory was simply not close enough to reality. Eventually, we found other ways of describing matter, and today we use ideas such as atoms, molecules, aggregates of molecules, etc.

We note some characteristics concerning the development of new theories:

- A theory is sacrificed when a theory that is simpler to use is found.
- A new theory often builds on earlier theories, enhancing them.

- A new theory often changes something dramatically. For example, the earth is not any longer at the center, matter is discrete rather than a continuum, and so on.

## THEORIES AND SOFTWARE DEVELOPMENT

*Those who cannot remember the past are condemned to repeat it.*

—George Santayana

If we try to apply the thoughts outlined previously to software development, we find that today we have ways of describing software, but the theories (methods) are not easy to use, and they often fail to help us. The point is that today we develop software in much the same way as Dalton tried to describe atoms, Ptolemy, the movement of celestial bodies, and Aristotle, matter.

But why should we construct theories about software development? Before we can handle something or make predictions about this something, we must first understand it. We construct theories to be able to make models of the area of interest. We do so to understand better the things we have in the area of interest, whether they are matter, celestial bodies, or the business items a customer is interested in. The theory and the model are thus our tools to understand and handle something. But, as our historical examples point out, it is not enough just to have a tool. The tool must also display at least the following two properties:

- The tool should make it easier for us to grasp the area of interest.
- It must be close enough to the real thing so that we can use it to make accurate predictions.

We thus find two main reasons why a theory fails:

1. A theory fails because it is too difficult to use.
2. A theory fails because it is not close enough to reality.

True, we can use the theories put forward by Ptolemy to describe the movement of planets quite accurately, but the theory soon becomes so complex to use that we need something else anyway.

True, an electron is neither only a particle nor only a wave, because it is a mix of both. But these models are still close enough to reality to be usable when explaining much of what happens when we use electrons.

This is not true for the Aristotelian theory of elements and qualities mentioned before.

The real excitement with object-oriented technology is that we with it have a better tool than ever before—although we have not yet fully understood how to use it. But we do have a tool that will not fail because it is too difficult to use or because it is not close enough to reality:

1. *It is easy to use* because it is closely related to the human thinking process with its three basic principles of modeling:
   - The object, with an identity, characteristics (attributes), and ways of handling it (methods).
   - Grouping objects together to make larger objects, just as we do with things we deal with in everyday situations (aggregation).
   - Modeling similarities with the class and the class structure.
2. *It is sufficiently close to reality,* because the ideas we use when thinking and dealing with things are easy to transform into objects. Reality is object-oriented.

Is everything perfect with object-oriented software development? Of course not. One improvement would be if we could free us more from the often text-related interface we use today. Object-oriented technology is one of pictures. Objects should not be described by text but by graphical figures. When we implement an object-oriented system, we should do it in a graphical way.

Another important improvement would be a clear understanding of how to find simple objects and then group these into larger objects. In the author's opinion, this is a key to the object-oriented revolution. However, our conclusion is that our tool is understandable and close enough to reality to meet the requirements of a successful theory. Everything is set for the revolution.

## THE KEY TO THE REVOLUTION

*I leave this rule for others when I'm dead, Be always sure you're right—then go ahead.*

— David Crockett

Before we see a true object-oriented revolution, the basic principles of object-oriented software development, as they are discussed in this book, must be fully understood and permeate every aspect of the software development process. But this is not enough. All new theories are incomplete at first, and we need to augment them. To reach the full potential of object-oriented software development, the theory must also explain in detail how to find reusable components and how to organize them. The real power with object-oriented technology is *not* found in ideas such as inheritance or polymorphism, but in the idea of the reusable component.

Finding components can be eased by a proper organization of the components and by having a computerized on-line information system, where we can search among available components by giving various search criteria. In the following, we discuss the organization of components.

In Chapter 8 we discussed some properties a reusable component must have. Here we will discuss the following three properties that objects must display if they are to be reusable:

1. They must be true encapsulated microworlds exchanging information only via a well-defined interface.
2. They must be usable together.
3. They must be organized in layers, each layer representing a family of components.

These properties are needed, because in other industrial fields, where reuse exists, we find such an organization of reusable components. This organization is late in the software community probably because software systems are complex and code is invisible in a way that something more tangible is not. This invisibility makes it hard to understand how the organization of reusable components should be set up.

A good example of an intelligent layering of components is found in electronics, where we have arrived at a set of very usable layers. We started to discuss this topic in Chapter 5 and we show Figure 5.11 again (as Figure 9.3) for easy reference.

We have a set of basic components such as integrated circuits, resistors, and so on. The components of this family have a lot in common, and so we have put them in a class structure. Each such component is an encapsulated microworld. The components of the family are also able to interact via a well-defined interface. Figure 9.3 also illustrates that we have several such families of components. The middle family represents a layer with more complex components, circuit boards. The components (classes) in the circuit board family are designed from components taken from the family of electronic components. Next we put these circuit boards together, forming a third set of reusable components, computers. In each such set or family of components, we find that each higher (more

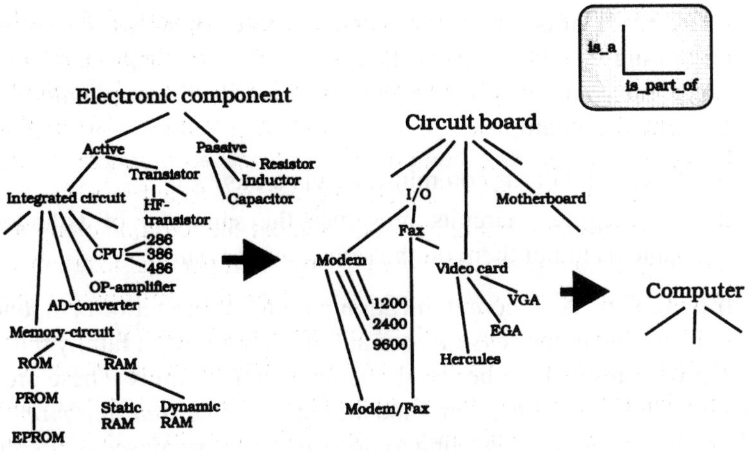


**Figure 9.3** Families of reusable components layered in several levels.

complex) set is designed by using lower set(s). Usually only the next lower set is used when designing the next (higher) layer. Looking at the integrated circuits we could, however, argue that they are made of components from their own family because they are composed of transistors, etc. But (in this case) it is not difficult to follow the rule that a set should be designed using components from lower set(s) only. We illustrate this in Figure 9.4, where we have taken away the part with integrated circuits and instead grouped them in their own family.

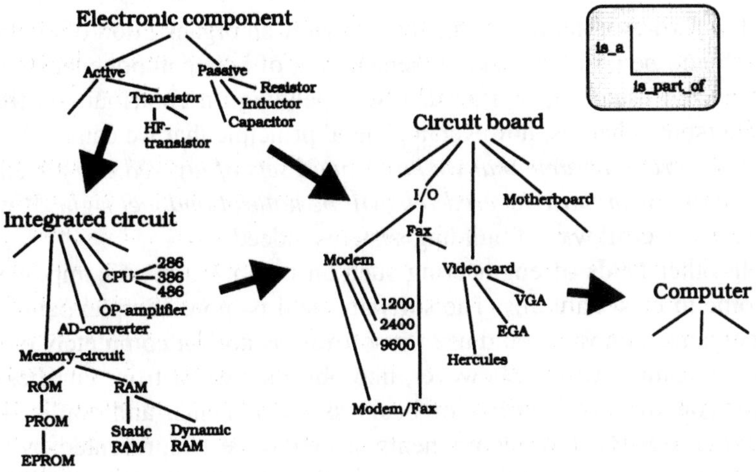


**Figure 9.4** Another view of our electronic components.

Each family of components (class structure) is enclosed by a set of rules describing how they are to talk to each other, that is, a standard that makes it possible for the components in a family to communicate and work together. For example,

- The circuit boards communicate via a bus.
- The integrated circuits must use the same set of voltages to enable us to put them on the same circuit board.

If there is no such communication paradigm, the set of components will not be usable in the sense we are aiming at here. Each family thus has a set of properties that applies to all members in the family. These properties include the communication standard but also other *relevant properties for the family in question*, relating to the way we are supposed to use them.

## REUSABLE COMPONENTS AND SOFTWARE

How should sets of interworking software components be built? We should, of course, apply the three properties of reusable components mentioned earlier:

1. They must be true *encapsulated microworlds* exchanging information only via a well-defined interface.
2. They must be *usable together.*
3. They must be *organized in layers,* each layer representing a family of components.

It is, however, hard to define exactly how an organization of components should be designed. The understanding of how components should be organized usually grows gradually, depending on contributions from many persons. There is, however, a general principle that we can apply:

*If we are to assume that we have found sets of layered components, then working with those layered sets will be natural and feel right.* It will be a very powerful way of building systems indeed.

In other fields of engineering such an organization of components has come to exist naturally. The software field is more complex, and the exact organization we should use for software is not yet completely clear. In an application we will, however, find objects created from families of generic components, families of business components, and application specific classes. Generic components are today best represented by the class libraries supplied with languages such as Smalltalk. Business components are sets of components created to suit a particular type of application, such as banking. Experience also shows that an application will have objects that are unique to the application. Thus some classes will be specific to the application and not reused elsewhere.

Because business components often represent a significant investment by a company, there appears to be little willingness to share such components with other companies. Thus, today few business components exist on the market. However, as we understand the basic principles outlined above in a conscious effort to organize the components, we should be able to draw up a plan for a component standard. Such a component standard would be a key to software reuse.

Next we look at some ideas that have emerged in connection with reuse and that we expect will be further refined in the future.

## IDEAS FOR REUSE

Today we see several trends introducing ideas and concepts that try to solve, to a lesser or greater degree, the problem of providing reusable code. Perhaps the simplest of these ideas is the toolkit, which is an outgrowth of the subroutine library concept. A *toolkit* provides basic functionality but seldom imposes any constraints on the architecture of an application. We write the application and call the toolkit code only when we need its functionality. The C++ I/O stream library is a typical example of the toolkit idea.

A *framework* is a set of cooperating classes. A framework specifies the main outline of an application typically specifying details such as how objects should work together, how the thread of control should be implemented, and so on. The framework thus specifies much of the overall structure of an application. Typically we adapt a framework to a particular application by implementing application-specific subclasses. The code we write is typically called by the framework. This is sometimes called the Hollywood principle—don't call us, we'll call you. The reverse is true when we use a toolkit: the code we write calls the toolkit code.

A *design pattern* is another idea intended to speed up the building of an application. However, a design pattern is a more abstract idea than a framework. Design patterns are thus less specialized than frameworks. In the book *Design Patterns* [35] 23 patterns are listed. Each pattern names and explains a design that typically occurs in object-oriented systems. For example, the book introduces a pattern called "Observer." This pattern is a more general solution to one of the problems solved by the MVC (Model/View/Controller) construction outlined earlier in this book. The MVC construction makes it possible to attach several views to the same (data) model and have appropriate updates be done automatically. The Observer pattern decouples objects so that changes to one object can affect other objects without requiring that the changed objects know details about other objects. Thus the Observer idea outlines a pattern that is a more general solution than the corresponding construction used in MVC. Design patterns represent smaller elements than frameworks. It is typical that a framework uses several design patterns.

Figure 9.5 shows how we can relate these ideas. We classify the ideas according to how much design structure they give us and according to how easy it is to reuse them directly.

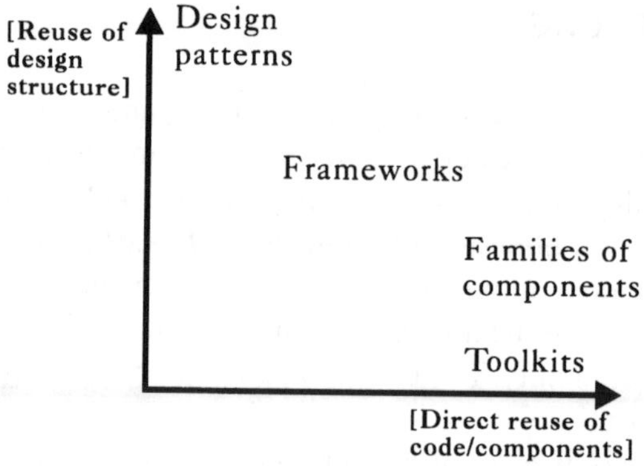


**Figure 9.5** Comparing different reuse ideas.

Design patterns are primarily directed to give us ideas for constructions that we can use to solve particular design problems. A design pattern is normally not reusable directly. Toolkits on the other hand are reusable directly, and they do not impose many architectural design demands on the application we build. We reuse the functionality supplied by them whenever we need it by calling appropriate methods found in the toolkit's concrete classes. Frameworks are somewhere in the middle. Often its classes are abstract and need to be subclassed before they can be used. On the other hand, the purpose of the *families of components* idea, discussed earlier in this chapter, is to supply readily instantiable classes, concrete classes. The classes are related by class structures and the class structures are nested. A difference between families of components and frameworks lies in their purposes. The families of components are supposed to give us components directly in the same way as integrated circuits can be put to use directly on a circuit board. The families of components idea imposes some design constraints on the application built with these components but these constraints are much less demanding than those imposed by frameworks. The framework represents a reusable design skeleton around which we build our application. It need not incorporate any concrete classes at all—even though it probably will include some concrete classes. A framework can be likened to a circuit board with holes in it. For example, on a framework for motherboards we are supposed to put a CPU in one of the holes. In other holes we are supposed to put RAM modules and so on. We can use different components—within specified limits—and set different parameters such as the clock speed for the CPU. However, the main design is set and cannot be changed. The families of components idea is less restricted and only presents us with a set of components that we can use together to build any type of circuit board. For example, the same family of components can be used to build different frameworks.

Several frameworks exist; however, the science of finding families of components is still immature. Thus, it appears that designing a framework is easier than designing a set of families of components.

## CONCLUSION

As pointed out in Chapter 8, "Soft Factors," there are many issues beside the purely technical issues. We have social and economic factors to deal with, for instance. One important economic factor concerning reusable components is the question of getting a working marketplace for the components. Specifically, we must solve the problem of paying those who design sets of reusable components. This problem is nothing new, but unfortunately it is harder to solve for software, because it is, for example, very easy to copy a program.

However, the revolution will occur, because the driving forces behind such a revolution are already here:

- We need more and more software with improved quality.
- The cost of hardware is decreasing dramatically.

In the foreseeable future, there will still be a place for the smart assembler programmer who can squeeze all power there is from some hardware. Regarding the bulk of software development, other questions will become important, however:

- Will software deliver what is needed and in an easy-to-use way?
- Will it work without crashing?
- Will it be available in time—That is, before the competitors have put it together?

Other restrictions, such as lack of understanding of the object-oriented technology, will also vanish as schools and universities teach the new object-oriented paradigm.

In the short term we will see more discussions about problems with object-oriented software development. Remember, however, that these problems are also, to a large extent, part of other software development techniques.

Building systems by putting objects together rather than by putting lines of code together equals a revolution. Only object-oriented software development has the potential of giving us such a much-needed revolution, but first we must get standardized sets of components and a working marketplace for them.

We have many advantages without this, however, so we feel there is no good excuse for postponing object-oriented software development in your company.

## SUMMARY

Looking at history, we find that a theory fails because

- It is too difficult to use.
- It is not close enough to reality.

We found some characteristics concerning the development of new theories:

- We stop using a theory when a theory that is simpler to use is found.
- A new theory often builds on earlier theories, enhancing them.
- A new theory often changes something dramatically.

Object-oriented theory fits into this scenario, setting the stage for a revolution.

Three important properties if components are to be reusable are

- They must be true encapsulated microworlds, exchanging information only via a well-defined interface.

- They must be usable together.
- They must be organized in layers, each layer representing a family of components.

Two remaining problems concerning reusable components are:

- How do we organize them?
- How do we get a working marketplace for them?

We believe these two problems to be the main hindrance for a large-scale object-oriented revolution. Unless we conquer these problems and learn how to build large applications object by object, we will have to reduce our ambitions or continue to incur extreme costs when developing large applications.

We briefly discussed some ideas dealing with reuse:

- The toolkit, which is an outgrowth of the subroutine library idea.
- The framework, which represents a reusable design skeleton around which we build an application.
- A design pattern names and outlines a design that typically occurs in object-oriented systems.
- A family of components presents us with a set of components that we can use together to build other more complex components and applications.

# Appendix 1

# Information Modeling

## *A Comparison*

*The philosophers have only interpreted the world in various ways; the point is to change it.*

— Karl Marx

## INTRODUCTION

The information modeling technique we have chosen to follow in this appendix is very close to the one suggested by Sally Shlaer and Stephen J. Mellor in their book *Object-Oriented System Analysis* [18]. We have chosen their approach because it is a fairly well known approach and because it is representative of the wide variety of information modeling techniques available today. This type of information modeling might better be termed data modeling. However, because Shlaer and Mellor prefer the term information modeling in their book, so do we.

The idea of the information model is to model a system with the following concepts:

- Entity types
- Attributes of those entity types
- Relationships between entity types

An entity is simply a thing in reality, an instance. An entity type is an abstraction of what is common with a chosen group of things. In information modeling this abstraction is captured in a table. This means that an entity type represented by a table, as in Figure A1.1, is very close to the idea of a class.

An attribute, in information modeling, is used to express *one* common characteristic of an entity type (our table).

A relationship (often also called a relation) shows how various entity types (tables) are related.

| Reg. no. | Make | Color |
|---|---|---|
| ABC 123 | Volvo | Green |
| CBA 321 | Saab | Blue |
| DEF 456 | Opel | Blue |
| GHI 789 | Volvo | Red |

**Figure A1.1** A table.

A common notation for information modeling is shown in Figure A1.2. A rectangle represents an entity type, and a diamond is used to represent a relationship. An arrow is often substituted for the diamond, and we use this latter approach in this appendix. Finally, a circle is used to represent an attribute type. Note that other words are often used for these concepts. For example, an entity type is sometimes referred to as an entity name or an entity set. We will not use these latter synonyms in this book, however.

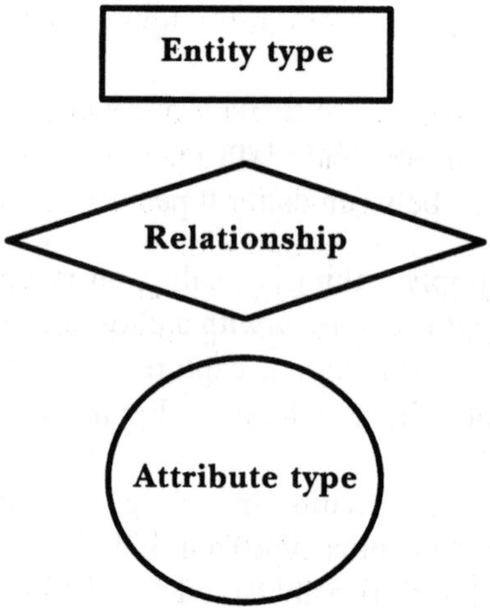


**Figure A1.2** A common notation used in information modeling.

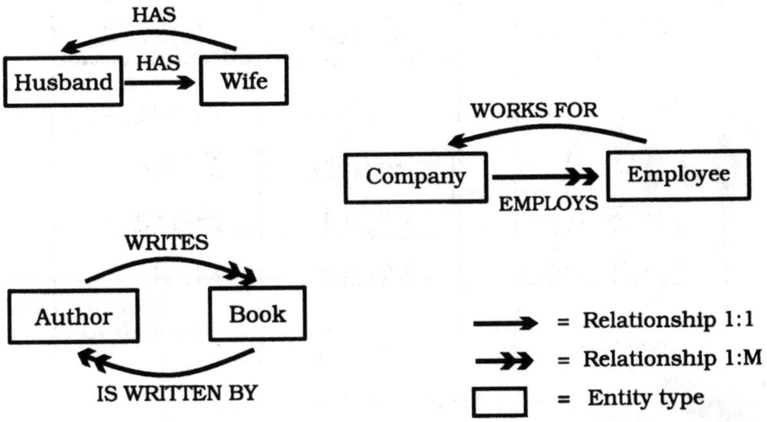


**Figure A1.3** Examples of relationships used in information modeling.

**Definition.** A *relationship*, in information modeling, is an abstraction of a set of connections that holds systematically between different entities (things). For example a group Person may be related to the group Dog, in that Person OWNS Dog. Attributes are used to implement such relationships.

We see some information modeling relationships in Figure A1.3. In the figure we show entity types with boxes and relationships with arrows. We see several types of relationships.

We soon find many similarities between information modeling and object-oriented modeling. For example, in object-oriented modeling we have classes and objects, and in information modeling we find tables and entities.

Objects and classes relate to each other in the same way as entities relate to tables. This is so because in object-oriented modeling, the class defines the attributes and methods for its objects, and in information modeling the table defines what attributes an entity (instance) shall have. Figure A1.4 illustrates that building an object model can—at least in the beginning—be very similar to building an information model.

## TWO PROBLEMS

The human being is very limited in his or her capacity to deal with several things simultaneously. The complexity a human being can handle is very trivial compared to the complexity we need to handle when modeling modern systems.

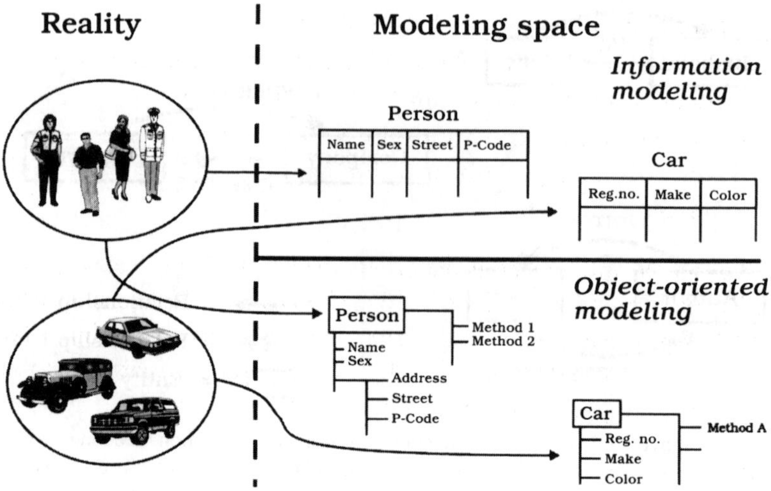


**Figure A1.4** Building information and object-oriented models, respectively.

Another problem when modeling is to choose words and ideas to describe the system and what we want the system to do. It is not easy for different persons to agree on ideas and words and what they really mean.

To conquer these two problems, we need something that can reduce the amount of detail we need to understand at a given moment as well as something that makes us speak the same language. In the following two sections we discuss these two aspects.

## Abstraction

The technique we use to reduce the number of details with which we have to deal at a given moment is called abstraction. As we showed earlier in this book, abstraction is used extensively in object-oriented modeling. Recapitulating, we remember that object-oriented modeling gives us

- The *class,* to keep groups of related attributes and methods together.
- The *class structure,* to relate and group classes.
- *Aggregation,* to keep related objects together in object structures.

Comparing object-oriented modeling and information modeling we find that

- The class defines both attributes and methods, whereas the table defines only attributes for its instances.
- Class structures are not normally used in information modeling, although some "styles" now incorporate that ability.
- Aggregation is not very well developed in information modeling. This is especially true for aggregation with information hiding.

We look a little closer at the comparison between the class and the table: Reality around us is full of "things," instances. If we use information modeling, we use tables to describe what these groups of things have in common. The row of values in a table represents a particular thing (instance) in reality. This makes two good abstractions:

- The *row* in a table is a group of values to describe a particular thing.
- The *table* is a refined abstraction, in which we consider only what is common with a set of similar things (rows) rather than each thing.

These two abstractions are good, but they are more fully developed in object-oriented modeling. The table can be regarded as a predecessor to the class used in object-oriented modeling. That is, the class defines the attributes just as in the table, but it also defines methods (see Figure A1.5). The class is our template used to produce objects, just as the table defines the entities (things) in information modeling.

The conclusion is that object-oriented modeling offers us better abstraction facilities than information modeling.

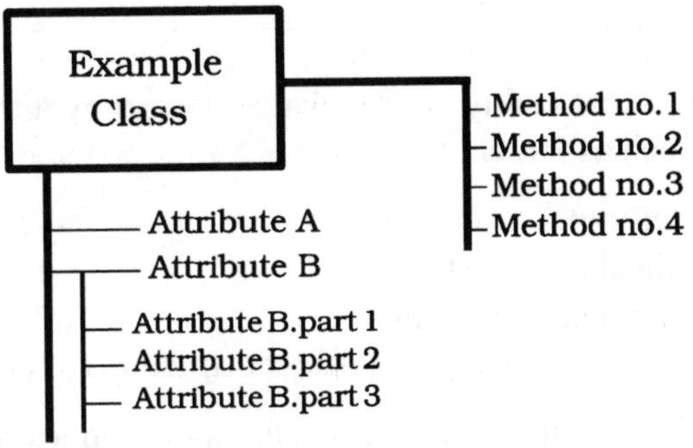


**Figure A1.5** A class.

### Modeling Ability

*Language is the dress of thought.*

—Samuel Johnson

What about the problem of selecting words and ideas when modeling? Simply stated,

*Speaking the same language means talking about objects.*

The fact that people tend to refer to reality in an object-oriented way has been reflected in our use of languages. For example, in all languages, we find that there are verbs, nouns, and adjectives. We saw in earlier chapters that we could often find a correspondence between nouns and objects, attributes and adjectives, and methods and verbs. This is a strong point in favor of object-oriented modeling.

Summing up, we can say that when people start talking about objects (instead of data and/or functions), they have a better chance of agreeing on the same model because humans are accustomed to talking about objects. Thus, things become easier when we start using the object idea in system development.

## OTHER COMPARISONS

We look at a simple example to find other points to compare.

---

**Example**

Consider a pen. We note (1) that we can refer to the pen, (2) that it has certain characteristics (weight, etc.), (3) that we can write with it, and (4) that it is related to the owner by being owned by him or her.

---

When we look at reality we find that almost everything we deal with has properties such as these:

1. We can refer to it.
2. It has certain characteristics.
3. We can do something with it.
4. It is related to other things in different structures.

If we think about it we can see that the same applies to cars, houses, people, invoices, and so on. There are also other things that we can say about the pen, but let us be content having found some more points to compare.

How do the preceding four points compare to our table and its things? Let us first restate our description in a more precise way and then look at each point. Using object-oriented terminology, we say that a thing (and let's call it an object from now on)

1. Has an identity (so that we can refer to it).
2. Has certain attributes and certain values for these attributes.
3. Has methods that define what we can do with it.
4. Is part of different structures.

We discuss these points, one by one.

## Identity of the Object

In information modeling we use the term *identifier* to identify a thing. We have the following definition.

**Definition.** An *identifier* is one or several attributes that can be used to distinguish each object (entity) *uniquely*.

In information modeling we thus identify an object through its attributes. In Figure A1.6 we have shown three possible identifiers. We use the attributes Library ID, ISBN number, and Title plus Author, respectively, to identify an object. (In information modeling an object may have one or several identifiers.)

An identifier is sometimes called a *candidate key*.

**Figure A1.6** Three possible identifiers.

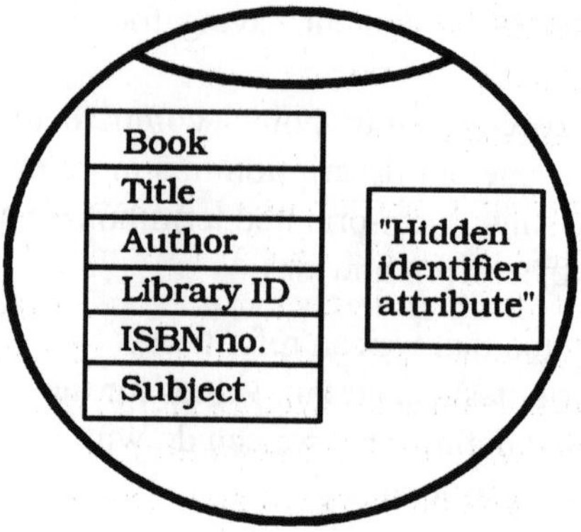


**Figure A1.7** The identity of an object cannot be changed.

An object has an identity, but it is not implemented using (ordinary) attribute(s). In object-oriented modeling the identifier exists independently of the attributes. We can regard the identity of each object in object-oriented modeling as an identifier created by adding an extra hidden attribute (see Figure A1.7). This hidden attribute is managed by the system, and it cannot be used in the same way as an ordinary attribute.

---

**Example**

We define a table representing a group of persons, and we set up an (information modeling) identifier using the attributes Name and Street in this table. The identifier "Sam Engelwood, Kings Street 126" identifies Sam Engelwood—but only as long as his name and the street address are unchanged. In object-oriented modeling, changing the attributes would not influence the identity of an object.

---

The object-oriented type of identifier is less prone to mistakes because it cannot be changed by the user of an object. (See also the discussion about surrogates in the section "Normalization" (later in this appendix).) The object-oriented type of identifier is therefore preferable.

### Attributes

Even though the basic idea behind the attribute in object-oriented modeling is the same, to a large extent, as in information modeling, there are some differences. Different styles of information modeling often recognize three different types of attributes:

- Descriptive attributes
- Naming attributes
- Referential attributes

*Descriptive attributes* provide us with facts about the object. They describe intrinsic facts about the object. Examples are age and weight. These are the typical attributes that we use in object-oriented modeling.

*Naming attributes* are arbitrary names and labels. Examples are employee ID, employee name, car license, and so on.

*Referential attributes* are used in information modeling to connect an object of one class with an object of another class.

We do not usually talk about naming attributes in object-oriented modeling, although we can have attributes equal to this type of attribute in object-oriented modeling. Also, we sometimes use state attributes in object-oriented modeling whereas this is uncommon in information modeling.

When we refer to an attribute in this book, we thus typically mean a descriptive attribute. However, they need not be what we call *fully factored*. In object-oriented modeling, attributes may have an hierarchical structure of their own, allowing us to group the attributes. For example the attribute Name may be made up of several other attributes. Figure A1.8 shows two attributes with an internal structure of their own: Name and Address.

Information modeling techniques normally state that an attribute must *not* contain an internal structure. This means that an attribute must capture a single separate aspect of the thing we are modeling. This is a consequence

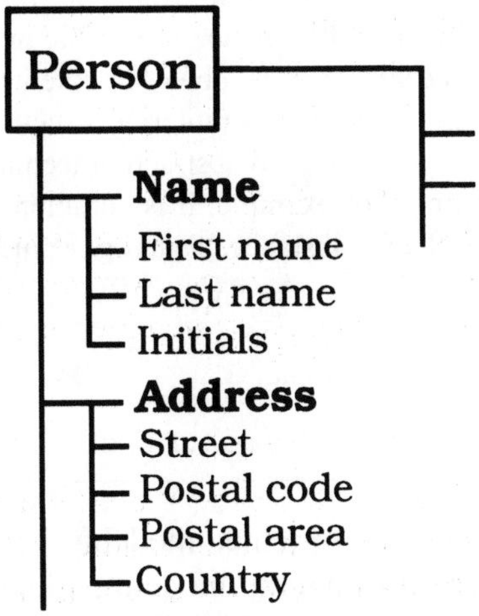


**Figure A1.8** A class.

```
Longstring  = packed array (1..40) of char;
Shortstring = packed array (1..5) of char;

Name = record
         First_name : Longstring;
         Last_name  : Longstring;
         Initials   : Shortstring;
       end;
```

```
Struct Name {
      Char* First_name;
      Char* Last_name;
      Char* Initials;
      };
```

**Figure A1.9** Typical implementations of composite attributes in Pascal and C, respectively.

of using a technique, called normalization, which is widespread in the data processing world. We discuss normalization later in this appendix. Attributes without an internal structure are often called *atomic attributes*. In object-oriented modeling, on the other hand, we can group data much as we put together records in Pascal or structs in C (see Figure A1.9). Such groupings of attributes are commonly called *composite attributes*. Information modeling would not allow us to make such attributes.

---

**Example**

We have a table with the attributes Name and Address. If Name includes first name, last name, and initials and all these details are not always used together, then Name is not fully factored. This is not acceptable in information modeling. It would, however, be acceptable with object-oriented modeling, because the attributes with this technique can have an internal structure. In fact, having such internal structures is considered a good abstraction technique and is encouraged in object-oriented modeling. For example, it is common that we can work with attributes on different levels. For instance, we assign values on a "high" level:

```
Name1 := Name2;
```

or assign parts of a composite attribute:

```
Name1.First_name := Name2.First_name;
```

---

It is acceptable in object-oriented modeling to let values depend on other values, whereas information modeling demands that attributes should be *mutually independent* (if fully normalized). Two or more attributes are mutually independent if none is functionally dependent on any combination of the others. This implies that attributes can be updated independently of each other.

---

**Example**

Looking at the class Person, described previously, we might decide that the postal code should include the country prefix—for example, S-741 41. Because we also have the attribute Country, the attributes are not independent because if we change the S in the postal code, we must change (the same information) in the Country attribute. Object-oriented modeling, on the other hand, encourages a mapping close to reality and does not care if things are mutually independent or not. The important thing is, instead, that we have a close mapping to the problem space. For example, if the customer has a reality where we use S-741 41 *and* Sweden then this is the correct modeling, rather than another modeling where attributes are mutually independent.

---

Attributes in object-oriented modeling are more powerful modeling constructs than in information modeling, because they allow grouping of atomic attributes to composite attributes and because they are encapsulated inside an object. (See the next section, "Methods.").

## Methods

Methods represent the behavior of an object. In object-oriented modeling, method implementations are put inside the objects, together with the attributes

Using information modeling, it is possible to write a piece of code that acts upon the values of the attributes and possibly also changes them (see Figure A1.10). We could call these code-pieces "methods." These methods would not be explicitly connected to a certain table, however. In information modeling we could thus have a set of methods and a set of tables, but the connections between them would have to be explicitly stated and these methods would not be connected to the table in the same way as methods belonging to an object are connected to the object.

In information modeling, attribute values are always accessible, whereas with object-oriented modeling, the values are not directly accessible. That is, if we follow the definition of an object, the values are hidden, and if we, for example, want to read a value, we must include a method in the object that can return the value of an attribute. Let us imagine an object A with the attribute State and another object B that needs to know that State; then B cannot directly access the attribute State but needs

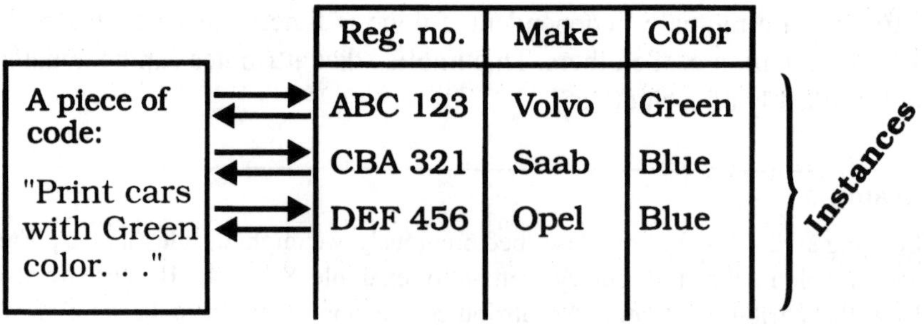


**Figure A1.10** In information modeling it is always possible to access values

a method in A that can return the state. In Figure A1.11 we have such a method: Return_state.

The values are accessible in the table (information modeling), but they are hidden in the object (object-oriented modeling), and can only be changed or accessed through a method. We say that attributes are encapsulated in object-oriented modeling.

Connecting behavior (methods) with things is as natural as connecting characteristics (attributes) with things.

We again conclude that object-oriented modeling is the more powerful modeling paradigm.

It is sometimes possible to simulate methods in information modeling. For example, in some variants of information modeling a concept called *daemons* (or *triggers,* in some database literature) is available. Daemons are procedures attached to a data structure that are fired (executed) when the data structure is accessed. They must, however, be regarded

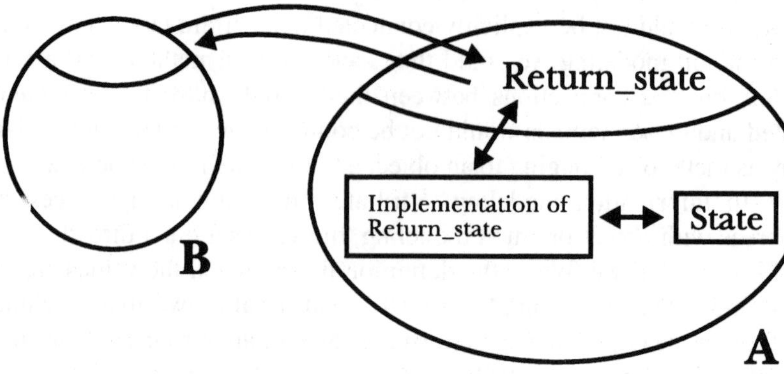


**Figure A1.11** An object cannot directly access an attribute value.

more as a special modeling construct than as a substitute for methods because they are activated when a data structure is accessed rather than when a message—possibly with parameters—is sent to an object.

## Structures

The class and the class structure exist in object-oriented modeling, but they are not normally available in information modeling, as we have already mentioned. Next, we discuss two other structures, relationships and aggregation of objects.

### *Relationships*

Because relationships are implemented by attributes, we can use relationships in object-oriented modeling, too. But relationships are much less in focus with object-oriented modeling.

We also have other options available. For example, we can hide associations to make them implicit. We presented an example of this earlier in the book when we made is_part_of associations implicit. See the section "A Major Problem with Associations," in Chapter 3.

At this point, we simply observe that the role of relationships can (and ought to) be greatly reduced in object-oriented modeling compared with how they are used in information modeling.

### *Aggregation*

If we want to keep track of what belongs together using information modeling techniques, we can use a table (see Figure A1.12).

Information modeling does not normally include the information hiding possibility of the object-oriented aggregation. Thus, the things in the aggregation are all directly accessible. We indicate *weak aggregation* (without information hiding) by using a dotted line (see Figure A1.13).

We call aggregation that also uses information hiding to encapsulate the things we aggregate *strong aggregation*. Strong aggregation would not allow us to refer to the internal objects. The same example as before but with strong aggregation is shown in Figure A1.14.

In the information modeling version, we have a set of tables that we relate via referential attributes. All the data are equally available. In the object-oriented modeling version, we have the option of seeing data on different levels. This way of grouping related data is what makes the object-oriented technique very efficient for CAD/CAM applications. When the user wants to have a drawing covering a part of the construction,

| Aggregate | Part |
|---|---|
| Plane 111 | Wing 011 |
| Plane 111 | Wing 093 |
| Plane 111 | Fuselage 01 |
| Car 4011 | Tire 1234 |
| • | • |
| • | • |
| • | • |

**Figure A1.12** A table with aggregation information.

all the data belonging to that part can be fetched in one "reading." If we instead have data in tables and relate them with tables, the underlying system would have to use these tables to find the relevant data (the data that belong to the part in question). This would mean that the system would first have to create a map of where the data are stored using joins and other operations. This map would then be used by the system to read the data distributed over the hard disk, moving the head to different tracks. This

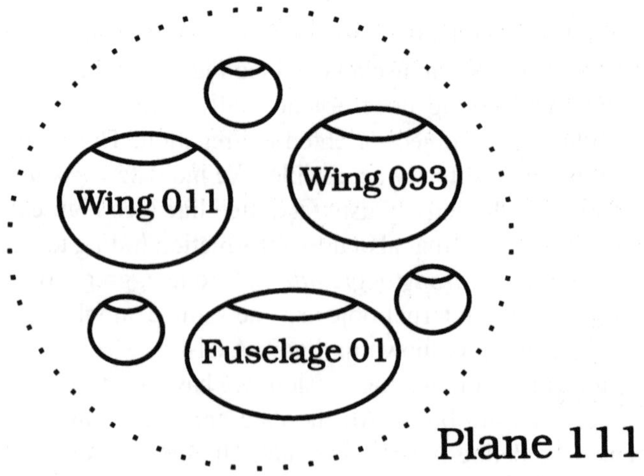


**Figure A1.13** Aggregation without information hiding is indicated by a dotted line.

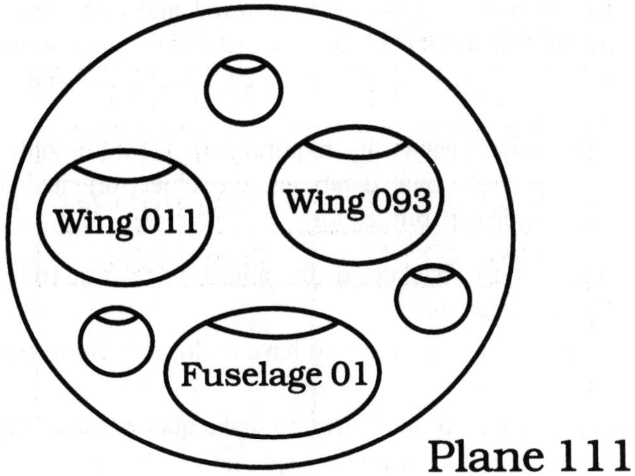


**Figure A1.14** Aggregation with information hiding.

would take more time than just reading all relevant data in one continuous reading.

These examples do not illustrate the whole idea behind aggregation, because we have left out the methods. The objects Plane 111, Wing 011, Wing 093, and Fuselage 01 are typical information objects. If we had been describing another example with system objects, the methods would have been more important, and our aggregation would have included methods on each level. That is, there would have been some methods available for the whole, other methods for the parts of the whole, and so on down to the lowest level. Each set of methods would use the subobjects on a lower level to achieve their goals.

In summary: Information modeling does not give us aggregation with information hiding or a natural leveling of objects into a hierarchy. Thus information modeling presents us with a form of aggregation that is inferior to what is possible with object-oriented modeling.

## DATABASES

### Introduction

A distinction can be made between what we call *hybrid* systems and *pure* (or true) object-oriented databases. The main difference is that hybrid systems have an underlying relational database. In these hybrid systems, there is a mapping layer that converts objects into traditional relational structures when they are to be stored, and vice versa. It should also be noted that object-oriented databases represent a mix of two separate technologies, conventional data management capabilities and object-oriented language technology.

Data management capability requirements are commonly regarded to be the same for relational databases and object-oriented databases. Requirements include capabilities for

- Restart/recovery/backup, or the ability to recover from software and hardware failure.
- Concurrency, or the ability to have multiple users working on the same data.
- Query facilities, or the ability to make queries via a simple interface.
- Security, or the ability to limit access to selected data.
- Integrity, or changes to the database without this leading to incorrect (or inconsistent) data.
- Data definition (schema) modification, or facilities to let data migrate easily to newly defined data models.

We do not elaborate more on conventional data management capabilitires but instead concentrate the discussion on some selected aspects concerning pure object-oriented databases. For a further discussion, the reader is referred to any of the many available books or documents discussing object-oriented databases. See the references in Appendix 5. For example, a detailed discussion can be found in *The Object Oriented Database System Manifesto* [31] and *Object Databases, An Evaluation and Comparison*, from ButlerBloor [32].

A database is used to store data (objects) that must exist between program executions. Such data (objects) that do not vanish when a program stops its execution are said to be *persistent*.

With a relational database there is an important difference in how we handle variables stored with persistence in the database and the variables we choose not to put in the database. The variables stored in the relational database must be retrieved and, when we have changed them, put back into the relational database using special software constructs. This process often involves a conversion between the data structure used in the programming language and the data structure used in the relational database. Thus, the programmer must write code that translates between the disk resident representation of data and the in-memory representation used during execution. It is not a straightforward procedure to transform between an object (or object structure) and a data structure suitable for a relational database. This problem is often referred to as the *impedance mismatch*.

The use of nonpersistent objects (in RAM) and persistent objects with a relational database management system (RDBMS) is illustrated in Figure A1.15. With a pure object-oriented database, the situation changes dramatically. No special constructs or very few such constructions are needed for storing and/or retrieving persistent data from the object-oriented database. Probably the best way to view a pure object-oriented database is to view it as something that is not there. By this we mean that code using persistent objects, stored in a pure object-oriented database, does not differ significantly from other code. The idea is illustrated in Figure A1.16.

A database exemplifying this is the commercial database ObjectStore™, made by OBJECT DESIGN, that needs few additions and changes to the code to use it.

Concurrent access by several users creates the possibility that updates will interfere with each other. ObjectStore™ manages this by providing a transaction construct. In ObjectStore™, a transaction is defined as a unit of work whose boundaries are determined by the developer. All

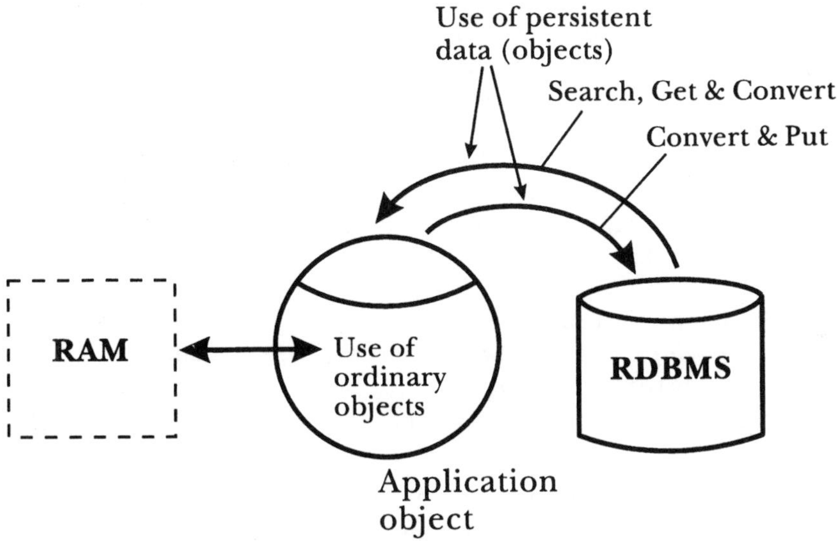


**Figure A1.15** Using data with a relational database. (RAM = Random-Access Memory).

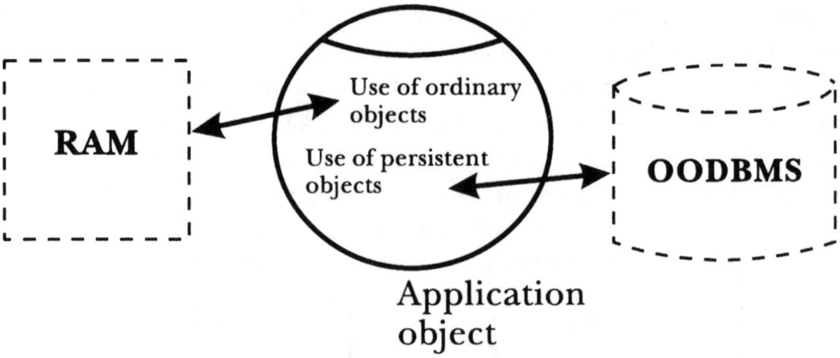


**Figure A1.16** Using data with an object-oriented database. (OODBMS = Object-Oriented Database Management System).

reading and writing to the database must be put inside this transaction. C++ code for this is

```
do_transaction() {
   /*something*/
   }
```

The following code examples are, with permission, adapted from the ObjectStore™ technical overview manual [29]:

```
#include <ostore/ostore.hh>
#include <records.hh>

main () {
database *db;
persistent<db> department *dept;
database* db = os_database::open("/company/
records");

do_transaction(); {
employee *emp = new (db) employee ("Fred");
emp->salary = 1000;
dept->add_employee (emp);
}
```

This code opens a database (db) and creates a new persistent object (emp) of class employee. The code also adds the employee to an existing department (dept) and sets the salary of the employee to 1000.

Memory is allocated and deallocated with the new operator and the delete operator, respectively, as usual in C++. The db argument to the new operator specifies that the created employee object shall be allocated in the database db. Data are allocated from persistent memory. Thus objects will be persistent in ObjectStore™ without making persistent part of the class of an object. In other object-oriented databases it is common to use multiple inheritance and let a class inherit from a class having the property of persistence. This technique is illustrated in Figure A1.17. With

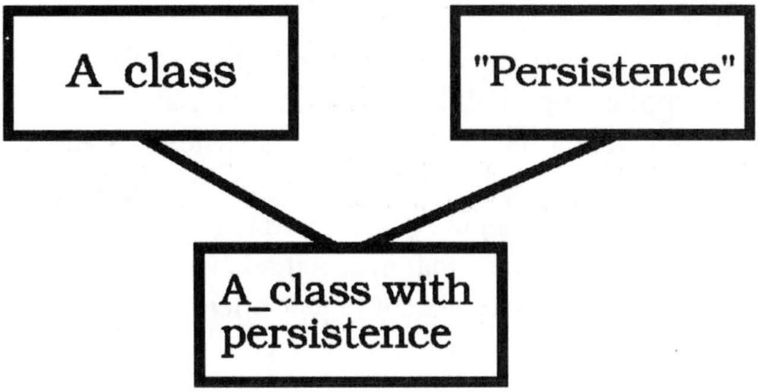


**Figure A1.17** Inheriting persistence.

ObjectStore™, on the other hand, persistence and the class structure will be orthogonal. There is no need to inherit from a special Persistence class. Different objects of the same class may thus be persistent or transient within the same program.

Manipulation of data looks like a normal C++ program in the previous code, even though the objects are persistent. The code will also compile the same way. We thus do not need to write two sets of classes or functions, one for transient data and one for persistent data. Note also that a programmer does not need be to concerned with managing locks. ObjectStore™ will automatically set read and write locks and automatically keep track of what has been modified.

In Smalltalk the same code would look like this:

```
|db dept emp|
db := ObjectDatabase open:'/company/records.db'.
ODBTransaction transact: [
   dept := db at:'department'.
   (emp :=  Employee newln: db)
      name: 'Fred'
      salary: 1000.
   dept addEmployee: emp
]
```

This Smalltalk code opens a database (db) and accesses an existing department (department). A new persistent object (emp) is created of class Employee and given values for name and salary. Finally, the new object (emp) is added to department.

Once persistent database objects have been created, they are used in the same way as objects that have been allocated in the Smalltalk image. (The image is all the Smalltalk objects that make up the Smalltalk environment.)

An example, quoted in the ObjectStore™ technical overview manual, states that an application module of 102 lines of code was reduced to 29 lines simply by deleting the explicit read and write lines and substituting calls to ObjectStore™. ObjectStore™ is an interesting development and is a good representative of a pure object-oriented database. ObjectStore™ also has some query facilities, that makes it an even more interesting product. A more thorough discussion of object-oriented databases is outside the scope of this book.

## Normalization

*The best ideas are common property.*

—Lucius Annaeus Seneca

Normalization is a technique used when designing relational databases. It is based on ideas by Chen [17]. For an in-depth discussion, the reader is referred to a text such as [10]. The purpose of the technique is to reduce redundancy in data and to ensure that manipulations of data will not make the database inconsistent.

The availability of a normalization technique for relational databases is often put forward as a significant advantage and a major reason why we should select a relational database rather than an object-oriented one. In the author's opinion, this argument is not as strong as it may at first appear. There are reasons for selecting a relational database, but the preceding argument is not a good one. Two arguments against normalization techniques as a reason for selecting a relational database are

- Object-oriented models tend to be fairly normalized.
- Normalization is only a part of database design, anyway.

It has been pointed out by other authors* that object-oriented models tend to be fairly normalized, even though we do not use normalization

*See, for example, Appendix 5 [7] (page 236).

techniques. It has also been pointed out by other authors* that the normalization process is really *only* formalized common sense. Formalizing common sense is of value, but this value is directly related to the need for formalizing. That is, if it is possible to use object-oriented technology and get fairly normalized models, we may not need to formalize common sense into a theory of normalization.

As we pointed out in Chapter 1, "Problems and Solutions," the world is consistent. Thus, if our model is not consistent, it is because the transformation from reality to model is defective in some way. Object-oriented development implies a very close mapping to reality explaining at least partially why object-oriented models tend to be normalized. Our conclusion is that if we model the world and think about potential redundancies and anomalies, we have a good chance of getting a normalized model when using object-oriented techniques.

The other part of the argument concerns the role of normalization when doing database design. The author has often heard the argument that relational database design has a theory—normalization—that object-oriented database design does not have. Therefore, relational database design is to be preferred. Even if normalization techniques are good techniques—and maybe needed in object-oriented database design too—it is clearly wrong to equate normalization and database design. Database design is still a subjective exercise, both for relational and object-oriented database design. It has been pointed out by other authors† that there are few principles available for database design. Figure A1.18 summarizes the last argument.

The aim of these arguments has been to reduce the importance of normalization as a reason for selecting a relational database rather than an object-oriented database. Next, we look at some reasons why we should not select a relational database and one reason why we should perhaps select one anyway.

The main argument against using relational databases is that normalization hides and destroys semantics. When we normalize, we are driven by considerations concerning computation or logic rather than about modeling the structure of the application. Normalized relations (tables) rarely correspond to any object in the real world. This is especially true for objects that have a complex structure. Also, relationships in relational models do not keep information and functions together. This results in a loss of application knowledge. Thus, normalization (and

---

*See, for example, Appendix 5 [10] (page 546).

†See, for example, Appendix 5 [10] (page 609).

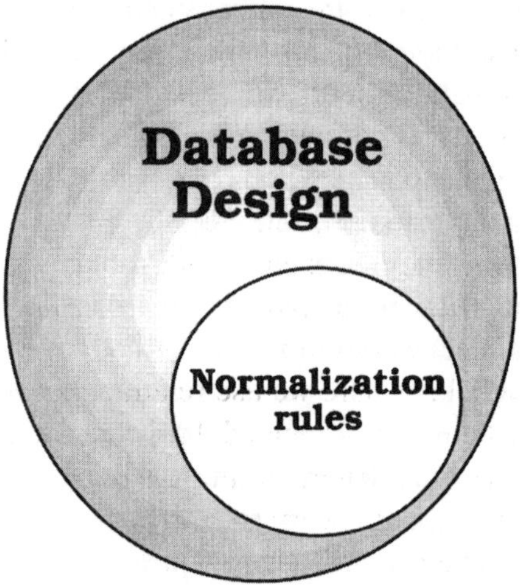


**Figure A1.18** Normalization is only part of database design.

relational modeling) destroys structures that naturally belong together. This can make retrieval of data very inefficient. Inefficient retrieval of data is the major reason why such areas as CAD/CAM are using object-oriented databases. In an object-oriented database, we know that the information representing an object such as an integrated circuit is going to be retrieved at the same time. This makes it easy to implement efficient retrieval algorithms because information can be collected sequentially from the hard disk. In a relational database, on the other hand, we have to retrieve information stored in different tables, slowly constructing the original object as we access data from different parts of the hard disk.

An argument *for* relational databases is that they enable us to retrieve data in a random way. It is possible to construct select statements (that is, retrieval conditions) in any way we want for the information stored in the database. If we want to have a list of everyone who owns a green house and has two pairs of brown shoes and this information is stored in the database, we can have it. In an object-oriented database the possible ways of accessing data are set when we model the data. If we do not know that Y wants to access data in a particular way when we make the model, Y will not be able to get the data. In practice, however, unusual ways of accessing data do not seem to be very common. That is, this argument for relational database design does not seem to be very strong.

There are also other problems with relational database design. One is the way of constructing the identifier using attributes. The use of something called *surrogate*s can solve some of the problems with the identifier.

Surrogates are purely logical object identifiers. They are generated using some algorithm. They are mapped to the physical address of an object using an index or something similar to an index. These surrogates are thus system-controlled keys closely resembling the identifiers we already use in object-oriented databases.

Relational databases will continue to exist. It is possible they will never be replaced when storing large amounts of information with simple structures. Object-oriented databases will continue to succeed where complicated data structures dominate, and it is a good guess that they will also be common in fields where we use relational databases today. Major reasons for this are that object-oriented databases are much easier to integrate with object-oriented programming languages and that the object-oriented modeling paradigm is very strong.

Important advantages of the object-oriented database are that it has increased modeling power, good support for information hiding, and low semantic gap and that there is no impedance mismatch. The main disadvantage is the absence of a good ad hoc query language.

The general rule when choosing between a relational database and an object-oriented database is that the more structure the data has, the more suitable the object-oriented database is. Because of the absence of a good ad hoc query language for object-oriented databases, the opposite of this rule is also true; the less structure the data has, the more suitable the relational database is. As object-oriented databases get better searching facilities, this latter rule will be less and less relevant.

## SUMMARY

Object-oriented modeling presents us with better modeling abilities than information modeling:

- Object-oriented modeling gives us much better abstraction techniques.
- Speaking the same language implies talking about objects.
- Objects are identified with an identifier that is *not* implemented by attributes, and because of this the identifier is less prone to mistakes with object-oriented modeling.
- Attributes in object-oriented modeling can easily be grouped, and consequently they can have an internal hierarchical structure.
- Methods are described along with attributes only with object-oriented modeling.

- Relationships can be used, but we need them less with object-oriented modeling.
- Aggregation is much more developed in object-oriented modeling.

Using pure object-oriented databases makes coding easier, because persistent variables can be coded in the same way as normal variables.

The availability of normalization techniques for relational database design is not alone a strong enough reason for selecting relational databases rather than object-oriented ones.

# Appendix 2

# Notation

## *Object and Class Structures*

*No rule is so general, which admits not some exception.*

—Robert Burton

### INTRODUCTION

An object structure describes an executable application, or part of an executable application, whereas a class structure describes the organization of some classes. The classes represent our reusable components, and we will thus normally use them in more than one application. This is a major reason why we separate the two structures. Thus, the object structure and the class structure are *not* described in the same model, as is common in some other object-oriented methods. Instead we make two separate models.

This separation does not mean that we must postpone noting pieces of class structures when we work with the object structure. However, the center of attention is always the object structure. When we find pieces of class structure(s), we note them but keep them separate from the object structure.

In Chapter 8, in our first two laws about software development, we noted that a notation should be simple, have few constructs, and should mirror the method being used. This is the basic reason for not just copying some existing notation. The notation used is a mix of the ones used by OMT [9], Coad and Yourdon [4] and others. Classes are drawn by a rectangle with the class name at the top. Methods and attributes are put below this name. We put the methods above the attributes in the style used, for example, in *Design Patterns* [35] rather than in the OMT style. Abstract classes are normally not indicated by italic (slanted type). Instead, the word abstract is added if this information is important. Objects are indicated by ellipses or circles rather than by rectangles with rounded corners because this makes the difference between objects and classes more distinct. (It is also easier to hand-draw ellipses than rectangles with rounded corners.) The OMT notation for inheritance is a line with a triangle. Because we do not mix class structures and object structures, we do not normally need this tri-angle. Thus, inheritance between classes can be indicated with a simple line where a class below another class inherits from the upper class.

Aggregation is mostly shown only for objects and then by encircling the aggregated objects with an ellipse or a circle. Thus, the OMT notation where a line, with a diamond at its base, goes to the aggregated element is not used in this book—but can be used if needed. The remainder of this appendix gives more details.

The constructions outlined in this appendix are sufficient for this book but may be inadequate when the reader is going to make models of his or her own. The reader is referred to [9] and [21] for more possibilities. An outline of the object-oriented analysis and design modeling approach we used in our two example chapters, Chapters 6 and 7, is given in Appendix 3.

In this appendix, we basically discuss the notation used in Chapters 6 and 7. Thus, we do not repeat the notation used for relationships here because we did not use it in those chapters. (Notation for relationships can be found in Chapter 3.)

## Naming Conventions

In this book we have adopted the following practices:

- The context determines whether a name refers to a class or an object—that is, it is obvious from the surrounding text or because we have defined a name as representing a class or an object.
- When we want to be particularly clear, we prefix the name of a class with a C. If we are referring to some object created from this class, we leave out the prefix. However, if we want to point out that we are referring to an object, we prefix the name with A_, An_, The_, or possibly, a_, an_, or the_.

For example, CError_report is a class name, whereas Error_report and An_Error_report refer to objects created from the class CError_report.

Names of classes, objects, methods, messages, and attributes normally begin with a capital letter, whereas names for variables are written using only lowercase letters. (Names starting with a_, an_, and the_ thus normally indicate variable names.)

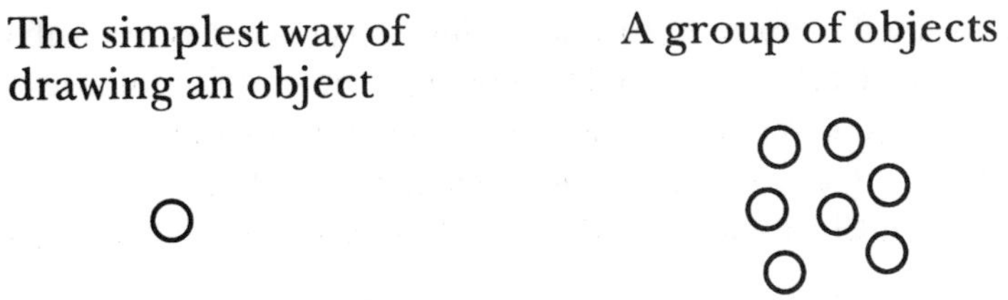


**Figure A2.1** Drawing objects.

## OBJECT STRUCTURES

An object is an occurrence of something. In this book the terms instance and object are synonyms. Each object has an identity, attributes, and methods. We use the class (see the following) to describe (or "produce") objects.

### Drawing Objects

If we just want to indicate the presence of an object or a group of objects, we do so with circles (or ellipses), as shown in Figure A2.1.

In Figure A2.2 we see five examples of drawing an object in a more detailed way. As indicated in the figure, we usually draw an object as a circle or as an ellipse, with a line used to divide it into two parts. Above the line we typically place names of methods belonging to the object. Below the line we place the name of the object if we do not place the

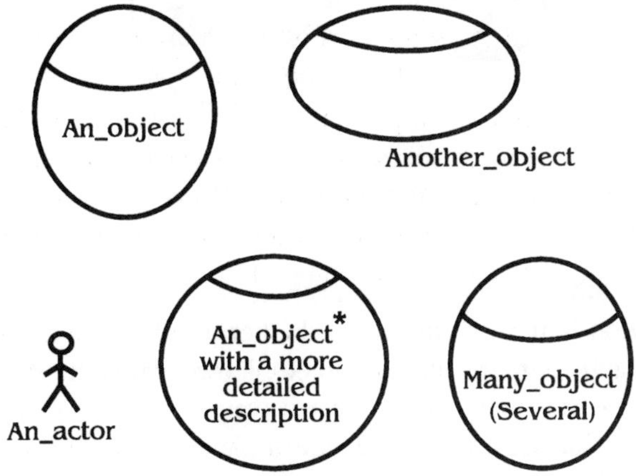


**Figure A2.2** More elaborate ways of drawing objects.

name outside the object to the right. The part above the line is the interface. Things placed there will be available to other objects for use. If the object in question represents a user role, an actor, we show this by drawing a symbol of a person.

Below the line we can put other information:

- *An asterisk* (*) means that a more detailed, exploded, description of the object is available.
- *A word inside parentheses* suggests some information. Examples are: (Several) and (Active). (Several) suggests that the object exists in more than one version. (Active) indicates that the object contains a task.
- *Other information* can be added if necessary, in the form of subobjects or something else that explains more of what the object is intended to do.

## Object Types

If the main role of an object is to represent some information, we shade the whole object and call it an information object. If the object contains several information objects and these are shown, we only shade the lowest level of objects (see Figure A2.3).

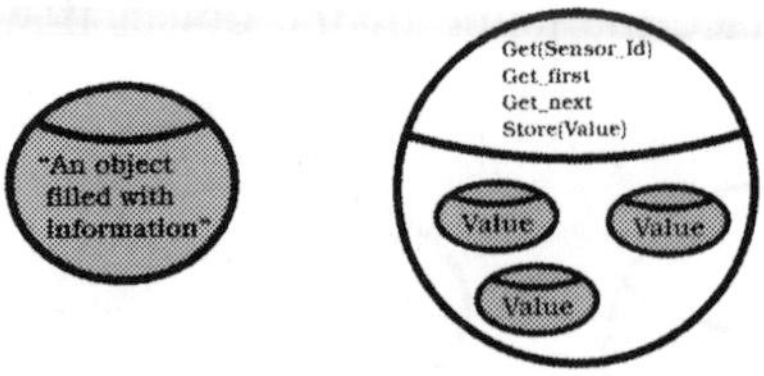


**Figure A2.3** Only the lowest level of shown information objects are shaded in gray.

In most other cases, no special notation is used. For example, no special notation is used to indicate whether an object is a client, server, agent, actor, active and/or passive object. However, as mentioned before, we can indicate the type of the object if we need to. For example, if it is active (that is, having a task) we can indicate this by writing the text "(Active)" inside the object. In the same way, we can also write: "(Server)," "(Client)," etc. We can, if necessary, detail this information—for example, "(Active, asynchronous)" or "(Active, synchronous)."

To each object we can also connect a comment if the information available in its class description is not enough. The comment should explain the object's obligations and responsibilities. A key question the comment should answer is, "Why does the object exist?" Comments are seldom put in the drawing. Instead, comments are typically put in separate documents.

## Methods

We place names of methods in the object above the line (see Figure A2.4). Above the line we show the *interface* of the object, what is available to other objects. A method is run by sending the object a message with a corresponding name. The set of messages an object accepts is called its *protocol*.

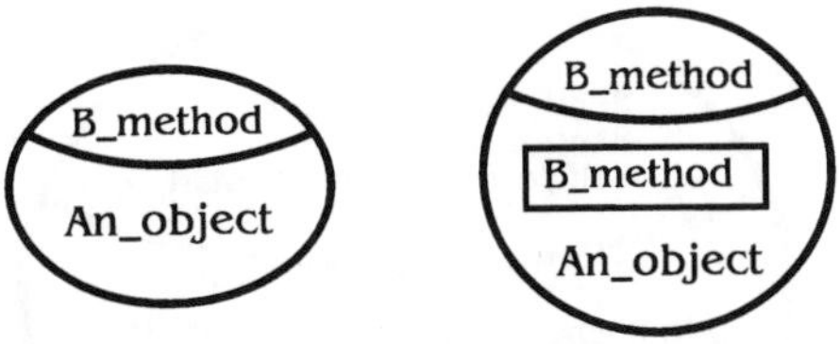


**Figure A2.4** Indicating method information in an object.

If we also want to show the implementation of a method, we repeat the name of the method inside a box placed below the line. Often we add the text "Implementation of:" inside the box, above the method name. The box is called the *body* of the method and represents the *implementation* of the method. The box is used in combination with lines and arrows to explain the implementation or part of the implementation of a method. For example, we can show how methods available in subobjects are called. Note that we, at a certain level of abstraction, normally draw only those parts of the implementation considered necessary for an understanding of the method at this level of abstraction.

## Mini-uses

If we have indicated one (or several) name(s) in the upper left corner, this implies that it is not "normal" method(s) we name but mini-use(s). A mini-use is a way of using an object. Names of mini-uses are placed in the upper left corner or inside an object (see Figure A2.5). If we put the names in the upper left corner, we give them the headline

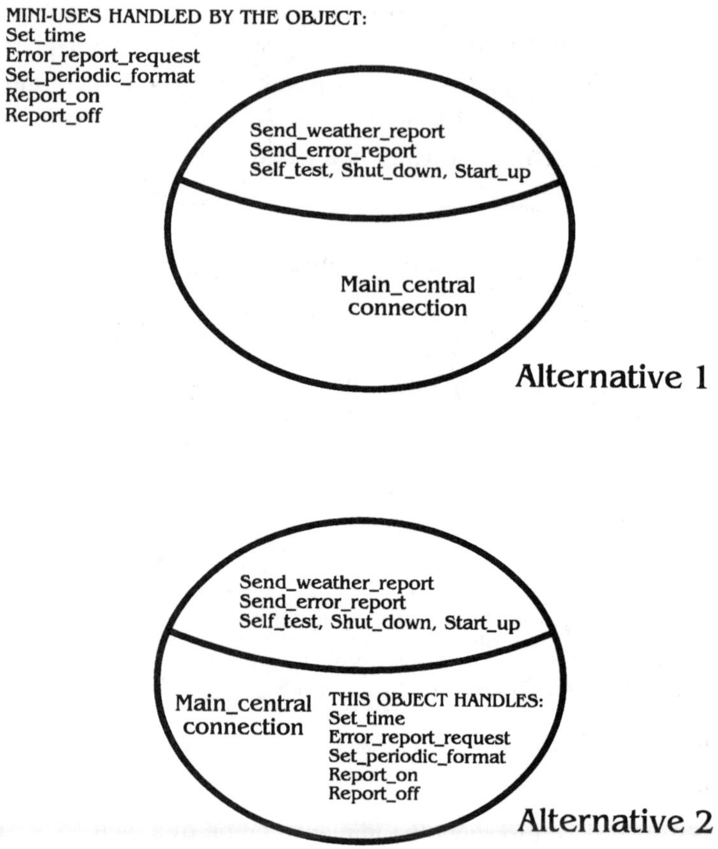


**Figure A2.5** Two alternative ways of indicating mini-uses handled by an object.

MINI-USES HANDLED BY THE OBJECT:. It is more common to put the names of the mini-uses inside the object handling them. A mini-use is not really part of an object's interface (the area above the line), so we put the text below the line, adding the headline THIS OBJECT HANDLES: and below this we list the names of the mini-uses, as illustrated in the figure. See also Chapter 4, section "Interface Objects," and Chapter 5, section "Describing Behavior," for further discussion.

## Communication

If object A sends a message to object B, we show this by drawing an arrow from A to B (see Figure A2.6). If B also calls methods in A, the arrow goes both ways or is drawn as a line without arrowheads. A line

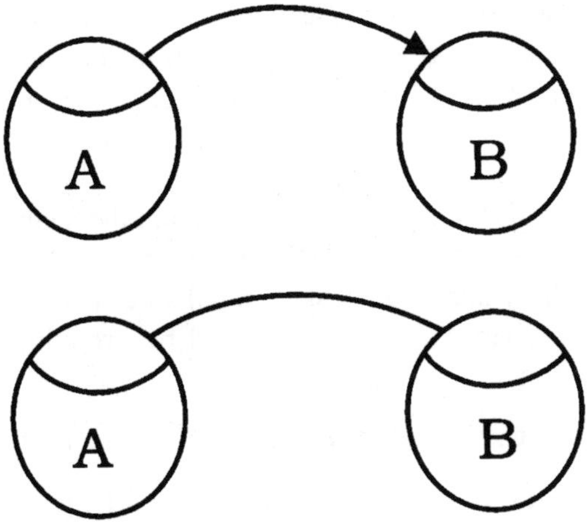


**Figure A2.6** Arrows and lines indicate message passing between objects.

without arrowheads thus suggests that two objects are communicating but does not specify the direction of calling. That is, a simple line can suggest any of the following communication cases:

- A is calling B.
- B is calling A.
- A is calling B and B is calling A.

This is a good starting point. At first we may be aware that two objects must be able to communicate, but we might not be sure of the best way of communicating.

### Attributes

Attributes are shown by putting them inside a box, often with the text "ATTRIBUTE(S)" at the top of the box (see Figure A2.7).

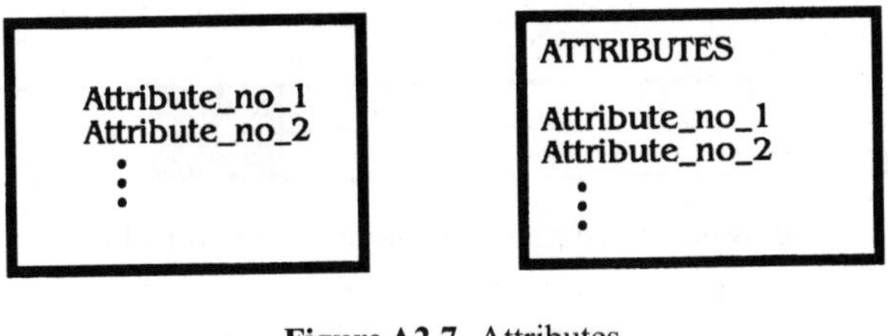


**Figure A2.7** Attributes.

The possible values of an attribute—the *domain*, or type, of an attribute—can be included and is then shown inside square brackets, for example, Integer [1..1000], Boolean [TRUE, FALSE] or Color [Red, Green, Yellow, Blue], or just: [1..1000], [TRUE, FALSE] or [Red, Green, Yellow, Blue].

A looser specification is sometimes used in the analysis and possibly also in the design, indicating only the type. Examples are [Integer], [Color], and [Weight]. (These domains must eventually be specified exactly.)

A complex attribute can be described by grouping several simple attributes inside brackets [ ]. An example is

[YearOfBirth, Name, *Age*, {Comment}]

where italic implies values that can be derived (*Age* = current year—YearOfBirth) and curly brackets { } implies one or several attributes of the same type.

In order to show the attributes of an information object in a simple and easily understood way, we sometimes use a *form*. An example of this is shown in Figure A2.8. The idea is to show the attributes contained in an information object in a way as close to reality as possible. A form should thus be close to what is shown on a computer screen, a paper, or something similar—representing the origin of the information.

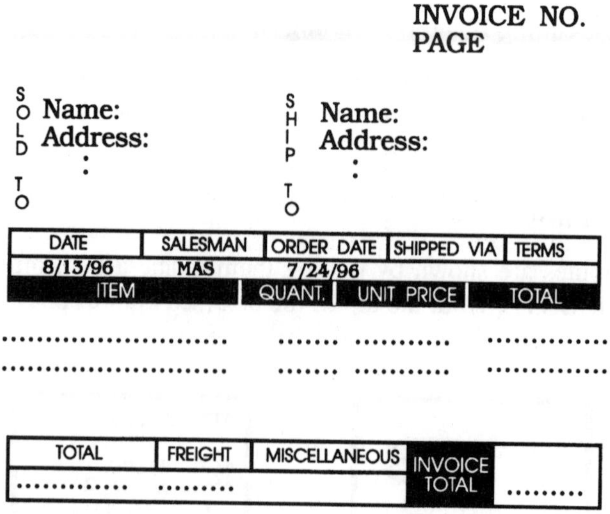


**Figure A2.8** A form shows attributes in a natural way.

**Figure A2.9** A broken line indicates objects executing in the same system.

## Systems

If we want to show that certain objects execute in the same computer and thus can communicate directly with each other, we show this by enclosing them with a broken line. We can also use this broken line to show that objects execute in the same process. This line is mostly used only if it is not clear from context which objects belong to the same system. This type of broken line used to enclose objects in the same system is shown in Figure A2.9.

Please note that a dotted line indicates aggregation without information hiding. See "A Dotted Line" later in this appendix.

If we have only one object, A, executing in a system, we usually call this system A_system. That is, we add "_system" to the name of the object.

# CLASS STRUCTURES

The class describes what attributes and methods an object will get.

## Drawing Classes and Class Structures

We show a class by putting its name inside a box. If we want to show more than one class, we put them in a hierarchy, connecting classes with lines (see Figure A2.10). Classes below other classes are called *subclasses,* whereas classes above other classes are called *superclasses*. If the class is abstract, we can show this by putting the text "(Abstract)" inside the box. (An abstract class does not have any instances. It is used only as a superclass.)

If we want to describe the attributes and methods of a class, we can do it in several ways. Figure A2.11 shows how we have split a box into four parts with horizontal lines. This is an augmented and changed version of the notation used by, for example, Coad and Yourdon. We put the

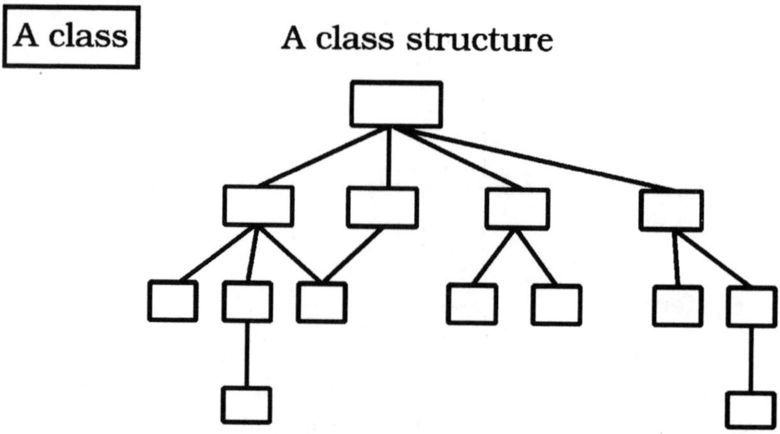


**Figure A2.10** Boxes indicate classes.

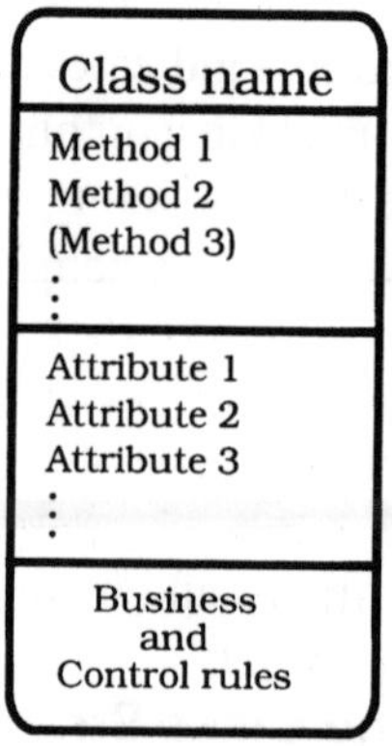


**Figure A2.11** A typical representation of a class.

methods above the attributes. The reason for this is that they typically represent the interface, and because we show the interface of objects at the top, we do the same for class descriptions. If a method is not available (public) to other classes (objects), we put the name inside parentheses (as we have done for Method 3 in the figures). At the bottom there is a box for comments. These comments include business and control rules. This idea is taken from a book by Ian Graham [7]. In this box we can put information about dependencies between attributes or comments explaining the responsibilities of the class. Here we can also put information about whether objects created using this class will be persistent or not. This is

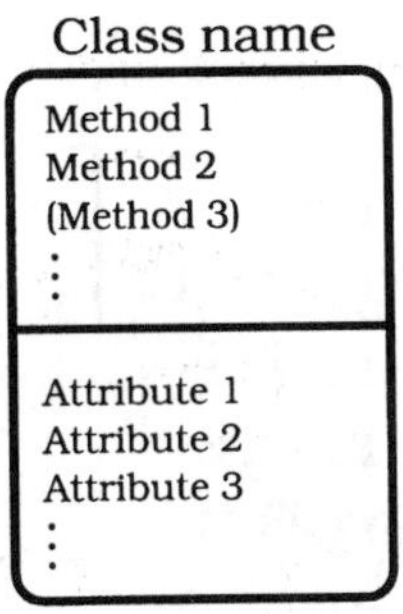


**Figure A2.12** A simplified class description.

also the place to put other types of descriptions pertinent to the class. Figure A2.12 shows a simplified class description.

If needed, we can let a class define an object structure. We refer to this type of class as a *complex class* when we want to point out that the class contains a definition of an object structure. A class description augmented with an object structure is shown in Figure A2.13.

Another way to draw a class, which at first may appear to be more complicated but actually is easier when we are hand-drawing a class, is shown in Figure A2.14.

Inside the box we put the name of the class. The attributes are placed below the box, and the methods are to the right. If we want to add a method or an attribute, we just make the corresponding vertical line longer. Attribute B illustrates how we can draw complex attributes.

If we want to draw a class structure in a simple way, without boxes, we draw it as shown in Figure A2.15.

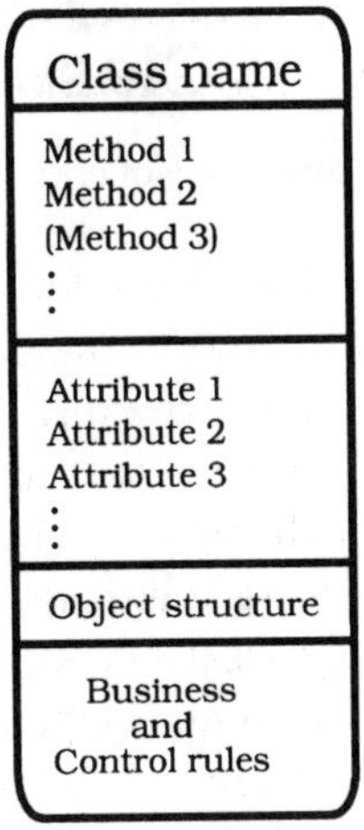


**Figure A2.13** A class description that also defines an object structure.

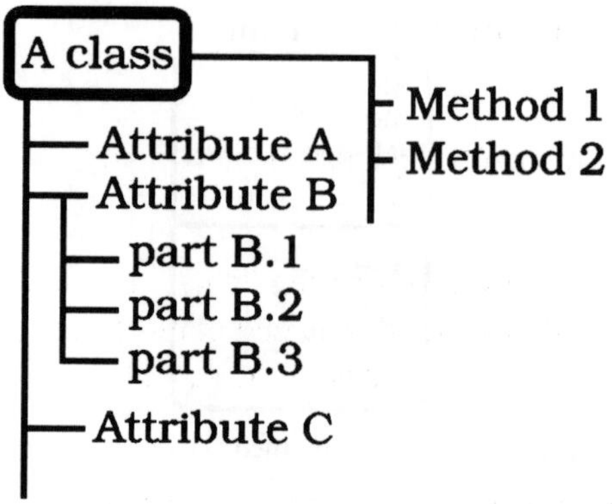


**Figure A2.14** A notation suitable for hand-drawing a class.

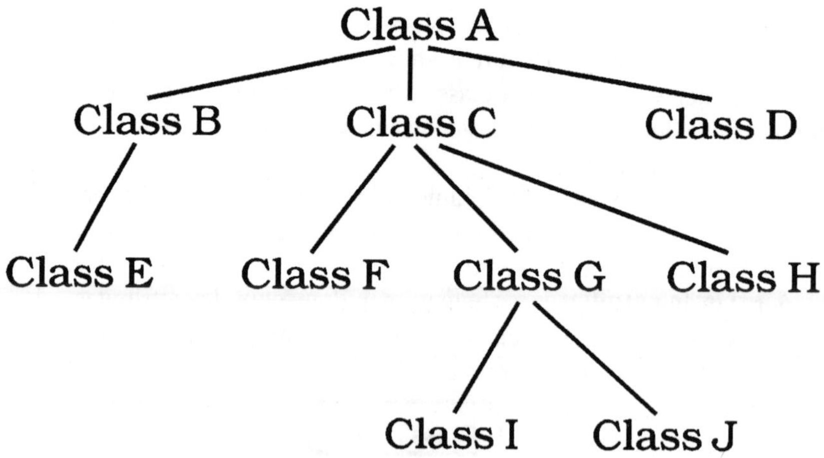


**Figure A2.15** A simple way of drawing a class structure.

## PSEUDOCODE

The pseudocode used in this book is not strictly defined but follows common sense. In the following examples, we show how we use pseudocode in this book, either by giving examples or by giving short comments about its use.

## Constructions Used

*;*

A semicolon indicates the end of a statement.

*{}*

A pair of brackets shows that the "code" inside them is to be comprehended as one unit. (When describing complex attributes curly brackets implies one or several attributes of the same type.)

*//*

Indicates a comment. The comment goes from the symbol to the end of the line.

---

**Example**

// ABCDEF

The "//" indicates that ABCDEF is a comment.

---

***Calling a Method***

A method "A_method" belonging to an object "An_object" is called if we write

```
An_object.A_method;
```

or if A_method has (two) parameters:

```
An_object.A_method(parameter no 1, parameter no 2);
```

If we need to point out the type or class used, we use constructions such as these:

```
a_method1(TEmployee);
a_method2(an_employee : TEmployee);
a_method3(CPerson);
```

where TEmployee and CPerson indicate the type of variable and class of object, respectively, that should be used.

*:=*

We assign values with ":="

---

**Examples**

```
a_value := "some calculation"
```

or

```
another_value :=
An_object.A_method_that_returns_a_value;
```

=

The equal sign (=) is used in boolean expressions.

>, <, >=, <=

These symbols are used in boolean expressions the same way as the equal sign.

*[]*

Enumeration of values is described by enclosing them with brackets. (These brackets are also used to describe composite complex attributes.)

**Example**

```
[Is_available, Is_not_available, Is_not_installed]
```

***IF***

```
IF "some condition" THEN
   line no a1
   .
   .
   line no b1
   ELSE
   line no x1
   .
   .
   line no y1.
END_IF;
```

If "some condition" is true, we execute lines a1 through b1. If the condition is false then lines x1 through y1 are executed.

The ELSE part can be left out:

```
IF "some condition" THEN
   line no a
   .
END_IF;
```

***WHILE***

The usage of WHILE is much the same as for IF:

```
WHILE "some condition" DO
   line no a1
   .
   line no b1
END_WHILE;
```

We execute lines a1 to b1 as long as "some condition" is true.

***FOR***

```
FOR "some condition" DO
   line no a1
   .
   line no b1
END_FOR;
```

The "some condition" explains under what conditions lines a1 to b1 are to be executed. If we want to give a more specified condition, it can be done in the following way:

```
FOR "something" := "start_value" TO "end_value" DO
   line no a1
   .
   line no b1
END_FOR;
```

Lines a1 to b1 are executed. The first time we execute them, "something" has the value "start_value."

The next time we execute the lines, "something" has increased one (relevant) unit. The actual value by which "something" is increased should be apparent from the context of the pseudocode itself. (We have pseudocode, not real code.)

However, if we want to show explicitly how much "something" is increased, we can add a WITH part:

```
FOR "something" := "start_value" TO "end_value"
WITH "some_value" DO
   line no a1
   .
   line no b1
END_FOR;
```

The "something" is increased by some_value each time the lines have been executed.

***EXIT***

EXIT indicates that we leave the enclosing loop, or as otherwise specified with a comment.

**Example:**

```
EXIT; // Exit method
```

### *CASE*

```
CASE "selector"
'value 1'      : Do something 1;
'value 2'      : Do something 2;
.
.
'value i'      : Do something i;
ELSE           : Do something default;
END_CASE;
```

Depending on the value of selector, actions will be taken. For example, if selector is equal to 'value 1', then Do something 1 (and only this) will be executed. There is thus an implicit EXIT after a Do something statement. If the selector does not contain a value corresponding to any of the values 'value 1' to 'value i', then the ELSE option is executed. The ELSE is optional.

## MISCELLANEOUS

### A Dotted Arrow

We use a dotted arrow to show in what direction an information object is being sent (see Figure A2.16).

### A Dotted Line

A dotted line indicates weak aggregation—that is, aggregation without information hiding. (Note: A *broken* line is used to enclose objects in

**Figure A2.16** An information object.

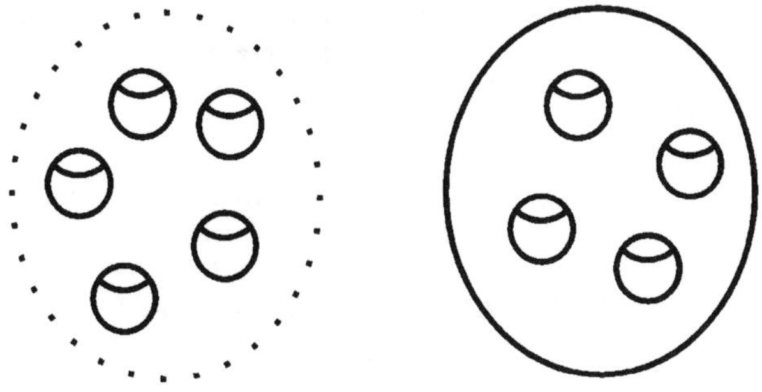

**Figure A2.17** Weak and strong aggregation.

the same computer or process). An unbroken line indicates information hiding (see Figure A2.17).

## Arrows

Arrows are normally used to show how objects call methods in other objects, but they are sometimes also used for other purposes. For example, in Figure A2.18 arrows are used together with numbers to indicate a sequence of actions. Arrows are also used to point to something in the normal way of using arrows, to indicate state transitions, and more.

## State Transition Diagrams

We can use techniques such as state transition diagrams if we feel the need to clarify some point. A simple notation is shown in Figure A2.19. This is the same notation as the one used by Coad and Yourdon [4].

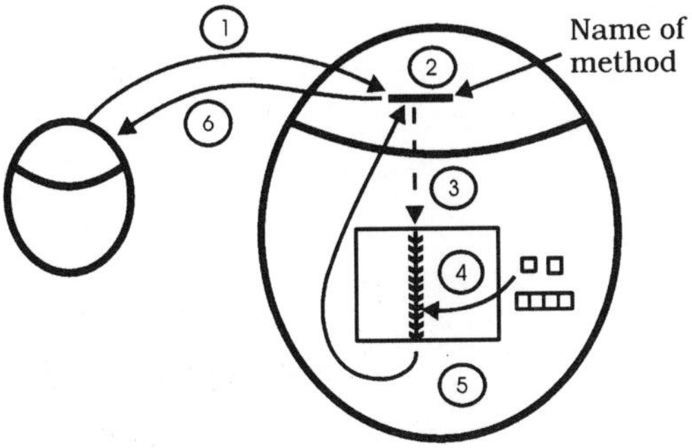


**Figure A2.18** Arrows are used in several different ways.

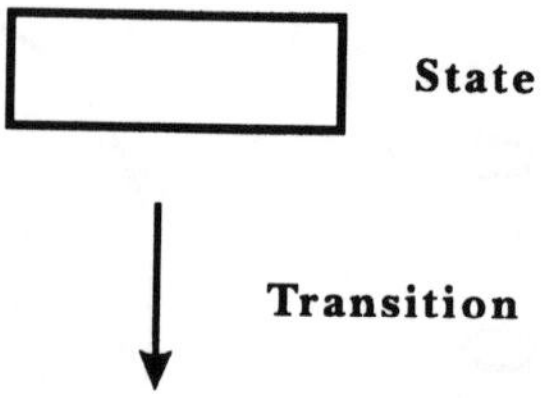


**Figure A2.19** State transition symbols.

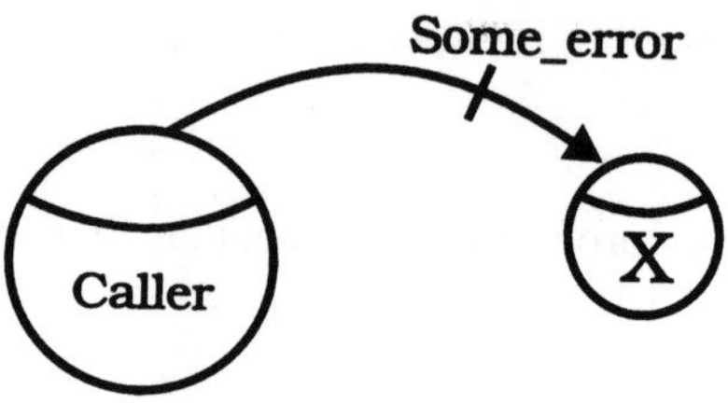


**Figure A2.20** Exception.

## Exceptions

If a call can raise an exception, the arrow indicating the call is crossed, and the name of the exception is put close to the arrow, as shown in Figure A2.20.

# Appendix 3

# Method

## *Analysis and Design Summary*

*Angling may be said to be so like the mathematics that it can never be fully learnt.*

—Izaak Walton

*And so it is with methods.*

—Added by the author

### INTRODUCTION

Describing a software development process in detail would involve writing several additional books, because it is a very complex process involving many different aspects and concurrent subprocesses. The intention of this appendix is thus not to give a full account of this process. For example, quality assurance and configuration management, vital when building large systems, will be discussed only briefly. The objectives of this appendix are, instead, the following:

- To give a feeling for how object-oriented analysis and design can be done, especially as we applied it in Chapters 6 and 7.
- To give some checklists for the software development process.
- To introduce some usable tools, such as standards, interviewing, brainstorming, and reviewing.
- Finally, to present two important documents.

This appendix must be adapted to the specific needs of a company and the particular company culture. Additional inspiration can be obtained from the set of available IEEE standards [30], which are displayed in Figure A3.1. Appendix 5 also has a number of helpful references.

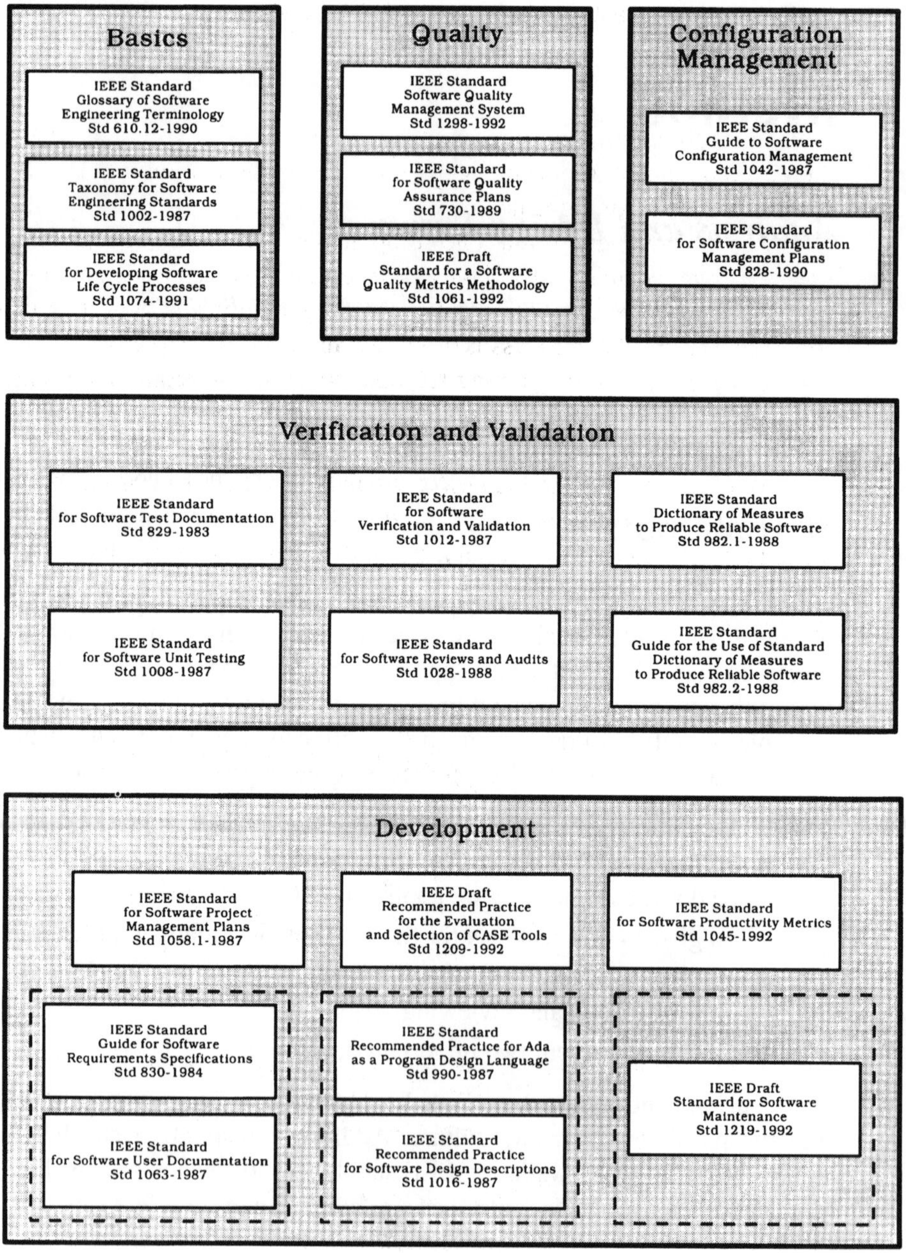


**Figure A3.1** IEEE standards contain a lot of usable information [30].

# THE SOFTWARE DEVELOPMENT PROCESS

## Overview

In a company we ought to find two main activities going on. One is the development of applications and the other is the continuing development of reusable components.

The development of reusable components is shown at the top of Figure A3.2, represented by the class structures there. Development of applications is represented by the increasingly larger groups of objects going from left to right. The process is discussed in detail in Chapter 4.

If we believe in developing reusable components, reuse is to a large extent a matter of organization. We outlined a way for this in Chapter 8, "Soft Factors."

When we try to map the object-oriented paradigm to a phase model, we find that in early phases we tend to find large objects. In later phases we simply tend to find smaller objects, until we eventually reach the code. Figure A3.3 illustrates the phase idea when doing object-oriented software development.

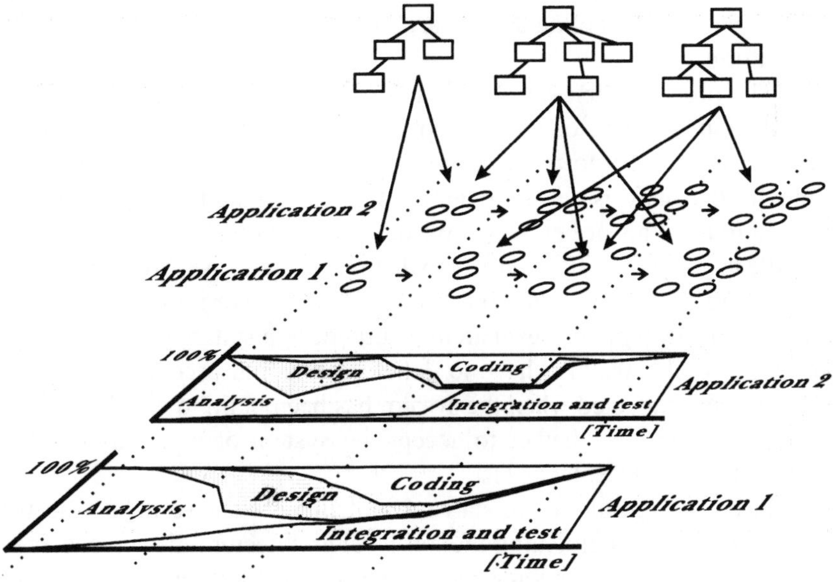


**Figure A3.2** The development process.

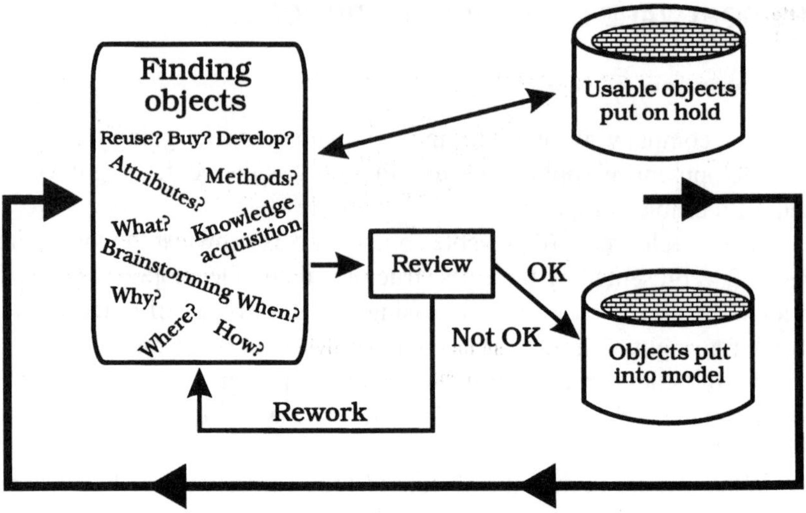


**Figure A3.3** An object-oriented phase.

The development is neither strict top-down nor strict bottom-up. The major effort is, however, top-down, because what is most important at the beginning is to define a good architecture (object structure) for the application.

The process often starts with a feasibility study to determine if we can develop a system or not. This phase is then followed by an analysis phase, where we try to understand in detail the problem(s) facing a customer. In the analysis phase we define a general solution strategy that can be used to meet his or her needs. We have to develop an understanding of who the users of the system are and what needs they have. We have to find out if there are any special constraints we must take into consideration and start to specify a top-level architectural design suitable for the system we aim to build. We also have to define testing and acceptance criteria. The latter is conducted when the system has been built, to enable the customer to determine whether to accept the system or not. This is often referred to as an acceptance test.

In the design phase we start to implement what we defined in the analysis phase by augmenting the top-level architectural design specified during analysis. In the coding phase, the main bulk of the coding takes place. As has been pointed out earlier, phases are not as strictly separated in object-oriented engineering as in earlier types of software development. The idea is illustrated in Figure A3.4. We still have the same basic

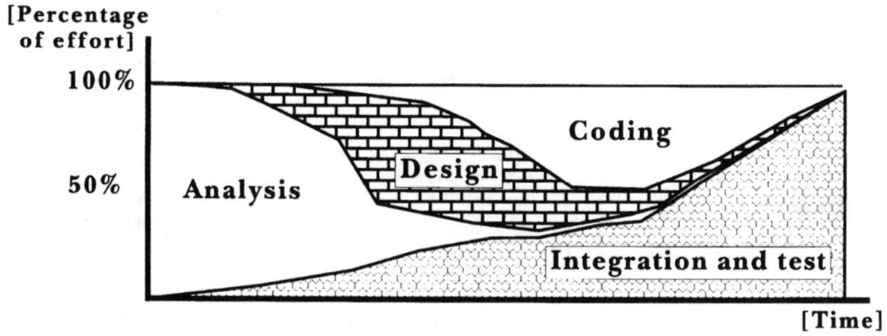


**Figure A3.4** Effort spent on different activities during object-oriented software development (example).

activities: analysis, design, coding, and integration and test but they do not necessarily follow each other strictly.

In Figure A3.5 we summarize the process. A customer with some needs is willing to invest to develop a system, and the process starts. Figure A3.5 implies a sequential development process, which is not completely true (see Figure A3.4). Typically, the process is sequential in the beginning (feasibility study and analysis), but then it turns into a mix of activities. For example, the reuse of an object immediately translates the object from analyzed to coded. Objects that are not reused are also typically implemented with different speeds. The vertical arrow indicates that integration is taking place continuously. The object-oriented software development process is further discussed in Chapter 4.

Actors, mini-uses, use-cases, and methods are normally first described with plain text. In the case of mini-uses and use-cases it is especially important to check this text with the user. The text is then refined into a structured text. The structured text can take the form of pseudo code or be text in a point-by-point fashion. If the customer has high technical competence, text may be written in a structured way from the beginning. The final stage is to develop the text into some exact text, a text including all necessary details. For example, in the case of methods, this exact text can be equal to code. In the following we take a more detailed look at the phases.

## Feasibility Study

Typically, we start with a *feasibility study*, in which we investigate the situation. We begin by determining who the users of a system are and what needs they have. The most important thing here is to develop a

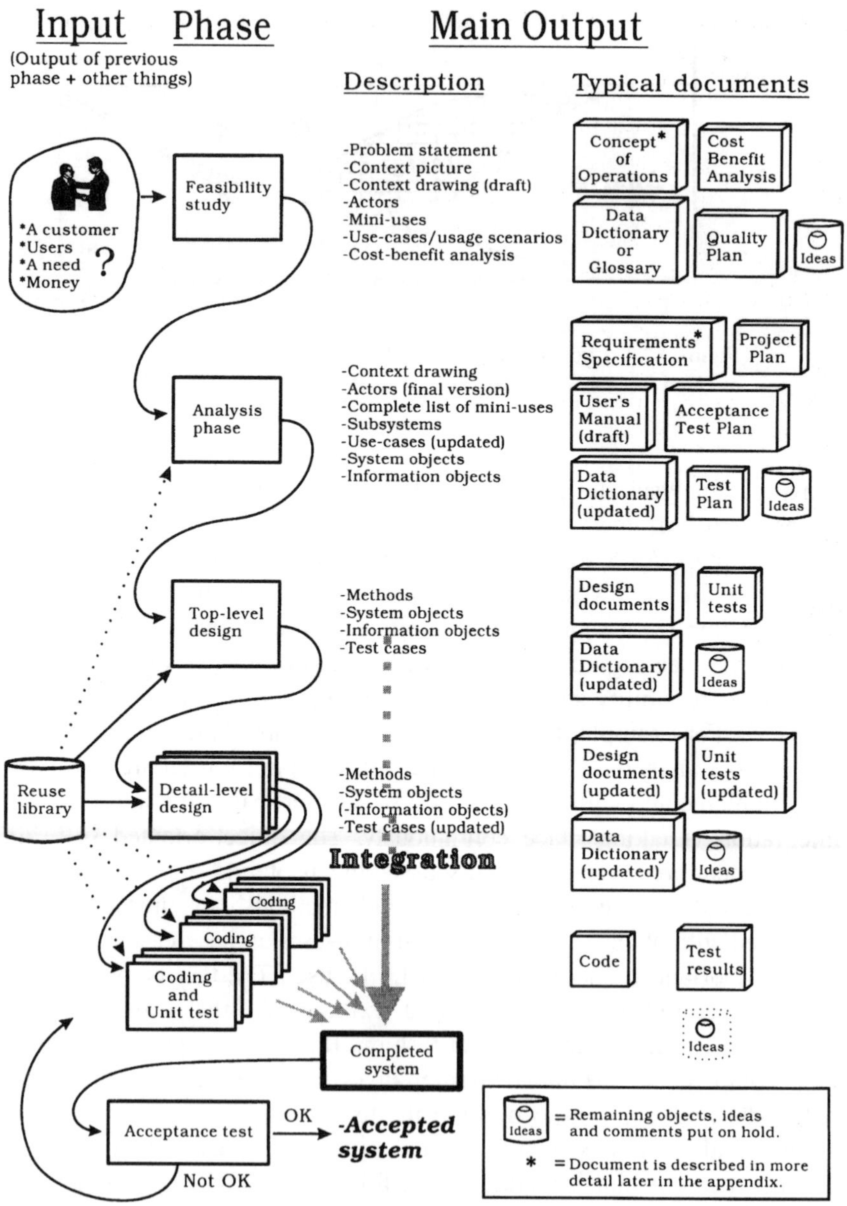


**Figure A3.5** Overview figure of the software development process. Objects need not be in the same state of completion. Thus, phases are not worked in a sequential manner. The process of developing applications is shown. The parallel process of developing, augmenting, and extracting components is not shown. Feedback loops to, for example, the QA and the methods department are not shown. Also, possible milestones are not indicated.

well-defined purpose. We define the purpose by writing a *problem statement,* using concepts familiar to the user/customer. The problem statement is a text describing as explicitly and clearly as possible why the system is needed, setting its context, and indicating what it should do. For small- to medium-sized systems, the problem statement can be as small as five to ten lines. Larger systems need from half a page to a full page of text. The problem statement is typically iterated on in several stages before a final version is reached. A good question to ask in connection with this iteration is, What is the system *not* supposed to do?

The feasibility phase is sometimes called a *business phase* because it is here we find out whether or not we have a business opportunity. Normally this phase involves a *cost-benefit analysis*. The purpose of a cost-benefit analysis is to see if the benefits of the system will outweigh the costs of building it. The output from the feasibility phase is shown at the top of Figure A3.5. An important part of this output is the *context picture.* The purpose of this picture is to set the system in an easily understood context to help us develop a conceptual picture of what function the system will fill when it has been developed. We show the context pictures used in Chapters 6 and 7 in Figures A3.6 and A3.7, respectively.

We also develop a draft *context drawing.* Whereas the context picture has the character of a photo, the context drawing is the first drawing

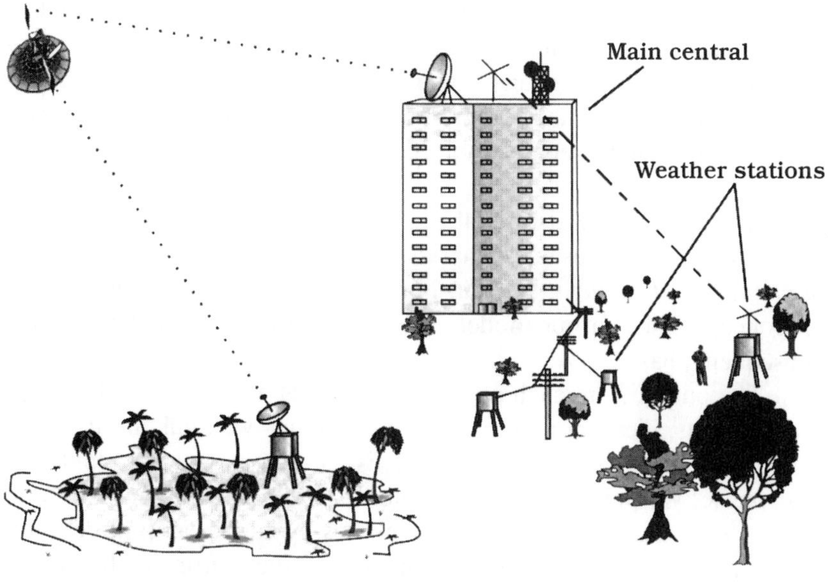


**Figure A3.6** Context picture from Chapter 6.

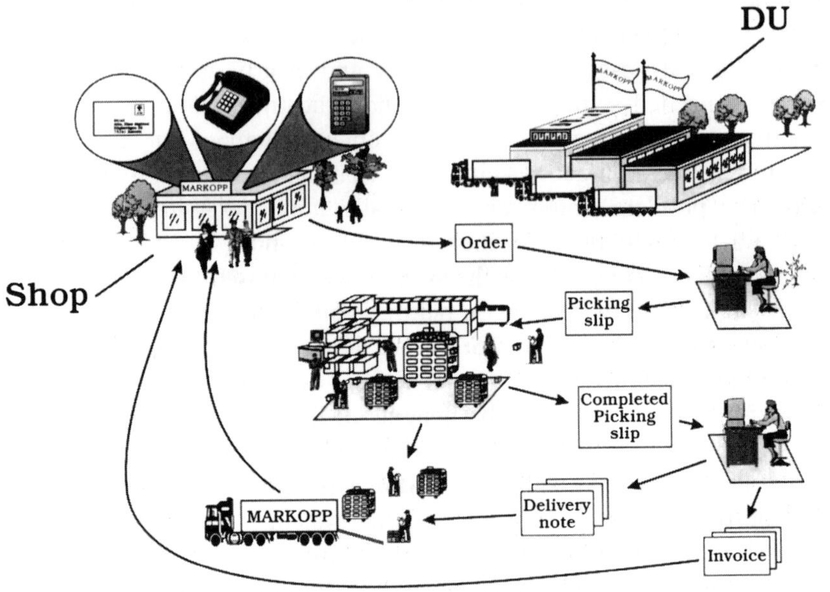


**Figure A3.7** Context picture from Chapter 7.

of the model we make of the system. The context drawing shows subsystems, information objects exchanged between subsystems, and, for each subsystem, the main actors using the subsystem. Important system objects and other details can also be put in this drawing. The draft context drawing, made during the feasibility study, includes the main parts of the system. Note that we separate objects into information objects and system objects.

In this phase we also list the mini-uses we find and give some sample use-cases and/or usage scenarios. All this is documented in a *concept of operations document*. We start our *data dictionary*, a dictionary listing all concepts used in our model. The data dictionary is updated in each consequent phase.

The output from each phase also includes potentially usable things, those objects, ideas, comments, and other things we think are usable but cannot use in the current phase. This list is then part of the input to the next phase. We put these parts "on hold" in a pool of potentially usable things, to be used if needed in later phases. Note that an indirect output from a phase often is some rework of the output from earlier phases. Object-oriented development will not eliminate such rework, but it will help to minimize it and the cost incurred by it. Quality assurance and configuration management are begun in this phase. (See the section "QA and CM" in this appendix.)

## Analysis Phase

If we decide to develop the system, an analysis phase follows. In the analysis phase we develop what we found in the feasibility study into something exactly defined. If we have a class structure with ready-made components, it is natural to look at it to see if we have any parts that we can reuse. The center of focus should always be the object structure, however. Higher levels of the object structure (subsystems) are the basis for deciding the project structure. A (sub)project typically develops only one subsystem.

The context drawing is completed during the analysis phase. The completed context drawings used in our two example chapters are shown in Figures A3.8 and A3.9, respectively.

The context drawing should now include all subsystems, all information objects exchanged between these subsystems, all actors, and all mini-uses. The context drawing shows the top level of the architectural design of a system. How to develop the architectural design is discussed in more detail in Chapter 5, in the section "System Architecture."

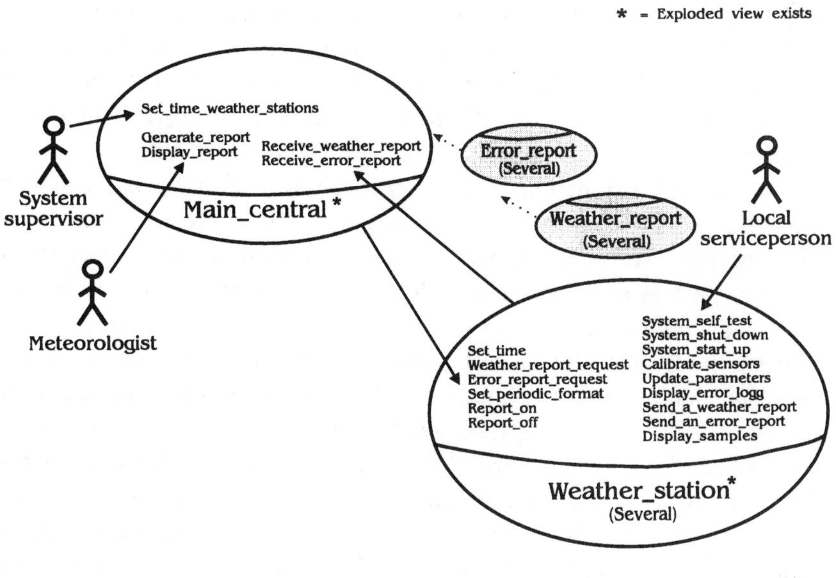


**Figure A3.8** Context drawing from Chapter 6.

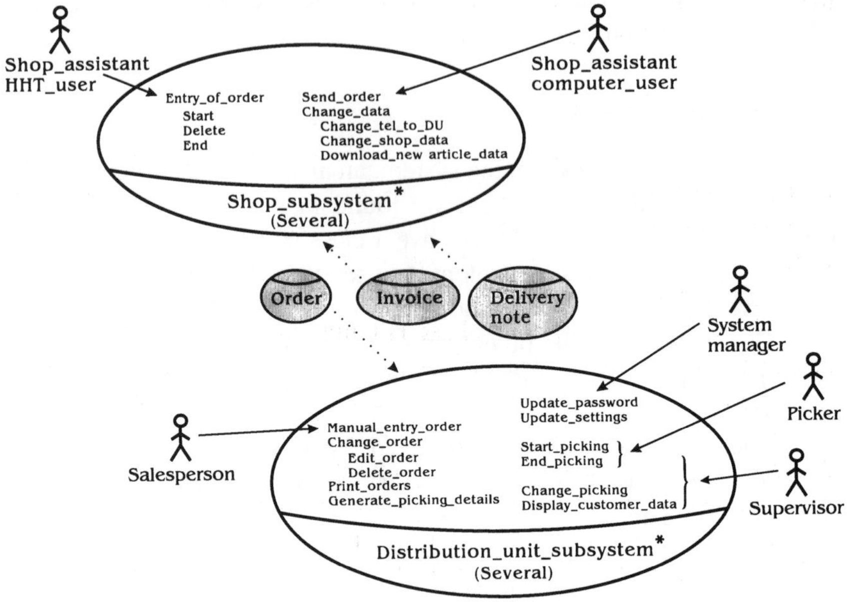


**Figure A3.9** Context drawing from Chapter 7.

If necessary, we augment the set of use-cases begun in the feasibility study to get a more complete set of use-cases. All this is documented in a (software) *requirements specification*, often referred to as an SRS. If a concept of operations document has been written, text from this is often copied into the requirements specification.

Note that the total sum of all mini-uses is basically equal to the functionality the system is expected to deliver. Changing a mini-use, once a contract has been signed on a requirements specification, is a question of renegotiation between customer and developer. Thus, even if it is true that object-oriented software development is not very sequential, we still need baselines such as one that includes approved mini-uses.

A *test plan* is also made. The test plan contains general information concerning testing and instructions for developing unit tests and integration tests. Here we start to plan the test cases we need to use later when we are to test. An acceptance test plan should also be developed.

We start to develop a user's manual and we update the data dictionary. The user's manual is often finished late in a project. This is a waste because the user's manual is an excellent tool for improving a requirements specification document. It is thus a good idea to start developing a user's manual as early as possible.

## Design Phases

The design is similar to the analysis. A basic difference is that instead of use-cases and well-defined purpose(s) to work the process, we now have something else that will push the implementation process forward: First the mini-uses and then, at lower levels, the methods will drive the implementation process.

Thus, when the analysis phase is completed, we start the top-level design phase, where we basically implement the mini-uses we defined during the analysis. When we do this, we will find new system objects and new information objects. We expand subsystems outlined in the context drawing by adding details showing how mini-uses will be realized. We thus add objects and methods to objects so that a mini-use can be realized by calling a sequence of methods. We also add other system objects, information objects, methods, and attributes as needed. Use-cases are used to develop test cases.

The next phase is a detail-level design. The basic difference between the detail-level design and the top-level design is that we implement methods and not mini-uses. We have to iterate this phase for as many levels of abstractions as we have in our system. That is, this step will be repeated for each layer of system objects until we reach the lowest level of objects needed. We thus build a nested object structure until we reach a level where we do not need to define any more objects. Figure A3.10 illustrates the idea of developing one level of methods in each iteration. Note, as has been pointed out earlier, the development is not strictly top-down. For example, low-level objects such as drivers are often developed early in a project.

We test or review when we have something to test or review. A document is thus reviewed when it is completed. Unit testing is done when a unit (object/class) is finished, and so on. Test cases are used to test how several objects behave together.

## Other Phases

We also have coding, an integration test and—in the end—an acceptance test. Other possible phases include a packaging phase and a maintenance phase. During the packaging phase we do what is necessary to

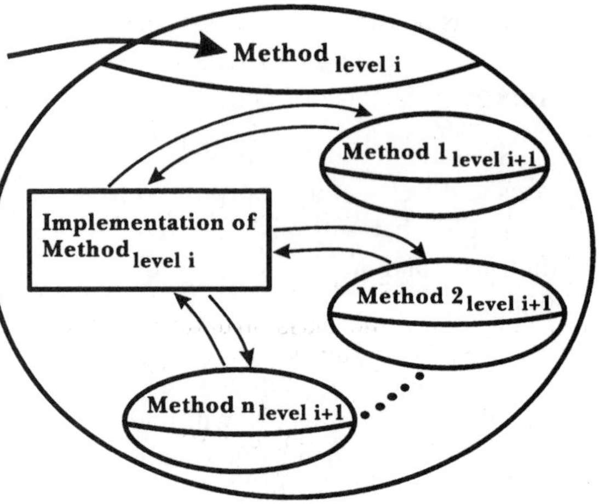


**Figure A3.10** A method at a certain level is implemented using methods at the next level of subobjects.

deliver our system or place it on the marketplace, if we have developed a commercial package to be sold by our own company. This phase can also include an evaluation of the project and a search for classes that we should turn into reusable classes, our components.

The maintenance phase is the time from the end of the project until the system is taken out of service. During this time we monitor the system for satisfactory performance and make necessary modifications to correct problems or to respond to changing requirements.

## Class Structures

A class structure is a modeling tool allowing us to keep similar parts together, needed when we design the object structure. This helps us beat complexity. A class structure is also a tool for reusing code.

If we use a class library such as one of those available in Smalltalk, Visual C++, or in Borland C++, for example, it will influence our class structures and probably also our object structures. Having such an existing class library is an asset but also a problem. It is an asset because it supplies us with ready-made components that can be incorporated into our object structure either directly or after some minor changes. It is a problem because such a class structure will influence our object structure, making us focus less on it. This does not necessarily increase the chances for a well-designed application. The main purpose with a class structure should thus be to model similarities between classes and not to reuse code, even though these two uses of a class structure are intermixed. It is very important that the modeling purpose governs the reuse aspect or we will get a very unorganized reuse of code, resulting in bad object structures—that is, an application with a bad architecture.

The systems developed in our example chapters, Chapters 6 and 7, were built without having a ready-made library with class structures from the beginning, so our object structures there were created without any influence from other class structures. We thus concentrated our attention on the object structure, not the class structure, following the principles laid out in this book. We "forget" the class structure when we build our object structure because of the experiences gathered in the studies [1] and [2]. These showed clearly that the object structure will be better if we do not let class structures dominate our work.

A drawback with this approach is that possible class structures are often not immediately apparent. Another drawback is that we do not reuse classes as much as if we had a class library available.

However, we again stress the point that the intention with this book is to help the reader think about objects—not classes. In a real project, we would probably take a more active interest in possible class structures during analysis and design than we have shown here. In the future, when class libraries become larger and we get more experience in using them, class libraries will play a more central role than in Chapters 6 and 7. However, the focus should always be on the needed object structure of the application. Our starting point when we make the class structure is then a knowledge of what the objects contained in the object structure are supposed to do. Our task is, in essence, very simple: What classes do we need to instantiate the objects? Can we design classes preserving a good object structure while reusing code?

## CHECKLISTS

*All experience is an arch to build upon.*

—Henry Brooks Adams

**Definition.** A *checklist* is a list of questions and instructions, compiled from experience, used to check that we have not forgotten to do something and that we have not done something in the wrong way or in the wrong sequence.

## General Checklist

This checklist contains general checks that can be applied to *all* phases:

- We should choose names with care. During early phases, we look for names on actors, mini-uses, and so on, that are descriptive and close to the user's terminology. Before we invent our own names, we check whether there is a name in the problem domain language that we can use. We stay focused on the real world. During later phases, we work hard on finding descriptive names on objects, classes, methods, etc.
- We should avoid vague words. Be sure agreement is reached on the precise meaning of words.
- Is the model good enough? A good solution is seldom reached in a first attempt. Iterating on a solution until a good model is reached is thus not a failure but rather the normal situation.
- It is important to keep a sense of humor and keep the group in a good mood. When the going gets tough, lighten up, take a break, and try a different approach.
- We should assign documents, objects, classes, etc., to someone. Ownership increases the quality of items, because we tend to feel responsible for what we "own."
- We should check the output of each phase for quality. This especially applies to the items that are most important, such as the problem statement and the requirements specification. Have we done necessary reviewing and testing?
- Trust your intuition. A good rule is to review a solution after a good night's sleep. Listen to the little voice inside yourself prompting you into an alternative solution that *feels* better.
- Have we included a textual description? Large items, such as systems or subsystems, need a full problem statement. Small items, such as an attribute or a method, may need only a line or two of comment, but a textual description should always be there.
- Have we avoided wish lists? Only real needs should be included. Needs should also be prioritized. The customer wants to add a new function. The design team invents a new, interesting method, and so on. This is often called *feature creep* and can cause great problems with deadlines and projects. Changing or adding a mini-use is a question of renegotiation with the customer: Who shall pay for it? This is an important reason why we want to have

traceability. If we have traceability (which presupposes configuration management) we can determine whether an item in the current phase can be justified from a requirement in an earlier phase. We should thus develop a skeptical attitude and never assume that an item is necessary until it is proven necessary. On the other hand, if we are implementing a (reusable) component, the question is often reversed: Is the component functionally complete?

- Does a fact contribute more to our understanding than it detracts by burdening our mental capacity? It is easy to repeatedly add details, resulting in a cumbersome system. Details should be discarded if possible or otherwise (preferably) abstracted away.
- We should make certain that each object has a well-defined purpose and responsibility. This is to make them independent of each other and to give them low coupling. The more an object takes on the character of an independent microworld the easier it will be to reuse it and to implement changes. We should thus put great effort into designing these responsibilities and the interfaces. A more general idea than low coupling is orthogonality, which can also be used to check methods, classes, and attributes. See Chapter 3.
- We must check the schedule. In each phase we update the schedule and set new goals and deliverables. Is the schedule reasonable?
- We should use what works! If we thoroughly understand object-oriented techniques, as they are outlined in this book, and we cannot describe a problem using these techniques, then we should use something else. There is only one rule that is always applicable and that is that there is no rule that is always applicable. On second thought, there may be an exception to that rule, too.
- Finally, if things get really hectic, an obligatory (minimal) 60-hour week is imposed for everyone and everyone is working as fast as they can, take a couple of steps backward into a quiet corner, relax, compose yourself and try to figure out what is important in this situation rather than just urgent at the moment.

## Checklist Feasibility Study Phase

This checklist contains checks applicable to the feasibility study phase. The checks in the general checklist should be *added* to these checks:

- Is the communication with the user working smoothly? Has the user been involved in the writing of problem statement, use-cases (and/or usage scenarios), and mini-uses? Echo solutions to the user. Get suggested solutions validated by the user. Writing a user's manual is one way of improving communication with the users. What's the attitude of the user? Is he or she aware of the project and positive to your efforts of defining use-cases and mini-uses?

- We should try to meet the real needs of our user(s). Immature understanding of what computers and software can do, problems in communication, etc., can make users suggest solutions that are not advisable. The actor concept, use-cases, and mini-uses help us focus on the real needs of the user and on getting the user involved.
- Are we dealing with the real users? Often there is a difference between the actual users and the decision makers who pay for the software development. When defining actors, mini-uses, use-cases, and/or usage scenarios, the real users are more important than the ones paying for the software development.
- Do the decision makers with whom we are working have the necessary power to make decisions, or do they only give the impression that they have this power?
- Have high-risk areas been defined? Note, the higher the risk, the earlier the risk must be tackled.
- Do not postpone decisions. If a user cannot give a clear description of what he or she needs, help by giving several suggestions. (If we present a user with only one suggestion, he or she might accept it not because it is the correct solution, but because of not seeing any alternatives).
- Have we avoided unnecessary constraints, such as computer and hardware details? We should at this stage be as free from technological constraints as possible. It is common to hamper developers by imposing unnecessary constraints. Thus constraints should be critically reviewed and analyzed before being accepted. However, important technological constraints should not be ignored. Ignoring fundamental design constraints might produce a nice model but a model that we cannot implement.
- Have concerned personnel been given enough training? This is especially important when training people in the new object-oriented paradigm. Note that managers must also be trained in the new object-oriented paradigm.
- Have we established a first schedule for the development of our system?

- Is funding available and sufficient for what we aim to do?
- Do we need to automate, or should parts of the system (or all of it) be implemented (or remain) as a manual process?
- Have we separated objects into information objects and system objects respectively?
- Have we established a balance between formalism and creativity in the project? The scale goes from extremely rigorous software engineering for the software in a passenger airplane to little discipline in a small and uncritical prototype project.

### Checklist Analysis Phase

This checklist contains checks applicable to the analysis phase. The checks in the general checklist and the checks applied during the feasibility study should be *added* to these checks:

- Have we checked the reuse library for components? This is an important question we should ask ourselves again and again during analysis and design. When we develop an application in an object-oriented fashion, we are supposed to build the application object by object rather than by line by line. If we do not check the reuse library each time we need an object, we will reuse much less. However, the focus should be on making a good object structure rather than on getting maximum reuse of code.
- Have we separated interface objects from application objects? Often the development of the interface for an application and pure application objects can be done in parallel. This is one important reason for separating interface and application objects. Another important reason for separating objects dealing with the interface and objects dealing with application logic is that it makes it easier to move the application to another computer system. A third reason is that changes to the interface (including a new radically different interface) will be easier to implement.
- Have we defined some use-cases and/or usage scenarios? Is our set of use-cases large enough to be a good starting point for writing test cases?
- Have we checked and thoroughly discussed use-cases (and/or usage scenarios) and mini-uses with our users?
- Have we avoided making optimizations too early? Optimizations are best done when we have a well-thought-out object structure for our application.

- Is the list of mini-uses complete? The list of mini-uses we define during the analysis phase is the key part of the requirements specification. Basically, the set of all mini-uses makes up the functionality we agree to deliver to the customer. Thus, the set of all mini-uses is the most important part of the contract we make with our customer. An unclear or incomplete requirements specification guarantees problems in later phases.
- Are mini-uses testable?
- Have high-risk areas been evaluated?
- Nonfunctional requirements should be checked for correctness and validity. This involves performance requirements, design constraints, security and much else. The IEEE Guide to software requirements specifications [30] is an excellent source of information about these nonfunctional requirements.
- Have subsystems been defined? The subsystems should be finalized during the analysis phase. How we partition the system into independent subsystems is the most important input when we decide about the project organization. It is thus very important that subsystems are clearly and finally defined as early as possible so that they will not change during the rest of the development process. (However, it is common that we have to make some changes to subsystems during the beginning of the design).

## Checklist Design Phase

This checklist is applicable both to top-level and detail-level design. The checks found in the general checklist should be *added* to these checks:

- Have we defined programming language, hardware and software platform, and database? (Sometimes this is done during the analysis phase instead.)
- Have we defined a good trade-off between hardware and software? Often a function can be implemented both by software and hardware. We must then construct a strategy for making choices between implementation in hardware and software, respectively.
- Have we checked the reuse library for possible components? The reuse library now comes more into focus.
- Do we continue to keep a clear separation between interface objects and application objects?

- Have the high-risk areas defined during the feasibility study and the analysis phase been finally evaluated and investigated? Have we developed plans for handling these high-risk areas?
- If we are designing an object, we should not be coding it. If we do any coding during the design, it should only involve sketching high-level structures of objects.
- Have we thrown away our prototype? A prototype is an excellent tool for increasing the quality of a requirements specification, but it should never be used for more than that. Thus a prototype should be thrown away.
- Have we avoided creating classes that reflect only a division of time? For example, we should not create a subclass modeling a new car and another subclass modeling a second-hand car.
- Have we avoided case statements? Too many case statements serve as a warning that we are probably not thinking in an object-oriented fashion. Case statements may, however, still appear. For example, case statements can be used when handling input in primitive interface drivers. For instance, a user has to enter one of options 1 through 5. The system can then be given a simple branching logic (implemented as a case statement) that takes appropriate action depending on the entered number.
- Have we got a good leveling of abstractions? When we try to understand the implementation of a method or a mini-use, we should have to look at only one lower level (layer) of the object structure. If we have to revert to complicated message traces again and again to understand a method, it is an indication that we have got a bad leveling of abstractions.
- Missing abstract classes? Overlapping responsibilities and similar classes could indicate missing abstract classes and/or subclassing possibilities.
- Have we avoided multiple inheritance and too many levels of inheritance? Multiple inheritance is difficult to use and too many levels of inheritance is bad design. An upper limit of four to eight levels is appropriate.

## Checklist Coding Phase

Because we do not deal much with coding in this book, we will not give an extensive checklist for this phase. However, a few important points concerning coding will be mentioned nevertheless:

- Have we used a coding standard?
- Have we avoided using too many case statements?
- Are we still using class structures as modeling tools? Class structures should never primarily be built to reuse code. Reusing code should be a nice secondary effect. (This point is not as important when building small systems as when building large to very large systems.)

## TOOLS

*Man is a tool-using animal . . . Without tools he is nothing, with tools he is all.*

—Thomas Carlyle

In this section, we discuss some interesting tools that can be used during the software development process to get information and to check the quality of deliverables. These tools are fairly complex; they should possibly be called techniques instead. However, we prefer the word tool, because that word puts them in the right perspective.

A special case of a tool is a computer program that supports the software development process. In this section, however, we look at other types of tools. Our definition of a tool follows.

**Definition.** A *tool* is something that aids us when we work with something.

Figure A3.11 shows when tools discussed in this section are most commonly applied. Note, these tools can often be applied in phases other than those indicated.

### Interviewing

*Reason is natural revelation.*

—John Locke

***What It Is***

Interviewing is a technique for information gathering. It is used mainly during the feasibility study and the analysis phase and can be regarded as a specific form of meeting or conference, usually limited to two persons.

| Tools | Feasibility study | Analysis phase | Design | Coding and Test | Acceptance Test |
|---|---|---|---|---|---|
| Interviewing | X | X | • | | |
| Brainstorming | X | • | • | • | |
| Use-cases | X | X | • | | |
| Test-cases | | | • | X | X |
| Noun/Verb strategy | • | X | • | • | |
| Reviewing | • | X | X | X | X |
| Static/dynamic testing | | • | X | X | X |
| Change control | • | X | X | X | X |

X = Main use of tool
• = Tool is usable

**Figure A3.11** Tools and where they are typically applied.

### *Main Steps During Interviewing*

- Select the person to be interviewed and schedule a time for the interview.

We should put some work into finding out whom to interview. To do this, it is best to start at the management level. Here we find people with an overall view, and this helps us find the people we need to interview. It is also important to interview the managers, because they decide what our system is all about. However, the most important persons for us to interview are the actual users of the system because they will define our mini-uses, use-cases, and/or usage scenarios.

- Prepare for the interview.

This involves doing some research, preparing some interview questions, and setting some goals for the interview. The goals should be clear but not written in too much detail, because this can reduce the possibilities of gathering information. On the other hand, an interview should not start from scratch. Some communications about the goals of the interview should occur before the interview—for example, through telephone calls.

- Conduct the interview.

The interview should be a dialogue—not a monologue. We should also try to switch between the abstract and the concrete continuously during the interview. Questions are preferable to statements when we gather information. Long multiword descriptions to describe concepts are acceptable during the interview, but better words should be found at the end of the interview or during the documentation of the gathered information. Main points are these:

- Start the interview by giving the interviewee the reason for the interview and by stating that his or her opinions and knowledge are important and will aid in the analysis process. Set clear goals for the interview, but don't assume anything.
- Establish a time frame and tell the interviewee when the follow-up will occur and how it will be done.
- Tell the interviewee what will happen to the information gathered and determine if there are any areas of restricted information.
- Assure the interviewee that nothing will be passed on until it has been checked with the interviewee.

■ Follow-up and document the information gathered during the interview.

The follow-up should include further communication with the person interviewed. A report is written and the contents of this should be checked with the person interviewed.

***Guidelines***

During an interview we should constantly verify and cross-check the information we receive. Thus, we should always verify understanding and take notes but don't be obtrusive about it.

We are there to gather information, so it is our task to do most of the listening.

A good idea is to make a list of all interviews and make it and the results of the interviews available to all involved.

## Brainstorming

*Criticism comes easier than craftsmanship.*

—Zeuxis

***What It Is***

Brainstorming is a meeting where we try to produce as many ideas as possible to solve a problem at hand. The key idea with a brainstorming meeting is to separate the creative act of thinking up ideas from the critical act of judging and selecting among them.

### *Main Steps During Brainstorming*

- Preparation.

Before we have a brainstorming meeting, we have to define the purpose of it. What problem do we intend to solve? We also have to select the participants. The group selected should not be too large, maybe five to six people. Next we have to select a moderator. The task of the moderator is to keep the meeting on track, finding ideas related to the purpose we have defined for the meeting. He should also enforce the rules we agree to follow in the meeting. Finally, we have to select a place for the meeting. As this is not a regular discussion, it is a good idea to select a place that differs as much as possible from normal meeting places.

- Brainstorming meeting.

We start the brainstorming meeting by clarifying the ground rules, especially the no-criticism rule. That is, we must outlaw all negative criticisms. Ideas should be stopped only if they are utterly out of context and have absolutely no relation to the problem at hand. Thus, if an idea has an even remote potential of solving the problem at hand, it is an idea fit for discussion in a brainstorming meeting.

As the meeting continues, we should make every effort to invent new ideas. Ideas should be recorded in full view of all the participants. This gives the group a feeling of achievement, and it helps us avoid repeating the same ideas.

When the main brainstorming session is over, we relax the no-criticism rule. Our task is now to select among the ideas. The most promising ideas should be selected for further discussion. The main task is now to improve on the selected ideas and make them as attractive as possible. The last thing to do in the brainstorming meeting is to select a time for a follow-up meeting.

- Follow-up meeting.

Our task at this meeting is to make a final judgment about the promising ideas we discussed in the end of the brainstorming meeting. We should decide which ideas we want to use and how to improve them further.

### *Guidelines*

In a way there are no guidelines for a brainstorming meeting as long as we produce ideas. However, one important rule is to avoid introducing any fear of sounding stupid or any other negative feelings in the brainstorming meeting. At the brainstorming meeting the task for everyone is to produce ideas and not to kill ideas by giving negative comments about them.

## Use-cases and Test Cases

A use-case is a way of using a system in order to accomplish some well-defined work. The main difference between a mini-use and a use-case is that a mini-use actually defines some functionality that we deliver to a customer, whereas a use-case is an example of how we apply mini-uses. The use-cases are used to find mini-uses and they are also the starting point for designing test cases. (See section "Describing Behavior" in Chapter 5 for a detailed discussion of use-cases and mini-uses.)

## Noun and/or Verb Strategy

The noun and/or verb strategy is a way of extracting objects, methods and attributes from text. Basically, nouns tend to give us objects, verbs tend to give us methods, and adjectives and other modifiers for nouns or verbs tend to give us attributes. (See section "Nouns, Verbs, and Adjectives" in Chapter 2 for a detailed discussion of this.)

## Reviewing

> *The practice of 'reviewing' . . . in general has nothing in common with the art of criticism.*
>
> —Henry James

### *What It Is*

A review is a basis for approving or not approving a document. It involves a procedure for checking and commenting on a document produced during software development. (Note that a software unit is also a document.) The purpose of having reviews is to increase quality and productivity in a company. The primary goals of a review are to check that a document has the correct technical content, follows standards, is readable, has a good layout, and is maintainable. Secondary goals of a review include giving feedback to help us refine our methods and gather statistical information. Other secondary goals are to educate those involved by letting them share the experience of others and to support the same understanding of the concepts used during software development. It is *not* a goal to review those who developed the documents. We should practice *egoless programming.** We are interested in finding errors in a document, not in criticizing its author.

### Review Participants

A moderator acting as a chairperson is a person with great technical skills. His or her main task, apart from normal chairperson responsibilities, is to decide what action to take when we find errors.

The author or authors of the document we review attend the meeting. Their task is to produce the document, to present it to the rest of the participants, and to correct it. They should also give ample warning if a suggested correction is of small value but will lead to a lot of rework.

Reviewers are people invited to review the documents because they have special technical knowledge and/or knowledge about how to review.

A meeting also normally includes other attendees. Experts include the review coordinator and other experts with special technical knowledge. A review coordinator helps the moderator with the administration. He or she distributes documents, checks that the review participants can come to the meeting, books the time for the meeting and so on. He or she also collects statistics to be forwarded to the quality assurance department and helps with the feedback to the methods department in order to refine review methods. Finally, he or she also checks that the review is done in a correct way. Experts also include document specialists, test experts, methods experts, and communication experts.

### Main Steps During Reviewing

- Start-up.

The moderator identifies the participants and the material to be reviewed. The material should not be too lengthy. Rough guidelines are no more than 200 hundred lines of code or about 20 to 30 pages of text at the same review occasion. The moderator also, together with the review coordinator, identifies necessary checklists, estimates the time needed for preparation, and decides place and time for the meeting.

Normally, only one document is reviewed at a time, but supplementary documents can be distributed together with the document

*Egoless programming is an approach to software development based upon the concept of team responsibility for program development. Its purpose is to prevent the programmer from identifying so closely with his or her output that objective evaluation is impaired. Having the document as a common group property, rather than as a personal possession, results in documents with higher quality.

to be reviewed. For example, checklists and/or references to checklists are typically sent out to review participants. The review coordinator distributes the material. The participants must have all necessary materials one to two weeks prior to the meeting.

- Presentation (optional).

At the presentation, the documents are presented by the author(s). Such a presentation should not last too long—not more than an hour. At this presentation we can also cancel the inspection meeting if we understand that the document(s) are not of adequate quality. The time and place for the inspection meeting can also be changed if necessary.

- Preparation.

During the preparation we read the document(s). It is seldom adequate to read a document only once to find important errors. A rule of thumb is that a document must be read at least three times if significant errors are to be found. The preparation thus takes time. To prepare the materials suggested here would take about four to eight hours. Checklists should be used during this preparation.

- Inspection meeting.

Each participant has a specific role in the meeting. The moderator leads the meeting by asking questions. In this way he or she encourages all participants to take an active part in the meeting. The review coordinator or a special secretary writes the protocol, and so on. Typically, the material is reviewed page by page or code statement by code statement.

The moderator starts the meeting with a check that all participants have prepared for the meeting by reading the documents that have been distributed. If the participants have not read the documents, the meeting, should be canceled and a new date set for the inspection meeting. If the reviewed document is of very low quality, the inspection meeting can be stopped and a new inspection meeting scheduled.

The moderator then continues the meeting by stating the purpose of the meeting, summarizing the method to be used for the inspection meeting, and summarizing the main points to be discussed during the meeting. Interruptions coming from mobile telephones, for example, should be indicated to be unacceptable. During the meeting unclear concepts should be defined and results should be clarified and summarized as they appear. It is essential that the meeting is not allowed to stray too far from the subject. The moderator is responsible for keeping the meeting on track. Writing results on a white board or something similar, verbally summarizing results, and asking appropriate questions all help to keep the meeting on track.

During the meeting, the task is to find, classify, and describe errors and to appoint someone—normally the author(s)—to correct them. We typically look for

- Errors. Errors are often classified according to some scale as more or less severe.
- Unnecessary items, such as redundant text.
- Missing items.
- Inconsistencies and ambiguities.

Some discussions concerning the errors can be allowed because this promotes an understanding of the errors and the causes behind the errors. However, it is not the purpose of the meeting to produce detailed solutions—that task is always delegated. The meeting should not last too long, and if it lasts more than an hour, short pauses should be inserted. The size of the group should not be too large, including at a maximum six to seven persons. The review coordinator arranges for feedback to the quality assurance department and the methods department.

The meeting is ended by the moderator summarizing all results and checking with the group that items noted in the protocol have been entered correctly.

- Rework and follow-up.

The author(s) rework the document(s) and a protocol is sent out. The moderator can schedule a follow-up meeting, if necessary. If a follow-up meeting is scheduled, the document will be approved (or not approved) during that meeting. Otherwise, the moderator has the responsibility of approving or not approving the document.

## Testing

*The man who makes no mistakes does not usually make anything.*

—Edward John Phelps

### *What It Is*

There are various types of testing. The most common ones are unit testing and integration testing. During unit testing we test an object (a class), and during integration testing we test how objects function together. We can also divide testing into dynamic testing and static testing. *Dynamic testing* is the traditional type of testing, in which we use test cases to execute a program. *Static testing* refers to all those other activities that find errors without running a program on a computer. Reviewing can be regarded as a special case of static testing. Here we will only mention a few points regarding testing; the reader is referred to the references for more information about testing. A good source of information is the book *The Art of Software Testing*, by Glenford G. Myers [11].

The best approach to testing is to try to find errors. If we try to prove that something is correct, we will probably do so. If we, on the other hand, take a more destructive approach, trying to show that something is in error, we will find errors. If we find errors (and remove them) we get paid for our work by an increase in the quality of what we are testing. Thus, we should take the more destructive approach.

Little is known about how the object-oriented paradigm will change the test situation. The early focus on interfaces, encapsulation, and other aspects should make the test situation more manageable. However, although this appears to be true for those using Ada, the experience of this author indicates that the test situation for those using C++ is still not more manageable compared with using non-object-oriented languages.

## Iteration

Iteration is not a separate tool but rather a supplementary technique that is applicable to other tools. We can thus use iteration during interviewing, brainstorming, reviewing, or when we try to describe or develop an item such as an actor, a mini-use, a method, or something else.

Iteration consists of two main steps that are repeated. The first step involves finding words, sentences, and pictures to describe something. We apply questions using words such as why, how, when, and what, taking a brainstorming attitude. What is the purpose and the role of the item?

The second step is to check and put some structure into what we found in the first step. To do this we use questions such as the following:

- Have we put things in the correct sequence?
- Is the description correct?
- Is our description complete or are details missing?
- Can we take away things? Do we have correct levels of abstractions?
- Can we use object-oriented structures to describe this?
- Are the names we have chosen appropriate?
- Is there someone who can help us check this?

The unstructured information we found in the first step is thus put into a more exact and structured form in the second step. The two steps are repeated until we are satisfied with the results.

## QA and CM

We defined QA (Quality Assurance) in Chapter 4.

**Definition.** *Quality Assurance.* (1) A planned and systematic pattern of all actions necessary to provide adequate confidence that an item or product conforms to established technical requirements. (2) A set of activities designed to evaluate the process by which products are developed or manufactured. [IEEE]

With QA we mean a *quality system* that is implemented in an organization with the purpose of ensuring that delivered products meet contractual requirements. Thus, the main purpose of QA is not to help in the software development process but to furnish an independent examination of products. In some cases this has led to the view that QA entails extra work for software developers and that QA interferes in a nonproductive way with the software development process.

There is a true tension between a more creative and chaotic way of working and the need for systematic development and control. As we have pointed out at various places in this book, object-oriented development has sometimes been taken as reason to abandon a systematic way of working. However, it is important to find a working balance between a systematic way of working and a more chaotic but creative way of working (see Figure A3.12).

QA covers all activities that are carried out to create a system and affects all personnel having anything to do with the development of the system. Typically a quality system is implemented using a *quality standard.* Such a standard is a document that states in a general way the requirements a quality system must meet. Often a *quality manager* is assigned, who is given the authority and responsibility needed to ensure that a quality system is functional. A quality manager also functions as an official channel between customer and developer acting as a focal point for resolving quality matters. The quality manager is accountable to the management level.

A quality system is planned early in a project, and its implementation is typically documented in a *quality plan*. All activities and all personnel in a project who affect quality of software must be identified and

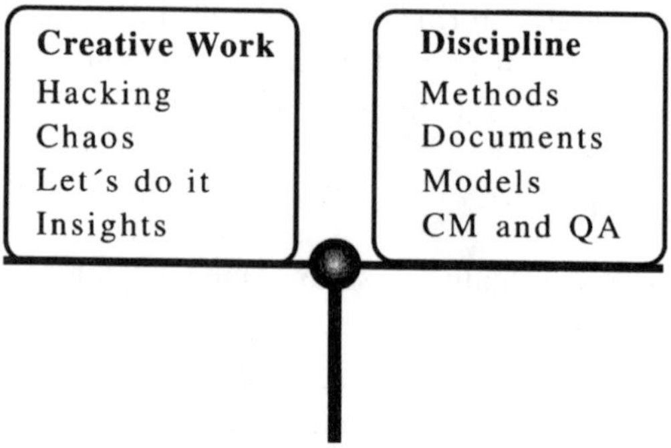


**Figure A3.12** A balance between chaos and order must be established in a company.

documented. A quality plan must have (or reference) procedures, which ensures that only software meeting contractual requirements will be delivered. This means that the quality system must describe (or reference) procedures both for the actual software development and for the quality system itself. A procedure, in this context, defines how to conduct the procedure, who will perform it, what will be examined, how and where the procedure will be done, to whom the result will be reported, and how any necessary corrections will be done. Activities include sitting in on design reviews, program walk-throughs, etc.

A quality standard does not identify any particular software procedures (methods) or a particular organization to be used to implement the quality system. It is up to the developer (and the customer) to describe this—the implementation of the quality standard—in the quality plan. The quality plan thus implements the quality standard by listing standards and procedures to be used for validation, verification, testing, reviewing, etc. For example, the checklists in this appendix could be referenced in a quality plan to be used in connection with different activities during software development. Thus, the quality of software is checked against existing standards, procedures, and checklists, as defined in the quality plan.

A quality system is subject to continual review and assessment to ensure its effectiveness. For example, it must implement procedures to make it possible to detect problems early that might lead to software that does not comply with contractual requirements. Note that purchased software and subcontractors must meet the same quality requirements as the main contractor if not otherwise explicitly excluded.

A developer must provide objective evidence that a quality system is functional. To do this it is necessary that minutes from reviews, test reports, and other types of documentation be maintained and cataloged. This necessitates a *configuration management* system, which we discuss next.

One of the major problem areas in developing software is the controlling of changes. Changes fall into two categories, minor and major. Minor changes can often be corrected without involving management. Major changes are those changes that either add, remove, or alter a contractual function, such as a mini-use. If the cost for such a major change is high, a decision must be made as to whether to accept the change or not and, if accepted, who is to pay for it. As we have tried to show in this book, object-oriented techniques help us to minimize problems related to making changes, but the problem is not eliminated by adopting object-oriented technology. A quality standard handles this problem by calling for CM (Configuration Management).

CM is a set of procedures by which software and changes to software are identified, documented, and controlled. *Configuration identification* collects software (and hardware) into units that can be handled by CM. We call these identified units CIs (Configuration Items). A typical CI is a document, an object, a class, or a group of such items. *Change control*—often called configuration control—is the process whereby changes are scheduled and tracked. The steps involved are roughly the following. A change is

1. Proposed
2. Evaluated
3. Approved or disapproved and, if approved
4. Implemented.

Typically a group of people is given the responsibility and authority to implement the change control. This group is commonly referred to as the CCB (Configuration Control Board). CM must be carried out according to established procedures in the spirit of quality assurance, as described here.

## DOCUMENTS

Figure A3.5 (page 388) shows an overview of typical documents used during software development. We outline two important documents used during the feasibility study and the analysis phase, respectively:

- Concept of operations
- Requirements specification

## Making a Concept of Operations Document

The concept of operations document is *not* a requirements document. The purpose of the document is to reduce uncertainty in a process where we echo solutions to users and decision-makers. When we are convinced we have a workable solution strategy, we finish the concept of operations document and the work with the requirements specification begins.

The concept of operations document is a description/view of the users and their environment and describes in a high-level fashion how the system interacts with the users and their environments. Making this document is often the first step in systems development. The document defines the goals, main uses, and main components of the intended system. Internals of system and subsystems are transparent to the users. The document should not include design-dependent constraints.

The overview section of the document should be done first. Two important parts of the overview section are the following:

1. A *problem statement*. This is a descriptive text of the system and the uses of the system, preferably made by the users themselves. The text should not exceed two pages. Half of a page is ideal.
2. A *context picture* of the system and the users. This picture should be made as lifelike as possible. It should resemble a photograph of the situation, except that it can include comments, lines, and arrows to enhance the understanding of the system. It should show the system and how it relates to other systems and users and make it clear why the system is needed. If the location is important, that should also be evident from the picture. See the examples earlier in this appendix.

When the overview section has been made, the rest of the document can be filled in, written by the developers together with the users.

### *Concept of Operations Document Outline*

1. Introduction
    - 1.1. Table of contents
    - 1.2. Purpose and scope of the document
    - 1.3. A description of the intended audience of the document
2. Overview
    - 2.1. The purpose of the system (problem statement)
    - 2.2. A context picture

2.3. Context drawing (draft)

For each subsystem, a subsystem problem statement should be written. These problem statements can be parts of the problem statement, describing the whole system, or more detailed versions describing particular subsystems.

3. Types of information units handled by the system
4. User description(s)
    4.1. User description I
    4.2. User description II

    .
    .
    .

5. Mini-uses
    5.1. Mini-use a
    5.2. Mini-use b

    .
    .
    .

6. Sample use-cases (and/or usage scenarios)
    6.1. Use-case 1
    6.2. Use-case 2

    .
    .
    .

7. Appendices
    7.1. Referenced documents

    Identify each document by title, report number, date, author, and publishing department/organization.

    Examples of documents:
    - User's manuals
    - Other documents presented by the users or customer

    .

    7.2. Abbreviations and acronyms
    7.3. Glossary or Data Dictionary
    7.4. Comments
    7.5. Index

***Comments***

The documents "DoD-STD-2167A Operational Concept Document" and "NASA, SMAP-DID-P100" can be used as inspiration when adapting this document to the needs of a particular company. Note that the process of writing the concept of operations document is as important or even more important than the produced document.

It is a good idea to start writing user's manuals at this stage, because they show how the users use the system. A user's manual should be clear, have step-by-step instructions, and include examples.

The checklist for the feasibility study can be used to check the concept of operations document. Brainstorming, use-cases and interviewing techniques are the most relevant tools when making this document.

## Making a Requirements Specification

A requirements specification must be a more exact document than a concept of operations document because we usually sign a contract to fulfill it. This document can be very extensive. We present only a simple template for such a document here.

***Requirements Specification Outline***

1. Introduction

   The text here is copied from the concept of operations document and rewritten to make it updated and more detailed.

2. Overview

   2.1–2.2. These sections contains parts copied from the concept of operations document rewritten to make them updated and more detailed.

   2.3. Context drawing.

   This drawing is now completed. It should now show all subsystems, important system objects, all actors, information objects, all mini-uses, and important comments.

   2.4. Selected programming languages, hardware, and database. (2.4 is optional.)

   2.5. General constraints, assumptions, and dependencies.

3. Types of information handled by system

   3.1. Information objects exchanged between subsystems.

   3.2. Information objects exchanged between subsystems and actors.

   3.3. Other important high-level information objects.

   Information objects can, alternatively, be presented together with other objects in Chapter 5, "Subsystems."

4. User description(s)

   This section contains updated material copied from the concept of operations document. We define actors and connect them with mini-uses, which are rewritten to make the descriptions complete and specific. We can add one level of system objects to show how mini-uses can be implemented. This is the starting point for the top-level design.

5. Subsystems

The set of mini-uses and actors should now be complete. Each mini-use should be described in a point-by-point fashion or by using pseudocode. We describe mini-uses either in connection with an actor or together with the connection or dialog object implementing the mini-use(s). We can also mix these ways of describing mini-uses. For each subsystem we describe objects, methods, and mini-uses in the way outlined next. Note that we prefix methods with a dot (.) whereas names for mini-uses are not prefixed. (Chapters 4 and 5 in the requirements specification can be combined into one chapter.)

Subsystem 1
Actor A (Description of Actor A)
Mini-uses: Actor A
Mini-use A.1
Mini-use A.2
.
.
.
Actor B
Mini-uses: Actor B
Mini-use B.1
Mini-use B.2
.
.
.
Interface object X
Mini-uses: Interface object X
Mini-use X.1
Mini-use X.2
.
.
.
Methods: Interface object X
.Method X.10
.
.
.

Other Object S
Methods: Object S
.Method S.1
.Method S.2
.
.
.
Other Object T
.
.
.
Subsystem 2
Actor AA
Mini-uses: Actor AA
.
.
.

6. Use-cases (and/or detailed usage scenarios)

   We add use-cases to the ones we had in the concept of operations document.

   Use-case 1
   Use-case 2
   Use-case 3
   .
   .
   .
7. Nonfunctional requirements
8. Appendices

   This section is copied from Chapter 7 in the concept of operations document and updated. For example, we update the glossary, and if we have not already transformed the glossary into a data dictionary, now is the time to do so.

***Comments***

Basically, the functionality is defined as the set of all mini-uses. However, sometimes it is convenient to include use-cases to explain some functionality. For example, in Chapter 5 we had a use-case that showed how the mini-use "Program" was used to set the time and channel for recording. Such a use-case ought to be included in a requirements specification because understanding the sequence of calling "Program" several times to program the videocassette is better explained with this use-case than by enlarging on the explanation of the mini-use "Program." On the other hand, a use-case built up by calling mini-uses such as "Open," "Cut," "Paste," etc. in some sequence showing a typical session on a wordprocessor would not have to be included because all its functionality is already defined through its mini-uses.

Objects S and T are objects that do not deal with interfaces or they are subobjects to other objects. Mini-uses and methods may or may not be numbered.

Subsystems and large (complex) objects can be described in separate documents.

The following documents can be used as inspiration when adapting a (software) requirements specification document to the needs of a particular company:

- IEEE Guide to Software Requirements Specification IEEE Std. 830-1984 [30]
- Software Requirements Specification, DoD-Std-2167A DI-MCCR-80025A
- System/Segment Specification, DoD-Std-2167A DI-CMAN-80008A
- System/Segment Design Document, DoD-Std-2167A DI-CMAN-80534

A requirements specification should be complete, including all actors, information objects, subsystems, and needed mini-uses. We make every effort to avoid ambiguity and overspecification. The checklist for the analysis phase can be used to check the requirements specification.

# Appendix 4

# About C++

## *And Readability*

*Common sense is not so common.*

—Voltaire

### INTRODUCTION

A professional C++ user will probably be aware of the problems outlined in this appendix and will (we hope) avoid many of the constructs used in the examples below. For example, the problem with the String class discussed should be a well-known problem to the professional C++ programmer. However, similar problems do occur with newly constructed classes, which sometimes escapes the professional C++ programmer, too. The aim of this appendix is only to illustrate why C++ again and again forces us to impose rules on our programming to avoid problems. The discussion will not be an in-depth look at C++.

There may be other languages equally difficult to use as C++, but that does not invalidate the points we are making about C++ in this appendix.

We start by discussing why C++ code is often hard to comprehend and then give some recommendations concerning the use of C++.

### LARGE SEMANTIC GAP

The main problem with C++ is that it does not map closely to how we think. That is, the semantic gap is large when we try to write a solution using C++. To illustrate this point, we will use examples. Our first example is the expression:

```
max = (a<=b) ? b : a;
```

What does this expression mean? We can guess that max will be given the maximum value of b and a, but we cannot be sure of this unless we are familiar with this construction. The following pseudocode could, however, be understood by most of us:

```
IF a<=b THEN
max := b
ELSE
max := a;
END_IF;
```

Another example is

```
i++;
```

Which means

```
i := i + 1; // Add one to i
```

These trivial examples show how C++ can give us compact code, but code that is difficult to understand. The following C++ code illustrates this point even better:

```
FOR (Animal *p = pz ; p ; p = p.next)
p.Draw ();
```

This code is very compact but hard to understand. The following pseudocode explains some of the mystery:

```
Animal *p; // p points to an object of class Animal
p := pz; // p now points to what pz points to

WHILE p <> 0 DO
   p.Draw(); // Call method Draw
   p := p.Next; // Let p point to next object
END_WHILE;
```

The loop thus ends when we get a pointer with the value 0. Note that this is something that is implicitly understood in the C++ version of the code. A programmer not aware of this would have problems understanding the code. The Boolean values True and False are not available in C++. Instead, zero is used to represent False, and a nonzero value represents True. This can often give us compact code, as illustrated by the preceding example. However, False and True are not integers and should not be mixed with integer values.

To illustrate further how C++ can make it hard for us when we try to write a solution, we assume the role of a mathematician. We start the example by assuming that we need an array v with 30 elements. With our assumed shallow knowledge of programming in C++ but in-depth knowledge of mathematics, the following code is a probable first attempt to define the array:

```
float v[30];
```

In this case we found a correct solution. We then try to convert an algorithm where we assign the first element in our vector the value 100—that is, v[1] := 100. It is then very possible that our solution to this would be

```
v[1] = 100;
```

This is not the correct solution using C++. In C++, an array always starts at zero. That is, our correct code should have been

```
v[0] = 100;
```

This error is so common, when programming in C and C++, that it has been given its own name: "off by one." Our problems increase if we need a multidimensional array, v2. For example, if we need a 30 X 10 array, it is probable that we would write

```
float v2[30, 10];
```

Again, this is incorrect using C++. A C++ compiler may reject this, but typically it will be interpreted as

```
float v2[10];
```

The correct code, using C++, is

```
float v2[30] [10];
```

Each problem is seldom a problem by itself. However, C++ is filled with problems of this type, and together they create a very difficult environment for us when we try to convert a solution into code.

The problems we have touched upon above are primarily problems of readability. For example, in another programming language, it is probable that we would have written a multidimensional array something like this:

```
v2b : array [1..30, 1..10] of float;
```

The advantage with such a solution is the high readability of it. With very little help from our imagination, we can read the line as: "v2b is an array with index 1 to 30 and 1 to 10 with elements of type float."

## LOW-LEVEL DETAILS

Apart from the problem of transforming a model into code and being able to read it, it is very clear that C++ is a language invented by people working very close to low-level details of computers. Most difficulties related to programming in C++ seem to come from the handling of pointers and memory allocation and deallocation. (In a language such as Smalltalk the handling of memory is automatic.) Let us illustrate the problem of handling memory using an example adapted from Bjarne Stroustrup's book, *The C++ Programming Language* [20]. We declare a class that can be used to create strings:

```
class String {
   char* p;
   int size_of_string;
   String(int sz) {p = new
   char[size_of_string=sz];}
   ~String() {delete p;}
};
```

Here, p is a pointer to chars and size_of_string is a variable of type integer. The expression, `String(int sz)`, is a so-called constructor. This constructor is called when we create an object of class String. The expression, `{p = new char[size_of_string=sz];}`, is the implementation of this constructor, and it results in a pointer, p, that points to an array of chars.

`~String()` is a destructor. It is called when a string is no longer needed. Its implementation, `{delete p;}`, deallocates the memory to which p points. We use this class in a function Foo, where we create two strings s1 and s2 and then assign one string to the other:

```
void Foo()
{
   String s1(15);
   String s2(25);
   s1=s2;
};
```

The problem with this code is that the assignment, `s1=s2`, destroys one of the pointers and doubles the other one. When we leave Foo, the destructor for this latter string will be called twice for the same pointer. This could have serious results in C++ programs. However, the fault is not really in our function Foo. With another implementation of the class String, Foo could have worked. Bjarne Stroustrup shows in his book how we can build a class able to handle functions such as Foo. However, he then shows how a slight change of our function Foo will give us similar problems again. This illustrates how C++ again and again forces us to consider problems that are really of no concern to us. We are interested in solving our problem—not problems that are due to idiosyncrasies of C++. For example, a mathematician is interested in converting his or her algorithm as easily and painlessly as possible into code and not in allocating and deallocating pointers in the correct sequence. When a project becomes large, the extra burdens connected with a language like C++ soon give us insurmountable problems.

In spite of all these problems, it is probable that many object-oriented projects will select C++ in the foreseeable future. An awareness of the limitations of a language like C++ then becomes something of the utmost importance.

## RECOMMENDATIONS

In the following we give some advice concerning the use of C++. More general advice can be found in Chapter 8 and in Appendix 3.

- Object-oriented thinking must be taught before C++ is taught. The major limitation is that C++ encourages programmers to form abstractions close to the hardware level rather than the business-application level. Thus, without proper training in object-oriented thinking, we will not get much object-oriented design or object-oriented programming if we use C++.
- Look for an alternative to C++. Small systems can often be built in Smalltalk, and Smalltalk with add-ons, which help us keep track of versions and subsystems, can be used to build at least medium-sized systems. It is true that Smalltalk is generally considered to be slower than C++ but consider (1) whether you really need the speed C++ can give you and (2) that much of the time needed to execute a system is due to the used database and GUI, time that will probably not change if we change programming language. Smalltalk is thus often fast enough. Note, the speed of a program also depends on the design of the program. The author has seen some examples in which equivalent programs were significantly faster in Smalltalk than in C++. It was simply much easier to get a good design in Smalltalk. Ada (9X) is an excellent choice if we are to build large or very large systems. Other alternatives also exist.

- If the decision is to use C++, discipline must be applied. C++ has a very free syntax, and if we do not restrict ourselves, C++ will help us to introduce errors. Style guides and rule checkers are tools that maintain discipline. A style guide contains sets of rules that tell us how to code in C++, and a rule checker is a software application that checks that C++ code has been coded in an agreed way.
- Compile a list of error explanations. Error reports generated by C++ compilers are often very cryptic, both at compile time and run time. For example, the error message "Syntax Error" at compile time probably means we are referring to a class that has not included its header file. Thus, it is important to compile a list of errors and their possible causes. If this is not done, programmers will spend a lot of time just trying to figure out what the real error is.
- Use more than one compiler. Many compilers for C++ are bad. For example, compiling with or without optimization can yield different results in functionality for the same code.
- A tool that can trace memory usage is as vital as a good compiler.
- Minimize the use of pointers. Pointers are a main source of problems; the less we use them, the fewer errors there will be in the system we build.
- Put a lot of work into the architectural design.
- Use code reviews to check code, to communicate experience, and to update error explanation lists.
- Make sure at least one professional C++ expert is available.

## SUMMARY

C++ is today a popular language often selected for object-oriented programming. However, because C++ does not really promote object-oriented thinking, the danger is that C++ programmers will start to crank out C++ code that is actually C code without any object-oriented design in it. C++ is not a simple language to understand or to program in. Object-oriented programming will thus not come from selecting C++ but through training in object-oriented thinking.

# Appendix 5

# References and Books

*You have to study a great deal to know a little.*

—Charles de Secondat, Baron de Montesquieu

## REFERENCES


[1] Sigfried, Stefan (1991).
*Förstudie objektorientering.*
Stockholm, Sweden:
Mekanförbundet.

[2] Sigfried, Stefan (1992).
*Objektorientering metoder och problemområden.*
Stockholm, Sweden:
Sveriges Verkstadsindustrier.
ISBN 91-524-1159-1.

[3] Sigfried, Stefan, Mats Göthe, and Erik Nyquist (1993).
*Ada och C++ vid objektorientering.*
Stockholm, Sweden:
Sveriges Verkstadsindustrier.
ISBN 91-524-1162-1.

[4] Coad, Peter and Edward Yourdon (1991).
*Object-Oriented Analysis,* 2nd edition.
New Jersey, USA:
Yourdon Press.
ISBN 0-13-629981-4.

[5] Coad, Peter and Edward Yourdon (1991).
*Object-Oriented Design.*
New Jersey, USA:
Yourdon Press.
ISBN 0-13-630070-7.

[6] Meyer, Bertrand (1988).
*Object-Oriented Software Construction.*
Cambridge, Great Britain:
Prentice Hall.
ISBN 0-13-629031-0.

[7] Graham, Ian (1991).
*Object-Oriented Methods.*
Kent, Great Britain:
Addison-Wesley.
ISBN 0-201-56521-8.

[8] Wirfs-Brock, Rebecca, Brian Wilkerson, and Lauren Wiener (1990).
*Designing Object-Oriented Software.*
New Jersey, USA:
Prentice Hall.
ISBN 0-13-629825-7.

[9] Rumbaugh, James, Michael Blaha, William Premerlani, Frederick Eddy, and William Lorensen (1991).
*Object-Oriented Modeling and Design.*
New Jersey, USA:
Prentice Hall.
ISBN 0-13-629841-9.

[10] Date, C.J. (1990).
*An Introduction to Database Systems,*
Vol. 1 (5th edition).
USA: Addison-Wesley.
ISBN 0-201-52878-9.

[11] Myers, Glenford J. (1979).
*The Art of Software Testing.*
New York, USA:
Wiley-Interscience.
ISBN 0-471-04328-1.

[12] Hetzel, William (1984).
*The Complete Guide to Software Testing.*
Massachusetts, USA:
QED Information Sciences, Inc.
ISBN 0-89435-110-9.

[13] Deutsch, Michael S. (1982).
*Software Verification and Validation (Realistic Project Approaches).*
New Jersey, USA:
Prentice Hall.
ISBN 0-13-822072-7.

[14] Booch, Grady (1983).
*Software Engineering with ADA.*
California, USA:
Benjamin/Cummings.
ISBN 0-8053-0600-5.

[15] Lippman, Stanley B. (1991).
*C++ Primer,* 2nd edition.
USA: Addison-Wesley.
ISBN 0-201-54848-8.

[16] Coplien, James O. (1992).
*Advance C++ Programming, Styles and Idioms.*
USA: Addison-Wesley.
ISBN 0-201-54855-0.

[17] Chen, Peter (1977).
*The Entity Relationship Approach to Logical Data Base Design.*
Massachusetts, USA:
QED Information Sciences, Inc.
ISBN 0-89435-020-X.

[18] Shlaer, Sally and Stephen J. Mellor (1988).
*Object-Oriented Systems Analysis.*
New Jersey, USA:
Yourdon Press/Prentice Hall.
ISBN 0-13-629023-X.

[19] Boehm, Barry W., TRW Defense Systems Group (May, 1988).
*A Spiral Model of Software Development and Enhancement.*
*IEEE Computer,* pp. 61–72.

[20] Stroustrup, Bjarne (1991).
*The C++ Programming Language,*
2nd edition.
USA: Addison-Wesley.
ISBN 0-201-53992-6.

[21] Booch, Grady (1991).
*Object-Oriented Design with Applications.*
USA: Benjamin/Cummings.
ISBN 0-8053-0091-0.

[22] Cattell, R.G.G. (1992).
*Object Data Management.*
USA: Addison-Wesley.
ISBN 0-201-53092-9.

[23] Perry, William E. (1983).
*A Structured Approach to Systems Testing.*
Massachusetts, USA:
QED Information Sciences, Inc.
ISBN 0-89435-061-7.

[24] Sully, Phil (1993).
*Modelling the World with Objects.*
Cambridge, Great Britain:
Prentice Hall.
ISBN 0-13-587791-1.

[25] Dillon, Tharam, and Poh Lee Tan (1993).
*Object-Oriented Conceptual Modeling.*
Australia: Prentice Hall.
ISBN 0-13-712952-1.

[26] Lorenz, Mark (1993).
*Object-Oriented Software Development.*
New Jersey, USA:
Prentice Hall.
ISBN 0-13-726928-5.

[27] Jacobson, Ivar et al. (1992).
*Object-Oriented Software Engineering—A Use-case Driven Approach.*
USA: Addison Wesley.
ISBN 0-201-54435-0.

[28] Modell, Martin E. (1988).
*A Professional's Guide to Systems Analysis.*
USA: McGraw-Hill.
ISBN 0-07-042632-5.

[29] *ObjectStore Technical Overview* (manual, 1994).
Burlington, Massachusetts, USA:
Object Design.

[30] *IEEE Standards Collection, Software Engineering.* (1993).
USA: The Institute of Electrical and Electronics Engineers, Inc.
ISBN 1-55937-253-2.

[31] Atkinson, Malcolm, et al. (1989).
*The Object-Oriented Database System Manifesto.*

[32] Potter, Carl (1994).
*Object Databases: An Evaluation and Comparison.*
Great Britain: ButlerBloor Ltd.
ISBN 1-874160-10-4.

[33] *Computer,* Vol. 27, No. 9, September 1994.
IEEE Computer Society.

[34] Boehm, B. W. et al. (1978).
*Characteristics of Software Quality. TRW Series of Software Technology.*
Amsterdam, Netherlands:
North-Holland Publishing Company

[35] Gamma, E. et al. (1994).
*Design Patterns, Elements of Reusable Object-Oriented Software.*
USA: Addison-Wesley.
ISBN 0-201-63361-2.

# BOOKS

## -Methodologies

Bassett, P.G. (1994).
*Frame-Based Software Engineering.* Prentice Hall.
ISBN 0-13-327859-X.

Benson, A., and G. Aitken (1992).
*OI Programmer's Guide: Version 3.0.*
Prentice Hall.
ISBN 0-13-631383-3.

Berard, E.V. (1993).
*Essays on Object-Oriented Software Engineering.*
Prentice Hall.
ISBN 0-13-288895-5.

Berard, E.V. (1994).
*Project Management Handbook for Object-Oriented Software Development.*
Prentice Hall.
ISBN 0-13-138611-5.

Blair, G. et al (1991).
*Object-Oriented Languages, Systems and Applications.*
Pitman.
ISBN 0-273-03132-5.

Booch, G. (1991).
*Object-Oriented Design with Applications.*
Benjamin/Cummings.
ISBN 0-8053-0091-0.

Booch, G. (1994).
*Object-Oriented Analysis and Design with Applications,* 2nd Edition.
Benjamin/Cummings.
ISBN 0-8053-5340-2.

Budd, T. (1991).
*Introduction to Object-Oriented Programming.*
Addison-Wesley.
ISBN 0-201-54709-0.

Carmichael, A., ed. (1994).
*Object Development Methods.*
SIGS Books .
ISBN 0-9627477-9-3.

Coad, P. and J. Nicola (1993).
*Object-Oriented Programming.*
Prentice Hall.
ISBN 0-13-032616-X.

Coad, P. and E. Yourdon (1991).
*Object-Oriented Analysis,* 2nd Edition.
Prentice Hall.
ISBN 0-13-629981-4.

Coad, P. and E. Yourdon (1991).
*Object-Oriented Design.*
Prentice Hall.
ISBN 13-630070-7.

Coleman, D., P. Arnolds, S. Bodoff, C. Dollin, H. Gilchrist, F. Hayes, and P. Jeremaes (1994).
*Object-Oriented Development: The Fusion Method.*
Prentice Hall.
ISBN 0-13-338823-9.

Computer Science Corporation/ Object Management Group. (1994).
*Object Technology Today.*
Wiley.
ISBN 0-471-10614-3.

Connell, J.L. and L. Shafer. (1994).
*Object-Oriented Rapid Prototyping.*
Prentice Hall.
ISBN 0-13-629643-2.

Cox, B. and A.J. Novobilski (1991).
*Object-Oriented Programming: An Evolutionary Approach,* 2nd Edition.
Addison-Wesley.
ISBN 0-201-54834-8.

Davis, A.M. (1993).
*Software Requirements: Objects, Functions, and States,* Revision.
Prentice Hall.
ISBN 0-13-805763-X.

de Champeaux., D. Lea and P. Faure (1993).
*Object-Oriented System Development.*
Addison-Wesley.
ISBN 0-201-56355-X.

Desfray, P. (1994).
*Object Engineering: The Fourth Dimension.*
Addison-Wesley.
ISBN 0-201-42288-3.

Dorfman, L. (1990).
*Object-Oriented Assembly Language.*
Windcrest.
ISBN 0-803-067620-1.

Ege, R.K. (1992).
*Programming in an Object-Oriented Environment.*
Academic Press.
ISBN 0-12-232930-9.

Eliens, A. (1995).
*Principles of Object-Oriented Software Development.*
Addison-Wesley.
ISBN 0-201-62444-3.

Ellis, J.R. (1994).
*Objectifying Real-Time Systems.*
SIGS Books .
ISBN 0-9627477-8-5.

Embley, D.W. et. al. (1992).
*Object-Oriented Systems Analysis: A Model Driven Approach.*
Yourdon Press.
ISBN 0-13-629973-3.

Entsminger, G. (1991).
*The Tao of Objects: A Beginners Guide to Object-Oriented Programming.*
Prentice Hall/MandT Books.
ISBN 13-882770-2.

Firesmith, D.G. (1993).
*Object-Oriented Requirements Analysis and Logical Design.*
Addison-Wesley.
ISBN 0-471-57807-X .

Goldstein, N. and J. Alger (1992).
*Developing Object-Oriented Software for the Macintosh: Analysis, Design and Programming.*
Addison-Wesley.
ISBN 0-201-.57065-3

Graham, Ian (1995).
*Migrating to Object Technology.*
Addison-Wesley.
ISBN 0-201-59389-0 .

Graham, Ian (1994).
*Object-Oriented Methods,* 2nd Edition.
Addison-Wesley.
ISBN 0-201-59371-8.

Graham, Ian (1991).
*Object-Oriented Methods: A Practical Introduction.*
Addison-Wesley.
ISBN 0-201-56521-8.

Gunter, C.A. and J.C. Mitchell (1994).
*Theoretical Aspects of Object-Oriented Programming: Types, Semantics, and Language Design.*
MIT.
ISBN 0-262-.07155-X

Halliday, A. and M. Wiebel (1993).
*Object-Oriented Software Engineering.*
R and D Publications/Prentice Hall.
ISBN 0-13-034489-3.

Hamilton, M. (1994).
*Object Thinking Development Before the Fact.*
McGraw-Hill.
ISBN 0-07-911802-X.

Harland, D.M. (1988).
*REKURSIV: Object-Oriented Computer Architecture.*
Ellis Horwood/E. Halsted Press.
ISBN 0-7458-0396-2.

Harmon, P. and D.A. Taylor (1993).
*Objects in Action.*
Addison-Wesley.
ISBN 0-201-63336-1.

Henderson-Sellers, B. (1992).
*A Book of Object-Oriented Knowledge.*
Prentice Hall.
ISBN 0-13-059445-8.

Hollowell, G. (1993).
*Handbook of Object-Oriented Standards: The Object Model.*
Addison-Wesley.
ISBN 0-201-63328-0.

HOOD User Group (1992).
*HOOD Reference Manual.*
Prentice Hall.
ISBN 0-13-396243-1.

Hutt, A. (1994).
*Object Analysis and Design: Comparison of Methods.*
Wiley.
ISBN 0-471-05276-0.

Jacobson, I. (1995).
*The Object Advantage: Business Process Re-engineering with Object Technology.*
Addison-Wesley.
ISBN 0-201-42289-1.

Jacobson, I. (1992).
*Object-Oriented Software Engineering: A Use Case Driven Approach.*
ACM Press/Addison-Wesley.
ISBN 0-201-54435-0.

Khoshafian, S. (1992).
*Intelligent Offices: Object-Oriented Multi-Media Information Management.*
John Wiley.
ISBN 0-471-54699-2.

Khoshafian, S. and R. Abnous (1990).
*Object Orientation: Concepts, Languages, Databases, User Interfaces.*
Wiley.
ISBN 0-471-51801-8.

Kiczales, G., J. des Rivieres, and D. Bobrow (1991).
*The Art of the Metaobject Protocol.*
MIT.
ISBN 0-262-61074-4.

Kiczales, G. and A. Paepcke (1994).
*Open Implementations and Metaobject Protocols.*
MIT.
ISBN 0-262-61103-1.

Kim, W. and F.H. Lochovsky (1989).
*Object-Oriented Concepts, Databases, and Applications.*
Addison-Wesley.
ISBN 0-201-14410-7.

Kirkerud, B. (1989).
*Object-Oriented Programming with SIMULA.*
Addison-Wesley.
ISBN 0-201-17574-6.

Knecht, K. (1993).
*Object-Oriented Programming with Turbo Pascal and Object Professional.*
Prentice Hall.
ISBN 0-13-630310-2.

Kristen, G. (1994).
*Object Orientation, The KISS Method.*
Addison-Wesley.
ISBN 0-201-42299-9.

Kurtz, B., S. Woodfield, and D. Embley (1992).
*Object-Oriented System Analysis and Specification: A Model Driven Approach.*
Prentice Hall.
ISBN 0-13-629973-3.

Lano, K. and H. Haughton (1994).
*Object-Oriented Specification Case Studies.*
Prentice Hall.
ISBN 0-13-097015-8.

Lipovski, G.J. (1993).
*Object-Oriented Interfacing to 16-bit Microcontrollers.*
Prentice Hall.
ISBN 0-13-629221-6.

Lorenz, M. and J. Kidd. (1994).
*Object-Oriented Software Metrics.*
Prentice Hall.
ISBN 0-13-179292.

Lorenz, M. (1993).
*Object-Oriented Software Development: A Practical Guide.*
Prentice Hall.
ISBN 0-13-726928-5.

Love, T. (1993).
*Object Lessons: Lessons Learned in Object-Oriented Development Projects.*
SIGS Publication.
ISBN 0-9627477-3-4.

Madsen, O.L., B. Moller-Pedersen, and K. Nygaard (1993).
*Object-Oriented Programming in the Beta Programming Language.*
Addison-Wesley.
ISBN 0-201-62430-3.

Martin, J. (1993).
*Principles of Object-Oriented Analysis and Design.*
Prentice Hall.
ISBN 0-13-720871-5.

Martin, J. and J. Odell (1992).
*Object-Oriented Analysis and Design.*
Prentice Hall.
ISBN 0-13-630245-9.

McCabe, F.G. (1992).
*Logic and Objects.*
Prentice Hall.
ISBN 0-13-536079-X.

McGregor, J.D. and D.S. Sykes (1992).
*Object-Oriented Software Development: Engineering Software for Reuse.*
Van Nostrand Reinhold.
ISBN 0-442-00157-6.

Mellor, S. and S. Shlaer (1991).
*Object Lifecycles: Modeling the World in States.*
Prentice Hall.
ISBN 0-13-629940-7.

Mellor, S. and S. Shlaer (1988).
*Object-Oriented Systems Analysis: Modeling the World in Data.*
Prentice Hall.
ISBN 0-13-629023-1.

Meyer, B. (1994).
*Reusable Software: The Base Object-Oriented Component Libraries.*
Prentice Hall.
ISBN 0-13-245499-8.

Meyer, B. (1994).
*An Object-Oriented Environment: Principles and Application.*
Prentice Hall.
ISBN 0-13-245507-2.

Meyer, B. (1991).
*Introduction to the Theory of Programming Languages.*
Prentice Hall.
ISBN 0-13-498510-9.

Meyer, B. (1989).
*Object-Oriented Software Constructions.*
Prentice Hall.
ISBN 0-13-629049-3.

Meyer, B. and D. Mandriolo (1991).
*Advances in Object-Oriented Software Engineering.*
Prentice Hall.
ISBN 0-13-006578-1.

Meyer, B. and J. Nerson (1993).
*Object-Oriented Applications.*
Prentice Hall.
ISBN 0-13-013798-7.

Moss, C. (1994).
*Prolog ++: The Power of Object-Oriented and Logic Programming.*
Addison-Wesley.
ISBN 0-201-56507-2.

Object Management Group (1993).
*Common Object Services Specification,* Vol. I.
Wiley.
ISBN 0-471-07684-8.

Parker, R.O. (1993).
*Easy Object Programming for the Macintosh using APPMAKER and Pascal.*
Prentice Hall.
ISBN 0-13-092974-3.

Parker, R.O. (1993).
*Easy Object Programming for the Macintosh using APPMAKER and THINK C.*
Prentice Hall.
ISBN 0-13-092966-2.

Pinson, L.J. and R.S. Wiener (1990).
*Applications for Object-Oriented Programming.*
Addison-Wesley.
ISBN 0-201-50369-7.

Pinson, L.J. and R.S. Wiener (1991).
*Objective-C: Object-Oriented Programming Techniques.*
Addison-Wesley.
ISBN 0-201-50828-1.

Robinson, P. (1993).
*Hierarchical Object-Oriented Design.*
Prentice Hall.
ISBN 0-13-390816-X.

Rumbaugh, J.M. et. al. (1991).
*Object-Oriented Modeling and Design.*
Prentice Hall.
ISBN 0-13-629841-9.

Schultz, R. (1992).
*A Comparison of Object-Oriented Development Methodologies,* 2nd Edition.
Berard Software Engineering.
ISBN 1-881974-03-0.

Schultz, R. (1992).
*A Program Management Handbook for Object-Oriented Development.*
Berard Software Engineering.
ISBN 1-881-974-00-6.

Schultz, R. and E. Berard (1992).
*A Complete Object-Oriented Design Example.*
Berard Software Engineering.
ISBN 1-881-974-01-4.

Smith, D.N. (1994).
*Concepts of Object-Oriented Programming: With Examples in Smalltalk,* 2nd Edition.
McGraw-Hill.
ISBN 0-07-059236-5.

Springer, G. and D.P. Friedman (1989).
*Scheme and the Art of Programming.*
MIT Press/McGraw-Hill.
ISBN 0-262-19288-8.

Starr, L. (1994).
*Practical Guide to Shlaer/Mellor OOA.*
Prentice Hall.
ISBN 0-13-207663-2.

Sully, P. (1993).
*Modeling the World with Objects.*
Prentice Hall.
ISBN 0-13-587791-1.

Taylor, A. and D. Shafer (1993).
*COOPERATION: An Object-Oriented Enterprise by NCR.*
Prentice Hall.
ISBN 0-13-088451-0.

Taylor, D. (1995).
*Business Engineering with Object Technology.*
Wiley.
ISBN 0-471-04521-7.

Taylor, D.A. (1992).
*Object-Oriented Technology: A Manager's Guide.*
Addison-Wesley.
ISBN 0-201-56358-4.

Tkach, D. and R. Puttick (1994).
*Object Technology in Application Development.*
Benjamin Cummings.
ISBN 0-8053-2572-7.

Tozer, J. (1992).
*Object-Oriented Enterprise Modeling.*
Prentice Hall.
ISBN 13-630286-6.

Treleaven, P.C. (1990).
*Parallel Computers: Object-Oriented Functional Logic.*
Wiley.
ISBN 0-471-92518-7.

Voss, G. (1992).
*Object-Oriented Programming: An Introduction.*
Osborne/McGraw-Hill.
ISBN 0-07-881682-3.

Walden, K. and J. Nerson (1994).
*Seamless Object-Oriented Software Architecture Analysis and Design of Reliable Systems.*
Prentice Hall.
ISBN 0-13-031303-3.

White, I. (1994).
*Using the Booch Method: A Rational Approach.*
Benjamin Cummings.
ISBN 0-8053-0614-5.

Wilkie, G. (1993).
*Object-Oriented Software Engineering: The Professional Developer's Guide.*
Addison-Wesley.
ISBN 0-201-62767-1.

Winblad, A.L., S.D. Edwards, and D.R. King (1993).
*Implementing Object Technology,* 2nd Edition.
Addison-Wesley.
ISBN 0-201-50847-8.

Winblad, A.L., S.D. Edwards, and D.R. King (1990).
*Object-Oriented Programming.*
Addison-Wesley.
ISBN 0-201-50736-6.

Wirfs-Brock, R., B. Wikerson, and L. Wiener (1990).
*Designing Object-Oriented Software.*
Prentice Hall.
ISBN 0-13-629825-7.

Yourdon, E. (1994).
*Object-Oriented Systems Design: An Integrated Approach.*
Prentice Hall.
ISBN 0-13-636325-3.

Zeigler, B.P. (1990).
*Object-Oriented Simulation with Hierarchical Modular Models Intelligent Agents and Endomorphic Systems.*
Academic.
ISBN 0-12-778452-7.

# Index